Transformational Trends in Governance and Democracy

National Academy of Public Administration

Terry F. Buss, Series Editor

Modernizing Democracy:
Innovations in Citizen Participation
Edited by Terry F. Buss, F. Stevens Redburn, and Kristina Guo

Meeting the Challenge of 9/11:
Blueprints for More Effective Government
Edited by Thomas H. Stanton

Foreign Aid and Foreign Policy:
Lessons for the Next Half-Century
Edited by Louis A. Picard, Robert Groelsema, and Terry F. Buss

Transforming Public Leadership for the 21st Century
Edited by Ricardo S. Morse, Terry F. Buss, and C. Morgan Kinghorn

Performance Management and Budgeting:
How Governments Can Learn from Experience
Edited by F. Stevens Redburn, Robert J. Shea, and Terry F. Buss

Innovations in Public Leadership Development
Edited by Ricardo S. Morse and Terry F. Buss

Reengineering Community Development for the 21st Century
Edited by Donna Fabiani and Terry F. Buss

About the Academy

The National Academy of Public Administration is an independent, nonprofit organization chartered by Congress to identify emerging issues of governance and to help federal, state, and local governments improve their performance. The Academy's mission is to provide "trusted advice"—advice that is objective, timely, and actionable—on all issues of public service and management. The unique source of the Academy's expertise is its membership, including more than 650 current and former Cabinet officers, members of Congress, governors, mayors, legislators, jurists, business executives, public managers, and scholars who are elected as Fellows because of their distinguished contribution to the field of public administration through scholarship, civic activism, or government service. Participation in the Academy's work is a requisite of membership, and the Fellows offer their experience and knowledge voluntarily.

The Academy is proud to join with M.E. Sharpe, Inc., to bring readers this and other volumes in a series of edited works addressing major public management and public policy issues of the day.

The opinions expressed in these writings are those of the authors and do not necessarily reflect the views of the Academy as an institution. To access Academy reports, please visit our Web site at www.napawash.org.

Reengineering Community Development for the 21st Century

Edited by Donna Fabiani
and Terry F. Buss

NATIONAL ACADEMY OF
PUBLIC ADMINISTRATION

TRANSFORMATIONAL TRENDS IN
GOVERNANCE AND DEMOCRACY

Routledge
Taylor & Francis Group

LONDON AND NEW YORK

First published 2008 by M.E. Sharpe

Published 2015 by Routledge

2 Park Square, Milton Park, Abingdon, Oxon OX14 4RN
711 Third Avenue, New York, NY 10017, USA

Routledge is an imprint of the Taylor & Francis Group, an informa business

Library of Congress Cataloging-in-Publication Data

Reengineering community development for the 21st century / edited by Donna
Fabiani and Terry F. Buss.
    p. cm. — (Transformational trends in governance & democracy)
  Includes bibliographical references and index.
  ISBN 978-0-7656-2289-1 (cloth : alk. paper) — ISBN 978-0-7656-2290-7 (pbk. : alk. paper)
  1. Community development. I. Fabiani, Donna, 1959- II. Buss, Terry F.

HN49.C6R45 2008
307.1'4—dc22   2007050821

ISBN 13: 9780765622907 (pbk)
ISBN 13: 9780765622891 (hbk)

Contents

Preface and Acknowledgments   ix

1. Whither Community Development: An Introduction
   Donna Fabiani and Terry F. Buss   3

Part 1. Community Development Financial Institutions

2. Evolving Roles of Mission-Focused and Mainstream Financial
   Organizations: Implications for the Scale and Sustainability of CDFIs
   Robin Newberger, Michael Berry, Kirsten Moy, and Gregory A. Ratliff   15

3. When Subsidy Becomes Scarce: Rethinking Community
   Development Finance
   Julia Sass Rubin   34

4. CDFIs "Make the Market" for Charter School Facilities Financing
   Annie Donovan   47

5. The Case for the Community Partner in Economic Development
   Anna Steiger, Tessa Hebb, and Lisa A. Hagerman   60

6. Research Design Issues for Measuring CDFI Performance and Impact
   Dan Immergluck   76

7. Social Performance Measurement for CDFI Banks
   David Porteous and Saurabh Narain   94

Part 2. Asset Building

8. Stubborn and Persistent Lending Disparities
   Joshua Silver   113

9. The Assets Framework: Moving Toward Transformative Transactions
    Hannah Thomas   132

10. Connecting Asset Building and Community Development
    William Schweke   143

11. Innovation in State Government: Pennsylvania's Financial
    Education Office
    Rene Bryce-Laporte and Hilary Hunt   157

Part 3. Capacity Building and Citizen Engagement

12. Community Capacity Building Through Strategic Philanthropy at
    the United Way
    *Yoel Camayd-Freixas, Gerald Karush, Melissa Nemon,
    and Richard Koenig*   169

13. Building Community Capacity Through Multisector Collaborations
    Jane F. Morgan   180

14. Southern Bancorp's Model for Community Economic Development:
    The Delta Bridge Project
    Ben Steinberg, Ben Goodwin, and Michael Rowett   198

15. Effective Civic Engagement: Lessons from the Seattle School
    District—A Memoir
    Norman Rice and Lynda Petersen   209

Part 4. Federal Policy

16. Reforming CDBG: An Illusive Quest
    Terry F. Buss   223

17. Rethinking Federal Low-Income Housing Policies
    F. Stevens Redburn   236

Part 5. Smart Growth and Land Use

18. Smart Growth and Community Investment: Confronting
    Suburban Decline in Baltimore
    Thomas J. Vicino   255

19. Positive Cycling: Riding Our Bicycles Down the Path to
Community Development Success
David W. Sears and Colin D. Sears 274

Part 6. Affordable Housing

20. Aging-Out and Foster Care: Housing Policy
James O. Bates 293

21. Would the Adoption of Land Value Taxation Drive Down the
Price of Land and Increase Housing Affordability?
Edward J. Dodson 301

Part 7. Crime and Development

22. Crime's Impact on the Viability of Young Urban Small Businesses
Timothy Bates and Alicia Robb 311

23. Courts, Equity, and Community Development
Brenda Bratton Blom, Kathryn Titford, and Elisabeth Walden 326

Appendix: Redevelopment's Trend Away from Eminent Domain
T. Michael Lengyel 337

About the Editors and Contributors 345
Index 357

Preface and Acknowledgments

This work is part of a series of edited books, *Transformational Trends in Governance and Democracy*, that capture the latest thinking in public management. The books represent what we believe are fundamental, transformational trends emerging in governance and democracy. Each book asks: How is governance or democracy being transformed? What impact will transformations have? Will forces arise to counter transformations? Where will transformations take governance and democracy in the future? The Academy sponsors the series in partnership with M.E. Sharpe, Inc. Many of the chapters in the series have been contributed by Academy Fellows and professional staff. We have also drawn on leaders in public management representing different ways of thinking about the issues. I am editing the series overall, with well-known experts editing individual volumes.

This edited book arises out of discussions Donna Fabiani, now with the Opportunity Finance Network, but late of the Community Development Finance Institutions Fund, and I had about changes in community development financing generally, and community development program performance management and accountability, and their implications for the field. We concluded that it would be a good time to marshal the opinions of practitioners, researchers, policymakers, and advocates to learn their views on trends in community development.

Acknowledgments

We would like to thank Jenna Dorn, President of the Academy, for her support and for marshalling Academy resources in developing and executing this project. We would also like to thank M.E. Sharpe, Inc., especially Harry Briggs, Elizabeth Granda, and Stacey Victor for their assistance and encouragement.

Terry F. Buss
Westport, Mass.

Reengineering Community Development for the 21st Century

1

Whither Community Development

An Introduction

DONNA FABIANI AND TERRY F. BUSS

In 2004, federal agencies spent about $45 billion on community development, as broadly defined. Federal transfers of funds made up about 70 percent of funding spent by states and localities on community development (Gerenrot, Cashin, and Paulson 2006). No one knows how much nongovernmental organizations, including nonprofits, foundations, and for-profit private-sector organizations, spent, but the amount is substantial. With this level of effort and with the changeover in leadership both in the House and Senate in 2007, the impending transition in the office of president in 2008, the unprecedented number of presidential candidates (most running since 2006), the expected turnovers among state and local officeholders, and the continuing evolution of the community development field, it seems a propitious time to take stock in this important issue.

In 2006–2007, the editors sent out a call for papers to policymakers, practitioners, researchers, and advocates, looking for chapter contributions about where community development stands as an issue, where it is headed, and how it might be reengineered to better meet the needs of various constituents and stakeholders. We left the definition of community development vague with the intention of including the broadest range of activities, including community economic development and community development finance. We were not disappointed. Leaders from a wide array of sectors responded (see other work on leadership in Morse, Buss, and Kinghorn [2007]).

Looking across the twenty-three chapters in the book, we are struck by three recurrent themes. First, policymakers, practitioners, researchers, and advocates interpret "community development" as encompassing many more domains than we would have anticipated. For example, David W. Sears and Colin D. Sears, in chapter 19, "Positive Cycling: Riding Our Bicycles Down the Path to Community Development Success," make a compelling case for promoting community and economic development through enhancement of bicycling as a way to reduce reliance on automobiles. James Bates, in chapter 20, "Aging-Out and Foster Care: Housing Policy," observes that only 50 percent of youth "aging out" of foster care are employed—but in low-wage jobs—and they lack affordable housing options. Community development, then, can easily mean just about anything policymakers and practitioners want it to mean. As such, as these chapters aptly demonstrate, the field is highly diverse, providing as yet unrecognized opportunities for synergistic collaborations.

Second, decreasing or redirected funding subsidies and evolving market forces have compelled community development organizations and programs—public and private—to rethink their missions and goals, reorganize their operations, offer new or improved products and services, and engage in partnerships for mutual benefit. In the field of finance, as illustrated especially in part 1, "Community Development Financial Institutions," community development financial institutions (CDFIs) are continually seeking to meet the evolving needs for financial products while maintaining their long-term sustainability, while banks seeking new revenues are taking a closer look at the markets CDFIs serve. This trend has challenged the field—often in positive ways—as organizations compete and partner in the market for community development finance.

Third, performance attainment—establishing that organizations and programs are having intended impacts and are efficient—has infused itself across the community development field. Federal community development programs—under the Government Performance and Accountability Act of 1993 and the Bush administration's Program Assessment Rating Tool begun in 2002—have made performance management, coupled with accountability and transparency, a requirement (see Redburn, Shea, and Buss 2008). But state and local governments, along with private organizations and nonprofits, have followed suit, motivated by their own desires to demonstrate their value and to hold responsible people accountable.

Where the Action Is in Community Development

Although such a diverse cross-section of chapters on community development can be organized in various ways, and many chapters easily fit under several headings, we arranged *Reengineering Community Development for the 21st Century* in seven parts.

Part 1. Community Development Financial Institutions (CDFIs)

The field of community development finance is evolving rapidly as CDFIs find innovative ways to capture investment opportunities and meet the needs in underserved communities. The six chapters in part 1 offer different perspectives on the changes in the field. Robin Newberger, Michael Berry, Kirsten Moy, and Gregory A. Ratliff, in chapter 2, "Evolving Roles of Mission-Focused and Mainstream Financial Organizations," take a comprehensive look at the community development finance industry. Building on a state-of-the-industry conference series, they examine how nine CDFIs' relationships with mainstream financial institutions increase the impact of the CDFIs individually and collectively, suggesting that these types of strategic partnerships and creative business models can help bring the industry to greater scale.

In chapter 3, "When Subsidy Becomes Scarce: Rethinking Community Development Finance," Julia Sass Rubin focuses on two types of CDFIs—community development loan funds and community development venture capital funds—that provide debt and equity capital in higher risk transactions. Rubin observers that changes in once-supportive economic and political environments have caused these institutions to reconsider their underlying business models.

CDFIs are innovative financial institutions. Annie Donovan, in chapter 4, "CDFIs 'Make the Market' for Charter School Facilities Financing," examines a relatively new investment opportunity for CDFIs: financing facilities for charter schools. Donovan's analysis shows the positive investment potential for charter school financing.

Anna Steiger, Tessa Hebb, and Lisa A. Hagerman, in chapter 5, "The Case for the Community Partner in Economic Development," look at issues and best practices in linking investment intermediaries and community partners to channel capital into underserved neighborhoods. Investment intermediaries "intervene between the investor and the community by pooling investments, spreading risk across investors, and pricing the transaction up to the associated risk." Community partners "draw on their specialized local knowledge to structure deals that ensure social benefits for low- and moderate-income residents." Effective community development will rely increasingly on these partnerships.

Two chapters look at performance management and accountability issues in community development finance. Dan Immergluck, in chapter 6, "Research Design Issues for Measuring CDFI Performance and Impact," addresses the methodological issues involved in evaluating CDFIs, including research design, impact measurement, data requirements, validity, and reliability. Although CDFIs pose numerous challenges in conducting evaluations, Immergluck lays out a framework that moves the field considerably in the direction of meaningful evaluation. David Porteous and Saurabh Narain, in chapter 7, "Social Performance Measurement for CDFI Banks," move from the theoretical/conceptual to an actual assessment of the "social performance" of community development banks using a variety of publicly available databases. Like Immergluck, Porteous and Narain review database limitations and offer an agenda for future research.

Part 2. Asset Building

Asset building is one of the newer innovative perspectives in community development undertaken over the last few years. The simple notion behind the concept is that assets, whether individual or community, are both ends and means to community economic development. As such, asset building must be a focus, or for some, *the* focus, of development initiatives. Joshua Silver, in chapter 8, "Stubborn and Persistent Lending Disparities," documents the extent and nature of disparities in loan pricing based on race and income levels in neighborhoods that arise from discrimination, market failure, and lack of consumer financial knowledge. Inability to obtain loans impedes wealth building and sustainable homeownership necessary for community development. Silver offers recommendations to remove barriers primarily through federal regulatory powers.

In chapter 9, "The Assets Framework: Moving Toward Transformative Transactions," Hannah Thomas looks at asset building from an institutional perspective in which a CDFI—Coastal Enterprises, Inc.—approaches development not only by financing deals but also by building wealth in communities. Thomas calls attention to the fact that many CDFIs have acted or are tempted to act more like mainstream banks, in the process diminishing their community development focus. Coastal Enterprises offers a model for CDFIs to consider before redirecting their community development missions.

In chapter 10, "Connecting Asset Building and Community Development," William Schweke develops a framework and comprehensive action agenda that promotes the linkage of asset-building strategies for individuals to broader community development approaches. In prominently linking asset building and community development, policymakers and practitioners can develop a whole new perspective on helping individuals and revitalizing communities, one that portends much success for those who engage it.

Rene Bryce-Laporte and Hilary Hunt, in chapter 11, "Innovation in State Government: Pennsylvania's Financial Education Office," provide a case study of how concerned Pennsylvania policymakers created a state-of-the-art financial education program intended to provide people with the skills they need to build assets. The authors show the necessity of building a broad coalition of decision makers and stakeholders in developing a sustainable program that yields great benefits in building communities.

Part 3. Capacity Building and Citizen Engagement

Capacity building in grassroots organizations and for citizens is critical if community development initiatives are to be successful in revitalizing neighborhoods and communities. Without capacity to effectively participate in community development planning and activities, some organizations will be ineffective and citizens will be frustrated as efforts fail. Four chapters look at capacity building in community development through very different lenses. In chapter 12, "Community Capacity Building Through Strategic Philanthropy at the United Way," Yoel Camayd-Freixas, Gerald Karush, Melissa Nemon, and Richard Koenig detail how a local United Way in Manchester, New Hampshire, reengineered itself to engage community development as a core part of its mission, in the process moving away from a traditional community chest model of philanthropy. The authors show how the agency built capacity within its own operations and among its member agencies to realize its new approach.

Jane F. Morgan, in chapter 13, "Building Community Capacity Through Multisector Collaborations," looks at a multisector collaboration between a Local Initiatives Support Corporation in Detroit and numerous organizations involved in community development, education, human services, and a variety of other sectors. The collaborative model, grounded in neighborhood planning and community development corporation approaches, shows how the Detroit Low Income Support

Corporation (LISC) took the lead and created Strategic Investment Areas to target funds in areas of greatest need to great effect.

In chapter 14, "Southern Bancorp's Model for Community Economic Development: The Delta Bridge Project," Ben Steinberg, Ben Goodwin, and Michael Rowett recount the efforts of Southern Bancorp—a community development bank holding company—to revitalize a rural community in the Arkansas Mississippi Delta region. The Delta Bridge Project illustrates how a bank can take the lead in stimulating participation across all sectors of a community, setting the stage for sustainable development.

Chapter 15, "Effective Citizen Engagement: Lessons from Seattle Schools—A Memoir," is a memoir offered by Norman Rice, former mayor of Seattle, and Lynda Petersen, recounting Rice's innovative effort to bring stakeholders—citizens and organizations—of Seattle together to solve the crisis in the city's schools—at the time a major community development issue in neighborhoods and citywide—through a broad-scale citizen engagement project. This exemplary citizen-participation effort helped turn the school system around and provides invaluable insights for others. (See Buss, Redburn and Guo [2006] for a review of citizen participation issues.)

Part 4. Federal Policy

Two federal issues—among many—caught the attention of those working in the community development field. In chapter 16, "Reforming CDBG: An Illusive Quest," Terry F. Buss analyzes reforms—some successful, others not so—in the $4 billion Community Development Block Grant (CDBG) program as it came under continued scrutiny for its performance under the eight years of the George W. Bush administration. (See Redburn, Shea, and Buss [2008] for an overview of performance management and budgeting issues.) F. Stevens Redburn, in chapter 17, "Rethinking Federal Low-Income Housing Policies," provides an in-depth review of why federal policies are so ineffective, then lays out a comprehensive strategy to reengineer low-income housing policy from the federal perspective.

Part 5. Smart Growth and Land Use

During the urban renewal of the 1930s to 1960s and the war on poverty in the 1960s, policymakers and planners concentrated on community development in moribund central business districts and inner-city neighborhoods devastated in part by the rise of suburbs. In recent years, concern has shifted to the suburbs, many of which are in decline in part because of urban sprawl, unplanned growth, and out-migration. Thomas J. Vicino, in chapter 18, "Smart Growth and Community Investment: Confronting Suburban Decline in Baltimore," looks at suburban decline in the Baltimore metropolitan area and Maryland's efforts to reverse downward trends by promoting "smart growth" policies, now in their tenth year. A central concern that permeates any discussion of smart growth is transportation. Many attribute suburban and urban decline generally to the increasing reliance on the automobile, especially among commuters to work. Much community development effort has focused on public mass transit as the solution. In a very innovative piece, "Positive Cycling: Riding Our Bicycles Down the Path to Community Development Success" (chapter 19), David W. Sears and Colin D. Sears convincingly suggest that communities might better realize smart growth if they pursued bicycle-friendly strategies that could, in their view, reduce reliance on the automobile.

Part 6. Affordable Housing

Affordable housing has always been central to community development, but despite Herculean efforts, it remains a problem for many Americans and communities. Two chapters address the issue of affordable housing in very different ways.

In chapter 20, "Aging-Out and Foster Care: Housing Policy," James O. Bates takes a look at a low-visibility, yet high-import affordable housing issue that has yet to attract much attention: what do youth in foster care do when they "age out" of the system, are unemployed, and have few housing options? Bates draws attention to the magnitude of the problem and offers policy prescriptions to address it.

Land prices and behavior of landowners are critical to many aspects of community development—nonprofits or governments try to amass tracts of land for affordable housing or open space siting, but find it difficult and expensive where land values are high. Edward J. Dodson, in chapter 21, "Would the Adoption of Land Value Taxation Drive Down the Price of Land and Increase Housing Affordability?" draws on the work of late nineteenth-century political economist Henry George to argue that land value taxation is an effective tool to stimulate community development, especially in the realm of affordable housing.

Part 7. Crime and Development

Conventional wisdom in community development has it that crime is a major deterrent to business development and viability and hence a contributor to urban decline. Timothy Bates and Alicia Robb, in chapter 22, "Crime's Impact on the Viability of Young Urban Small Businesses," decided to test this proposition empirically with Census Bureau surveys of small business owners, finding that although crime certainly provides the context for business in urban areas, scaring away businesses that fear crime, the businesses that remain tend to thrive. This chapter makes a major contribution to this sensitive community development issue.

Brenda Bratton Blom, Kate Titford, and Elisabeth Walden, in chapter 23, "Courts, Equity, and Community Development," look at the issue of crime in community development through the lens of the criminal justice system, especially the courts. They review the evolution of the criminal justice system from its early roots in England under the Normans to the present-day need to reconsider a system that incarcerates so many offenders to the detriment of themselves and the community.

Aftermath of Eminent Domain

In the appendix, "Redevelopment's Trend Away from Eminent Domain," T. Michael Lengyel argues that with the decline of eminent domain powers precipitated by the backlash of a 2006 Supreme Court decision (see next section), communities will have to rely on incentive-based community development programs, which he summarizes.

Community Development Issues to Watch

Several community development themes could not be addressed in this book, either because they are too new or because they have not yet attracted much attention. Nonetheless, these issues are important in a survey of the field.

New Markets Tax Credit

Although it received surprisingly little attention when launched under the Clinton administration in 2000, the New Markets Tax Credit (NMTC) is arguably the largest community and economic development program in existence today. As of January 2007, the CDFI Fund awarded $12.1 billion of NMTC authority to 179 community development entities (CDE) (GAO 2007a). In 2007, the Fund launched a multiyear evaluation of NMTC. Whether the program is producing the level of benefits intended will spur intense debates about community development in years to come.

Immigration

The recent influx of 10 to 12 million undocumented or illegal immigrants may eventually, if it has not already, substantially change some traditional aspects of community development (see, e.g., Fernandez 2003). Living below the radar of government scrutiny because of their legal status, immigrants are forced to work off the books in the hidden economy, often for very low wages with no benefits and with considerable discrimination and exploitation. They often live on the margins of society, without a lot of hope for the future. These immigrants present challenges for community development in that they have needs and could access services were they not legally prohibited from doing so. The bottom line: communities could invest a lot of funding and resources into development that may not reach those in need.

Mega Disasters—Natural and Man-made

The September 11, 2001, terrorist attacks on the United States and Hurricane Katrina in 2005 highlighted the need for community development organizations to develop the capacity to revitalize large sectors of communities, many that were economically once viable, after natural and man-made disasters. Eerily, the terrorist attacks and Hurricane Katrina have many things in common: planning for redevelopment was complicated, delayed, apparently ineffective, and largely beyond the capacity of local and state public and private actors to undertake successfully even with substantial federal assistance. Community development experts now have a good idea of the magnitude of the problems they will face in future mega-disasters, but they are much less certain about what to do about it (see CRRR 2005; GAO 2007b; NAPA 2007).

Microenterprise

Microenterprise development was a favorite topic in community development during the late 1990s, but in recent years, it has not received as much attention as other issues in the field. That may change now that the guru of microcredit, Muhammad Yunus and the Grameen Bank he founded, won the 2006 Nobel Peace Prize for leadership on the issue in Bangladesh and internationally (see http://nobelprize. org/nobel_prizes/peace/laureates/2006/press.html). There is renewed interest in microenterprise development that may catch on in the United States and may provide an opportunity for community development practitioners to learn from the major advances the international microfinance field has achieved in the last decade.

Eminent Domain

Perhaps the most salient land use issue affecting community development in decades was the 2005 U.S. Supreme Court ruling on eminent domain that supported communities whose officials wished to appropriate land from private owners to benefit other private investors. Although the ruling stands, at least twenty-nine states, feeling political pressure from virtually all quarters, have promulgated their own laws and regulations that try to nullify the Court's decision (GAO 2006). Individual communities, even though they have the law on their side, are opting not to pursue eminent domain because of the political backlash. It is unclear how the ruling will affect community and economic development initiatives generally.

References

Buss, Terry F., F. Stevens Redburn, and Kristina Guo, eds. 2006. *Modernizing Democracy: Innovations in Citizen Participation*. Armonk, NY: M.E. Sharpe.
Commission on Recovery, Rebuilding and Renewal (CRRR). 2005. *After Katrina*. Baton Rouge: Governor's Office (December 31).
Fernandez, Catherine. 2003. *Community Development in Dynamic Neighborhoods*. Washington, DC: Neighborhood Reinvestment Corporation.
Gerenrot, Julie, David B. Cashin, and Anna L. Paulson. 2006. "Community Development Spending, 1981–2004." *Chicago Fed Letter* (Federal Reserve Bank of Chicago) #232 (November).

Government Accountability Office (GAO). 2006. *Eminent Domain.* Washington, DC: GAO #07–28.

———. 2007a. *NMTC Appears to Increase Investment.* Washington, DC: GAO #07–296.

———. 2007b. *Preliminary Information on Rebuilding Efforts in the Gulf Coast.* Washington, DC: GAO #07–809R.

Morse, Ricardo, Terry F. Buss, and C. Morgan Kinghorn, eds. 2007. *Transforming Public Leadership for the Twenty-first Century.* Armonk, NY: M.E. Sharpe.

National Academy of Public Administration (NAPA). 2007. *The Small Business Administration's Disaster Loan Program.* Washington, DC: NAPA.

Redburn, F. Stevens, Robert Shea, and Terry F. Buss, eds. 2008. *Performance Management and Budgeting: How Governments Can Learn from Experience.* Armonk, NY: M.E. Sharpe.

Part 1

Community Development Financial Institutions

2

Evolving Roles of Mission-Focused and Mainstream Financial Organizations

Implications for the Scale and Sustainability of CDFIs

ROBIN NEWBERGER, MICHAEL BERRY, KIRSTEN MOY, AND
GREGORY A. RATLIFF

In 2005, the Federal Reserve System and the Aspen Institute's Economic Opportunities Program launched a national conference series to explore the state of the community development finance industry. A further goal was to document lessons and practices primarily from the for-profit sector and introduce product-, organization-, and industry-oriented innovations to increase the impact of community development financial institutions (CDFIs) and other community development organizations.[1] Prior research by Moy and others formed the basis for the series. This research showed that environmental changes related to public policy, changes at the point of community development impact[2] (where, how, and why community development investments occur), and sweeping advances in the mainstream financial services industry have significant implications for community development financial intermediaries. Research identified strategic partnerships and creative business models that the industry should consider to achieve greater scale (though not necessarily organizational size) and effectiveness. The conference series and attendant industry design and discussion sessions among practitioners, researchers, and policy groups have given rise to new research initiatives, of which this is one.

Financial Industry Developments and Trends

This study's purpose is to examine whether and how community development finance institutions increase their impact individually and collectively by building on and learning from relationships with mainstream financial institutions. Changes affecting the community development finance field, notably reduced federal funding and greater focus on CDFI performance by potential financial partners, as well as dramatic changes in the mainstream financial sector, have brought CDFIs face to face with new strategic opportunities for working with the mainstream financial system. In the past, mainstream financial institutions and CDFIs were separated by the populations they served and the products they offered. The dominant sentiment within the community development finance field was that banks were the perpetrators of disinvestment, and the first partnerships between banks and CDFIs were greeted with suspicion and doubt. Over several decades, that thinking has changed almost completely. Today, development finance organizations have become fluent in the language of business and command more and better resources to accomplish their mission. Many have adopted risk-management and administrative practices resembling those of mainstream institutions.

At the same time, financial markets have evolved to securitize credits and supply liquidity to credit markets once considered too risky or obscure. Mergers, refined risk-modeling capabilities, and heavy reliance on specialized, outsourced services have impacted the role of mainstream financial institutions in supporting and financing community development and providing financial services in low- and moderate-income communities. Public-sector support of community development has come increasingly in the form of federal tax credits to induce investments by banks, other corporations, and individuals. Although CDFIs have not broadly adopted the tactics that have led to efficiencies and growth in the industry, today's community development finance industry is more integrated with the conventional financial system than ever before. The mainstream financial sector has become the most important source of funding for community development. These developments have blurred the line between mainstream and development institutions, at least in their support for community development.

Future Niche of CDFIs

The participation of conventional lenders in the community development field is in many ways evidence of success for the development finance industry. The case is often made that the goal of development is not only to initiate and fund projects in lower-income neighborhoods but also to attract traditional commercial lending through the success of nontraditional capital. However, the success of the development finance industry raises new questions about the appropriate role of development finance organizations in today's market. The growing involvement of mainstream financial institutions in markets that were previously underserved has created the need to redefine, or at least reexamine, the position of community development financial institutions in the financial sector.

Through interviews with representatives of nine CDFIs as well as with officials at mainstream institutions, this study explores how interaction with conventional financial institutions enhances the impact of CDFIs. It addresses the ways integration and collaboration currently take place and which CDFI characteristics mainstream financial institutions value in forming relationships. It also touches on some of the challenges to CDFIs with respect to profitability and sustainability. This study is not intended as an exhaustive industry analysis but provides insights on some key industry trends.

Methodology

This study explores innovations from a cross-section of CDFI organizations, most of which have long operational histories and a diverse set of relationships with their mainstream financial partners. The group includes the Community Reinvestment Fund (CRF), Community Preservation Corporation (CPC), Low-Income Investment Fund (LIIF), Nonprofit Finance Fund (NFF), Center for Community Self-Help (Self-Help), ShoreBank Corporation, The Reinvestment Fund (TRF), ACCION New Mexico (ACCION-NM), and the National Community Investment Fund (NCIF); see Figure 2.1. All have weathered numerous changes in the mainstream financial services market, public policy, and the general economic climate and adapted to these environmental changes. Two of the participant organizations are mission-focused depository institutions and, as such, have at least one steady capital source (deposits). ACCION-NM and NCIF, both established in the mid-1990s, provide interesting cases of the use of existing banking infrastructure and perhaps insights for a possible future state of the development finance industry.

Roles described in the next section are drawn from personal interviews with the CEO and senior staff of each organization, as well as from background research and literature reviews. While we worked from a list of questions covering organizational history and financial relationships, each discussion went in its own direction. We also spoke with representatives of banks, foundations, and government agencies to gain some external perspective on these relationships. All interviews were conducted between June 2006 and April 2007.

Interactions Between CDFIs and Mainstream Financial Institutions

We draw from our interviews with the participant group to present current examples of collaboration with banks, government-sponsored enterprises such as Fannie Mae, and investment banking organizations. While we identified a range of CDFI activities vis-à-vis mainstream institutions, we focus here on roles and activities that represent reasons for organizational success in attracting and deploying capital and on those that represent advancements or innovations with ramifications for the community development finance field. Several examples illustrate how CDFIs bring liquidity and more competitive pricing to credits targeted to lower-income populations. We also summarize ways CDFIs align interests of multiple actors, including lenders, investors, and government agencies, and thereby increase and better leverage resources that go to development projects in impoverished communities.

The CDFI roles are grouped into broad areas: (1) extend through diverse constructs the ability of mainstream institutions to lend beyond profitability constraints to nontraditional borrowers in the primary market; (2) expand capital markets to include community development credits; (3) develop new areas of lending that mainstream institutions eventually serve independently; (4) perform civic

Figure 2.1   **Brief Descriptions of CDFI Organizations Interviewed**

Nonprofit Finance Fund (NFF) provides loans, credit enhancements, and grants to nonprofits. Increasingly, the organization is moving away from facilities financing and toward lending (and other funding), training, and consulting services that build capacity of its nonprofit clients.

The Reinvestment Fund (TRF) is a national leader in the financing of neighborhood revitalization. TRF finances housing, community facilities, commercial real estate and businesses across the Mid-Atlantic. TRF also conducts research and analysis on policy issues that influence neighborhood revitalization and economic growth.

Community Preservation Corporation (CPC) is a nonprofit bank consortium that facilitates affordable housing development and redevelopment. CPC offers construction, rehab, and refinancing loans, and provides technical assistance to borrowers, which include public, private, and nonprofit developers. CPC is sponsored by eighty banks and insurance companies, and its geographic scope includes the states of New York, New Jersey, and Connecticut.

The Center for Community Self-Help (Self-Help) focuses on mortgage and small business lending to people of color, women, rural residential and low-wealth families, and communities that are not served adequately by other financial institutions. Self-Help operates the Center for Responsible Lending, a nonprofit created to explain and promote responsible lending advocacy at the national level. Self-Help is based in Durham, North Carolina. It operates offices in cities across North Carolina as well as in Washington, D.C. and Oakland, California.

The **Community Reinvestment Fund (CRF)** is the development finance industry leader in opening channels to capital markets. CRF operates a national secondary market for community development loans, more broadly connecting local development lenders with capital markets to increase their liquidity and impact.

The **Low-Income Investment Fund (LIIF)** provides capital and other assistance for affordable housing, child care, education, and other community building facilities and initiatives. LIIF finances all development phases, including permanent mortgages, as well as operating lines of credit for nonprofit organizations. LIIF operates mainly in three metropolitan areas: San Francisco, Los Angeles, and New York City.

ShoreBank Corporation was the first community development bank in the nation. It is a multistate banking and community development organization comprising two banks and seven nonprofit subsidiaries in Chicago, Detroit, Cleveland, and Ilwaco, Washington. Having pioneered the concept of community development banking and the "double bottom line" of both mission and profit goals, ShoreBank developed in the 1990s the concept of a "triple bottom line" that also encompasses environmental goals.

The **National Community Investment Fund (NCIF)** was established in 1996 as an independent fund to make investments in depository institutions around the country. These institutions are community banks, thrifts, and some credit unions that have a primary mission of community development.

ACCION New Mexico (ACCION-NM) provides business credit, microloans, training, and other resources to further the goals of emerging entrepreneurs in the state of New Mexico. ACCION-NM is part of an international network of independent ACCION organizations.

Note: More information about each organization can be found in an appendix at www.napawash.org.

intermediary functions by helping to contextualize public and private investments from regulatory and economic development viewpoints and capture public funds to attract mainstream participation in community development; and (5) help to build community (development) banking by leveraging existing infrastructure and capital, and increasing the number of CDFI banks. We explain the importance of each strategic area, and then provide examples that reflect the function at selected CDFIs. Many of these functions are common to more than one organization in our participant group. Some of the activities we describe illustrate several functions or roles in the same example. In addition, not all the broad strategic functions apply to all of the organizations in our study group. ShoreBank, the only (community development) bank in our sample, has larger banks as investors, but the relationship has little in common with that of loan funds or even the only other depository in the group, Self-Help.

Primary Market

Extending the ability of regulated, mainstream financial institutions to lend and invest in community development beyond profitability and risk constraints through diverse CDFI/bank constructs is a classic CDFI function. CDFIs (more precisely, community development loan funds) borrow bank and other funds to lend at below-market rates to higher risk, less experienced, or unproven customers at a small profit. These loans are often smaller, riskier, more specialized, and comparatively less profitable than typical bank products; many banks cannot underwrite such loans on a continual, cost-effective basis. Borrowers include nonprofit organizations and developers who cannot meet underwriting criteria at conventional institutions.

Lending Consortia, Pools, Syndications

In addition to one-on-one relationships between CDFIs and mainstream financial institutions, CDFIs organize lending consortia, pools, syndications, and other risk sharing that use specialized lending, local/regional market, and policy expertise. These arrangements bring more capital for community development and enable CDFIs to generate more and larger loans. They allow banks to participate in and thereby spread risk across portfolios of community development loans, earn profit, and earn Community Reinvestment Act (CRA) credit. They extend further than one-on-one relationships the ability of mainstream financial institutions to lend and invest in community development beyond profitability constraints, potentially to a broader geographic area, and with greater impact.

CPC is one of the earliest examples of a loan consortium for community development purposes in the nation. Unlike other examples we cite, in which a nonprofit lender uses consortia as one of multiple strategies, its organizational structure is a loan consortium. CPC was founded in the 1970s in response to the long-term deterioration of the affordable housing stock in New York City boroughs. CPC traces its origins to a study conducted under the auspices of (David Rockefeller at) Chase Manhattan Bank in the early 1970s that looked to redress almost three decades of disinvestment in the housing stock of neighborhoods in Brooklyn and the South Bronx. After much earlier middle-class flight to the suburbs from these areas, banks had become leery of lending in them. Thrift institutions, which served some blighted areas, did not have the capacity or expertise to finance and carry out large rehabilitations. The study concluded that only a nonprofit funded with bank capital and dedicated to improving specific neighborhoods could turn around this long-term deterioration. A consortium of about sixty banks provided lines of credit to CPC. Today, these lines total about $460 million, are renewed every five years, and a single agent bank, Deutsche Bank, lends to CPC directly under a revolving credit arrangement.

Another example of a pioneering consortium was developed by the NFF in the mid-1990s. When wholesale banks came under CRA regulation in 1995, banks such as JPMorgan recognized that working with an intermediary was the best and perhaps the only way to meet CRA lending requirements. Wholesale banks were not structured to make small, customized loans. With an understanding that these loans would not be profitable for banks to do on their own, NFF structured a loan syndication with wholesale banks as funders. This arrangement was pivotal to NFF's growth; at the same time, it was a relatively straightforward relationship. All the banks lent with the same set of covenants. A single bank, JPMorgan, acted as the syndication agent. The terms of the consortium made NFF the underwriter. Banks lent to the consortium unsecured, without collateral, but with full recourse, meaning that NFF could be compelled to make good on (i.e., buy back) nonperforming loans. They made the loan decisions and decided the terms of the loans, incurring the related due diligence and servicing costs.

Variations of the pool/consortia model have allowed CDFIs to move away from making relatively small loans to one in which larger pooled arrangements facilitate financings that banks would still not underwrite alone, sometimes for specific purposes, such as construction, or for specific types of collateral, such as charter schools. In 1994, TRF organized a consortium of bank lenders, called the Collaborative Lending Initiative, to finance large construction projects—larger projects than TRF could finance using its own capital. The Collaborative Lending Initiative is a direct lender to housing, community facilities, and commercial real estate projects. Starting at $13 million and growing to $30 million, the Collaborative Lending Initiative marked the first time TRF turned ad hoc loan participations into a system. The consortium initially consisted of twenty-two different lines of credit managed by TRF. Small banks were most interested in participating because the consortium gave smaller institutions that did not have their own real estate departments a way to receive CRA credit. When the Collaborative Lending Initiative turned into a true syndication in 2002, larger banks joined with a different motive: to outsource the smaller deals (less than $500,000) that they could not do profitably on their own. Chase assumed the role of managing these credit lines in 2002.

Deploy Off-Balance-Sheet Capital

The broad goal of community development loan funds to grow their lending and impact has in some cases pushed individual institutions past the point where it remains practical to borrow and then deploy money. Two principal obstacles inhibit lending growth among loan funds: they have finite core capital (and sources of funding available to grow capital have diminished), and bank funding above a certain level is too costly. Banks can often underwrite credits that in the past required an intermediary, reducing their incentive to lend at any discount to market. Some CDFIs accordingly engage in "off-balance-sheet" lending, deploying funds of other institutions directly. This model enables the CDFI to increase its lending impact in an environment where growing internal capital has become more difficult. It also enables a mainstream partner to leverage the local market knowledge, expertise, and high-touch servicing of a CDFI, but usually with some level of recourse.

LIIF provides an example of this type of arrangement. Within the past few years, LIIF determined it could realize its goal of increasing its lending capacity more efficiently by lending funds of other entities that it need not control directly. LIIF originates and services loans for mainstream financial institutions, which are held on the books of the mainstream institutions. For example, LIIF originates and underwrites charter school loans for Royal Bank of Canada, one of the most active banks in the California charter school financing market. Another source of off-balance-sheet capital for LIIF is the Fannie Mae American Communities Fund. Fannie Mae reviewed and approved LIIF's underwriting standards, and LIIF sells loans to Fannie Mae without review, but with 5 percent recourse, meaning Fannie Mae can compel lenders to buy back that portion of (nonperforming) loans sold to the fund. Currently, about 60 percent of the $300 million in capital LIIF has available to finance community development projects is not on its balance sheet but under the CDFI's (sole) purview. LIIF's CEO described the organization's role as moving toward one of supplying intellectual capital (market expertise) in isolation versus expertise coupled with financial capital that it raises and deploys.

Employ Variations of Traditional Partnership Roles to Facilitate Broader CDFI Reach

A very different way of extending the reach of CDFIs is the ACCION-NM model. In 1999, after five years of operation, ACCION-NM expanded its geographic footprint from the greater Albuquerque area to the entire state of New Mexico. ACCION-NM recognized that small-business lending and microlending were badly needed among cash-starved entrepreneurs with blemished credit histories or none at all, but traveling great distances to originate and close very small loans would create too much expense for ACCION-NM to survive. Therefore, ACCION-NM became adept at using the network of offices of banking institutions around the state (Wells Fargo; First State Bank, a First Community Bank subsidiary; and more recently First National Bank of

Santa Fe) to identify borrowers, often would-be bank customers, who do not meet bank underwriting criteria. These banks have become the principal distribution system for ACCION-NM, even representing the organization at loan closings. In some instances, credit is extended without any face-to-face contact between ACCION-NM staff and actual borrowers; the bank office serves as a communication and funding channel, but ACCION-NM underwrites and funds the loans. These relationships between ACCION-NM and the banks set up the opportunity for ACCION-NM's customers to "graduate" to a direct relationship with the bank at a later time.

Secondary Market

The secondary market promotes open channels to capital markets for community development loans to facilitate greater liquidity and reliable funding sources for community development lenders. Much of the dialogue related to scaling and to some degree mainstreaming the development finance field revolves around the topics of liquidity and access to reliable, stable, and predictably priced sources of capital. Capital markets create liquidity and reduce pricing once risks associated with an asset type are identified and quantified, and the CDFI industry has made significant inroads toward accessing secondary market capital on a continual, if not yet broad, basis. There are still numerous challenges to this endeavor. Many of the loans originated by CDFIs do not fit normal secondary market criteria, loan volume is insufficient to attract interest among investment bankers, and there is a scarcity of data to inform risk-management models. To the extent CDFIs can adapt their lending practices, capital markets represent an efficient and ready funding source for an industry that has historically depended on uncertain government and foundation funding and specialized relationships with banks.

Create Capital Markets Channels for Non-SBA-Qualifying Small Business Loans

As an organization founded on the principle of bringing capital to community development lenders through the secondary market, the CRF works to demonstrate and develop secondary markets for loans that do not fit current secondary market criteria. For many years, the Small Business Administration (SBA)-insured portion of qualifying loans was the only secondary market for business loans. Lack of similarity between business loans was a barrier to secondary market sales. CRF saw a niche in devising ways to pool non-SBA-insurable loans—loans to small business owners originated through revolving loan funds whose growth would otherwise be constrained because of the slow return of funds to relend to subsequent borrowers. CRF purchases loans under specified agreements from nonprofit or publicly sponsored small business lenders around the country and packages them into securities. These loans are secured by real estate, but typically their loan-to-value ratios are too high or the collateral has a second lien, and therefore they do not qualify for

SBA 504 guarantees. CRF sells these securities predominantly to banks investing for CRA purposes. In 2004, CRF reached an important milestone, receiving a Standard and Poor's rating for its roughly $50 million securitization, 87 percent of which was AAA (highest) rated. Buyers included institutional money managers and insurance companies. Another rated security followed in 2006. Banks seeking CRA credit continued to invest in the lower rated tranches of these issues.

Securitize Nonconforming Mortgages

Another important innovation for accessing the secondary market is one developed by Self-Help. Self-Help began its secondary mortgage market program in 1994 to address the need for greater liquidity in the lending market to nonconventional mortgage customers. In Self-Help's secondary mortgage market program, the supplier network is mainstream financial institutions. Self-Help purchases nonconforming "CRA-qualifying" mortgage loans and securitizes them through Fannie Mae. These are high-loan-to-value mortgage loans to households that may have blemished credit histories and/or difficulty documenting income and do not qualify for conventional ("A credit") mortgage financing.[3] This program began with Self-Help's purchase of Wachovia's $20 million nonconforming portfolio. The terms of the transaction required Wachovia to relend the sale proceeds of its portfolio in low- and moderate-income communities. Funding from the MacArthur Foundation in 1997 allowed Self-Help to buy additional loans from Wachovia and other institutions. In 1998, this pilot led to a national program to sell nonconforming loans to Fannie Mae. Fannie Mae made a $2 billion dollar commitment to securitize the loans originated by twenty-two financial institutions. Self-Help obtained a $50 million Ford Foundation grant to serve as a loss reserve. The $2 billion mark was reached in 2003, and the commitment was renewed at $2.5 billion with a new five-year term. Presently, the mortgage-backed securities derived from these loans (issued by Fannie Mae) account for about two-thirds of Self-Help's portfolio.[4]

Expand Loan Securitization to New Types of Assets

An even more recent development in CDFI secondary market activity is exploratory work on securitizing charter school loans. CDFIs have been making charter school loans since 1997. Planning is under way among members of the Housing Partnership Network (HPN), a consortium of affordable housing developers, lenders, and other development finance organizations, to explore the feasibility of a bond securitization program for charter schools. Five of the CDFIs involved in HPN are among our participant group: CPC, CRF, TRF, Self-Help, and LIIF. Under the direction of Minneapolis-based consultant Wilary Winn, which also advises CRF individually, the group has assembled data about its loan portfolio and is working with potential investors and partners. The expected launch of a pooled transaction is the second half of 2007.[5]

Innovator/Pioneer

An innovator/pioneer is one who develops new areas of lending that mainstream institutions can eventually take on with or without intermediaries, in part by identifying and helping to address related risks. Over the years, a case has been made that a key role of CDFIs relative to mainstream financial institutions is that they demonstrate the viability of the community development finance market. Indeed, CDFIs often see themselves as laboratories and regularly adapt their products in response to economic, social, and institutional changes. They make the case for lending and investment in underserved communities, demonstrating the value of the collateral they are creating, so that a part of this market can later be taken over by mainstream financial institutions. CDFI innovations are shared or "spun-off" to larger, often private, financial players that are better able to commercialize fully a promising new product or service. Some in the industry have a goal of changing the behavior not just of lenders in the primary market but of investors in the secondary market as well.

Mortgages to Lower-Income Households

A classic example of this "demonstration effect" is nonconforming and subprime mortgages. Community development banks and credit unions, as well other intermediaries, began underwriting mortgages to lower-income households as early as the mid-1970s. Although the subprime market is currently in crisis because of overly relaxed underwriting standards and aggressive marketing of nontraditional (e.g., low/no documentation, interest-only, 2/28[6]) subprime loans to inappropriate borrowers as of spring 2007, CDFIs were among the first to demonstrate that nongovernment-insured mortgages could be extended to lower-income households that do not qualify for prime, conventional loans. The secondary market for subprime mortgages expanded in the 1990s, and Government Sponsored Enterprises (GSEs) began purchasing the least risky ("A-minus" credits) of these loans. Today, mainstream institutions have overtaken mission-oriented organizations in providing mortgage loans to low- and moderate-income borrowers. Construction and permanent financing for affordable multifamily housing comes from banks and less often from CDFIs.

Loans to Charter Schools

A more recent example is loans to charter schools (see also Chapter 4, "CDFIs 'Make the Market' for Charter School Facilities Financing"). In the early days of charter schools, there was no connection made to CRA by banks or, formally, by bank regulators. Banks moved slowly into the field through participations organized by CDFI intermediaries. Later, CDFIs noted that some of the banks they worked with started making these loans directly. For example, Citibank was one of the banks to help CRF negotiate its first charter school loan pool. It took that knowledge and then made five or six charter school loans as the sole lender. Despite some idiosyncrasies, the larger loan sizes (some over $5 million) help banks clear at least one profitability hurdle common to community development loans.

The concept of CDFIs as being fundamentally demonstration organizations can be oversimplified, however. Often, CDFIs do not exit a market after mainstream banks have joined. As TRF explains, it does not cede lending markets to banks once the related risks and idiosyncrasies are commonly understood. TRF remains a player, financial and otherwise, and works to inform and integrate aspects of public policy, civic involvement and awareness, and related development and services to the betterment of its local markets. For some CDFIs, the justification for remaining in a market relates to sustainability; the time and energy to understand and develop a lending market represents a significant investment, and CDFIs seek a return on that investment. Others question whether it is in the best interest of the community development borrower to hand over the market to mainstream financial institutions. In Wilary Winn's view, the charter school market is still an emerging, inefficient market, and CDFIs have a duty to consider whether a bank loan of five to seven years is necessarily the best type of funding for a charter school.

CDFIs also consider the permanence of mainstream institutions in these niches. As profit-motivated institutions, banks may temporarily or permanently vacate a product line if a certain margin is not met or if the bank changes its orientation after a restructuring or merger. CDFIs have seen this as an argument for staying in a particular market or product line to ensure that certain types of credit remain available. Leaving a market when banks move in during strong economic times creates the risk of leaving a lending vacuum not easily filled during weaker economic times if the CDFI has divested itself of the infrastructure and capacity to operate in that niche. ShoreBank, for example, competes with mainstream banks for market share in the rehab loan market and remains the dominant lender in the bank's original market, Chicago's South Shore neighborhood, even as other banks have entered and left the market.

Civic Intermediary/Aggregator of Public Funds and Resources

Civic Intermediary/Aggregator of Public Funds and Resources capture and manage available public moneys to enable and/or enhance community development finance. By virtue of their social missions and nonprofit status, as well as their expertise and market awareness, CDFIs are positioned not only to attract subsidy capital but also to provide input on government subsidy program design and deployment. Generally, to bring deals or programs to fruition, CDFIs must assemble subsidy, nonfinancial commitments, and community support and must form long-term (and informed) relationships with government officials, investors, and clients. CDFIs often assume the role of subordinate lender and take the first-loss risk and/or apply for and bring public, foundation, or other ancillary funding to bear to provide loss reserves and mitigate risk to their mainstream partners. The CDFI intermediary assumes the role of trustee (of sorts), and must not only assure the highest level of integrity and skill in deploying public (subsidy) resources but also use them efficiently, leverage private capital, and align the interests of all parties toward achieving the desired outcome. In most CDFI deals, banks would not otherwise lend or invest.

As CPC explains, one of its roles is to devise finance structures that dovetail private finance with tax incentives, grants, or low-interest loan subsidies. CPC has also addressed barriers to investing in multifamily housing by, for example, aligning guidelines common to city subsidy programs with its own underwriting criteria, eliminating the need for developers to meet multiple criteria and benchmarks, and providing technical assistance and support for borrowers/developers and building residents. These efforts have attracted more private-sector investors in affordable housing.

CDFIs also help to shape policy priorities. For example, NFF played a major role in broadening the types of loans for which banks receive CRA credit beyond housing finance. A breakthrough aspect of NFF's initial loan syndication in the 1990s was that it brought together bank funds to support community development activities outside of the housing sector. Prior to the early 1990s, banks did not expect to earn CRA credit for funding things like a nonprofit's operating credit line or arts facilities. NFF argued that nonprofits that support homeless shelters, drug treatment centers, community centers, and the like, should all be included in CRA. With some help from the New York and San Francisco Federal Reserve Banks, which held forums to raise awareness of NFF's efforts, the definition of *CRA-qualified loans* was extended beyond mortgages. NFF's advocacy led to increased bank lending to nonprofits in New York and across the country.

CRF's work to open capital markets to community development finance provides another illustration. As a secondary market investor, CRF envisioned ways the New Markets Tax Credit might be used as part of a strategy to enable capital markets funding. Its strategy reduced costs to end borrowers and produced loans suitable for investment-grade securitizations. Even though CRF's National New Markets Tax Credit Fund Inc. (the entity that receives the tax credits) is a for-profit institution, and it purchases loans from public loan funds (not uniquely nonprofits), it qualified for New Markets funding because it sought and received a private letter ruling that allows CRF to buy loans from non–community development entities (CDEs) as long as they are subject to an advance commitment (i.e., CRF reviews the loans and issues commitment letters).[7] New Markets enabled CRF to raise subordinate capital by applying for tax credit allocations and selling the credits to persons or organizations with sufficient federal tax liability. CRF became the first multi-investor fund in the marketplace to use the credit in this way. (CRF has been allocated roughly $400 million in credits in three rounds.) The fund creates capacity to purchase loans, and the structure allows CRF to improve pricing to end borrowers by roughly 150 basis points compared with market-rate pricing for the typical borrower. The New Market Tax Credit (NMTC)-financed limited partnership facilitates investment-grade ratings for the largest portion of CRF's securitizations.

Further, CDFIs see themselves as having a responsibility to protect consumers or play a watchdog role in the community development finance field. For example, Self-Help launched a subsidiary, the Center for Responsible Lending, to counter predatory lending practices through research, studies, and policy work. More recently, to counter predatory lending in the subprime market, two prominent organizations in the development finance industry are rolling out new subprime mortgage programs positioned as alternatives to predatory lenders that include secondary market components and fair pricing policies. The HPN is forming a conduit for "responsibly priced" subprime mortgages, and the Opportunity Finance Network, a trade association for CDFIs, is planning to offer a "turnkey" mortgage lending platform for CDFIs that wish to participate. TRF's self-described role as a civic intermediary goes to the heart of CDFIs as gatekeepers for community development projects in their service areas. From city and state politicians to local venture capitalists, local leaders seek TRF's advice and participation based on TRF's network of civic and policy relationships as well as its expertise and experience.

Demonstrate Community Banking Models and Expand the Development Banking Industry

The relationship between the community development bank in our sample, ShoreBank, and mainstream institutions, is distinct from that of other examples, which are primarily community development loan funds. Even banks such as ShoreBank that identify themselves as "community development" institutions do not get funding from or cofinance with larger, mainstream banks and may compete with mainstream banks in the same market for certain credits. If one metaphor for a CDFI is a bridge that connects community development borrowers to capital, CDFI loan funds start on one side of the river and CDFI banks on the other. CDFI banks are regulated depositories attempting to create a new business model for community banks. In effect, they are redesigning the financial system for low- and moderate-income populations and places from the inside. They serve customers who may find traditional banks intimidating or not welcoming and who may need some counseling or technical assistance to use the banks' account services and borrow and repay loans successfully. Community development banks are organizations with mission goals as well as profitability goals. ShoreBank has a triple bottom line of profit, community development, and the environment.

For ShoreBank, a bank is a very different "change agent" from other types of community development intermediaries. All banks must comply with an array of regulations relating to their liquidity, management, earnings, and exposure to market and interest rate risk (as well as CRA and consumer regulations). However, once these criteria are met, a community development bank can leverage capital to a far greater degree than a loan fund. From the bankers' perspectives, this allows community development banks to have greater overall impact. Leverage is seen as an important tool to operate at scale.

ShoreBank operates with a distinct philosophy as well. According to its theory of change, the individual and the private sector, not the nonprofit, are the most important agents of change. Few bank borrowers identify themselves as "community developers." They usually have a profit motive. Therefore, ShoreBank does not generally consider whether or not a prospective borrower is engaged in a textbook definition of economic development. If a loan can give people the opportunity to own a home that they might otherwise not be able to finance, and the bank can make the underwriting work, ShoreBank will provide it. Through its purchase/rehab lending in South Shore, ShoreBank has helped to create substantial wealth for some of its clients.

Another key aspect of ShoreBank's strategy is that it bundles nonprofit affiliates within a larger holding company structure. The ShoreBank structure includes non-profit and for-profit affiliates that complement the bank work, much like nonprofit CDFIs complement the work of mainstream financial institutions. ShoreBank's management recognized early on that regulatory requirements would constrain the bank from extensive lending to nontraditional borrowers with blemished (or no) credit profiles and/or insufficient assets. Establishing affiliates within the same bank holding company enables ShoreBank to reach deeper into low- and moderate-income populations. ShoreBank's affiliates have complementary roles to those of the bank and exist to help the bank achieve its mission goals as opposed to simply facilitating community development lending to meet regulatory requirements. The nonprofits raise grants and supplemental funding for redevelopment projects, provide technical assistance and training to entrepreneurs and others, and provide financing that the bank could not (easily) make directly. The nonprofits also benefit from the expertise, infrastructure, and underwriting discipline that come from af-filiation with a regulated bank.

Finally, ShoreBank's effort to remodel at least a segment of the mainstream financial system is evident in its mission to create examples of profitable products and services that other banking institutions can emulate. ShoreBank is the principal advisor and trustee to NCIF, which makes investments in community banks serving low-income populations and underinvested communities nationwide. ShoreBank has no ownership interest in NCIF but helped create the organization after NationsBank (now Bank of America) approached ShoreBank in the mid-1990s for ideas about how to invest in community banks. NCIF looks to leverage the existing infrastructure and delivery system of community development banks to have greater community impact but, like ShoreBank, is focused on profitability and disciplined management as well as mission goals.[8] The rationale is that many community banks around the country already have many characteristics of community development-focused and mission-focused institutions, even if they do not identify themselves as such. As financial institutions with existing funding infrastructure, insured deposits, and delivery systems, these institutions have higher barriers to entry and are accordingly fewer in number but control a much larger collective pool of assets than other CDFI types.[9] NCIF makes direct investments in community banks and encourages them to seek CDFI certification from the U.S. Treasury's CDFI Fund, thereby availing themselves of resources. In addition to direct investment, NCIF, which is a U.S. Treasury–designated CDFI and an NMTC CDE, also aggregates NMTCs on behalf of banks and credit unions with a community development focus. NCIF conducts workshops and extensive training for community banks that wish to pursue the CDFI designation. Research efforts by NCIF and others are ongoing to demonstrate the impact of community banks in community development lending, whether or not they identify themselves as having a mission focus.

Implications for the Scale and Sustainability of CDFIs

Funding Innovations Impacting Scale

While this chapter highlights a diverse set of institutions, ultimately our examples look at partnerships and relationships that enable these organizations to operate at a greater scale. The idea of greater scale is difficult to define precisely but might broadly be characterized as serving more people and communities and having a larger impact. Collaboration with large mainstream financial institutions allows CDFIs to have a greater financial, geographical, and political reach. Beginning with lending consortia, CDFIs have developed a series of innovations to attract funding from banking institutions for community development purposes. Off-balance-sheet financing—brokering loans for banks and others while still bringing market and program expertise to bear—has become a way for CDFIs to increase lending impact when they cannot grow internal capital rapidly enough to pace their own lending goals. The expanding use of secondary market mechanisms to fund community development loans is an important, more recent industry trend. It is one way that CDFIs work to institute efficient, reliable funding sources that ostensibly will lead to, in addition to greater scale, less reliance on customized, one-off financial relationships between CDFIs and banks. For CDFI depositories, the link between the financial mainstream and CDFI expansion follows a different model. Self-Help has forged key relationships with banks and Fannie Mae, but banks make up the distribution system more than the funding base. ShoreBank's integration of nonprofit and for-profit entities and support of the community banking industry have ramifications for the growth of development finance.

Some of these measures, particularly efforts to use capital markets, are intended to grow not only the capacity of individual CDFIs but community development lending capacity, broadly speaking. Indeed, CDFIs often position themselves to help mainstream institutions expand their customer base as well as meet their CRA obligations. A number of the CDFIs in this study market themselves as organizations with a high caliber of talent, large balance sheets (that carry sufficient loan loss reserves), and the know-how to ensure that projects get completed. Similarly, CDFIs highlight their ability to act as the community development face for large financial institutions. As large banks have grown even larger, resources and personnel devoted to affordable housing and other community development activities have decreased relative to the increasing size of these institutions. CDFIs offer themselves as partners to mainstream financial institutions, to develop "hand-crafted" deals based on specialized market knowledge and qualitative personal relationships with customers. CDFIs play the role of "retailers" who complement the role of large-bank "wholesalers." The most efficient partnerships are viewed as organizations that can deliver broad impact at a regional or national scale.

Importance of CRA

There is nothing inevitable about this collaboration. As noted in various parts of study, the CRA is a primary motivator for banks to work with CDFIs. Most large institutions look to earn a top CRA grade through a combination of in-house lending and investment and lending through CDFI intermediaries. CRA does not compel banks to support CDFIs, but its requirements motivate banks to seek efficient methods to meet credit needs. For CDFIs situated in places that are not big-bank CRA markets, however, CRA and bank support may never really be a factor for achieving scale. Put differently, where local conditions diminish the CRA incentives—areas with low population density outside of large-bank service areas—mainstream financial institutions may not be the path to scale and impact at all. Mandates within the socially responsible investment industry may bring more institutional funding. Among the CDFI depository organizations we interviewed, for example, socially responsible investors are an important source of capital not derived from CRA.

Similarly, the influence of CRA will wax and wane over time with the vagaries of politics and alternating trends within the financial system. Revisions to the CRA passed during the Clinton administration led banks to pull ahead of insurance companies in their support for community development finance institutions. In the past five years, the broad view of consumer advocates is that enforcement of CRA has been less stringent, and there are fewer banks seeking out CDFI partnerships. With the slowdown of merger activity in the mainstream financial sector, there is also less incentive in the banking sector to focus on the punitive consequences of a low CRA grade. CRA enforcement—more than simply the existence of the regulation—may affect the propensity of banks to seek out relationships with intermediaries.

Challenges to Sustainability

An additional issue to consider with respect to collaboration between CDFIs and mainstream financial institutions involves the goal of sustainability. Diverse organizations in our study have made tremendous strides in developing sustainable business models. They represent, largely, a segment of the CDFI industry that has become adept at financial management and that has moved closer to a mainstream financial institution model than ever before. Many of the organizations have adopted risk-management and administrative practices that closely resemble those of mainstream institutions. They hired former bank officials as chief financial and lending officers. Among the organizations in our study, ability to deploy community development assets in a prudent way is another reason they have attracted mainstream financial institution support. When financial institutions supported CDFIs in the mid-1990s, they tended to see these relationships more as philanthropic gestures than profit-making ventures. Now, mainstream institutions impose gradations of performance screens on community development.

These changes notwithstanding, CDFIs have expenses that mainstream institutions do not—counseling, technical assistance, high-touch loan servicing—which they cannot always cover in the pricing of their loans. CDFIs also need another type of low-cost (or no-cost) funding for credit enhancements to achieve end-pricing goals for lower-income borrowers and meet the risk-management needs of large financial institutions investing in essentially unstable or unproven assets. NMTCs have been used creatively and efficiently for this purpose but may not be available in sufficient quantity or at all at some later time to facilitate bringing the community development finance field to greater scale. In addition, CDFIs cannot always extract or recapture the value they create for mainstream financial institutions. Despite the direct and indirect assistance that CDFIs provide to mainstream financial institutions, many institutions do not always recognize, let alone pay for, these services. Part of the problem may derive from the nonprofit culture. CDFIs, like many nonprofits with a mission to help people, are not as cost conscious as for-profit ventures. If CDFIs don't know their unit costs, their value, they cannot convey the value to others nor expect to recover these costs (although some organizations in our participant group, such as TRF and CPC, have worked to quantify and recover their costs and/or remained aggressively in lending markets that banks serve independently). Community development depositories such as Self-Help and ShoreBank have a funding and thereby a sustainability edge in the form of deposits. ShoreBank's Development Deposits, drawn from individuals and organizations worldwide, make up almost half of the bank's deposits.

In addition, in the current climate, banks would rather avoid giving below-market-rate money to CDFIs and often screen development loans—even those for which banks receive CRA credit—for performance metrics and profitability. At many institutions, the community development borrower is compared to every other customer. A bank's treasury desk is the same for all departments. For the mainstream financial institutions that still provide below-market loans, internal discussions on pricing is increasingly controversial. Arguably, CDFIs would need less subsidy if they were properly compensated and more adept—industrywide—at quantifying their various costs, or phrased differently, their added value.

Conclusion

The CDFIs in our sample have managed to survive, and even thrive, in the changing financial services environment. The idea of change is so much a part of the environment in which CDFIs work that one CDFI describes it not as of changing ground but as a river. Banks that might have stood on a far shore at one time now stand on the same ground where development finance entities once stood, offering similar products potentially at much greater scale. However, nothing prevents them from retrenchment—market conditions or bank reorganizations may indeed precipitate banks' abandoning product lines and services. The future of the community development finance industry more broadly hinges on determining the appropriate relationship(s) with the mainstream financial industry, perhaps a more symbiotic association not entered into (or maintained) because of regulatory requirements. Our goal was to explore the work that has occurred and is ongoing to move the development finance industry that approaches this ideal. The overriding goal for development financial institutions is to produce organizations that can reach more people, tap into economies of scale, become more sustainable, and ultimately do more to redevelop low-income communities.

Notes

1. We use the acronym CDFI in some instances to refer broadly to organizations that provide their financial services to lower-income or special-needs populations or to organizations that serve those populations, whether or not they have the Treasury Department designation of Community Development Financial Institution and its benefits.

2. Borrowing from the TRF motto, "Capital at the Point of Impact."

3. Traditionally, a conforming loan had a loan-to-value ratio of not more than 80 percent. Over time, the GSEs have purchased and securitized higher loan-to-value loans, with proper documentation and mitigating (underwriting) factors.

4. This arrangement illustrates how access to the secondary market can reduce the cost of capital to a CDFI. Rather than sell the securitized loans to Fannie Mae for cash, Self-Help takes the mortgage-backed securities (MBS) themselves—a highly liquid form of collateral that allows Self-Help to borrow from the Federal Home Loan Bank (system) at the most favorable rates. With rated MBS, Self-Help can obtain relatively low-cost financing through the repurchase ("repo") market. Under a typical repo transaction, an investment bank accepts the securities as collateral for a loan of a specified term. At the end of the term, Self-Help "repurchases" the security for the amount of the loan plus interest.

5. See Housing Partnership Network Webpage at http://www.housingpartnership.net/lending/mortgage_conduits/ (Accessed 2–5–08.)

6. Low- or no-documentation loans have terms that do not require borrowers to fully document income and/or assets; interest-only loans do not require borrowers to pay down principal on an ongoing basis, and in some cases borrowers can pay less than interest due, causing the loan balance to increase by amounts of unpaid interest; 2/28 loans have an initial low rate but adjust sharply upward after two years.

7. NMTC legislation awards credits to taxpayers who make qualified equity investments in privately managed investment vehicles called community development entities (CDEs).

8. CDFI banks represent about 8 percent of all CDFIs but over 50 percent of CDFI assets. Additional information is available from the National Community Investment Fund Web site: www.ncif.org/aboutus.php?mainid=2&id=27 (accessed 2 May 2007.)

9. See the CDFI Fund Web site (www.cdfifund.gov) for a numerical breakdown of CDFIs by type.

3

When Subsidy Becomes Scarce

Rethinking Community Development Finance

JULIA SASS RUBIN

This chapter focuses on two types of community development financial institutions (CDFIs): community development loan funds (CDLF) and community development venture capital (CDVC) funds, which provide debt and equity capital for transactions that conventional capital sources consider too risky. CDLFs and CDVCs primarily fund organizations, including businesses, housing and real estate developers, and nonprofit community groups, with the objective of furthering economic development of distressed communities by creating high-quality jobs and infrastructure.

The late 1990s was a hospitable economic and political environment for CDFIs (Benjamin, Rubin, and Zielenbach 2004). Like all CDFIs, CDLFs and CDVCs grew significantly both in absolute numbers and in capitalization levels. However, the environment has changed dramatically since 2000, leaving many CDLFs and CDVCs struggling to survive as the subsidized capital necessary to fund their operations largely has evaporated. This environmental change has sparked a conversation within the industry and among its supporters regarding future business and industry models for these organizations.

This chapter begins by reviewing the structures and current activities of CDLFs and CDVCs. It then discusses the historic sources of subsidized capital and why they have shrunk, reviews potential new and underutilized sources of capital as well as the organizational ways that CDLFs and CDVCs are responding to their changed environment, and concludes with recommendations for policymakers and funders.

The chapter is based on interviews with CDLF and CDVC staffs, foundation and bank officers, and policymakers involved with the field. It also is based on documents from individual CDLF and CDVC institutions, on contemporary press accounts, and on organizational-level data from the CDFI Data Project (CDP). To protect their confidentiality, most of the individuals interviewed are not identified.

Part I: CDLF and CDVC Structures and Current Activities

Community Development Loan Funds

CDLFs lend capital to businesses, for-profit and nonprofit real estate and housing developers, nonprofit organizations looking for facility or operating capital, and increasingly individuals looking for financing to purchase or rehab homes. Most organizations and people financed by CDLFs are not able to obtain capital from more traditional sources or cannot obtain it on terms they can afford.

As of 2005, there were about five hundred CDLFs in the United States, with more than $3.5 billion in assets.[1] CDLFs financed more than $2.6 billion of activities that year, with more than $2.3 billion in additional financings outstanding. These figures are somewhat misleading, however, as a few large organizations accounted for most of this activity. The five largest CDLFs, for example, accounted for 52 percent of total loan fund capital and 58 percent of all direct financing outstanding. The top twenty CDLFs held 77 percent of all capital and were responsible for 79 percent of all financing outstanding. Most CDLFs are small, with median capital of $8.9 million as of 2005 (CDFI Data Project 2007).

The CDLF model emerged from a variety of origins, including efforts in the late 1960s and 1970s, by a few community development corporations and a group of revolving loan funds, to make loans to businesses to promote economic development (Grossman, Levere, and Marcoux 1998; Rubin 1998). In addition to business lending, many of the early CDLFs focused on financing construction of low-income housing in response to the lack of alternative sources of capital.

Although housing and business loans still make up the bulk of CDLF financing, accounting for 66 percent and 17 percent of all CDLF dollars outstanding, many CDLFs have diversified their offerings, providing operating and facility construction loans to nonprofits—including charter schools, childcare centers, healthcare facilities, social services agencies, and arts organizations (CDFI Data Project 2007). As with their business and housing finance activities, CDLFs began providing capital to nonprofits because more traditional capital sources viewed the nonprofits' revenue streams as too unpredictable to make them good credit risks. The newest area of CDLF activity is home loans to individuals. As of 2005, twenty-two CDLFs reported providing housing loans directly to individuals, a growing trend (CDFI Data Project 2007).

CDLFs, which are legally nonprofits, rely on loans and grants to capitalize their activities. Loans, mostly below market rate, accounted for 68 percent of all CDLF capital under management as of 2005. They were provided by banks and thrifts (49.6 percent); foundations (16.3 percent); federal (9.5 percent), state, and local (4.6 percent) governments; religious institutions (6.4 percent); nondepository financial institutions such as pension funds (4.0 percent); individual investors (2.9 percent); national intermediaries such as Opportunity Finance Network (2.5 percent); and corporations (2.5 percent). CDLFs relend loans and grants at market or near-market rates, using the spread—or difference—to help finance their operations. Most

CDLFs also must find ongoing subsidies to pay for technical assistance (TA) they provide to borrowers, high-cost predevelopment and microloans, and other aspects of their operations that the spread on lending does not cover.

CDLFs lend independently and in conjunction with conventional lenders. When lending in partnership with more conventional institutions, CDLFs generally take a subordinate position, absorbing most or all of the risk. Because most CDLF loans are riskier than those made by banks, and at times unsecured, CDLFs also provide extensive pre- and postinvestment TA to their portfolio companies. TA is used both to help potential borrowers qualify for capital and to assist them with various aspects of operations after they have received that capital. TA includes help with writing business plans, creating marketing strategies, and developing financial systems.

An aspect of CDLF activity that has received little attention is the role they play in demonstrating financial viability of low-income communities to traditional financial institutions. In the area of small business lending, for example, both through successful solo lending and by taking the higher risk portions of joint deals, CDLFs have encouraged banks to lend to small business customers located in low-income markets, a group banks previously had rejected (Rubin and Stankiewicz 2001).

In the area of multifamily housing, CDLFs have helped bring banks into multifamily projects and demonstrated that such deals could be successfully and profitably underwritten. CDLFs also have helped banks understand how to lend within those communities. Banks now consider lending to multifamily development projects reasonably safe because of the underlying physical collateral; presence of subordinate, risk-alleviating financing such as CDLF loans, Low-Income Housing Tax Credit equity, and public loans; and extensive organizational and project-based counseling and TA that the CDLFs provide to the borrowers (Zielenbach 2006). As a result, conventional financial institutions have become much more involved in projects that previously were financed primarily or exclusively by CDLFs. Construction and permanent financing now comes frequently from banks and less often from CDLFs. In certain markets, CDLFs and their bank supporters compete for the same multifamily loans.

As banks have moved into markets once served entirely by CDLFs, the latter have had to take on increasingly risky investments (Rubin and Stankiewicz 2001). In real estate finance, for example, as conventional lenders have become more willing to take on more of a project's financing costs, CDLFs have often been pushed further into making early-stage, higher-risk loans. This heightened risk position, coupled with a lower interest rate spread associated with higher interest rates, has caused many multifamily CDLF lenders to revisit their loan pricing so as to make it closer to market cost. CDLFs are less willing and able to offer deeply discounted monies and more willing to provide market-rate financing, particularly if their dollars are effectively the only ones available for seed/gap capital (Zielenbach 2006).

Community Development Venture Capital Funds

CDVC providers make investments of equity and near-equity in small businesses. An equity investment consists of cash a company receives in exchange for partial ownership of that company in the form of preferred or common stock. A near-equity investment consists of a loan with special features—warrants, royalties, or participation payments—which enable the lender to participate in the upside if the company receiving the capital is successful. Both equity and near-equity are forms of patient capital, giving young firms funds needed in early years without requiring immediate repayment of those funds, as is the case with most loans.

The earliest CDVC providers were Title VII community development corporations, which, in the early 1970s, began making equity investments in businesses as part of their economic development work. Other CDVC funds were begun by individual states, intending to stimulate business growth in low-income areas, and by CDLFs, which expanded into equity provision to meet needs of their debt clients (Rubin 2001).

There were more than sixty CDVC providers either active or in formation as of the end of 2006, with about $1 billion under management (Rubin 2007). This is a substantive increase from the six providers with less than $100 million under management that existed just a decade earlier (Rubin 2001). This dramatic growth reflects the overall growth of CDFIs during this time, due in large part to the Clinton administration's active support of the industry. In the case of CDVCs, growth also reflects the overall positive perception of venture capital during the late 1990s, as traditional venture capitalists made record-breaking profits for their investors via a strong economy and an unprecedented public appetite for initial public offerings.

CDVCs differ from traditional private venture capital funds and small business investment companies (SBICs). Most importantly, unlike the majority of traditional venture capitalists and SBICs, which have an exclusively financial returns objective, CDVCs invest with both social and financial goals. Thus, they consider a company's potential for significant high-quality job creation for low-income individuals, as well as its likelihood of rapid economic growth, before making an investment. As a result of this dual bottom line, CDVCs are willing to invest in companies in numerous industries, stages of development, and locations, setting them apart from traditional venture capitalists, which tend to specialize by industry and stage and to invest almost exclusively in a handful of domestic technology corridors, such as California's Silicon Valley and the Boston area's Route 128.

The earliest CDVCs also differed in their legal structures. Unlike traditional venture capital funds, which are for-profit and usually structured as either limited liability companies (LLCs) or limited partnerships (LPs), the early CDVC providers utilized a multitude of nonprofit, for-profit, and hybrid legal structures. Since the late 1990s, however, CDVC providers have begun adopting the more conventional LP and LLC legal structures for their investments. This helped them raise larger funds by attracting bank investors familiar and comfortable with these traditional venture capital models.

Another major source of CDVC capital has been the federal government, through the New Markets Venture Capital (NMVC) program and the CDFI Fund. Foundations were an important early source of CDVC capital. Most foundation investments, however, have been in the form of program-related investments structured as low-interest debt versus the equity dollars that venture capital investing requires. Furthermore, foundations appear to have moved away from supporting individual CDVC funds, investing in few of the most recently capitalized CDVC funds (Rubin 2007). This trend is discussed in Part II.

Many of the CDVCs using the for-profit LP and LLC models have created nonprofit subsidiaries, enabling them to raise grant funds to offset operating expenses. CDVCs tend to have higher operating expenses because they provide portfolio companies with TA. TA is necessary because CDVC funds often have a more limited number of investment prospects, whether because of geographic restrictions or the social screens many of them impose to meet other objectives (e.g., a company's environmental or labor practices). This limited deal flow may require funds to invest in companies with less experienced management and then work with them to increase their levels of knowledge and market readiness (Rubin 2001).

Like traditional venture capitalists, CDVC providers must exit their investments in order to make a profit and free up capital for new investments. In general, they tend to hold their investments for a longer time than do traditional venture capitalists, tying up valuable capital and management time and decreasing their financial returns. The longer holding times reflect both the greater difficulty of exiting from the types of companies in which CDVCs invest and the unwillingness of many CDVC managers to force an exit that would be detrimental to a company's overall survival or to the survival of any jobs the company could have created. This longer holding time, combined with the industry's relative youth, has meant that most CDVC funds are still holding the bulk of their investments.

Part II. Challenges Facing the Field

Of all the challenges that CDLFs and CDVCs currently face, by far the greatest is raising capital necessary to fund operations. The economic and political environment for community development finance has changed dramatically since 2000, making it increasingly difficult to raise capital at subsidized rates. Part II reviews existing sources of subsidized capital for CDLFs and CDVCs and why they have shrunk.

Community Development Financial Institutions (CDFI) Fund

The CDFI Fund is one of the few sources of grant and equity capital for community development finance. Under the Bush administration, the CDFI Fund was dramatically reduced, from $118 million in FY 2001, the last budget under President Clinton, to $55 million in FY 2007. Additionally, a large portion of the Fund's appropriation is devoted to administering the New Markets Tax Credit (NMTC) program, leaving even fewer dollars to fund CDFIs.

Conventional Financial Institutions

Commercial banks have been a very important source of capital for CDFIs, since the 1995 regulatory revisions to the Community Reinvestment Act (CRA), which instituted the investment test and expressly recognized community development financial institutions as qualifying CRA investments and borrowers (Pinsky 2001). Recent changes to the CRA, however, reduced the number of banks expressly evaluated for their investment activities. This change, in combination with the dramatic consolidation in the banking industry and the growth of alternative options that meet the investment test while providing a market-rate return, made it more difficult for CDFIs to raise subsidized capital from banks.

Foundations

Foundations have been a small but important source of capital for CDVCs and CDLFs for the difficult-to-obtain operating support and equity dollars. In the last few years, foundation support for community development finance declined partly because of the stock market decline that began in 2000, which shrank foundation assets and led to an overall reduction in foundation giving. More significant, however, have been decisions by the most active foundation investors to change the nature of their support for the sector or to withdraw support entirely. Foundations generally view their dollars as seed money, intended to catalyze other sources of capital and ultimately lead to organizational or project sustainability. For CDFIs, this has meant subsidized dollars foundations provided to many organizations in the industry's beginnings have become rare or unavailable.

Some foundations pulled back entirely, no longer funding CDFIs except when the work of individual organizations overlaps with their other programmatic interests. Others focused resources on organizations or programs perceived to be the most innovative and likely to bring about the next wave of significant development. Even those few foundations that have continued to fund CDLFs and CDVCs evaluate these investments relative to the range of other options available that promise comparable social impact and a market rate of return.

New Markets Tax Credit Program

NMTC combines public- and private-sector resources to bring $15 billion in new investments to impoverished rural and urban communities. The program was enacted as part of the Community Renewal Tax Relief Act of 2000, along with NMVC. In 2006, the program was extended through 2008, with an additional $3.5 billion credit allocation.

The CDFI Fund, which administers NMTC, allocates a set pool of tax credits to financial intermediaries, called community development entities (CDEs), on the basis of a competitive application process. The CDEs then offer the credits to investors in exchange for equity capital investments. The credit is equal to a 39 percent cumulative tax reduction for the investors and must be used over seven years—allowing for a 5 percent reduction in taxes in each of the first three years and a 6 percent reduction in each of the remaining four years.

The program came into existence with strong encouragement and support from the CDFI industry. When the program was being designed, there was great hope that it would be a significant new source of equity capital to fund business lending and investments. Because of several statutory and regulatory provisions, however, the program has so far been primarily used to finance real estate–related transactions (Rubin and Stankiewicz 2005), making it of very limited applicability for the CDVC industry.

The NMTC has been a more useful tool for CDLFs, many of which have come to rely on it for critical fee income they use to subsidize operations. Initially, the competitive nature of the program and the expense and expertise required to meet its legal and compliance requirements precluded all but the largest and most sophisticated CDFIs from being able to take advantage of NMTC. Some of the smaller CDFIs, however, have been able to access the program by partnering with larger entities. Nevertheless, the future of the NMTC past the 2008 allocation is still uncertain, and its usefulness for CDVC and non–real estate debt transactions is limited.

New Markets Venture Capital and Rural Business Investment Programs

NMVC and Rural Business Investment Company (RBIC) programs were designed to increase the supply of equity and near-equity capital flowing into distressed communities. Both programs are administrated by the Small Business Administration, which selects NMVC and RBIC entities that are provided with matching debenture capital. Both programs went through one round of funding during which six NMVC and one RBIC funds were created. Subsequent funding was rescinded by Congress, but efforts are ongoing to approve new authorizations.

Part III: Opportunities and Industry Response

In response to the increasingly challenging environment CDLFs and CDVCs face in raising subsidized capital, they have turned toward finding ways to reduce their ongoing reliance on such capital by becoming more sustainable. For many organizations, sustainability is associated with growing their size. While some small CDLFs and CDVCs can survive because of ongoing local subsidies, overall it is difficult to cover operating expenses with a small capital base. To grow their size, CDLFs and CDVCs are exploring new sources of subsidized capital, such as state-level initiatives. They also are identifying ways to access new sources of capital—pension funds and individual investors—that historically have not been significant for community development finance. Finally, CDLFs and CDVCs are rethinking the way they do business and repositioning themselves to become more sustainable by cutting costs and by finding ways to utilize market-rate capital and access traditional capital markets to fund operations.

State and Local Governments

Although economic conditions in the states are uneven, they generally offer a more receptive policy environment than the current federal level. Community organizations also have a track record of successfully lobbying for state-level CDFI Funds, CRAs, and tax credits designed to encourage community economic development. The power of state-level initiatives is best illustrated by California, where public-sector activity over the last decade encouraged creation of innovative sources of capital to fund community development:

- Insurance industry–funded Community Organized Investment Network (COIN), which both certifies and funds state-level CDFIs.
- Twenty percent tax credit for qualified deposits of $50,000 or more in CDFIs.
- Double bottom line: Investing in California's Emerging Markets initiative, launched in 2000 by State Treasurer Philip Angelides "to direct investment capital—through state programs and the State's pension and investment funds—to spur economic growth in those California communities left behind during the economic expansion of the past decade" (Angelides 2001, 2). The initiative led two of California's largest public pension funds, the California Public Employees' Retirement System (CalPERS) and the California State Teachers' Retirement System (CalSTRS), to make substantial investments in real estate and businesses located in the state's poorest communities.

Pension Funds

Historically, most pension-fund assets have been conservatively invested in fixed income, public equities, and real estate. In the last few decades, pension funds have expanded to include "alternative" investments such as venture capital. Pension funds now account for over 50 percent of all venture capital (National Venture Capital Association 2006).

Some pension funds also have incorporated economically targeted investments (ETIs) into their portfolios, which have both financial and social objectives. To date, most of the pension-fund ETI investments have been in fixed income and real estate. The real estate focus has created an opportunity for some CDLFs to access this capital if they can provide the scale and rate of return that pension funds require.

Pension funds generally have been reluctant to make private-equity ETI investments because of the greater risk involved. Only a few of the most innovative pension funds have expanded their ETI investments to include private equity, including several investments into CDVC funds. While pension investments in CDVCs are still the exception, they are likely to increase if the CDVC funds can demonstrate an appropriate risk-adjusted rate of return and an ability to absorb larger investments.

Individual Investors

Individuals have been a source of capital for community development finance from the field's beginnings. At present, community development banks and credit unions rely on individual investments for approximately three-quarters of their capital (CDFI Data Project 2007). Much of this capital is in the form of government-insured certificates of deposit (Phillips 2006). For nondepository CDFIs, however, socially responsible investors make up a fairly small percentage of all capital sources. In 2005, for example, CDLFs received only 3 percent of their investment capital from individuals (CDFI Data Project 2007). Although there is anecdotal evidence that some CDVC funds recently have been able to attract larger investments from individuals, they accounted for only 6 percent of all CDVC investments as of 2000, the last year for which these data are available for the entire industry.

Individuals can invest in specific CDFIs directly via an equity investment in a CDVC or a loan to a CDLF. Individuals also can invest in CDFIs via intermediaries, such as the Calvert Foundation, which aggregate the capital and provide due diligence on different CDFIs. Some CDFI trade associations also serve as investment intermediaries for both large and small individual investors. The Community Development Venture Capital Alliance (CDVCA), for example, has a fund that accepts individual loans of as little as $10,000 for a period of ten years.

CDLFs and CDVCs face a number of challenges in attracting individual investors, including an inability to offer insured deposits, a diversity of difficult-to-explain products, and investor perception that community investments are higher risk. Nevertheless, a growing number of CDLFs and CDVCs are trying to access this potential source of investment capital.

Accessing Market-Rate Capital: Securitization and Structured Financings

Given the decreasing availability of subsidized capital, energy is being focused on market-rate capital and the traditional capital markets. Two possibilities that have proven effective for CDLFs are the use of structured financings and securitization. Structured financings enable certain assets with more or less predictable cash flows to be isolated from the originator and used to mitigate risks and thus secure a credit (Hew 2006). Securitization consists of aggregating loans with similar characteristics and selling them to investors.

Selling loans to free up capital is not a new concept for CDLFs. Historically, however, they have sold their loans to a limited group of socially motivated investors. Despite their historically low loss rates, CDLFs have had to discount these loans in order to overcome the perception that they are lower performing than conventional loans.

To make their loans a viable option for the much larger number of institutional investors, CDLFs had to demonstrate to such investors that their loans performed comparably to those made by conventional financial institutions and to offer a product that was at a scale of $50 million and above, which is the size necessary to make a public placement cost efficient (Dunlap, Okagaki, and Seidman 2006). The solution was to combine loans from multiple organizations and to have them rated by a Wall Street rating agency, making the investment attractive to mutual funds, insurance companies, and pension funds.

A number of loan pools were created between 1999 and 2006, demonstrating that the traditional capital markets can bring new investors. There still are obstacles, however, to making this an ongoing source of capital for CDLFs. These barriers include a lack of standardization in loan-performance data, documentation, and underwriting procedures; a lack of infrastructure to support these transactions; a lack of models for forecasting future borrower demand for community development loans; a lack of capacity among some community development lenders; and the belief on the part of many lenders that loans will be discounted in the securitization process (Stanton 2003; GAO 2003). A number of initiatives are under way to overcome the remaining barriers and make securitization a viable, ongoing way for CDLFs to access market-rate capital.

Repositioning and Rethinking

In addition to identifying innovative ways to attract capital to make growth possible, CDLFs and CDVCs are rethinking their business models in order to become more sustainable and less reliant on subsidized capital. Toward that end, many of them have undertaken strategic planning processes to determine how to reach this objective (Dunlap, Okagaki, and Seidman 2006). For CDLFs, the resulting innovations included the following:

- Forming partnerships, networks, and mergers to increase impact and cut costs.
- Identifying and focusing on the most lucrative and socially meaningful activities, while outsourcing others, such as loan processing and back-office operations, in order to cut expenses.
- Increasing their levels of off-balance-sheet transactions in which CDLFs invest funds for other organizations in exchange for origination and servicing fees.
- Diversifying their base of borrowers and mix of products.

CDVCs also are considering alternatives to enable them to access new sources of capital. However, the industry is divided on how to proceed. Many current and potential investors associate CDVCs with smaller capitalization levels, tightly drawn geographic target areas, small deals, and low financial returns. Those CDVC funds that have moved away from this model want to reframe the industry to change perceptions and make it possible to raise more capital. They point to other socially oriented venture capital that CDVCs could incorporate—minority- and female-focused funds or funds that invest in clean technology. While having both social and financial objectives, these venture funds market themselves as able to deliver competitive financial returns and have attracted billions of dollars from traditional investors.

Other CDVC managers advocate that the industry include funds that make double bottom line equity investments in real estate, such as the UrbanAmerica and Genesis funds, which have raised hundreds of millions of dollars. Others suggest that CDVCs reposition themselves to fill the void of equity investments of under $5 million in geographies not served by traditional venture capital, arguing this could become attractive as the number of SBIC funds making equity investments shrinks in response to the elimination of SBA leverage for participating security SBICs. While individual funds have pursued these ideas, the industry has yet to embrace them.

Conclusions

CDLFs and CDVCs are at a critical junction. The economic and political environment of the late 1990s, which facilitated their growth in numbers and size of assets, is unlikely to return. The last few years also have brought increased competition for capital in the form of new financial products that promise both community impact and market-rate returns.

To be able to access new capital in this environment, CDLFs and CDVCs must better understand and document social and financial outcomes, including their role as policy advocates on behalf of low-income communities, innovators that demonstrate to conventional financial institutions the viability of this market, intermediaries that bring together other sources of capital to make projects and programs possible, and direct providers of financial products, services, and education.

Given the limited pool of subsidized capital, CDLFs and CDVCs must find new ways of using market-rate capital. However, they also should continue to pursue new sources of subsidized capital, such as the states and individual investors. At the same time, funders cannot lose sight of the field's ongoing need for subsidy. Without such subsidies, the ability of both CDLFs and CDVCs to serve low-income communities would be greatly diminished.

Finally, the federal government must stop abrogating its critical role in serving the financial needs of low-income communities by reinvigorating the CRA and appropriating significantly more capital to the CDFI Fund. Regulatory changes to the Employee Retirement Income Security Act (ERISA) also are needed to make pension funds more accessible sources of capital for CDFIs.

WHEN SUBSIDY BECOMES SCARCE 45

The low- and moderate-income communities that CDFIs were designed to assist are facing an increasingly difficult environment. The problems of economic inequality and poverty have worsened; funding of services for the country's neediest has shrunk; and predatory financial service providers have come to view low-income communities as market opportunities, reversing the wealth-building efforts of CDFIs. The products, services, and knowledge that CDFIs provide are needed more than ever.

Note

1. The total number of CDLFs is an estimate provided by the Opportunity Finance Network. This chapter is focused on a subset of CDLFs for whom microloans—of $35,000 or less—constituted less than 50 percent of their financing activities.

References

Angelides, Philip. 2001. *Double Bottom Line: Investing in California's Emerging Markets.* Sacramento: California State Treasurer.
Benjamin, Lehn, Julia Sass Rubin, and Sean Zielenbach. 2004. "CDFIs: Current Issues and Future Prospects." *Journal of Urban Affairs* 26 (2): 177–95.
CDFI Data Project. 2007. "Self-Reported Annual Organizational-Level Data on CDFIs for the 2005 Calendar Year." Washington, DC: The CDFI Fund.
Dunlap, Helen, Alan Okagaki, and Ellen Seidman. 2006. "Review of the Current State of Community and Economic Development Finance: A Memo to Funders." White paper prepared for the John D. and Catherine T. MacArthur Foundation (December 7).
Government Accountability Office (GAO). 2003. "Community and Economic Development Loans: Securitization Faces Significant Barriers." Washington, DC: GAO # 04–21.
Grossman, Brian, Andrea Levere, and Kent Marcoux. 1998. *Counting on Local Capital.* Washington, DC: Corporation for Enterprise Development.
Hew, David. 2006. "Structured Finance Deals: How Do They Work and Will They Work?" www.unescap.org/drpad/projects/fin_dev/hew.ppt. (Accessed 7 July 2007.)
National Venture Capital Association. 2006. "The Venture Capital Industry—An Overview." www.nvca.org/def.html. (Accessed 7 July 2007.)
Phillips, Ron. 2006. "New Approaches in Social Investing." *Communities & Banking,* Winter.
Pinsky, Mark. 2001. "Taking Stock: CDFIs Look Ahead After 25 Years of Community Development Finance." *Capital Xchange* (December). www.brookings.edu/metro/capitalxchange/article9.htm. (Accessed 7 July 2007.)
Rubin, Julia Sass. 1998. "Public Policy and High Growth Firms: The Role of Institutional Forces in the Creation and Growth of Hybrid Social Enterprises." Paper presented at the Babson College-Kauffman Foundation Entrepreneurship Research Conference, Gent, Belgium, May.
———. 2001. "Community Development Venture Capital: A Double-Bottom Line Approach to Poverty Alleviation." Proceedings of the Changing Financing Markets and Community Development, Second Federal Reserve System Community Affairs research conference, 121–154. Washington, DC: Federal Reserve System, April. www.chicagofed.org/cedric/files/cfmacd_rubin.pdf. (Accessed 7 July 2007.)
———. 2007. "Community Development Venture Capital." Working paper.

Rubin, Julia Sass, and Gregory M. Stankiewicz. 2001. "The Los Angeles Community Development Bank: The Possible Pitfalls of Public-Private Partnerships." *Journal of Urban Affairs* 23 (2):133–153.

———. 2005. "The New Markets Tax Credit Program: A Midcourse Assessment." *Community Development Investment Review* (San Francisco Federal Reserve) 1 (1): 1–11.

Stanton, Gregory. 2003. "Unblocking Obstacles to Capital Markets for Community Development Lenders." School of Community Economic Development, Southern New Hampshire University Working Paper in Community Economic Development.

Zielenbach, Sean. 2006. Personal correspondence with author.

4

CDFIs "Make the Market" for Charter School Facilities Financing

ANNIE DONOVAN

This chapter examines the role community development financial institutions (CDFIs)[1] play in supporting the growth of public charter schools, one of the most significant education reforms in decades. CDFIs are financial institutions whose primary mission is to provide capital and development services to meet the needs of low-income people and communities. CDFIs fill market niches underserved by traditional banks and investors. Charter schools are publicly funded but operate independently of school districts. They receive funding for operations but usually are not provided a facility and must find and finance one on their own.

The rapid growth of the charter school movement has created a financing demand estimated to exceed several billion dollars.[2] Banks and other financial institutions have been reluctant to lend to charter schools for a variety of reasons. Chief among them is the experimental nature of the charter movement and the attendant risks that come with start-up ventures. With expertise in high-risk lending and innovative problem solving, CDFIs have stepped in to provide much-needed capital and technical assistance. In the process of responding to the considerable demand for facilities financing, CDFIs have propelled their own growth and are finding a path to reach investors in the capital markets. Their work is a case study of how CDFIs can "make the market"—that is, how their investment activity can establish the viability of an emerging market and nurture its development to the point of market acceptance.

Central to the success of CDFIs in the charter space has been the participation of the federal government through the Credit Enhancement for Charter School Facilities Program (CECSF). Enacted first as a demonstration in 2001 and later authorized under the No Child Left Behind Act, the program makes funding available to induce investment in charter school facilities. As of 2007, the U.S. Department of Education (DoE) has awarded $160 million under the program, 83 percent of which has gone to CDFIs. While the program was not intended specifically for CDFIs, they have proven to be the most effective vehicles for organizing and delivering capital to this emerging market. Data compiled by The Charter Coalition shows that for every $1 of federal funding, program grantees have raised $8 of private capital, or nearly $1.3 billion (www.thechartercoalition.org). The availability of credit enhancement has not only helped charter schools gain access to capital, it has created an opportunity for CDFIs to grow, innovate, and move the development finance field to the doorstep of the capital markets.

Public Charter Schools Defined

Charter schools are public schools that are permitted through state law to operate outside of the rules and regulations that govern traditional public schools. In exchange for greater autonomy, charter schools agree to be held accountable for academic achievement. The expectation is that charter schools will meet the terms of their charter or face closure by their authorizing bodies. Funding for charter schools is determined at a state level. Typically, schools receive funding based on their enrollment, commonly called "per pupil" with additional funding for special education and other populations.

Begun as an experiment in Minnesota in 1991, charter schools were created to address the decline in performance of public schools. Since the publication of the landmark study *A Nation At Risk* in 1983, education reformers have struggled to address what the report cites as "disturbing inadequacies" in our public school system that threaten to erode the foundations of American society. Further, despite the promise of school desegregation, since *Brown vs. The Board of Education,* the "achievement gap" between white and minority students has remained a persistent problem. According to the *National Assessment of Education Progress,* in 2000, 70 percent of African American students scored below "basic," the lowest level of proficiency, in math compared to 58 percent of Hispanic students, 29 percent of white students, and 26 percent of Asian American students. In reading, 48 percent of African American students scored below basic compared to 41 percent of Hispanic students, 28 percent of Asian American students, and 22 percent of white students (NCES 2007).

While many worthy experiments have been undertaken to spark changes in public school performance, no other innovation has been as widespread as the creation of charter schools. As of September 2006, forty states and the District of Columbia have charter laws. Figure 4.1 shows the pace of charter law adoption since 1991. Approximately four thousand schools operate across the United States (Figure 4.2) with enrollment of over 1.1 million children (Figure 4.3) (Center for Education Reform 2007).

Many feared that charter schools would create chasms in public education because charters would "cream" affluent, white students from the traditional system. On the contrary, the National Charter School Research Project concluded that "nationally, charter schools serve a larger proportion of minority and low-income students than is found in traditional public schools" (Lake and Hill 2006). Many students enter charter schools several grade levels behind.

Charter school performance data can be difficult to decipher, but recent research increasingly demonstrates effectiveness. A 2004 Harvard University study compared the reading and mathematics proficiency of charter school students to that

Figure 4.1   **States with Charter School Laws**

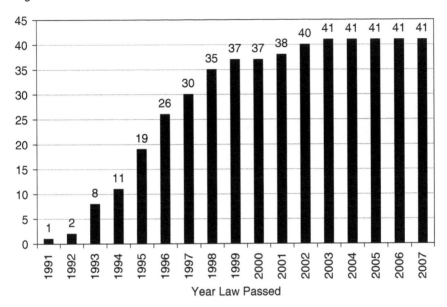

Year Law Passed

Figure 4.2   **Operating Charter School Growth**

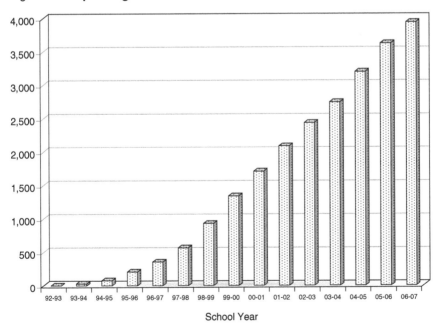

School Year

Figure 4.3   **Charter School Enrollment over Time**

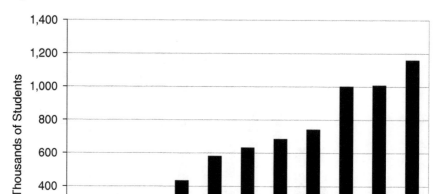

Beginning of School Year

of their peers in neighboring traditional public schools. Compared to students in the matched regular public school, charter students were 5.2 percent more likely to be proficient in reading and 3.2 percent more likely to be proficient in math on state assessments. In states where charter schools were well established, charter school students' proficiency was even greater (Hoxby 2004).

The Harvard study focused on aggregate data at the national level. When looked at individually, many charter schools are showing gains that are much less marginal. The DoE study *Charter High Schools: Closing the Achievement Gap* describes eight dramatic examples of schools that are closing the achievement gap between urban, minority, and low-income students and their better funded suburban counterparts (DoE 2006). Most first-rate charter school student graduates are accepted to college; many are the first in their families to attend.

Why Charters?

Most CDFIs do not identify themselves as education reformers. So what motivated them to enter the charter schools market? First is simply the *demand for development capital.* As described previously, charter schools receive funding for operations on a per-pupil basis, but most states do not offer either a school building or funding to support facilities. From the outset, charter schools have identified finding, developing, and paying for a facility as one of the top three obstacles to starting and expanding their schools (DoE 1998).

The reasons traditional financial institutions were reluctant to lend to charter schools are not surprising. Charter schools in need of financing, especially in the early years of the movement, were likely to be start-up or early-stage ventures with an unproven financial track record. The terms of their charters are usually three to five years, yet they may require a fifteen- or twenty-year amortization schedule to make debt service affordable. The very nature of the charter contract is to be subject to closure for failure to reach academic goals. The bar is raised even higher because charters tend to enroll low-performing students. Another risk factor is that charter school buildings are often single-purpose assets with limited reuse potential, located in low-income communities where real estate values may not support the cost of redevelopment. Finally, charters usually face opposition at the state level from stakeholders within the traditional public school system. Objections are most passionate around the autonomy and resources granted to charter schools. For all these reasons, traditional investors were reluctant to even spend time gaining an understanding of the market. If there is such a thing as a "classic" development finance market, charter schools qualify. CDFIs saw an opportunity to add value.

A second factor is that, although created to improve the quality of public education, charter schools are proving to be an *effective tool for community development.* Because they serve low-income, minority students, charter schools are disproportionately located in urban areas that are financially underserved, a prime market for CDFIs. Charter schools often redevelop underutilized or dilapidated properties and convert them into attractive spaces. The schools create jobs and attract ancillary businesses and services to neighborhoods.

The third factor, and perhaps the most compelling, is that charter schools are *improving the quality of education for low-income students* in many communities. Most charters are founded by parents, teachers, educational entrepreneurs, and other community leaders seeking better educational outcomes for poor and low-income children who have no other choice than to be subjected to an educational system that almost everyone agrees is failing them. Data from the Center for Education Reform show that 42 percent of charter schools serve populations where 60 percent or more of the students are consider "at-risk". In communities where half the children fail to complete high school, charters are preparing and sending low-income children to college. This is a significant poverty alleviation strategy.

What CDFIs Have Accomplished

CDFIs began addressing the needs of charter schools shortly after the first law was enacted. According to *Charter School Facility Finance Landscape* (LISC 2007), there are now twenty-five private nonprofit organizations offering financing to charter schools for their facilities. Collectively, these organizations have provided over $600 million in direct financial support to date. All of the twenty-five organizations surveyed in the report are either certified as CDFIs by the CDFI Fund or are

Figure 4.4   **Charter School Loans** (in millions)

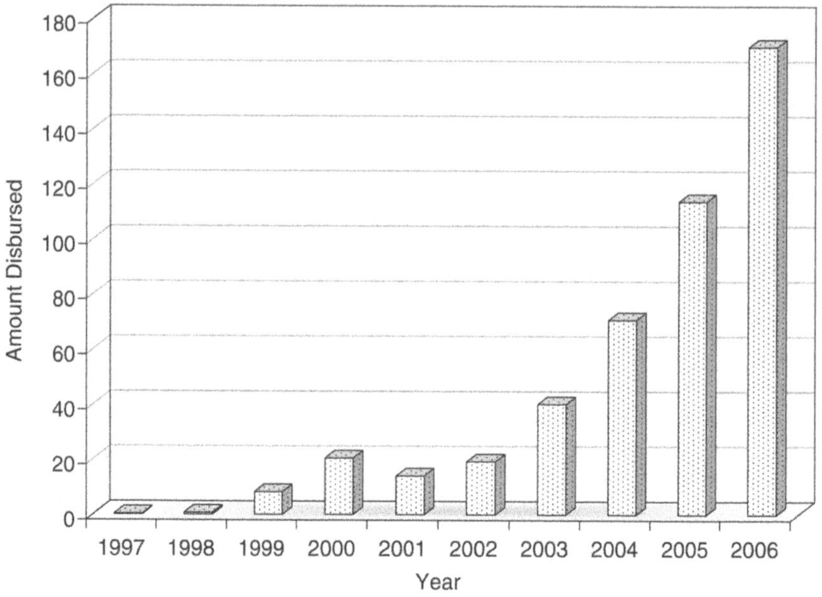

nonprofit organizations with common missions of providing development finance to one or more underserved markets.

When CDFIs entered the charter market, banks were absent from the scene, the option of tax-exempt bond financing was unthinkable, there were no public resources to address the facilities problem, and school founders were struggling to find solutions. Not only were financial resources scarce, most charter school operators were educators with little knowledge of how to develop and finance a school facility.

Figure 4.4 shows the aggregate growth of charter lending volume among the nine most active CDFIs, including Southwestern Pennsylvania Community Loan Fund (CLF), Illinois Facilities Fund (IFF), Local Initiatives Support Corporation (LISC), Low Income Investment Fund (LIIF), NCB Capital Impact, La Raza Development Fund, Nonprofit Facilities Fund, Self-Help, and The Reinvestment Fund (TRF). From 1997 to 2006, CDFI disbursements grew from $275,000 to $170 million. Cumulative disbursements over this period exceeded $460 million, a volume that approaches sufficient scale to impact an industry and attract attention of the capital markets. There were 436 loans made, financing over 200,000 school seats. Over 80 percent of the schools financed serve a majority of low-income children. CDFIs provided a range of products—loans for mortgages, leasehold improvements, and working capital. Loans were made in both senior and subordinate positions.

In the earliest days of the charter movement, schools had to open using their own funds. By 1994, however, the Clinton administration established a role for the federal government by creating a program to provide start-up seed funding under Title X of the Elementary and Secondary Education Act. This program alleviated the need for very high-risk start-up working capital loans. The problem of finding, leasing, or buying and renovating space then rose to the top of the list as the biggest barrier to opening schools. The first studies of charter schools commissioned by the DoE in the late 1990s showed they tended to be smaller than the average public school, with seven out of ten leasing space. This remains true today; average charter school enrollment is 40 percent less than conventional public schools, and only 30 percent of charter schools own their buildings (Center for Education Reform 2007). When it came to space, many schools had to improvise, occupying temporary spaces, church basements, vacant storefronts, or unused public school buildings. Accordingly, CDFIs made leasehold improvement loans as well as first mortgage loans to schools capable of owning their facilities. Loan amounts tended to be in the $250,000 to $2 million range.

Charter school portfolios held by CDFIs were performing well, as they continue to today, despite the perceived risks of the market. Most CDFIs were experiencing default rates of less than 1 percent, with no history of loan losses. Borrowers were beginning to establish creditworthiness; however, banks were still reluctant to get involved, and not more than a handful of bond deals had been executed. In 1999, Moody's Investment Services published its first analysis of the charter school market. Standard and Poor's and Fitch Ratings soon followed. While the bond market was beginning to pay attention, many were skeptical. Most bond deals were rated below investment grade, which meant charter schools were still paying relatively high rates for capital. In 2002, Fitch Ratings asserted that despite strong demand, "schools without three to 10 years of successful operating history or substantial credit-enhancing features will remain hard pressed to earn investment-grade ratings. Most proposed bonds in the sector possess credit features consistent with the 'BB' or 'B' rating categories." The continued growth in charter school demand put more pressure on those already willing to make charter loans.

When CDFIs first entered the market, they were making loans from their own balance sheet. However, demand for seats in new or existing charter schools continued unabated. Enrollment continues to grow at double-digit rates (see Figure 4.3). At the same time, charter schools began gaining more permanence in their communities. Charter operators needed room to grow and also wanted to upgrade their space to reflect their changing status. Occupying permanent space was a way to achieve both. Transaction sizes began to climb as a result, requiring CDFIs to find even more creative solutions to serve the market. Fortunately, the federal government devised a useful way to help.

Role of the Public Sector

To address the stubbornness of the traditional financial markets in responding to the needs of charter schools, Congress appropriated $25 million in 2001 to create a credit-enhancement demonstration program. After a successful first year, the CECSF program was authorized under the No Child Left Behind Act and funded at approximately $36 million annually thereafter. As of 2007, over $160 million in grants have been awarded to sixteen organizations; CDFIs have received $133 million, or thirteen awards.

The purpose of the demonstration was to find innovative, market-based solutions to the facilities financing problem. The program is proving to be an effective impetus for attracting traditional capital to charter schools. For example, TRF and NCB Capital Impact collaborated to create the Charter School Capital Access Program (CCAP) Fund. TRF and NCB Capital Impact used a $6.4 million CECSF grant as a first loss reserve to create a $45 million lending pool capitalized by leading national and international banks such as Citibank, JPMorgan Chase, Washington Mutual, and Bank of America. For many of the participants in the fund, CCAP was their first foray into charter school lending. Part of the goal for TRF and NCB Capital Impact was to demonstrate that charter loans could be prudent investments.

The request to participate in CCAP was easier for financial institutions to consider than a direct loan to a charter school. First, banks did not have to make the loans themselves and therefore did not have to understand the industry in as much depth. TRF and NCB Capital Impact each had at least five years' experience in the market, a collective portfolio at the time of nearly $40 million, and no loan losses to date. The two organizations had underwriting criteria that was consistent and time tested. Second, the first loss reserve protected investors fully for the first $6.4 million of loan loss. Third, TRF and NCB Capital Impact each invested $5 million into CCAP in a subordinate position to further protect the senior lenders. Under such a scenario, it became highly unlikely that investors would suffer losses. Transaction efficiency also improved. To date, the CCAP Fund has performed well. There have been very few delinquencies, no defaults, and no losses.

Since the creation of CCAP, banks in the program have continued to lend to charter schools, mostly through CDFIs. The *Charter School Facility Finance Landscape* (LISC 2007) reports that Bank of America and Citigroup have each invested between $100 million and $150 million in the market to date. The statutory requirement limiting CECSF program eligibility to nonprofit and public agencies has created an important advantage for CDFIs in designing and implementing approaches that leverage capital from traditional financial institutions.

CECSF spawned many other innovative programs and products. NCB Capital Impact created the Enhancement Fund with $40 million from a single pension fund investor, the first such institutional investor to enter the charter market. Because the pension fund is a "buy and hold" investor, NCB Capital Impact was able to create twenty-five-year fully amortizing loans. On an "all-in" basis, pricing is competitive with tax-exempt bonds and in many cases beats the tax-exempt market. The IFF is using the program to enhance tax-exempt bonds for charter schools in Chicago. Most charter bond transactions have credit enhancements, usually in the form of bond insurance or letters of credit from banks. Through its Illinois Charter Capital

Program (ICCP), created with an $8 million grant from the CECSF, IFF facilitated bond issuances in 2006 for two charter operators by funding loss reserves that reduced the cost of bond insurance. Transactions totaling $18.7 million created four new campuses serving 1,873 children, approximately 90 percent of whom qualify for subsidized meals through the U.S. Department of Agricultures School Lunch Program. The bonds are twenty-five-year fully amortizing notes. One is priced all-in at 5.9 percent, the other at 6.2 percent.

TRF is creating a unique partnership with PNC Bank and a local Philadelphia tax-exempt bond issuer to credit-enhance bond transactions. For more mature charter schools, especially those that have gone through at least one renewal of their charter by the authorizing body, access to capital is beginning to broaden. Local banks are offering more favorably priced, longer-term loans, and investment bankers are structuring bond transactions. TRF will accelerate this market momentum by purchasing participations from PNC in letters of credit that back the bonds. By taking the highest risk, TRF will facilitate bond transactions for schools that could not otherwise qualify. In addition to getting cheaper capital, borrowers will pay lower transaction costs because the bonds will be placed in a pool and cost will be shared.

These are but a few examples of the ways in which CDFIs have made use of the CECSF program to create innovative programs and products. Without the credit enhancement, CDFIs would not have achieved the level of scale and innovation they have attained, and fewer charter schools would have been able to start up and grow. Today, the market is recognizing charter schools as creditworthy. The top echelon of financially viable schools is now reaching the tax-exempt bond market where they can get the best rates and terms available to them. There have been roughly seventy rated bond issuances totaling nearly $1 billion (LISC 2007). As a matter of parity, many feel that charter schools, as public schools, should be able to access the bond market under the same conditions as traditional public schools. Because they are stand-alone organizations without taxing authority, they are not treated in the same manner as public schools by the capital markets. This is not likely to change for the foreseeable future. Charter schools will have to earn their way into the capital markets through their own financial performance. However, as momentum builds toward greater access to capital, it is wise to question the future role for CDFIs.

As the market evolves, CDFIs should not give up their role as leaders and innovators. There is much more work to be done. The job of CDFIs is now to move "down market" where there are still plenty of schools struggling to develop and finance their facilities. CDFIs should find a way to add value as players in tax-exempt bond transactions. Of the four thousand charter schools in operation, less than 2 percent have accessed the bond market. More charter schools need access to tax-exempt bonds. CDFIs can secure their position in the charter school market by collaborating with each other to facilitate access to the tax-exempt bonds for schools that are not otherwise able reach this market. As the data show, CDFIs are collectively originating enough loan volume annually to be significant to the capital markets. Their task is to find ways to standardize products, consolidate infrastructure, and achieve more efficient transaction executions.

The Future of CDFIs in the Charter Market

In March 2006, a group of leading CDFIs facilitated by the Housing Partnership Network (HPN) gathered in Chicago at the MacArthur Foundation to discuss ways of working together to gain greater access to the capital markets. A variety of strategies were discussed, ranging from creating a CDFI-owned bank to aggregating and securitizing pools of loans. The conversation was not specific to charter schools but included all asset types originated by CDFIs. To find common ground and move forward, meeting participants submitted data on lending separated by asset type. Data revealed the growth of CDFIs in the charter market but had not yet been quantified by participants (see Figure 4.5). CDFIs were building enough scale to be taken seriously by the capital markets. To further pursue the concept of securitizing charter school loans, a subgroup was created that included LIIF, NCB Capital Impact, Raza Development Fund, Self-Help, TRF, HPN, and CRF, a national nonprofit financial intermediary that securitizes economic development loans.

With the help of Wilary Winn LLP, a Minneapolis-based firm, the group is creating the Charter School Financing Partnership (CSFP). CSFP will function as a cooperatively owned conduit that will accumulate charter school debt and sell securities backed by the debt into the capital markets. CSFP will be owned by the CDFIs originating product, with HPN playing a facilitation role. Ideally, CSFP is seeking to issue rated, tax-exempt pass through securities backed by pools of tax-exempt bonds issued on behalf of individual charter schools. The pools will have a "senior/subordinate" structure, meaning that some investors in the securities will have a senior position in the cash flows of the pools and will be paid their principal first at a lower rate of interest. Other investors will have subordinate positions and will be paid more slowly at higher rates of return. If successful, the pooling mechanism will result in charter schools receiving better rates and terms than would otherwise be possible. Schools that might be rated below investment grade, in the B to BB range, will enjoy access to tax-exempt bonds priced as if they were B to BB or higher, that is, at an investment-grade level.

While the asset-backed securities (ABS) market is well established at an estimated $1.6 trillion in 2006 (*Barclay's Capital Research 2007 Outlook*), only one securitization of tax-exempt issuances has been issued. CSFP must be prepared for market resistance. To help overcome these obstacles and to improve efficiency, CSFP is seeking credit enhancement from CECSF as well as other forms of socially motivated capital.

The CDFI field has been engaged in dialogue about accessing secondary markets for community development assets. While the benefits of securitization are well understood and considered desirable among most CDFIs, there have been few tan-

Figure 4.5 **The CDFI–Charter School Market**

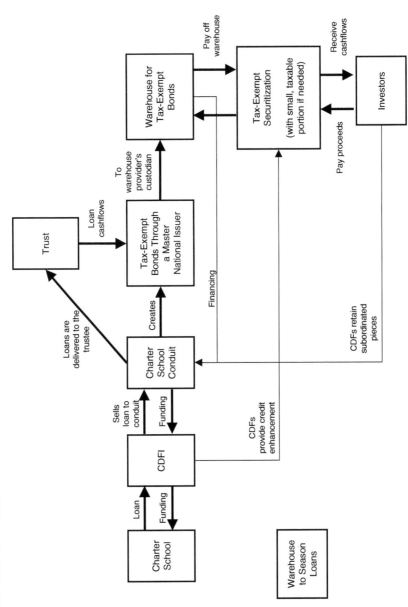

gible opportunities as ripe as the charter school market to pursue securitization. To accomplish CSFP goals, its members will have to begin building the infrastructure the field has been discussing for all these years but has not commenced constructing. CSFP must create a common originations and servicing platform. CDFIs will have to agree on and adhere to one set of underwriting criteria. They will have to use standard documents and contract with a master servicer. Selling assets into a conduit will mean that CSFP members will not hold those assets in portfolios. This will affect the revenue model and balance sheet for participating CDFIs. Fees will replace earning assets, and liquidity will improve. To make the model work, increasing volume will be essential. Customized loan structuring as a way of doing business, a hallmark of CDFIs, will be challenged.

Not only is the market ripe for CDFIs to experiment with securitization, time is of the essence. As the charter market matures, CDFIs are beginning to lose deals before they are closed or see their deals refinanced with tax-exempt bonds. This is likely to become a trend. CDFIs must make strategic adjustments in a timely manner to continue to add value in a marketplace they helped build. All indications are that CDFIs are prepared to do just that.

Conclusion

Tracing the growth of CDFIs through the charter school market makes plain the value that development finance institutions can play in correcting market inequalities and bringing about social change. Charter schools have made their mark on the education reform landscape. They are not without controversy or immune to legitimate criticism in some cases. But there is nothing more inspiring than seeing a young American at risk of ending up a teenage mother, a ward of the prison system, or just stuck in a low-wage job head off to college. CDFIs have helped make this important innovation happen by responding to the critical need charter schools have for facilities development and financing. As a result, CDFIs have fueled their own growth and have produced important innovations for the community development finance field.

The role of the federal government in providing credit-enhancement funding to organizations such as CDFIs cannot be understated. Without these incentives, and without CDFIs to effectively structure and administer them, the growth of the charter movement would have been slowed. The CECSF provides a model of how best to use social policy to address the deficiencies in a market-based system that leaves some communities financially underserved.

CDFIs are poised to innovate in the charter school market. Collaboration is key to success. If CDFIs are able to make securitization of charter school loans a reality, it will improve their acceptance in the capital markets. It may also pave the way for inclusion of other community development assets in the future—affordable housing, health care, and other community facilities. With access to the broader capital markets, CDFIs will come much closer to accomplishing the core mission of improving the lives of low-income people and communities.

Notes

1. CDFIs are organizations whose primary mission is to use financial and development services to create access to capital for underserved markets and communities. The CDFI Fund certifies CDFIs. Not all CDFIs are certified by the CDFI Fund.

2. Because no formal estimates exist, the author estimated demand on the basis of the percentage of schools seeking financing each year, average school size, average enrollment, and the cost of development per square foot. The range is $1.3 to $3 billion per annum.

References

Barclays Capital. 2007. *Barclays Capital Research 2007 Outlook.* http://www.barcap. com/sites/v/index.jsp?vgnextoid=f840d65126b6b010VgnVCM1000002e14480aRCRD. (Accessed 2-5-08.)

Center for Education Reform. 2007. *Annual Survey of America's Charter Schools.* Washington, DC.

Hoxby, Caroline. 2004. "Achievement in Charter Schools and Regular Public Schools in the United States: Understanding the Differences." Harvard University and National Bureau of Economic Research. http://www.heritage.org/Research/Education/wm622. cfm#_ftn1. (Accessed 2-12-08.)

Lake, Robin J., and Paul T. Hill. 2006. *Hopes, Fears and Reality, A Balanced Look at Charter Schools in 2006.* National Charter School Research Project, University of Washington's Center on Reinventing Public Education.

Local Initiative Support Corporation (LISC). 2007. *Charter School Facility Finance Landscape.* www.lisc.org.

National Center for Education Statistics (NCES). 2007. *National Assessment of Education Progress.* Washington, DC: U.S. Department of Education.

National Commission on Excellence in Education. 1983. *A Nation at Risk.* Washington, DC: DoE.

U.S. Department of Education (DoE). 1998. *National Study of Charter Schools: Second-Year Report.* Washington, DC: DoE.

———. 2006. *Charter High Schools: Closing the Achievement Gap.* Washington, DC: DoE.

5

The Case for the Community Partner in Economic Development

ANNA STEIGER, TESSA HEBB, AND LISA A. HAGERMAN

Large institutional investors are increasingly placing capital in *community invest-ments*,[1] seeking high financial returns while spurring economic growth in under-served areas. They look to invest large amounts of capital into easily replicable financial instruments that generate risk-adjusted market-rate returns. In contrast, investments in underserved communities are small, illiquid, and specialized to meet community needs. The challenge has been to find ways to funnel large amounts of institutional capital to community investments that have both high financial returns and meaningful benefits for communities.[2]

Hagerman, Clark, and Hebb (2007) set forth the role of intermediaries in com-munity-based investing, noting that investment intermediaries or "investment ve-hicles" and community intermediaries or "community partners" are needed to link the institutional investor to the economic development area. Investment vehicles intervene between the investor and the community by pooling investments, spread-ing risk across investors, and pricing the transaction up to the associated risk. They also link with community partners, who draw on their specialized local knowledge to structure deals that ensure social benefits for low- and moderate-income residents. As such, the partnership between the investment vehicle and community partner act to unlock value for institutional investors and communities alike.

In this chapter, we argue for the necessity of the partnership between the in-vestment vehicle and the community partner. There are various arrangements that establish the relationship between the two. We discuss the strengths and weaknesses of different business models of partnerships. We find two scenarios are particularly successful at yielding tangible benefits for the community. In the first scenario, a not-for-profit community partner owns or contracts with the for-profit investment vehicle. In the second, the for-profit investment vehicle affiliates with a not-for-profit community partner. We argue that investments made in partnership with a community development corporation (CDC) or community development financial institution (CDFI) provide some of the strongest community benefits.[3]

Using two case studies, we illustrate how investment vehicles and community partners work with each other. The first case study interrogates the model of a for-profit investment vehicle, The Urban Strategies America (USA) Fund, and its partnerships with two not-for-profit CDCs in the Boston area. The second case study examines Coastal Enterprises, Inc. (CEI) of Wiscasset, Maine, a not-for-profit CDC and CDFI, which owns several for-profit subsidiaries that create investments in low-income areas using the New Market Tax Credit (NMTC) program.[4]

Public pension funds in California, New York, and Massachusetts were early adopters of economic development policies that place capital with an investment vehicle. Lessons learned from these cases demonstrate that these investments yield both high financial returns and social returns (Hagerman and Hebb 2005). To date, public pension funds have committed $11 billion of their capital to urban or economic development investments (Hagerman, Clark and Hebb 2007).[5] Investments from other types of institutional investors, such as foundations, are increasing as well. Market-rate, mission-related investments from foundations grew at a 19.5 percent compound annual rate since 2000 and are funded from both program funds as well as endowment funds (Cooch and Kramer 2007).

While in some cases it is still too early to report on the financial returns of these investments, they are already yielding tangible social returns to communities. Opportunities exist to increase the flow of institutional capital into underserved communities. This chapter illustrates how the investment vehicle and community partner work together to create investments that meet the needs of both investors and communities, for the purpose of promoting models that successfully leverage institutional capital to promote economic development.

The Investment Vehicle and the Community Partner Relationship

The community development finance industry is looking to tap institutional investors —insurance companies, large commercial banks, public sector pension funds, foundations—as new sources of capital. Such investors can provide the patient capital needed for community investments, many of which do not yield returns for several years out. The underlying assumption is that engaging the financial markets in economic development is an effective way to transform lower-income communities. Several market barriers have traditionally prevented institutional investors from allocating capital to these types of investments. Daniels and Economic Innovation International (2005) cites five reasons that capital does not flow easily to low-income neighborhoods: (1) insufficient risk pricing, pooling, and spreading mechanisms; (2) high information and transaction costs; (3) market prejudice; (4) insufficient market competition; and (5) market-distorting government policies.

Institutional investors seeking to deploy capital to underserved areas do not have the time or expertise to actively manage these specialized investments. Investment vehicles intervene by using their financial expertise to pool assets and lower transaction costs. By creating scale, the investment vehicle produces the high financial return and large-size investments required by institutional investors. These investors allocate capital to economic revitalization through three asset classes: fixed income, equity real estate, and private equity (Hagerman, Clark and Hebb 2007).[6] Many community developments are multiuse projects, which are seen by investors as inherently more difficult to evaluate and implement. Investors consequently favor larger, more experienced fund managers and developers for these types of projects (Gyourko and Rybczynski 2000).

The community partner links the investment vehicle to the neighborhood. It uses its local knowledge to identify investment opportunities, enlist the participation of other partners such as developers, and assemble the support of civic leaders, government officials, and residents. The community partner also works to ensure that the investment yields benefits for the local neighborhood rather than lead to the displacement of lower-income residents—which occurs when revitalization projects raise property prices to the point that local residents can no longer afford to live and/or work in the community. Generally, community partners have previous experience promoting economic development through assembling smaller-scale investments in affordable housing, mixed-use real estate, community facilities, and small businesses.

Structures of Investment Vehicles

The investment vehicle links the institutional investor to the revitalized area through a variety of operating models. Daniels (2004) identifies four approaches to the oversight of an investment fund (see Table 5.1). We suggest that two models, the contractual model and the ownership model, hold the greatest promise for unlocking value for institutional investors and communities alike. In the contractual model, a not-for-profit community partner or "sponsor," such as a registered 501(c) (3), contracts with a well-established for-profit investment fund manager. In the ownership model, a not-for-profit community partner (often a well-established CDC or CDFI) owns the for-profit fund manager. The legislative model has been effective in Massachusetts, but it is dependent on supportive legislatures. The fund manager model is effective in aggregating investment for institutional investors but can lack grounding in the community unless it affiliates with a community partner. We find that most funds currently operating in this investment space fall into the fund manager model and may or may not affiliate with a community partner.

The contractual, ownership, and fund manager models draw on the strength of the for-profit fund manager to aggregate investments that allow for the scale and track records necessary for institutional investor engagement. Such for-profit fund managers often establish a commingled fund structured as a limited partnership or limited liability company. Often, reciprocal targeted investing is a feature of a commingled fund.[7] Another for-profit fund manager structure used in private equity investing in underserved capital markets is a fund-of-funds to achieve scale and diversification. An institutional investor can have small investments in ten funds but makes only one large investment in the single fund-of-funds (Hagerman, Clark and Hebb 2007). This lowers the degree of due diligence required by the investor, who selects only the fund-of-funds vehicle rather than each of the smaller vehicles that receive funding.

Table 5.1

Structures of Investment Vehicles

Legal Model	Structure	Strengths	Weaknesses	Examples
Contractual	Not-for-profit community partner sponsors or affiliate contracts with a proven fund manager to serve as fund manager; project can be structured either as an LLC or limited partnership	Proven outside fund manager	Fund manager can run off with the idea with no accountability to not-for-profit sponsor or affiliate, if ongoing funds are not built into the contract	Genesis LA Funds, Bay Area Family of Funds, San Diego Capital Collaborative, Nehemiah Sacramento Valley Fund
Ownership	Not-for-profit community fund sponsor owns for-profit fund manager	Not-for-profit community fund sponsor has control over fund manager	Institutional investors may not have confidence in the not-for-profit manager	Community Preservation Corporation (owns CPC Resources, Coastal Enterprises (owns CEI Ventures), MA Housing Investment (owns MHIC Equity LLC)
Legislative	Fund criteria and tax deal codified in state legislation	Good option with a sympathetic legislature	Not an option with an unsympathetic legislature	MA Life Initiative, MA Property and Casualty Initiative
Fund Manager	For-profit fund manager operates without a not-for-profit sponsor or affiliate*	Investors like returns, fund managers, and double bottom line concept	Who is monitoring second bottom line?	American Ventures, CA Urban Investment, Urban Strategy America Fund, New Boston USA Fund, Urban America, Canyon Johnson Urban Fund

Source: Adapted from Daniels (2004).
*We present in this case study an example of a for-profit fund manager that affiliates with a not-for-profit CDC, as shown in the case of the New Boston USA Fund affiliating with Lena Park CDC and the Asian CDC.

The Community Partner "Toolkit"

Community partners work with the investment vehicle and the community to un-lock both the financial and social benefits of investments. Community partners are organizations and businesses that are rooted in the community and have an explicit mission to promote community benefits. Community partners also make use of various "tools" to help structure community investments. The first set of tools is *financial tools*. Community partners have access to tools that affect the financial value of investments, such as land zoning and encumbrances, Low Income-Housing Tax Credits (LIHTCs), NMTCs, philanthropic grants provided by foundations and private donors, and other types of public and private subsidies.[8] Not all com-munity investments require these types of subsidies, but in some cases these tools help to create investments that otherwise might not have occurred or to provide greater social returns than otherwise might have been possible. The second set of tools is *social and political tools*. Community partners are rooted in the local area and often have a track record of contributing to local economic development. As a result, they have earned the community's trust and have extensive ties with key community stakeholders that can be called upon to help get a development project approved and to leverage resources. The third set of tools is *material tools*. A com-munity partner may own or manage the land or community facility that underpins the investment opportunity.

Types of Community Partners

Community partners by definition are rooted in the local community and are mis-sion-driven. We categorized partners into five types: not-for-profit fund sponsors; other not-for-profit affiliates; mission-driven wholesale lending intermediaries—either not-for-profit, for-profit, or public intermediaries; local governments and public officials; and underserved businesses, including minority- and women-owned businesses and state-certified local, small, and disadvantaged business enterprises (LSDBEs) (see Table 5.2).

Not-for-profit fund sponsors and affiliates—CDCs and CDFIs—are the stron-gest community partners because their mission is closely aligned with the needs of underserved areas and because they have access to the broadest sets of tools described. Mission-driven wholesale lending intermediaries can play the roles of either community partner or investment vehicle, depending on the investment. However, these institutions often have a more focused mission and role than a CDC (e.g., to assemble housing loans), which can limit their ability to bring diverse community benefits to an investment. The public sector can bring resources to an investment but may not be focused on securing benefits for lower-income and other underserved groups. Finally, underserved businesses can also be community partners in as much as they provide investment opportunities tied to public incentives for investors but have a limited set of tools with which to create community impact.

Table 5.2

Types of Community Partners

Type	Key Roles/Tools	Strengths	Weaknesses	Examples
Not-for-profit fund sponsors (such as civic organizations organized as 501 [c] 3s)	Create a fund and select a fund manager; help identify and structure deals Tools: • Social and political—ties to community stakeholders • Financial—philanthropic funding/NMTC/LIHTC	Robust community benefits that are often tied to regional priorities	Difficult to start, fewer examples	Bay Area Council sponsorship of the Bay Area Smart Growth Fund (of the Bay Area Family of Funds); Genesis LA sponsorship of the Genesis LA Family of Funds
Not-for-profit partners or affiliates (such as CDCs and CDFIs)	Help identify and structure deals Tools: • Social and political—ties to community stakeholders • Financial—philanthropic funding/NMTC/ LIHTC	Robust community benefits; well-established CDCs and CDFIs have been successful in partnering with for-profit investment vehicles	Varying organizational capacity	Coastal Enterprises, Inc.; Lena Park CDC; Asian CDC
Mission-driven wholesale lending intermediaries (such as state housing finance agencies)	Help identify and structure deals; provide housing finance: loans, guarantees, tax credits Tools: • Financial—loan guarantees, LIHTC, and other tax credits	Strong institutional capacity	Narrow mission (i.e., housing finance)	Illinois Housing Authority (with the AFL-CIO HIT): senior housing project in Chicago; Mass Housing Investment Corp (with Access Capital): Holyoke Housing Center

(continued)

66

Table 5.2 *(continued)*

Type	Key Roles/Tools	Strengths	Weaknesses	Examples
Local governments and public officials (such as mayors)	Use zoning/permitting authority for community benefits *Tools:* • Social and political—ties to community stakeholders • Financial—zoning/permitting authority	Ability to recruit public and private resources to deal	Not necessarily looking to maximize benefits for the underserved or low-income	Canyon Johnson and Mayor of Miami: down payment assistance for city workers)
Minority or women-owned businesses or businesses in underserved areas (such as local, small, and disadvantaged businesses [LSDBs])	Entrepreneurial activity *Tools:* • Financial—some states offer incentives to investors such as loan guarantees	Public incentives tied to LSDBE investment opportunities	Limited set of tools	LSDBE program in Washington, DC

In areas that do not have a strong presence of not-for-profit partners like CDCs or CDFIs, underserved businesses can provide opportunities for institutional investors seeking to make community investments.

Investment vehicles can partner with multiple community partners to augment the social returns of a project. The contractual model lends itself to multi-institutional partnerships. In this model, the fund sponsor—sometimes a council of local organizations (e.g., Bay Area Council)—works closely with local stakeholders to identify investment opportunities and recruit additional private, not-for-profit, and public resources. The fund sponsor often has a regional focus and connects investment decisions to regional economic priorities (Flynn et al. forthcoming).

Case Studies

Here, we examine two case studies that illustrate how the investment vehicles work with the community partners to develop investments with social returns. We also highlight the benefits accrued to the community partners.

The Urban Strategy America Fund

The USA Fund is an example of a for-profit fund manager model that takes a triple bottom line approach, seeking financial, social, and environmental returns on investments. The USA Fund was founded in 2004 by the New Boston Fund, a middle-market equity real estate investment fund started in 1993. With $170 million under management, the USA Fund participates in projects as direct investments or joint ventures on a scale of $10 million to $70 million or more in New England and the Mid-Atlantic. In addition to its real estate investment expertise, the USA Fund brings development expertise via the New Boston Developers group. The USA Fund counts among its institutional investors national banks, foundations, insurance companies, and public pension funds.

The USA Fund's Financial Engineering Model

The USA Fund provides preconstruction dollars as well as risk-adjusted equity to its community investment partnerships. The fund's financial expertise and ability to supply capital also provides credibility with the public sector, which is important for securing approvals and public and/or subsidy financing. In a typical deal, the USA Fund is responsible for obtaining third-party debt financing of up to 75 percent of project cost. Joint venture partners (developers and/or community partners) may provide up to 20 percent of project equity through cash, third-party predevelopment expenses, or contribution of land. In return, local partners receive a development fee commensurate with development expertise as well as profit participation after equity investors receive a preferred 12 percent rate of return.

Olmstead Green

Olmstead Green is a joint effort between the USA Fund and its not-for-profit community partner, Lena Park CDC.[9] Olmstead Green is being built on the former site of the Boston State Hospital, land that had been undeveloped for twenty-five years. In 2001, Lena Park CDC decided to reenter real estate development and hired Kirk Sykes, an architect, to help them think through a detailed strategy for the Boston State Hospital site. Together with Sykes, they interviewed twenty-nine developers and decided to go with New Boston Real Estate because of its proven track record working with community-based organizations on One Brigham Circle, a mixed-use real estate project in the Mission Hill section of Boston. Sykes subsequently was hired at New Boston, and the company formalized its triple bottom line strategy by creating the USA Fund. Olmstead Green was the fund's first investment. The project broke ground in May 2006. E. Lorraine Baugh, executive director of Lena Park CDC, explains, "Neither of the partners could have done the deal without the other." The USA Fund brought the equity and know-how of a large real estate fund and development firm. According to Sykes, Lena Park CDC brought knowledge of the local needs and the "hearts and minds of the community."

Olmstead Green will create 287 workforce housing condominiums and 153 affordable rental units. Four hundred jobs in construction and four hundred permanent positions will be created. The design is energy efficient and includes green public spaces. Lena Park CDC will also develop eighty-three units of senior housing, a 123-bed skilled nursing care facility, an urban farm, a Heritage House mental health center, a job training center, a fitness facility, and a community center, which will house Lena Park's newly renovated offices.

The Lena Park CDC has made its foray back into real estate development with its participation in Olmstead Green. This has helped the CDC strengthen its organizational capacity and is expected to provide a revenue stream that will cross-subsidize Lena Park's health and human service activities. The project will also help cement Lena Park's role in the community. According to Baugh, the experience also taught the CDC how to "partner with the private sector without getting swallowed up."

Parcel 24

Parcel 24 is a joint initiative of the USA Fund and the Asian CDC.[10] The land that Parcel 24 will sit on had been taken from 300 Chinatown residents in 1962 by the City of Boston as part of the Massachusetts Turnpike extension project. In 2000, the Asian CDC led a comprehensive organizing, community planning, and legislative effort to have the site returned to the community as part of the completion of the Central Artery/Tunnel Project commonly known as the "Big Dig." According to the Asian CDC's executive director, Jeremy Liu, the group was able to capture the social value of the land by getting encumbrances placed on the site that ensured it would be used for affordable housing and open spaces. As a result, the Asian CDC found itself in the position of looking for a partner that could help unlock the financial value of the land, given the encumbrances. The Asian CDC brought the deal to New Boston Real Estate/USA Fund and was impressed with the fund's willingness to have an ongoing conversation about how to balance the risk of the project with the need to ensure community benefits. The USA Fund and the Asian CDC formed Parcel 24, LLC, and won the designation for the project from the Massachusetts Turnpike Authority in April 2006. Parcel 24 is scheduled to break ground in 2009.

Parcel 24 will create 324 residential units, including 70 affordable rentals and approximately 85 affordable and 169 market-rate condominiums. The mixed-use design will feature 165 parking spaces, an urban park, and 11,000 square feet of retail and community space. The project will also create approximately 700 construction jobs and up to 40 permanent jobs in retail, community organizations, and property management. This development will be a "green construction" with a LEED project certification.[11]

Liu indicates that what the Asian CDC learned about developing large-scale projects through its partnership with the USA Fund has helped the CDC "emerge out of an era where projects happen to us" and become more forward-looking. The Asian CDC has experienced several key growth milestones over the past few years, many of which were made possible through its participation in Parcel 24. Some of these milestones include a larger staff and a more diverse representation of expertise reflected by board members; a first ever for the organization: a five-year strategic plan that includes an operating pro forma; a budget of over $1,000,000 in 2007–2008 compared with $200,000 in 1997–1998; and real estate pipeline prospects in three municipalities outside the City of Boston.

Coastal Enterprises, Inc.

Our second case study illustrates the ownership model. CEI, founded in 1977, provides financing and support in the development of small businesses, natural resources industries, community facilities, and affordable housing. CEI takes a triple bottom line approach (seeking financial, social, and environmental returns) and works in rural areas in Maine, northern New England, and upstate New York. CEI operates as both a community partner and an investment vehicle through three for-profit subsidiary companies: CEI Capital Management, LLC (CCML); CEI Ventures, Inc.; and CEI Community Ventures, Inc. We focus our discussion on CCML because of the ways in which its business model relies on relationships with community partners.

CEI Capital Management (CCML)

CCML is the entity set up to manage CEI's $129 million NMTC allocation, operating in eligible low-income, primarily rural, areas in New England and New York. CCML identifies investment opportunities in these areas through its network of community partners. In recent years it has extended this network and is now looking to do NMTC deals in rural areas across America. Charlie Spies, managing director of CCML, explains that the NMTC is a critical instrument for this type of investing. He says, "The NMTC provides the missing piece, which is equity, in these types of investments. While we might have had a state guarantee in the past, the NMTC has proven to be essential for these deals." Institutional investment in CCML deals has come from national and local banks, foundations, and private investment companies.

CEI's New Market Tax Credit Model

CCML plays an important role in the community development finance industry through its capacity to structure NMTC investments in rural areas. Health centers in rural communities face big hurdles in recruiting and retaining physicians. Tight quarters had hampered Mid-State's ability to add services and operate efficiently. The facility had to move to attract good doctors and grow, but it could not afford a conventionally financed building. Mid-State CEO, Sharon Beaty, turned to Capital Regional Development Council (CRDC), a statewide not-for-profit economic developer, for help. CRDC understood the health center needed a below-market lease to stay viable and brought the opportunity to CCML. CCML and CRDC crafted an investment using NMTCs whereby CRDC constructed a new building that they lease to Mid-State at an affordable rate. Investors in the new building include CRDC, a consortium of three community banks, the New Hampshire Community Development Finance Authority, and others. Mid-State's 19,000-square-foot state-of-the-art health center opened in 2007. With the new clinic space, Mid-State will be able to integrate behavioral health services such as counseling with telemedicine—the use of technology to facilitate consultation between two medical specialists in different locations. The clinic also plans to have on-site daycare for children of staff as well as children of community members. According to Beaty, "Our job is to protect access to primary care. This building is exciting for our community." CRDC's participation with CCML in the Mid-State Health Center has influenced its strategic planning. CRDC is looking to do additional NMTC investments with CCML as well as other organizations. CRDC is also talking to the parent company, CEI, about partnering on other initiatives, such as on the delivery of SBA 504 loans.

The Role of the Investment Vehicle

This section uses examples from our cases to illustrate three central roles that investment vehicles play in community-based investing: sourcing deals, financial engineering, and developing a niche industry.

Sourcing Deals

Investment vehicles engage in two types of deal flow strategies (Flynn et al. forthcoming). Top-down strategies leverage relationships with mayors and other government officials and executives of banks, real estate firms, and insurance companies. Bottom-up strategies look for specific deals and development opportunities, often before they are on the market. Sources included developers, real estate professionals, and community partners. In our cases studies, the investment vehicles work closely with community partners to source deals. CCML's business model is explicit about community partners taking a lead role in sourcing deals; the partnership agreement between CEI and the community partner establishes a fee structure to be paid for successful deals brought to CCML. Notwithstanding, CCML equips the community partners to source deals by providing presentation materials and participating with them on investment road shows. For both the USA Fund and CCML, once the deal comes to the investment vehicle, the vehicle is responsible for undertaking a due diligence review process, structuring the transaction, monitoring development, and creating an exit strategy.

Financial Engineering

The capital structure of an investment fund is developed through complex financial engineering. The structure can involve a debt component that helps bring the deal to scale. This is an important factor in understanding how the investment vehicle provides scale that leads to a transformation of neighborhoods and significant investment in growth companies. A successful real estate development includes a well-structured capital source. This is outlined in a pro forma detailing the sources and uses of funds. Funding sources include a combination of equity and often a bank loan for construction financing and other third-party debt financing. Equity is leveraged with mortgage financing to generate substantial capital in new developments. The role of subsidies is another component in the capital structure of private equity funds. While the second and third generations of funds have moved away from a reliance on public subsidies, they can still continue to play a role. Examples of financial engineering by the investment vehicles were presented in the previous section. As mentioned, the USA Fund and CCML are responsible for obtaining the bulk of third-party financing, while joint venture partners may provide some of the remainder of the financing. CCML uses the NMTCs as incentives for investors. Both investment vehicles work with community partners to secure other types of subsidy financing.

Developing a Niche Industry

Investment vehicles engaged in community-based investing are attentive to their participation in an emerging, niche industry. The investment vehicle works to increase demand for and supply of community investments by educating potential investors, community partners, and other stakeholders about how these investments work and typical returns to these investments. Investment vehicles also actively recruit resources to strengthen the industry, such as technical assistance providers to work with entrepreneurs and researchers who help catalog the financial and social returns for investors and communities. The investment vehicles we examined have worked to overcome market prejudices in a number of ways. New Boston Real Estate Fund had developed proof of concept in a traditional investment fund before moving to triple bottom line investments with the USA Fund. As mentioned, CCML works closely with its community partners to educate potential investors and growing businesses about the NMTC.

The Role of the Community Partner

This section uses examples from our cases to illustrate two central roles that community partners play in community-based investing: sourcing deals and ensuring community benefits.

Sourcing Deals

Community partners work with investment vehicles to identify investment opportunities. Community partners are aware of local needs and draw on this knowledge to pursue resources and partners that help address these needs. The community partner may also recruit smaller, local investors and/or invest themselves in the projects. Rural Opportunities Enterprise Center, Inc. (ROECI), a community development and human services not-for-profit based in Rochester, New York, has worked with CCML since 2005 to identify eligible NMTC opportunities in upstate New York. ROECI markets NMTC and does the preliminary screening of investment opportunities for financial viability. In 2005, ROECI brought the Brooks Landing project to CEI, an opportunity to revitalize a section of city waterfront in Rochester. Using $10 million in NMTC allocations, CEI and ROECI leveraged an additional $10 million in public and private funds, helping create an extended-stay hotel linked to Strong Memorial Hospital and the University of Rochester, commercial and office space, a public boardwalk, and boat-docking facilities.

Ensuring Community Benefits

Community partners ensure that the community investment has social returns for local residents, a responsibility that aligns well with a community partner's mission to promote local development. The community partner is more closely linked to the community than the investment vehicle and more likely to be held accountable for delivering these benefits. The community partner has in-depth knowledge of local needs and leverages its "tools" to garner resources for the investment. Its social and political tools may provide the "credibility pass" needed for the project to get approval, and, as mentioned, the financial tools may help overcome market barriers or create greater social returns than would otherwise be the case. The Nature Conservancy, a global conservancy organization with strong ties to the state of Maine, is a good example of how a community partner can employ financial tools for community benefit. The Conservancy worked with CCML to create a financing scheme using $32 million in NMTCs that allowed the Great Northern Paper Company in Millinocket, Maine, to preserve and/or reactivate 620 jobs. The Conservancy used its industry expertise to craft sustainability covenants into the loan agreement, resulting in Great Northern transferring 41,000 acres of land to the Conservancy and placing a conservation easement on an additional 200,000 acres of land.

In addition to the social metrics normally tracked, we found that the community partners participating in these deals also received direct benefits to their organizations. First, community partners participating in these large-scale projects *strengthened their organizational capacity.* A simple example is how the fees earned by CCML for assembling NMTC deals are used to cross-subsidize CEI's other activities. Second, we found the community partners were looking to engage in more complex project and products after participating in deals with the investment vehicle. As such, these partnerships had helped to *foster innovation* in the community partners. For example, after working with CCML to develop "River Valley," a food co-op in Northampton, Massachusetts, the Western Mass Enterprise Fund (WMEF) began looking at other ways to offer equity-like products to customers. They then decided to roll out royalty options, products that combine debt with an equity-like feature, namely, a right to a percentage of the company's future sales. Third, community partners *increased their collaborative efforts* after working with investment vehicles. Across the board, the community partners examined in this study said that after partnering with investment vehicles, they had a greater appreciation for the value that large collaborative efforts could have for their communities and their organizations.

Conclusion

There are opportunities to attract larger amounts of institutional capital to the emerging domestic markets while promoting the mechanisms that help ensure these investments have a meaningful impact on underserved communities. This study shows that the partnership between the investment vehicle and community partner acts to unlock value for institutional investors and communities alike. The investment vehicle and the community partner form a symbiotic relationship that allows for scale to effectively transform neighborhoods and yield financial returns to the institutional investor. Without the investment vehicle, large pools of capital would not be placed in the economic development area.

Investment vehicles and community partners work to overcome market barriers in a number of ways. One of the most important ways investment vehicles do this is by pooling assets and investors. Another important way investment vehicles and community partners overcome market barriers is by leveraging public incentives. Just as the LIHTC program opened the door to significant amounts of institutional capital for affordable housing, the NMTC program is attracting hundreds of millions of dollars to investments in businesses and mixed-use real estate. Additional research on the costs and benefits of these programs could help assess the value of the incentives for attracting institutional capital as an engine for economic development and poverty alleviation.

Lessons learned from early adopters among institutional investors demonstrate that these investments yield both high financial and social returns. The amount of capital committed by institutional investors is growing. Nonetheless, challenges remain. Deal flow remains a problem, and the relative complexity of these investments makes it difficult for some investors to classify them. The ability of investment vehicles to partner with community organizations is essential for generating more deals and successfully placing institutional capital in the underserved areas. We argue that the community partner toolkit that includes the financial, social and political, and material tools is the leverage that not-for-profit community partners bring to community-based investing. Opportunities remain for investment and community intermediaries to find new avenues for funneling institutional dollars into community investments such that these investments will provide robust benefits for investors and communities alike.

Notes

The views expressed in this publication do not necessarily reflect official positions of the Federal Reserve Bank of Boston or the Federal Reserve System.

1. These are investments targeting geographic areas and businesses that have traditionally had difficulty attracting private sector capital. Most of these investments are in lower-income urban areas, but some are targeted to rural areas as well. Other terms to describe these investments include *emerging domestic markets, urban revitalization,* and *investments in underserved areas.*

2. Community benefits comprise (1) economic returns: creation of jobs, affordable housing, and other real estate developments; (2) social returns: creation of community facilities, open spaces, and services for local residents; (3) environmental returns: promoting mixed-use, transit-oriented, and "green" developments as well as sustainable practices in local industries. Collectively, all these are *social returns.*

3. CDC is a resident-owned and resident-controlled organization engaged in affordable housing, business and commercial development, and providing community services in low- and moderate-income areas. Most are nonprofit, tax-exempt 501(c) 3 organizations. A CDFI is a financial institution whose primary mission is to promote community development in low- and moderate-income areas. CDFIs provide comprehensive credit, investment, banking, and development services. Some are chartered banks, others are credit unions, and many operate as self-regulating, nonprofit institutions that gather private capital from a range of investors for community development or lending.

4. NMTC, established by Congress in 2000 and administered by the CDFI Fund at the Department of the Treasury, gives individual and corporate taxpayers the opportunity to earn credits against income taxes by investing in qualified community development entities (CDEs). Investors can earn attractive rates of return while meeting a community need, qualified businesses gain access to development funds at reasonable rates, and CDEs fulfill their mission by helping stimulate economic growth and job creation.

5. The figure includes programs to stimulate economic activity in underserved markets but does not include broad in-state targeted investments.

6. Public pension funds investments include three asset classes: fixed income, equity real estate, and private equity (early- and later-stage venture capital).

7. The fund manager targets investments in geographic areas based on the limited partner's investment percentage in the fund, while the investor receives a return based on the total portfolio, not just its own geographic target.

8. Subsidies for economic development come in a variety of forms, including grants, loans, loan guarantees, the provision of in-kind products and services, regulation, and tax credits. Land zoning includes land use regulation; easements are land preservation agreements between a landowner and a municipality or a qualified land protection organization on conservation lands; the LIHTC is run by the IRS and allows companies to invest in low-income housing while receiving ten years of tax credits; and the NMTC permits taxpayers to receive a credit against federal income taxes over a seven-year period for making qualified equity investments.

9. Lena Park CDC is a health and human services organization with a thirty-five-year history of serving low-income families in the Dorchester, Mattapan, and Roxbury areas of Boston.

10. The Asian CDC, established in 1987, develops affordable housing and promotes economic development and financial education in the Chinatown area of Boston.

11. The Leadership in Energy and Environmental Design (LEED) is a nationally accepted benchmark for the design, construction, and operation of successful green buildings.

References

Cooch, Sarah, and Mark Kramer. 2007. *Compounding Interest: Mission Investing by U.S. Foundations.* Social Impact Advisors. http://www.fsg-impact.org/images/upload/Compounding%20Impact(3).pdf. (Accessed 2-5-08.)

Daniels, Belden, and Economic Innovation International, Inc. 2004. *Market Assessment and Investment Strategy for a Northwest Louisiana Community Development Fund, Shreveport, Louisiana.* Boston, MA: EII, Inc.

———. 2005. *Market Assessment and Investment Strategy for a Maryland Community Development Fund.* Boston, MA: EII, Inc.

Flynn, Erin, et al. Forthcoming. *The Double Bottom Line Handbook: A Practitioner's Guide to Regional Double Bottom Line Investment Initiatives and Funds.*

Gyourko, Joseph E., and Witold Rybczynski. 2000. "Financing New Urbanism Projects: Obstacles and Solutions." *Housing Policy Debate* 11 (3): 733–750.

Hagerman, Lisa, Gordon L. Clark, and Tessa Hebb. 2007. "Pension Funds and Urban Revitalization: Competitive Returns and a Revitalized New York." Oxford: Oxford University Centre for Environment, WP 05–13.

Hagerman, Lisa. Forthcoming. "More than a Profit? Measuring the Social and Green Outcomes of Urban Investments." Oxford University Centre for Environment Working Paper.

Hagerman, Lisa and Hebb, Tessa. 2005. "California Case Study: A Private Equity CalPERS' California Initiative." Oxford: Oxford University Centre for Environment, WP 05–15.

6

Research Design Issues for Measuring CDFI Performance and Impact

Dan Immergluck

Community development financial institutions (CDFIs) represent a key innovation in community development. CDFIs are loan funds, venture capital funds, microloan funds, credit unions, and banks that include community development at the core of their mission. Federal, state, and local governments, as well as private foundations and financial institutions, have invested billions of dollars in CDFIs over the last twenty years to revitalize communities through improved access to affordable capital and credit. Both private social investors as well as governments are increasingly asking for evidence of CDFIs' impacts.

While recognizing the substantial limitations and constraints of program evaluation in this field, I address major research design questions for CDFIs:

1. What is the appropriate level at which to examine the impacts of CDFIs? Should we measure impacts at the level of the entire subsector, a product line, or a specific product? Can we identify product lines that are relatively better candidates for impact evaluation?
2. What are some of the fundamental methodological approaches that might be used to conduct summative impact evaluation for specific CDFI product lines?

CDFI Borrower-Investee Types, Product Groups, and Product Lines

It is important to develop a typology of CDFI products and services, critical for understanding the context in which to measure impacts and to prevent an overaggregation of different products. Literature on CDFIs is widely available, much focused on distinguishing types of CDFIs first and then, within each CDFI class, examining projects—business, housing, nonprofit facilities, for example—financed by that category of CDFI (CDFI Data Project 2004; Tholin 1994). While the literature sometimes focuses on specific products, little effort has been made to disaggregate them into predominant products.

Approaching questions of CDFI outcomes by first thinking about the different types of institutions (e.g., community development bank versus community development loan fund) encourages a focus on financial performance measures (PMs), such as financial health. This may not be a bad thing to do, especially if financial sustainability is of interest. If questions concern the mission-oriented outcomes of the CDFI sector, however, it may be more productive to begin with outcomes, not delivery systems and their financial strength.

Some researchers think about the types of borrowers and investors that CDFIs target (Benjamin, Rubin, and Zielenbach 2004). This focus is closer to the approach taken in this chapter. I first consider the sorts of borrowers or investees that CDFIs target, then I examine the products offered.

Table 6.1 provides a typology of CDFI product lines by financial product group and borrower/investee ("customer") and financial product: households, microentrepreneurs, low-to-moderate growth firms, emerging or high-growth small firms, nonprofits (excluding housing development organizations), and real estate developers (both for-profit and nonprofit). The table does not include every product or service and technical assistance or educational services. It also does not consider any broader community development or community building activities not involving financing. These services could be added to the typology, but they were omitted to focus on financial products and services.

Financial product groups include bank accounts and related products, unsecured consumer loans and car loans, single-family mortgages, multifamily real estate loans, commercial real estate loans, business equity financing, and business term loans and lines of credit. These groups are defined by the structural characteristics of the products (e.g., mortgages versus term loans). Some CDFI product groups focus on one customer (e.g., low-cost bank accounts), while others serve multiple customers (e.g., commercial real estate loans).

The table lists specific product lines. For example, for the household customer category, the single-family mortgage group is disaggregated to include home purchase, home improvement, and refinance loans. Even within these categories, we can disaggregate further. For example, home purchase loans might include junior as well as senior mortgages.

The versatility of some product groups across multiple customer types is indicated by the vertical arrows, which signify that a group covers more than one customer type. For example, CDFIs may extend term loans to microenterprises, small firms (from low- to high-growth), or nonprofit organizations. While the rates and terms of these loans may vary by customer type, the basic loan structures are likely to be relatively similar.

Another important component of Table 6.1 is the set of acronyms at the bottom of the table, identifying types of CDFIs offering products. Identification of product lines and their organization into customer and product groups will assist with thinking about measuring outcomes and gathering data on comparable non-CDFI products.

Table 6.1

A Typology of Major CDFI Financial Product Lines, Excluding Technical Assistance and Education

Financial Product Groups

Type of Borrower/ Investee	Bank Accounts	Unsecured Loans & Auto Loans	Single-Family Mortgages	Multifamily Real Estate Loans	Commercial Real Estate Loans	Business Equity/Quasi-Equity	Business Term Loans & Lines of Credit
Households	Low-cost savings and checking accts CU, CB	Payday alternatives Overdraft products Student loans Auto loans CU, CB	Purchase • senior/junior Improvement • senior/junior Refinances • rate/term • antipredatory LF, CB, CU				
Microentrepreneurs					Construction loans Land financing Purchase • senior/junior Refinance • senior/junior Predevelopment grants/ recoverables LF, CB, CU	Equity; unsecured debt; royalty financing VC	Term loans • senior/junior Lines of credit LF, CB, CU ML for micro-entrepreneurs
Low- to Moderate-Growth Small Firms							
Emerging, High-Growth Small Firms							
Nonprofits/Charter Schools/Public Facilities (Excluding Housing Developers)							
Real Estate Developers (For-Profit and Nonprofit)				Construction loans Purchase • senior/junior Refinance • senior/junior			

Key to institution types: LF—loan funds; CB—community development banks; ML—microlenders; CU—CDCUs; VC—CDV

Figure 6.1 **A Simple Logic Model for a CDFI Home-Improvement Loan Product Line**

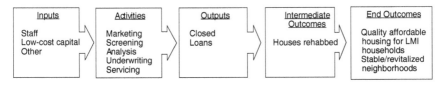

Performance Measurement Versus Summative Impact Evaluation

When people talk about CDFI "impacts," what do they mean? Some may mean "outcomes" in PM (Hatry 2007). Outcomes are the *purported* effects of completed CDFI activities—called *outputs*. They are the concrete, desirable conditions a program hopes to bring about for individuals and communities. PM distinguishes between end outcomes, intermediate outcomes, and outputs, with the former being defined by the CDFI mission and objectives. End outcomes include access to quality, affordable housing, decreased unemployment or underemployment, and higher wages. Intermediate outcomes are recognized as good in and of themselves but are most important in their critical role in bringing about desired end outcomes. An example is the expansion of firms in a region expected to lead to reduced unemployment or underemployment in a community. Outputs are completed program activities, which in themselves have little intrinsic value. They are desirable only in that they lead to intermediate or end outcomes.

Outputs and outcomes are tied to logic models, describing and analyzing program theory, operation and performance. A logic model for a hypothetical CDFI with a home improvement loan product line is presented in Figure 6.1.

Those adopting the PM perspective focus on defining and distinguishing outputs, intermediate outcomes, and end outcomes and in obtaining data needed to constitute sound, quantitative indicators. Distinguishing outputs and intermediate outcomes, for example, can be a key to PM.

In discussions of CDFI outcomes, *impact* frequently appears to be used when what is really meant is *end outcome*. This confusion occurs perhaps because an outcome is indeed a *purported* effect; that is, PM does not require that evidence support the notion that the program *caused* the outcome.

Strictly speaking, *impact* is best left to the domain of summative impact evaluation (SIE). SIE attaches a meaning to the term impact that is linked to causality. Measuring impact requires measuring the difference between CDFI outcomes and whatever would have occurred without CDFI intervention—the "counterfactual." SIE identifies causality between the program and the outcome and involves measuring the extent of that causality, or how much of the measured outcome can be attributed to the program.

To SIE practitioners, the challenge becomes identifying the counterfactual or developing a reasonable estimate of it. Although the evaluator would prefer measuring impacts on end outcomes, she may be willing to settle for measures of impact on intermediate outcomes or outputs if she can be confident of establishing a counterfactual for them. This is true if there is a strong, well-established link between these more proximate effects—outputs or intermediate outcomes—and end outcomes. For example, if evidence demonstrates that access to capital is a key driver of a desired outcome, an evaluator's concerns might lie chiefly in whether, in the absence of CDFI activity, borrowers would have access to capital from elsewhere and, if so, at what costs and conditions compared to the CDFI products that they received.

Some SIE practitioners may look upon PM with skepticism. They may view efforts to measure outcomes without identifying the extent to which such outcomes can be attributed to CDFIs as a hollow task. PM practitioners are more pragmatic, arguing that, together with qualitative and interpretive knowledge of an initiative and its context, PM can support a reasonable argument that impact is likely or unlikely and perhaps tell us something about the scale of any likely impact. PM can be used as a heuristic tool that, when combined with other, often less formally or quantitatively acquired knowledge, can contribute to assessing impact.

Regardless of whether an analytical exercise provides a strong measure of impact in a given product line, comparing CDFI outcomes to contextual data regarding needs or similar market activity can be useful. It can give us some sense of how much aggregate difference a program *might* be making at its current scale. For example, assume we know that all of the microenterprise lenders in Big City A made a total of ten microloans in a recent year and the lenders in Big City B made a total of 200 microloans in the same year. Let us also assume that the cities were similar in size, economic demography, and bank lending. This information would be useful in comparing microlending across cities. Moreover, it seems fair to say that microlenders in Big City B were *likely* to be having a greater overall impact on access to capital for very small firms than those in Big City A. Of course, the SIE practitioner might question whether microlenders in either city were actually having any impact, and that is a reasonable question. However, the point here is simply to consider outcomes and their context and not to quantify or prove impact. It seems that in many cases, even this limited information would provide us with a good deal more information than we currently have. Of course, it is important not to draw definitive conclusions from such analyses that microlending programs in Big City A "don't work." We have not been presented sufficient information to determine impact.

Depending on the intermediate and end outcomes of the CDFIs in a particular subsector, we might look for data to place these outcomes in an appropriate context. If the microlenders, for example, are looking to influence the behavior of conventional banks toward microenterprises (e.g., encourage them to make more loans to very small firms)—what might be called an *institutional* or *structural* impact—it is important to understand the scale of outcomes relative to the activity of the industry that is the target of influence.

Relative scale is just one context. Others include the relative challenges of working in different places. It may be that in one place, a certain outcome would be quite impressive, while in another, it would not be so remarkable. To complement quantitative measures of performance or outcomes, qualitative data, including information from informant interviews, could prove helpful.

In the realm of institutional impacts, scale matters for reasons beyond just the subsector's ability to deliver more capital to firms or households. Scale matters because the subsector becomes substantial enough to affect lender behavior. Mainstream lenders' (e.g., banks, thrifts, finance companies) actions are affected by a complex set of forces derived not only from traditional competitive pressures but also from regulatory obligations, reputational concerns, policy developments, and their involvements in the corporate and civic life of a community. The presence of an active microlender may encourage bankers to view microenterprise as an important activity, to value becoming more involved with smaller firms, and to partner with a CDFI they see as bringing reputational or Community Reinvestment Act (CRA) benefits.

My intent is not to take sides on the PM versus SIE perspective but rather to assess what may be achievable from both. PM is less ambitious and more feasible than SIE for most CDFI applications. It will be sufficient in gaining confidence that a CDFI is headed in the right direction and is likely—or not—to be having some meaningful impact. Systematic, quantitative evidence of impact is not always required or appropriate.

PM can provide information that, together with a broad and perhaps less than systematic set of other, often less quantitative knowledge, gives decision makers comfort that a program is making a difference. PM provides just one heuristic tool that, as part of what Schorr (2003) calls "multiple ways of knowing," can contribute to a much less systematic but more pragmatic and perhaps achievable way to discern—if not precisely measure—impact.

Although SIE studies may promise more systematic and quantified impact measures, their greater ambition brings with them greater risks for error. As in any social science research, studies should be rigorously reviewed and never be considered conclusive in and of themselves.

At the same time, to dismiss the potential for research that may give us better information than we currently have on CDFI impacts may condemn the field to a sort of purgatory of "we can never convince skeptics that we are making a real difference." In the end, in a world of many programs and policies competing for scarce resources, merely resigning to an inability to measure impacts may not be good enough to sustain the field. It is important to recognize the limits of impact research, especially as it exists today, but it is also important to invest in improved data and methods so that the CDFI field has an opportunity to document the differences it makes in lower-income and disadvantaged communities.

Unit of Analysis: Household or Firm Versus Neighborhood or Community

In considering issues of outcome measurement and impact evaluation, we might consider measuring outputs or outcomes at the level of households, firms, or place. In conventional social program measurement or evaluation, data are generally desired at the individual or household level. However, for a variety of reasons, households may be either an infeasible or undesirable unit of analysis when it comes to the evaluation of CDFI activity.

For some CDFI product lines and outcomes, we may want to measure outcomes for households or, in the case of business-oriented activities, for firms. As Hollister (2004) argues, however, identifying appropriate comparison groups can be very challenging. Moreover, obtaining data from members of treatment groups—either firms or individuals—can be daunting. In the case of employment-focused business development, for example, gathering data on workers, and not just firms receiving assistance, can be difficult.

For other product lines and outcomes—particularly those with high degrees of relative spatial density—we may expect neighborhood or geographic effects, perhaps out of accident (the programs just happen to be clustered spatially) or out of design. Some CDFI activities are tied—to a lesser or greater extent—to some notion of place. Although she was not considering CDFIs per se, Ladd (1994) provided a typology for alleviating problems of lower-income people and places. First, people-based strategies focus on helping people but do not pay any attention to the places where they live. Examples might include CDFI minority business-financing programs that lend to firms regardless of their location throughout some large metropolitan area or state.

Second, place-based-people strategies focus on places—perhaps certain neighborhoods or types of neighborhoods—to increase the well-being of people living in such areas. But there is no primacy given to changing quality of the place. Place is a tool for helping local residents. Third, place-based strategies aim to improve physical and economic vitality with little attention to the impact on current residents. The condition of residents is not seen as the end so much as a means to improve the geographic community. Differentiating, for example, between a neighborhood that "improves" via incumbent upgrading and one that improves via inmigration and outmigration is not of concern.

Figure 6.2 provides a conceptual map of this strategic space. Particular product lines can be positioned within this triangular space. Some may be more likely employed as part of people-based strategies, while others (e.g., real estate–related programs) are pure place-based to place-based-people strategies. Yet others are quite flexible, strategically: a small business loan might be employed in a targeted, place-based strategy to revitalize a retail strip or might be used to encourage employment over the CDFI's entire service area.

Distinguishing among strategic approaches is critical to developing outcome

Figure 6.2 **Strategic Space: Targeting Places, People, or Both**

measures. Product lines employed as part of a place-based strategy are better candidates for geographic evaluation, while products used as part of a pure people-based strategy are less appropriate.

Related to spatial targeting are market size, mobility of capital and labor, and capitalization of benefits in residential property values. The size of labor markets, for example, can make targeting of employment effects in neighborhoods problematic. Firms can hire from broad distances, and there is some evidence that firms in minority neighborhoods tend not to draw their workforces from near their facilities as much as do firms in other locations (Ihlanfeldt 1999). The geographic scale of labor markets means benefits of employment-oriented CDFI interventions will be more spatially diffuse as compared to housing market investments.

Moreover, because business lending or investment frequently focuses on increasing a firm's stock of relatively mobile capital (equipment, inventory) or human resources, less goes into permanent improvements in spatially fixed real estate. Housing investment is more spatially fixed. Of course, some of the benefits of housing investment may diffuse spatially, especially over time, as beneficiaries move on to different residential locations, perhaps partly as a result of earlier CDFI interventions—for example, as new homeowners become established homeowners and move into a larger house. Overall, however, a larger portion of the benefits from housing investment is likely to accrue locally as compared to investments in job creation or retention.

When considering measuring effects spatially versus individually, it is important to keep in mind the general phenomenon of the capitalization of neighborhood amenities into residential property values. As various aspects of the quality of life of a neighborhood improve, residential values are expected to rise. In essence, the future value of those improvements are at least partially capitalized into property values. If many residents fix up their homes, for example, we expect to see an increase in property values (Ding, Simons, and Baku 2000).

Of course, property values should be used with some caution as a measure of neighborhood quality of life. If values appreciate very quickly, displacement of existing residents or speculative price bubbles are a concern. Moreover, many nonmarket neighborhood qualities, including various forms of social capital, may not be fully capitalized into property values.

Notwithstanding these limitations, moderate levels of appreciation—and avoidance of falling values—are seen as a positive neighborhood indicator. It is important to note that this signal of neighborhood quality of life is not relevant only to homeowners. Because property values reflect improvements in the quality of life for residents, it is expected that the quality of life for renters would also improve, assuming that increases in rents or taxes are not excessive.

Experimental Methods for Impact Evaluation of CDFI Product Lines

Experimental methods are generally considered the first-best option in program evaluation. In such evaluations, "treatment" and "control" groups are randomly selected from some broader population. While experimental designs are more often associated with household- or firm-level data, it is possible to conduct experiments at the neighborhood or community level.

When applied to CDFI activity, experimental impact evaluation might look something like this: A randomly chosen subset of applicants would be provided with CDFI products or services, while the remaining applicants would not. Thus, the CDFI services are actually withheld from a control group. The experimental group cannot consist of all households or firms that express a desire for CDFI products. Otherwise, a selection bias problem would exist, because applicants are likely to possess some traits (e.g., motivational characteristics) that make them more likely to do better (or worse) on the chosen outcome measures. Given sufficient numbers of applicants in each group, randomization will insure that the two groups are "mean equivalent" on both measured and *unmeasured* characteristics. Given adequate randomization, outcome data can be collected on each group, and differences in mean outcomes are attributed to the program.

There are a number of challenges to implementing experimental studies for CDFIs. First, gathering outcome data from members of the experimental and, especially, the control groups can be difficult. Acquiring data on the firms or individuals receiving assistance is conceptually straightforward, albeit not without substantial challenges and expense. It is even more challenging to gather data on firms or households that do not receive loans or assistance. What incentives do they have to provide data and comply with research requirements? A second problem is the difficulty of denying services to control group firms. Some CDFIs may view such denial as unfair, although such experiments may be easily justified in a context of scarce resources. Another problem is that denying services to otherwise eligible firms may be politically difficult. Finally, for some programs, the deal flow may be so weak that there are insufficient firms or households to constitute a control group.

Experiments Using Geographic Areas

In addition to experiments at the individual level, researchers can conduct experiments structured by geographic clusters such as neighborhoods. The classical experiment can be conducted by identifying the universe of eligible geographies—based on programmatic criteria—and then randomly assigning areas to treatment and control groups. As in the case of the individual-level experiment, services would be withheld from the control group areas and differences in outcomes between the two groups would be tracked. One advantage of geographic experiments is that it is often easier to withhold the offering of a product line from some set of otherwise eligible geographic areas rather than attempting to withhold services from different individuals or firms. A CDFI could randomly choose, from a larger set of eligible neighborhoods, a group of neighborhoods in which its products or services would be made available. This might not be done for all products but for a specific product line. Politically, such an approach might prove more feasible in the case of new products that are not already offered in a region.

Another advantage of geographic analyses is that outcome data, while perhaps not plentiful, are not being collected from individuals. Rather, census or other, more frequently collected small-area data may be sufficient to provide quantitative indicators for key outcomes. This is advantageous in the case of control groups, from which data may be hard to gather.

One challenge that immediately arises with group or geographic randomization is the requirement to choose large enough numbers of geographies in both experimental and control groups that sufficient randomization is ensured. Bartik (2002) suggests a rule of thumb of at least twenty areas in each of the treatment and control groups, though he provides no justification. Bloom (2005) suggests that, depending on the statistical power desired, groups of twenty geographies may be less than sufficient for randomization.

Quasi-Experimental Methods for Measuring Impact

When experimental methods are not feasible, researchers typically use quasi-experimental methods to identify programmatic impacts. While quasi-experimental methods are typically not immune from validity threats (Hollister 2004), some methods may provide a sufficient degree of rigor—or at least provide us with information that is expected to, on average, give us substantially more accurate information than we had without the use of such methods.

There are a variety of quasi-experimental evaluation methods that may be appropriate for assessing CDFI impact. Not all potential methods and their faults are reviewed here. Much of that has been done elsewhere (Dickstein and Thomas 2005; Hollister 2004; Hollister and Hill 1995). Rather, the focus here is on approaches that get serious attention in the literature.

These methods fall into three groups. First is econometric simulation, in which multivariate methods are used to control for differences between nonrandom treatment and comparison groups, including the difference in the likelihood of applying to or being recruited into a program. This latter difference is key. If we merely attempt to identify differences in groups that we believe will affect the outcome variable, we may not adequately control for selection bias. Conventional econometric methods are used either to predict some raw level of outcome indicator or to explain the "difference in differences" between the treatment and comparison groups. That is, multivariate estimation is used to explain differences in gain (or loss) in a key outcome measure following program intervention (e.g., receiving CDFI loans of some kind) between the treatment group and a comparison group.

The second nonexperimental category of methods used to measure impact is called propensity-score matching. This approach is related to econometric methods that explicitly control for selection bias. A propensity score is the probability that, given certain features, a household, firm, or geography will receive "treatment" (e.g., receive a loan or investment). Households, firms, or geographies are grouped according to propensity scores. Within each group, outcomes for those receiving treatment are compared with those not receiving treatment.

Propensity-score-based matching studies have been used in economic development evaluation. Greenbaum and Engberg (2000) used this method to evaluate the impact of enterprise zones on housing markets in six states by comparing changes in prices for zip codes that contain enterprise zones to those that do not. O'Keefe (2003) used propensity-score matching to measure the impact of the California Enterprise Zone program on census tracts. Differences in growth between the zone tract and the nonzone tract were then used as estimates of program impact.

Propensity-scoring techniques are not without their critics. Hollister (2004) argues that propensity-score-matching techniques have not provided estimates of impact that are "consistently close" to those obtained from experimental methods. However, there appears to have been relatively little testing of these methods for geographic applications.

The last general category of approaches reviewed here is that of geographically based adjusted interrupted time series (AITS) analysis, which is a special subset of the econometric simulation approaches (Galster, Temkin, Walker, and Sawyer 2004). In this approach, outcome data for geographies receiving treatment are compared to those not receiving treatment. However, in AITS, researchers utilize time series data over a relatively substantial period of time (e.g., several years or longer) that are frequently collected (e.g., annually or more frequently) and that provide us with many observations over the study period—the more the better. This approach allows for the measurement of not only preintervention levels of the outcome indicator for treatment and comparison geographies but also the trends of the indicators in both groups before and after intervention. By being able to control for the differences in both the *levels* and *trajectories* of the treatment and comparison groups before and after the intervention, researchers can effectively control for omitted characteristics that might influence the outcome indicator.

Predecessors of AITS approaches include methods that seek to match geographies using more limited historical data and so are likely to do a poorer job of controlling for selection bias. Instead, selection bias is discounted as a problem as long as the comparison group is found to be in no better a position in terms of outcome indicators before the intervention as compared to the treatment group. A relatively well-known example of this approach is Isserman and Rephann's (1995) study of the Appalachian Regional Commission (ARC) in which the authors measured the impact of the ARC on county population growth by identifying a matched "twin" county for each ARC county. Matching was based on both level and trajectory data from 1959 and 1950 to 1959 before the beginning of the ARC in 1965. The accuracy of the match between the treatment and control group twins was then compared by identifying how well each pair was matched on 1959 to 1965 growth—again before the ARC was established. Because this method does not require the frequency of data that the AITS requires, it may prove more feasible in some cases. However, the approach is more vulnerable to selection bias.

Measuring Structural Impacts via Financial Output Variables

Many analytical approaches discussed so far might be aimed at determining whether CDFIs are having impacts on crosscutting social and economic outcomes—housing conditions, property values (which may indicate broader conditions), employment, income, or other phenomena.

However, there are reasons it may be useful to look at CDFI impacts on more intermediate outcomes—or even outputs—rather than at broader socioeconomic end outcomes. First, as one moves further down the logic model continuum from output to end outcome, it is harder to attribute outcomes to CDFIs because a greater number of other factors affect outcomes. For example, even if CDFI activity spurred the flow of capital to underserved firms, it may be difficult to identify how many jobs should be attributed to the provision of this specific amount of capital. Second, CDFIs are likely to report output or intermediate outcome data than end outcome data. Moreover, if we are placing CDFI data in the context of data on other mainstream financial providers, it is less likely we will have data on end outcomes associated with such providers. Third, CDFI activity may have institutional or structural impacts on some segment of financial markets. CDFIs may encourage conventional lenders to behave differently. Banks may learn from partnering with CDFIs. They may discover that borrowers or projects they believed to be too risky were not so risky after all. Even if banks do not partner with CDFIs directly, just witnessing CDFI activity may change how a bank or conventional lender views or approaches a market.

Some argue that CDFIs are simply "gap fillers," making loans banks are unlikely to make. As banks reach farther into less traditional market segments, such a model may imply a substitution from CDFI activity toward bank activity. Such a model would imply that bank activity and CDFI activity might be negatively correlated. Other models for the sector suggest that CDFIs influence the behavior of conventional financial institutions in ways that encourage these institutions to become more involved in the market segments targeted by CDFIs. Under such models, we might expect CDFI and bank activity to be positively correlated.

Anecdotally, this second model has often been associated with ShoreBank, a well-known community development bank. Prior to ShoreBank's targeted lending to multifamily apartment rehabbers in Chicago's South Shore in the 1980s, few conventional lenders appeared interested in funding low- and moderate-income projects (Goldwater and Bush 1995). After the bank fostered this market and the scale of rehab activity grew, larger, conventional lenders became much more active.

To have institutional or structural impacts, CDFIs may need to reach some minimum scale in a product line. Scale may matter for reasons beyond just the ability of CDFIs to deliver more capital to the target firms or households. Scale matters because CDFIs become substantial enough to affect lender behavior. Mainstream lenders are affected by a complex set of forces that are derived, among other things, from regulatory obligations, reputational concerns, policy debates, and their involvements in corporate and civic life.

Structural impacts might best be detected at the level of financial market areas, such as at the level of metropolitan areas or counties. These market areas are similar to the geographical areas that the Federal Reserve and other agencies use for evaluating competition in considering mergers and acquisitions. The general approach to such a study would be to measure CDFI activity in a particular product line across a large number of metropolitan areas. Because CDFIs may be more likely to operate on a more substantial scale in central cities, however, it may make more sense to use central cities (each within its unique metropolitan market area) as the geographic unit of analysis. Mainstream financial institution (banks, finance companies, etc.) activity in closely related product lines would be measured for each city. Models would be developed to explain the level of desirable financial end outcomes that CDFIs might encourage.

Another method for potentially testing for the influence of CDFI activity on mainstream financial institutions would be to develop measures of financial product innovation among CDFIs and banks or other mainstream lenders. Retrospective historical analysis of innovations in product design, pricing, or terms could identify whether new products and terms introduced by mainstream lenders were preceded by similar products or terms developed by CDFIs.

Research Methodology and Data Availability in Key CDFI Product Lines

To identify prospects for developing some reasonable measures of CDFI impacts within product lines, I evaluate types and quality of the data available, or that might be made available at reasonable cost, for some major financial product groups.

Single-Family Mortgages

Within this group there are different product lines, including senior and junior home purchase loans, home improvement loans, and refinance loans. Some CDFIs, especially those with a major homeownership focus, offer more than one product line. Perhaps the best-known examples are the NeighborWorks affiliates around the country. Because many programs focusing on single-family lending may include community development outcomes among their primary objectives, and because there is significant evidence that home improvement (Ding, Simons, and Baku 2000) and homeownership (Haurin, Dietz, and Weinberg 2003) result in positive neighborhood spillover effects, they may lend themselves well to geographic impact analysis.

One evaluation approach would use a geographic experiment. After identifying potential census tracts that meet the criteria for a new CDFI single-family lending program, researchers would randomly divide tracts into treatment and control groups. It would be critical for the selection process to be truly random and not corrupted by political or other criteria.

Quasi-experimental methods may be required. In analyzing the impact of New York City investments in housing on property values, Schill, Ellen, Schwartz, and Voicu (2002) employed a model moving neighborhood location and time of property sale to control for the fact that properties in different neighborhoods will likely be subject to different trajectories in property values. In this way, they controlled for selection bias. Galster, Tatian, and Accordino (2006) used property sales data for Richmond, Virginia, to determine if efforts and those of the area's Local Initiatives Support Corporation to concentrate community development investments strategically in certain neighborhoods had any positive effect on property values. They utilized AITS to measure the impact of nearby community development investments on the level and trajectory of property values.

It should be acknowledged that the data requirements for such property-value impact models, especially ones that do a good job addressing the issue of preintervention trajectories and selection bias, can be quite demanding. Not only are sales transaction data over time generally required, researchers may need information on property attributes—typically from a property tax assessor or a multiple listing service when available.

Multifamily Real Estate Loans

Estimating the impact of CDFI multifamily lending activity on local outcomes is conceptually feasible. However, one critical issue is determining what, if any, crosscutting outcomes might be identified in the case of multifamily lending activity. Some CDFIs may view community development outcomes—perhaps measured by neighborhood stability indicators such as property values—as a desired product of multifamily lending. Such would be the case for programs focusing on the repair and improvement of dilapidated multifamily properties. When small-area community development goals are the focus, analyses looking at local property value effects, such as the single-family lending model described earlier, may be feasible.

However, many CDFIs making multifamily loans focus more on the aggregate production of affordable rental housing, with less regard to neighborhood impacts. Moreover, because little good data—other than the decennial census—are available on vacancy rates or affordability measures at the small-area level, analyses at the neighborhood level are difficult.

Small Business Term Loans and Lines of Credit

CDFI lending to small businesses appears to be a weaker candidate for geographic impact evaluation. Many CDFIs that do small business lending do not target their programs at small-area levels, nor do they generally seek small-area impacts. At larger geographies, the lack of relative density is unlikely to allow for the discernment of geographic impacts. Hollister (2004) and Caskey and Hollister (2001) reviewed some attempts to evaluate the impact of what they call "business development financial institutions." They found existing efforts lacking and are less than optimistic in suggestions for additional research in this area.

In terms of quasi-experimental approaches, there at least two possible routes, both of which appear quite challenging given existing data sources. First is a model that would attempt to measure the structural effects on small business lending markets on an intermetropolitan level. The goal would be to determine whether increased CDFI small business lending is related to increased small business lending by conventional lenders. While CRA small business lending data may prove sufficient for this task, the data are not without problems.[1] The second approach would be to attempt to estimate neighborhood-level impacts of small business lending by CDFIs on neighborhood outcomes. Again, the problem is the weakness of small business lending data, as compared to mortgage data. Another problem is that many of the more active CDFI small business lenders do not target their loans spatially, so these programs are likely to achieve fairly low levels of relative density at the neighborhood level.

Conclusions and Implications for Policy

This chapter probes the possibilities for new research on impacts among CDFI subsectors and product lines. It focuses on research designs that might be used to measure impact, especially in the context of moving beyond evaluations of single CDFIs. I recognize the many formidable challenges involved in measuring impact, either through experimental or quasi-experimental methods. Moreover, I have argued that in many situations, well-implemented PM, which does not attempt to identify a convincing counterfactual, is preferable to impact evaluation, which is more ambitious and more vulnerable to error.

Recognizing that philanthropic and government funders and investors are under increasing pressure to allocate resources based on evidence of impact, this chapter attempts to move beyond the current state of affairs by proposing some potential research designs and methods that may provide us with more evidence than we currently have about CDFI impacts. Unfortunately, in some product-line areas, there appear to be very few prospects for feasible research in the near- to midterm. In some other areas, however, especially single-family housing lending in which spatial, neighborhood-level impacts are a substantial focus, there may be feasible methods for reasonably accurate impact evaluation.

Granted, these techniques are fairly sophisticated and have sizable data requirements. At the same time, data required are available in many places, sometimes at a sizable but usually not insurmountable cost. Moreover, in some places, county governments may provide the necessary data at a much lower cost, particularly to nonprofit or public-sector users.

Some may come away, understandably, with pessimism regarding the ability to demonstrate CDFI impacts. However, the intent is not to discourage but rather to provide a sober view of the challenges involved. Just as it takes resources to develop the CDFI field, it will take a significant investment to develop the data and methods needed to measure impacts. In my view, it makes sense to pursue the more feasible methods in the near term while exploring the possibility for improved data systems and availability for those areas and product lines where such data do not exist.

In considering the potential for research on CDFI impacts, one certainly needs a long-term view. There is a small but fairly steady stream of innovative research being conducted in the community development arena—some of it described in this chapter—that should continue to evolve. More applications of such methods could be applied to the CDFI sector. There is also a potential for more applications of true experiments, including geographically based experiments. Finally, improvements in data, especially in small-area data, will hopefully continue to develop and expand the tools available to conduct reasonable evaluative research.

Note

I would like to thank Valerie Chang, Deborah Schwartz, and Michael Stegman, of the MacArthur Foundation, for commissioning this work and for providing feedback; Julia Sass Rubin for exchanges we had about topics in this chapter; Carla Dickstein, George Galster, and Robinson Hollister for commenting on earlier work; and practitioners and scholars who met at the MacArthur Foundation in March 2006 to discuss issues addressed here. I remain responsible for any errors, omissions, and opinions herein.

    1. Thanks to Michael Stegman for making this suggestion.

References

Bartik, T. 2002. "Evaluating the Impacts of Local Economic Development Policies on Local Economic Outcomes: What Has Been Done and What Is Doable?" Upjohn Institute Working Paper No. 03–89. Kalamazoo, MI: Upjohn Institute (November).

Benjamin, L., J. S. Rubin, and S. Zielenbach. 2004. "Community Development Financial Institutions: Current Issues and Future Prospects." *Journal of Urban Affairs* 26: 177–195.

Bloom, H. 2005. "Randomizing Groups to Evaluate Place-Based Programs." In H. Bloom, ed., *Learning More from Social Experiments: Evolving Analytical Approaches.* New York: Russell Sage Foundation.

Caskey, J., and R. Hollister. 2001. "The Impact of Business Development Financial Institutions: A Review of Three Studies." Unpublished manuscript.

CDFI Data Project. 2004. "Providing Capital, Building Communities, Creating Impact." Washington, DC: Author. www.cdfi.org/Uploader/Files/cdp_finalfy03.pdf. (Accessed 29 November 2006.)

Dickstein, C., and H. Thomas. 2005. "Measuring Impacts in Practice: A Case Study of Coastal Enterprises, Inc.'s Experience." Unpublished manuscript. October.

Ding, C., R. A. Simons, and E. Baku. 2000. "The Effect of Residential Investment on Nearby Housing Values: Evidence from Cleveland, Ohio." *Journal of Real Estate Research* 19 (1): 23–48.

Galster, G., P. Tatian, and J. Accordino. 2006. "Targeting Investments for Neighborhood Revitalization." *Journal of the American Planning Association* 72 (4): 457–474.

Galster, G., K. Temkin, C. Walker, and N. Sawyer. 2004. "Measuring the Impacts of Community Development Initiatives: A New Application of the Adjusted Interrupted Time Series Method." *Evaluation Review* 28: 502–538.

Goldwater, S., and M. Bush, 1995. "CRA Boosts Multifamily Lending in Chicago." Reinvestment Alert. Chicago: Woodstock Institute.

Greenbaum, R., and J. Engberg. 2000. "An Evaluation of State Enterprise Zone Policies." *Policy Studies Review* 17: 29–46.

Hatry, H. 2007. *Performance Measurement: Getting Results,* 2nd ed. Washington, DC: Urban Institute Press.

Haurin, D., R. Dietz, and B. Weinberg. 2003. "The Impact of Neighborhood Homeownership Rates: A Review of the Literature." *Journal of Housing Research* 13: 119–151.

Hollister, R. 2004. "Measuring Impact of CDFI Activities." Paper prepared for the Community Development Conference. Federal Reserve Bank of New York. December 8–10.

Hollister, R., and J. Hill. 1995. "Problems in the Evaluation of Community-Wide Initiatives." In *New Approaches to Evaluating Community Initiatives,* ed. J. P. Connell, A. Kubisch, L. B. Schorr, and C. H. Weiss. Washington, DC: Aspen Institute, pp. 127–172.

Ihlanfeldt, K. 1999. "Are Poor People Really Excluded from Jobs Located in Their Own Neighborhoods? Comments on Reingold and Some Additional Evidence from the Multi-City Study of Urban Inequality." *Economic Development Quarterly* 13: 307–314.

Isserman, A., and T. Rephann. 1995. "The Economic Effects of the Appalachian Regional Commission." *Journal of the American Planning Association* 61: 345–365.

Ladd, H. 1994. "Spatially Targeted Economic Development Strategies: Do They Work?" *Cityscape: A Journal of Policy Development and Research* 1 (1): 193–218.

O'Keefe, S. 2003. "Job Creation in California's Enterprise Zones: A Comparison Utilizing a Propensity Score Matching Model." Paper presented at Federal Reserve Community Affairs Research Conference: System Seeds of Growth Sustainable Community Development, Washington, D.C., March 27–28, 2003, www.chicagofed.org/cedric/files/2003_conf_paper_session4_okeefe.pdf. (Accessed 29 November 2006.)

Schill, M., I. G. Ellen, A. E. Schwartz, and I. Voicu. 2002. "Revitalizing Inner-City Neighborhoods: New York City's Ten Year Plan." *Housing Policy Debate* 13: 529–566.

Schorr, L. 2003. "Determining 'What Works' in Social Programs and Social Policies." Washington, DC: Brookings Institution. www.brook.edu/dybdocroot/views/papers/sawhill/20030226.pdf. (Accessed 29 November 2006.)

Tholin, Kathryn. 1994. *Community Development Financial Institutions: Investing in People and Communities.* Chicago: Woodstock Institute.

7

Social Performance Measurement for CDFI Banks

David Porteous and Saurabh Narain

How can one assess the social performance of community development banking institutions (Cdbis)? The National Community Investment Fund has developed the term *social performance* to mean those depository institutions that attain positive social impact while remaining financially strong. CDBIs include banks, thrifts, and credit unions but are not restricted to those accredited by the U.S. Department of Treasury's Community Development Financial Institutions Fund (CDFI Fund). In this chapter, our analysis focuses on banks and thrifts (hereafter collectively called CDFI banks) but not credit unions.

Two problems stand in the way of better performance assessment. First, while there are methods to assess financial performance of banks, CDBIs are, by definition, "double bottom line" institutions that balance profit making with positive social impact. CDBI shareholders and management consciously make trade-offs between the two bottom lines—or the three, if one includes environmental impact, as is increasingly common (e.g., the Global Reporting Initiative, www.global-reporting.org/Home). As a result, measurement of the financial bottom line and comparison with "single bottom line" banks based on financial performance alone are inadequate. Second, even within the universe of depository entities concerned with social impact, there is no standard system of performance measurement. Instead, a multitude of approaches is used, often requiring collection of considerable additional information.

Efforts have been made to collect better data about the CDFI sector; however, some of these efforts—such as the CDFI Data Project (www.cdfi.org/cdfiproj. asp)—have focused on compiling aggregate data rather than comparing individual institutions. The CDFI Assessment Rating System (CARS) (www.opportunityfi-nance.net) provides standardized means of rating CDFI loan funds only and does not cover CDBIs. Also, the CARS relies on self-selected methods of determining impact and, like most rating services, requires collection of specialized information.

If CDBIs are to be a standard class, able to tap wider sources of retail investment, then there is a need to create standardized means of performance assessment so that CDBIs can be included in the broader universe of banks. This could enable investors to make investments on the basis of their own balance of objectives between financial and social return. Entities offering an attractive combination of both may benefit from greater access to capital and even a lower cost of funds than is possible in the absence of calibrating the investment trade-off. However, any approach to measuring social performance across banks must rely on publicly available data, since costs of collection would limit the universe of entities to a small self-defined set. Fortunately, there are rich sources of public data relating to the activities of home lenders—the Home Mortgage Disclosure Act (HMDA)—and depository institutions—Community Reinvestment Act (CRA) or the Federal Deposit Insurance Corporation's (FDIC) Summary of Deposits (SOD).

What then are the limits to which such publicly available data can be pushed in the cause of meaningful performance management for CDBIs? Can data be used to assist in performance measurement of CDBIs? To do this, we first survey performance assessment approaches, then assess the scope and usefulness of public data sources. Then, we access publicly available databases to create a profile over time of the sixty-one depository institutions accredited as CDFIs in July 2006. Our sample focuses on the period since the creation of the CDFI Fund in 1996, when the CDFI designation was started. We test and demonstrate the value of two measures derived from these databases. In the presence of sufficient data, these measures may be used as social performance metrics in themselves; certainly, they can function as lenses that enable better categorization and comparison of like with like. This categorization is an essential step in better performance comparison across entities, often missed.

The CDFI Fund Web site (www.cdfifund.gov) reported the names of sixty-one certified banks and thrifts in July 2006. While these entities were certified at various dates during the past ten years (and it has been impossible to secure a date of first certification in all cases from the CDFI Fund), we use the July 2006 cutoff to define the CDFI bank dataset for which we collect and report retrospective performance data.

To make the volume of data more tractable, three years were selected to represent the start, middle, and end points of this period: 1996, 2000, 2004. Table 7.1 compares the size distribution of our CDFI bank sample with all U.S. banks in 2004. In addition, it is relevant to compare lending activity undertaken by CDFI banks. Figure 7.1 reports the percentage of outstanding loans at year end in each of the subcategories related to real estate lending for CDFI banks on the left and small banks (less than $1 billion in assets) on the right.

Figure 7.1 shows real estate lending as the largest category for both CDFI and small banks as a whole—close to 70 percent by 2004. The difference between the two groups of banks is in composition of real estate lending: for CDFI banks, share of single- and multifamily loans has fallen from 43 percent of all loans to 36 percent (with a much higher share for multifamily); in their place, share of commercial real estate grew dramatically to a third in 2004 from a fifth in 1996. Small banks have increased single- and multifamily lending (50 percent to 52 percent), and home equity lending (although this remains a small proportion).

Table 7.1

Relative Size Comparison of CDFI Banks (Number of Banks Unless Specified Otherwise)

Gross Assets End 2004	CDFI Banks	All U.S. Banks
< $250 m	50	7,029
> $250 m; < $1 bn	10	1,350
> $1 bn	1	597
Average total assets	$173 m	$168 m

Figure 7.1 **Composition of Real Estate Portfolio of CDFI Banks Versus Small Banks**

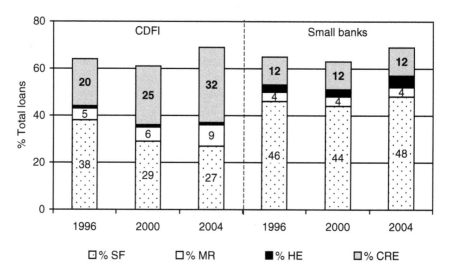

Because of the focus on CDFIs, we used the CDFI Fund definition of qualifying Investment Area.[1] This status is conferred by the CDFI Fund on the basis of census results that show unemployment and poverty rates against national benchmarks and median income lower than area median. The latest list of investment areas is based on 2000 Census results, published in 2001. Unfortunately, we were unable to obtain the list of qualifying areas for prior years. Hence, we re-created the prior list using similar underlying measures of poverty, unemployment, and relative income based on 1990 Census data. This gave us some 20,000 qualifying tracts for the earlier two years and the official number of 24,795 in 2004. Area definitions also were adjusted to allow for changes in the 2000 Census data, using a specific translation algorithm.

Approaches to Performance Measurement

Social Performance Measurement

There is a wide, if not yet deep, literature on social performance measurement for financial institutions, a review of which yielded several conclusions. First, need for credible social performance measurement of financial institutions is growing as a result of increasing demands by investors for social investment opportunities and because of pressures on mainstream financial institutions to report on a double or triple bottom line, which means that "we are all double or triple bottom line now." Specifically, new and existing investors need simple, credible measures to distinguish the social performance of financial institutions more broadly.

Second, true impact measurement is increasingly regarded as too expensive and difficult to achieve because of problems in adequately defining a control group outside of ideal experimental conditions, including randomized assignment of cases. Rather, the focus has moved towards measuring forms of outcome (for example, see Chapter 6, "Research Design Issues for Measuring CDFI Performance and Impact"). An outcome is a desired change resulting from an output or series of outputs. Output and outcome need to be linked by a theory of change that explains causality. While outputs are easy to measure—for lending banks, volumes of loans granted constitute output—outcomes are much harder. If the causal chain between output and outcome were demonstrated for a product, one could rely on collecting output measures alone.

The evidence that increased financial intermediation at a local microlevel—such as a census tract—leads to positive social outcomes at that level has not yet been demonstrated. This is in part because of the limitations of outcome-related data at tract level and, more so, because of the perennial questions about spillover effects across boundaries that may dilute the evidence, though not the reality, of impact within an area. Recent empirical work by Galster, Hayes, and Johnson (2006) on parsimonious indicators of neighborhood vitality may lead to the definition of tractable indicators that accurately measure changes in neighborhood characteristics over time.

While there is little or no strong evidence yet of positive outcome effects of intermediation activity at a tract level, there is finance literature that has demonstrated a causal link between volume of intermediation and economic growth at the national and international levels (summarized in Levine 2005). Only in recent years has the direction of causality been definitively isolated: while the effect is clearly bidirectional, it is now accepted that financial intermediation has a "first-order positive causal impact on economic growth." However, this relationship is not simple or linear. In fact, in one of the few empirical studies done at the state level, Dehejia and Llevas-Muney (2003) found evidence of positive causality in distant history but suggest that this effect exists only within bounds. For example, overlending as the result of a credit bubble will usually have a negative outcome on subsequent growth. World Bank researchers Beck, Demirguc-Kunt and Levine (2004) extended this theory of change further than impact on economic growth alone. Using a cross section of fifty-two developed and developing countries from 1960 to 1999, they showed that increased intermediation is related causally to other socially desirable outcomes—reduced poverty and income inequality.

Macrolevel findings give more credibility to the claim that "output" measures of intermediation volumes are linked to positive outcomes, although this is not definitive. However, neither can output-related measures be dismissed as irrelevant to the search for parsimonious performance indicators for CDFIs that operate on a local or regional level.

In the literature, there are a variety of approaches that capture direct outcomes, but as yet, none provides a widely accepted way of comparing social performance of financial institutions across a broad spectrum (Clark, Rosenzweig, Long, and Olsen 2003; Kramer and Cooch 2006).

As methods have proliferated, even financial institutions committed to social impact are increasingly sensitive to the cost in time and resources of complying with reporting regimes for measuring performance and impact (e.g., Coastal Enterprises 2006). This underlines the need to use existing data sources as much as possible, accepting the likely trade-offs between precision and the cost of data collection. An example from a related, although very different, sector—mutual funds—shows how widely used performance measurement tools can be developed on the basis of publicly available data alone.

Mutual Fund Rating: An Example

Morningstar started its mutual fund rating services in 1986, using publicly available information on fund performance to create Morningstar ratings used by retail investors to navigate the increasingly complex range of products and offerings. Morningstar's methodology is relatively simple (http://corporate.morningstar. com/US/asp/detail.aspx?xmlfile=279.xml):

- *Step 1: Create consistent categories* within which meaningful peer-group comparison can be undertaken. Morningstar currently has some sixty-two categories of funds, based on characteristics affecting performance such as the size and focus of fund, and has a methodology to control for movement between categories.
- *Step 2: Measure risk-adjusted return within each category.* Morningstar uses moving averages of risk-adjusted return, which for mutual funds are easily available and relate to the investment experience of retail investors.
- *Step 3: Rank funds within each category using this criterion.* in fact, for ease of investor use, Morningstar assigns stars on a bell curve so that a few top performers get five stars, most get three stars, and so on.

For Morningstar and others, the hardest parts of the process are not the latter steps but the first: creating a credible and robust means of peer classification. This is a challenge for CDBIs, which differ in size, focus, and approach.

Publicly Available Performance Data

Financial Performance

Two bank financial performance measures are commonly accepted as comparable indicators of profitability: return on equity (ROE) and/or return on assets (ROA). Of the two, ROA may be preferable for CDFI banks because they often have lower "gearing ratios" due to the nature of their business and hence are unable to earn higher ROEs. These measures may vary year to year, so if one is interested in long-run performance, averages must be calculated over time. For depository institutions, data necessary to construct such measures are available through publicly accessible databases such as FDIC's Statistics of Depository Institutions (SDI).

Dobbs and Koller (2005) go further, suggesting in addition to ROE, compound revenue growth over time is also an important measure of the long-run financial performance of a business. Using the sixty-two accredited CDFI Fund institutions in 2006, we experimented with possible composite measures of financial performance that blend a number of underlying dimensions of financial performance, including ROE, ROA, efficiency ratio, tier 1 leverage ratio, charge offs to loan book, and loan loss to reserves.

We ranked the CDFIs in each category for each year, then calculated the average of the six rank scores. However, perhaps not surprisingly, there is a strong correlation (0.76) between ROE and the composite financial performance measure, since most of the measures feed into an ROE or ROA result. Furthermore, it requires an a priori judgment to assign scores in certain categories: for example, should higher charge offs necessarily lead to lower rankings if this is the result of a decision to enter riskier markets, and if the risk-adjusted return is still adequate? Consequently, we have reverted to the simple, consistent option of using ROA averaged over a preceding five-year period as a long-run financial performance measure for CDFI banks.

Social Performance

Table 7.2 summarizes publicly available databases relevant to social performance. FDIC's SDI database, which provides only financial information, is not used in our analysis. Each database has some limitations:

- *HMDA:* While most (but not all) of the CDFI Banks report HMDA data, this captures only home lending, which is a declining proportion of most CDFI banks' real estate portfolios: single- and multifamily lending has declined from 43 percent to 36 percent of total loans outstanding between 1996 to 2004; cor-

Table 7.2

Summary of Public Data Bases

Database	Maintained By	Who Reports	What the Data Tell Us
1. Community Reinvestment Act (CRA)	FFIEC	All supervised banks with assets above $250 m pre-2005 required to report loan data; annually; threshold now $1bn in assets	Originations of loans in developmental categories (to small business; agriculture) by county/census tract; CRA exam ratings, undertaken periodically by supervisors provide an indication of official rating of development performance
2. Home Mortgage Disclosure Act (HMDA)	FFIEC	All depository lenders and other qualifying mortgage lenders in general with home purchase loan originations exceeding $25 m annually	Applications for and *originations and purchases* of home loans by type and by characteristics of borrower by census tract as opposed to loans outstanding
3. Summary of Deposits (SOD)	FDIC	All FDIC-insured institutions; annually	Location of branches and deposits booked per branch
4. Statistics on Depository Institutions (SDI)	FDIC	All FDIC-insured institutions; quarterly	Only financial information

respondingly, commercial real estate, which may only be picked up in CRA reports, has become increasingly important (32 percent in 2004, up from 20 percent over the same period). This means that HMDA is picking up less and less over time of the real estate–related development lending of CDFIs.

• *CRA:* Up until 2004, only entities larger than $250 million in assets were required to complete the detailed CRA reports, which enable new lending to small businesses to be identified separately by area. The rise in the reporting threshold to $1 billion from 2005 and the change in the methodologies mean that most CDFI banks, and indeed most small banks in general, will no longer be required to report origination at a tract level, so whatever the historic value of this information, its value as a source of detailed data on small banks has already diminished. (In 2005, there were only 1,103 CRA reporting banks, only 59 of which had assets less than $249 million.)

• *SOD:* Differential practices on booking deposits distort the information value of data on the value of deposits by branch. Therefore, a measure of

Table 7.3

Number of Observations Found in Each Database in Each Year

Database	1996	2000	2004
1. CRA	1	6	5
2. HMDA	34	36	43
3. SOD	47	57	58
4. SDI	52	59	61

percentage of branch offices in qualifying areas was used as a proxy for the focus of banking presence.

To construct a database for CDFI banks, considerable effort was necessary to extract data from the different databases and combine them. The SOD and SDI data for each year and for all institutions in the CDFI bank dataset are available at the FDIC Web site. The underlying HMDA and CRA datasets used in this analysis were available at the Federal Financial Institutions Examination Council (FFIEC) Web site for years after 1999 and could be ordered on CD-ROM for the earlier year in our sample. The transactional databases for CRA and HMDA raw data are large, requiring considerable manipulation to obtain usable data that combines the information by institution. While there are some commercial services that provide links across the databases by institution to facilitate such comparison, we found these to be very expensive; hence, we decided to test accessing these data directly from source.

Not all CDFI banks existed in 1996; and many of those that did, because of their size, were not required to report in each year (see Table 7.3). So few CDFI banks qualified to undertake detailed CRA reporting during this period that we could not use these data.

Given these limitations, what use can be made of these data related to social performance in particular? One of the key differences between CDFI banks and others is, in theory at least, that they do a sizable proportion of their business, whether lending or deposit taking, in qualifying areas. Business undertaken in such qualified areas is considered development-related business, which qualifies for consideration under the CRA lending test. Using databases mentioned earlier, differences should be measurable over time and can be calibrated to enable better comparison among entities that do relatively more, or relatively less, business in these areas. Specifically, we proposed two social performance measures (SPMs), which allowed us to distinguish among CDFIs and within broader groups (see Table 7.4):

- Development Lending Intensity (DLI), which should apply to all categories of lending deemed to have positive social impact (such as housing, SME, rural, commercial real estate) measured at a qualifying area level.

Table 7.4

Social Performance Distinguishing Features

Measure	Definition/s	Meaning
1. Development Lending Intensity (DLI)	The total value of development-related loans originated and purchased by a bank in qualifying areas in a year as a percentage of total loans originated by bank *i* at time *t*. DLI may also be calculated relative to some measure of size, such as tier 1 equity or total assets	A higher DLI value means relatively more of a bank's lending takes place in qualifying areas; a DLI value increasing over time indicates an intensifying focus on lending in qualifying areas
2. Development Deposit Intensity (DDI) (i) DDI(t)	(i) The value of deposits booked in qualifying areas as a percentage of total deposits; or	(i) The extent to which the bank draws its resources from qualifying areas
(ii) DDI(b)	(ii) Percentage of total offices located in qualifying areas	(ii) The extent to which the bank provides deposit and retail financial services in qualifying areas

- Development Deposit Intensity (DDI), which considers deposits taken or branches located in qualifying areas, similar to the service test considered as part of a CRA examination.

In many ways, these measures are at the heart of the CRA examination. The CRA examination report records the originations of home loans and small business loans by number and value, differentiated by geography of the borrower and even income of the borrower for home loans. This profile is compared against averages for a regional comparison grouping of banks to form an opinion on the reasonableness of the distribution of bank lending patterns. Similarly, for the location of retail service points, the current spread of branches and the trend in branch openings and closings in different income areas is considered in coming to an assessment of the performance of the institution.

The outcome of a CRA examination, conducted every three years or so, is a rating on a four-point scale. Examination methodology has been standardized across the bank supervisory agencies to attempt to make CRA ratings more comparable. Nonetheless, ratings are highly clustered in the upper two categories (outstanding, satisfactory) and are used only for regulatory purposes. They have not, to our knowledge, been used for investment purposes, because the CRA rating does not, nor does it seek to, systematize the underlying information in a way that can be used by investors to understand social performance. Instead, the derivation of DLI and DDI measures on a consistent basis is relevant to categorizing and comparing the social performance of banks with one another and over time.

The DDI measure is accessible annually through the FDIC's SOD database. However, the calculation of DLI from publicly available data presents a challenge: very few of the CDFI banks (five, from Table 7.3), or small banks under $1 billion in general, are required to produce annual lending reports for CRA. Because of lower exemption thresholds, many more are required to report HMDA data: forty-three in 2004 (Table 7.3). However, to calculate DLI on one asset class alone may create a misleading picture of the development lending of a bank: the bank may undertake little housing lending in investment areas because the bulk of its business is SME or commercial real estate investment in these areas. Since at present we can calculate only the DLI measure for home lending, this measure has descriptive power only for those entities that focus on home lending. We therefore distinguish DLI on the basis of HMDA alone as DLI (HMDA) and apply it for lenders for which home lending is more than 50 percent of their loan portfolios in 2004. For those lenders that are not housing focused, DLI (HMDA) provides a guide only to their housing activity, which is relatively small, and says nothing about their social performance.

Application of SPMs to CDFI Banks

Financial Performance

It is possible to compare the financial performance of the CDFI Banks with the rough peer group of banks with less than $1 billion in assets using SDI data. This cutoff was made simply because of tractability; ideally, other criteria would define the small-bank category more narrowly as community banks, as de Young, Hunter, and Udell (2004) and de Young (2006) have done.

A few results are immediately apparent from these data. First, at the bottom-line level of ROA, CDFI banks have been less profitable on average than small banks in general throughout the period, although the differential is less pronounced when the median is calculated, suggesting some outliers. The gap has also closed somewhat over the period (see Figure 7.2). Certainly, CDFI banks have increased median and average ROA over the period.

The difference in performance between CDFIs and the larger peer group of small banks appears to be due to several factors, explored more fully in de Young (2006). For example, although CDFI banks show a consistently lower median charge-off rate than small banks and earn a consistently higher gross interest margin (4.6 percent versus 3.6 percent), these positive factors are not sufficient to outweigh the effects that draw down profitability. These include the following:

- The efficiency ratio of CDFIs is more than a third higher than that of small banks in general (76 percent versus 56 percent in 2004), reflecting in part

Figure 7.2   **Return on Assets: CDFIs and Small Banks Compared**

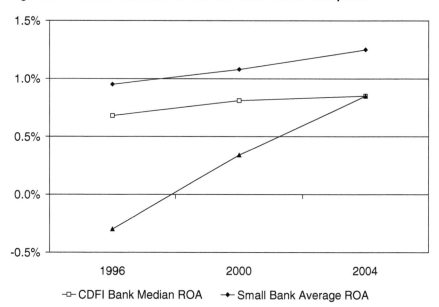

-□- CDFI Bank Median ROA   -◆- Small Bank Average ROA

lower average size of the CDFIs compared to the banks in the under $1 billion asset category; and

- CDFIs are consistently less geared (tier 1 leverage ratio of 9.2 percent versus 8.7 percent) and less lent out (loans to deposit ratios of 77 percent versus 104 percent), reflecting in part the less commoditized, more specialized nature of CDFI lending.

Social Performance

Figure 7.3 shows a scatter plot of DDI and DLI measures we calculated for the sample of CDFI banks in 2004. As explained earlier, DLI could only be calculated using HMDA data, that is, for home lending. This is a significant factor, since only thirteen banks in the sample can be described as housing focused, with single- and multiple family lending constituting more than 50 percent of assets in 2004. Figure 7.3 shows a scatter across the DDI–DLI space, indicating housing-focused lenders, for which DLI (HMDA) is a more useful measure, with diamond shapes. There is a notable grouping along 100 percent on the DDI line. Indeed, the median DDI for CDFI banks is 100 percent; that is, the median CDFI bank has all its branches in qualifying areas. The bulk of CDFI banks sit in the northwest quadrant, that is, have DDI and DLI above 50 percent.

However, the significance of an arbitrary segmentation—above and below 50 percent alone—may be questionable. We require benchmarks for these measures

Figure 7.3   **DDI (Branches) Versus DDI[b] Breakout by Housing Focus**

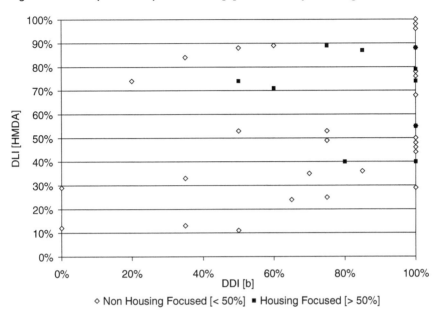

◇ Non Housing Focused [< 50%] ■ Housing Focused [> 50%]

from other categories of entities to make meaningful distinctions as to what level is low or high. Table 7.5 gives initial equivalent calculations for other categories of banks.

It is clear from Table 7.5 that CDFI banks are different from large U.S. banks and indeed even from smaller banks in general. Using norms for small or community banks, we could define four quadrants, with the expectation that CDFIs would then more clearly be clustered in the top right-hand quadrant, although, given that the DLI numbers are HMDA only, not all CDFIs will be located there: some may not do much housing lending, and the lending they do may be deliberately done in middle-income areas as a strategy to diversify risk or raise income to pursue development impact by other means. However, we would be surprised to find CDFI banks in the bottom left-hand quadrant—below median or average on both counts.

Seen through these DDI and DLI lenses, have CDFI banks changed over time? Figure 7.4 summarizes the average of these two measures for the CDFI bank category over the sample period. The DDI measure shows little variation over the period, returning to its 1996 average by 2004. However, there is evidence of an upward trend in DLI, which has risen from 45 percent to 55.2 percent, although it has fallen from the peak shown in 2000.

Underlying these averages are of course the stories of forty-two individual CDFI banks, which have adjusted their business models over time, presumably in response to many factors, including competition and desire for impact. If we define a material change in terms of the 2004 number being more than 10 percent

Table 7.5

DDI and DLI Comparisons

Category	Number in Category	DLI (HMDA) Average	DDI Average
Top 10 U.S. banks by assets	10	16.6%	31.44
Small banks (< $1bn)	1,142	NA	44.80
All minority-owned banks	189	49.6%	61.67
CDFI banks	42	55.2%	75.34

Figure 7.4   **CDFI Banks: DDI and DLI over time**

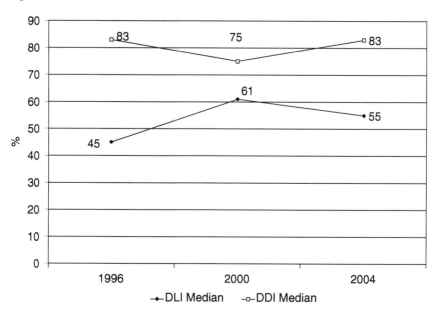

different from the 1996 number, then twenty-three banks saw no material change over this time, while twelve had a material rise in DLI and seven a material decline. The vast majority maintained or increased their development lending focus in housing; and for those that did not, it is not possible to say whether this is the result of, for example, increasing emphasis on other development lending such as commercial real estate.

How do we bring all this information together in an indicative performance rating? Earlier we argued that a long-run average ROA may be the best financial performance measure. In Table 7.6, we report on the CDFI banks that have performed best according to this measure in the period 2000 to 2004, but using the DLI and DDI lenses to create robust comparison groups.

Table 7.6

Performance Measurements for CDFI Banks Using Social Performance Lenses

	Housing Focused	No. of Banks
Above CDFI bank median DLI HMDA	ShoreBank: 1.04% Pacific Global Bank: 1.02% Seaway National Bank of Chicago: 0.97%	9
Below CDFI bank median DLI (HMDA)	Carver Federal Savings Bank: 0.70% Mutual Community Savings Bank, FSB: –0.10%	2
Above CB median DDI	11 Banks—Top 3: ShoreBank: 1.04% Pacific Global: 1.02% Seaway National: 0.97%	26 Banks—Top 3: Central Bank of Kansas City: 2.63% International Bank of Chicago: 2.12% University National Bank: 1.75%
Below CB median DDI HMDA	None	6 Banks—Top 3: Community Commerce Bank: 1.88% Park Midway Bank: 1.77% Inter National Bank: 1.54%

First, Table 7.6 reports a segmentation using above and below CDFI bank median DLI, which, as discussed earlier, is relevant only for housing-focused lenders, a relatively small group, and then, the median DDI for community banks as a whole is used, and banks are further categorized according to their lending focus—whether or not a majority of loans in 2004 was for single- and multifamily housing. Of course, "not" covers several major categories we cannot distinguish from these available data alone. The table reports only the top three institutions in each category, ranked by the average ROA for the last five years.

This categorization could inform and assist a double bottom line investor who seeks the best financial return possible from investing in banks that, for example, focus on housing and are more "present" in poorer communities. These criteria would be a good starting point for further analysis by the investor. Providing an easy starting point for investment decisions is all mutual fund rating services seek to do.

Conclusions

Our work has been exploratory, seeking to understand how CDFI banks performed over the past decade and the extent to which publicly available data can assist in measuring its performance. Based on the same logic underlying the lending test and service test undertaken as part of a CRA examination, we propose that DLI and DDI can be useful SPMs because they standardize comparison of a bank's underlying business model.

We have plumbed the limits of readily available public data. The SOD provides a useful profile of the location of deposit-taking operations of all banks, which can be summarized in the DDI measure proposed here. On the lending side, for banks focused on home lending, HMDA remains a very useful source of data, which may be used to calculate the DLI (HMDA) measure reported here. However, for those banks not focused on housing (and even for those that are but undertake substantial other development lending activities), the available public data are not adequate to develop benchmarks.

We have also demonstrated the possible use of these measures: creating consistent, relevant categories using these new measures in order to more fairly compare financial return measured by ROA across a broader category of institutions. While publicly available data do not allow for the calculation of SPMs per se, they can enable more meaningful comparison of financial measures across different types of banking institutions as we have demonstrated. These measures also help to track the focus of a bank's service model over time—highlighting whether it is becoming more or less development focused on these terms in a way that would invite further investigation.

Our findings suggest that the DLI and DDI measures are useful SPMs warranting further exploration. First, it is essential to fill out the DLI measure to include other categories of lending than those available from HMDA alone. CRA examination reports provide some data for each institution, although these are published on a three-year cycle publicly available in a pdf format and have to be accessed for each lender. Nonetheless, there is more relevant public data to be accessed, although the method of access is time consuming. However, the potential value of the DLI measure suggests that such effort may be worthwhile for CDFI banks at least. If these data cannot be accessed, then the alternative is to consider the incentives and inducements for lenders to self-report it.

Second, even if limited to using the more restricted DLI (HMDA) measure, it would be worth applying the DLI and DDI criteria as screens to identify a possible wider universe of CDFI banks beyond the small number of banks that have presently chosen to apply for CDFI status. DDI and DLI thresholds can be applied as the first cut toward identifying those banks with the potential for higher social performance. Of course, further exploration would be necessary to establish definite potential in each case. However, even to make the first cut requires investment in the hardware and software capacity to manage substantial volumes of data.

Third, changes in DDI and DLI observed over time deserve closer investigation because we lack an empirically verified theory of how double bottom line banks change over time. For example, do some banks move upmarket from necessity, opportunity, or even success in their development mission as depressed areas turn around and no longer qualify? Do others intentionally pursue high development intensity over time? In our opinion, it would be worth following up with banks that have shown increases or declines in DLI to determine the underlying factors for and results of these changes over time.

Note

David Porteous, Director, Bankable Frontier (www.bankablefrontier.com), and Saurabh Narain, Chief Fund Advisor, National Community Investment Fund (NCIF) (www.ncif.org), would like to acknowledge the hard work of Corinne Bradley, Joe Schmidt, and Benecia Cousin and the advice from numerous others, including trustees of NCIF, George Surgeon, Ron Grzywinski, Mary Houghton, Ellen Seidman, Dan Immergluck, Malcolm Bush, Bob de Young, and Mike Berry. This chapter was commissioned by NCIF with the kind support of the F. B. Heron Foundation and the CDFI Fund. NCIF expects to use the methodology discussed in this chapter for creating a direct link between availability of more capital/funding and community development outputs. *Development Lending Intensity* and *Development Deposit Intensity* are terms used by NCIF to measure social performance of community development banks.

1. Other screens would be low and moderate income (LMI), published annually by HUD, which considers tract income relative to area median, and more recent categories of financially distressed and financially underserved areas declared by FFIEC in terms of recent regulation. While this measure will be updated more regularly than CDFI investment areas, it has become available only recently and covers only nonmetropolitan counties.

References

Beck, T. A. Demirguc-Kunt, and R. Levine. 2004. "Finance, Inequality and Poverty: Cross-Country Evidence." World Bank Working Paper 3338.

Clark, C., W. Rosenzweig, D. Long, and S. Olsen. 2003. "DBL Project Report: Methods Catalog." www.riseproject.org/DBL_Methods_Catalog.pdf. (Accessed 2 July 2007.)

Coastal Enterprises, Inc. 2006. "Measuring Impact in Practice." www.ceimaine.org/images/stories/pdf/measurement.pdf. (Accessed 2 July 2007.)

De Young, R. 2006. "Is Community Development Banking Profitable?" Paper presented at NCIF Conference, Chicago.

De Young, R., W. C. Hunter, and G. F. Udell. 2004. "The Past, Present, and Probable Future for Community Banks." *Journal of Financial Services Research* 25 (2/3): 85–133.

Dehejia, R., and A. Llevas-Muney. 2003. "Why Does Financial Development Matter? The United States from 1900 to 1940." NBER Working Paper 9551.

Dobbs, R. and T. Koller. 2005. "Measuring Long-Term Performance." *McKinsey on Finance*, vol. 16.

Galster, G., C. Hayes and J. Johnson. 2006. "Identifying Robust, Parsimonious Neighborhood Indicators." *Journal of Planning, Education and Research* 24: 265—280.

Keystone. 2006. "The Keystone Method." www.keystonereporting.org. (Accessed 2 July 2007.)

Kramer, M., and S. Cooch. 2006. "Investing for Impact: Managing and Measuring Pro-active Social Investments." Report prepared for Shell Foundation.

Levine, R. 2005. "Finance & Growth: Theory and Evidence." *Handbook of Economic Growth*. Vol. 1, Part 1. Elsevier.

Morningstar. 2003. *The Morningstar Rating Methodology*. www.morningstar.com. (Accessed 2 July 2007.)

Part 2

Asset Building

8

Stubborn and Persistent Lending Disparities

JOSHUA SILVER

Community development often focuses on affordable housing and economic development projects as key for community wealth building. A parallel requirement is that family and community wealth be protected against predatory lenders. Predatory lenders steal equity through high fees and abusive terms and conditions.

Responsible high-cost lending serves legitimate credit needs. High-cost loans compensate lenders for the added risk of lending to borrowers with credit imperfections. However, wide differences in lending by race, even when accounting for income levels, suggest that more minorities are receiving high-cost loans than is justified based on creditworthiness. In fact, National Community Reinvestment Coalition (NCRC) observes that racial differences in lending increase as income levels increase. In other words, middle- and upper-income (MUI) minorities are more likely relative to their MUI white counterparts to receive high-cost loans than low- and moderate-income (LMI) minorities are relative to LMI whites. When minorities receive a disproportionate amount of high-cost loans, they lose substantial amounts of equity through higher payments to their lenders.

Since racial disparities have been stubborn and persistent over several years, this chapter also describes a number of programmatic and policy reforms. Community groups and financial institutions should engage in more partnerships to devise counseling programs and lending products that are fairly priced and affordable for minorities and working-class Americans. Congress must pass a comprehensive antipredatory law that prohibits steering or price discrimination and that outlaws a range of equity-stripping and abusive practices.

Literature Review and Introduction

A substantial body of research documents significant disparities in loan pricing based on the race, age, and income levels of neighborhood residents. These disparities result from discrimination, market failure, and other factors among minorities and the working class.[1] Discrimination and market failure impede wealth building and the creation of sustainable homeownership for residents of underserved neighborhoods.

Significant disparities in loan pricing reflect the growth of subprime lending. A subprime or high-cost loan has an interest rate higher than prevailing and competitive rates in order to compensate for the added risk of lending to a borrower with impaired credit. NCRC defines a predatory loan as an unsuitable loan designed to exploit vulnerable and unsophisticated borrowers. Predatory loans are a subset of subprime and nontraditional prime loans.[2]

A predatory loan has one or more of the following features: (1) charges more in interest and fees than is required to cover the added risk of lending to borrowers with credit imperfections, (2) contains abusive terms and conditions that trap borrowers and lead to increased indebtedness, (3) does not take into account the borrower's ability to repay the loan, and (4) violates fair lending laws by targeting women, minorities, and communities of color.

Lending discrimination in the form of steering high-cost loans to underserved borrowers qualified for market-rate loans results in equity stripping and has contributed to inequalities in wealth. According to the Federal Reserve Survey of Consumer Finances (FRSCF), the median value of financial assets was $38,500 for whites but only $7,200 for minorities in 2001. Whites had more than five times the dollar amount of financial assets than minorities. Likewise, the median home value for whites was $130,000 and only $92,000 for minorities in 2001 (Aizcorbe, Kennickell, and Moore 2003). By 2004, according to the FRSCF, the median net worth of minorities was 17.6 percent of that for all other families. In addition, the median net worth for African Americans was the same at $20,400 in 2004 as it was in 2001 ($20,300) (Bucks, Kennickell, and Moore 2006).

Since subprime loans often cost $50,000 to $100,000 more than comparable prime loans, a neighborhood receiving a disproportionate number of subprime loans loses a significant amount of equity and wealth. Using a mortgage calculator from Bankrate.com, a $140,000 thirty-year mortgage with the current prime rate of 6.25 percent costs about $862 a month, or about $310,320 over the life of the loan. In contrast, a thirty-year subprime loan with an interest rate of 8.25 percent costs $1,052 a month, or approximately $378,637 over the life of the loan. The difference in total costs between the 6.25 percent and 8.25 percent loan is $68,317. Finally, a thirty-year subprime loan at 9.25 percent costs $1,152 per month and $414,630 over the life of the loan. The difference in total costs between a 6.25 percent and 9.25 percent loan is $104,310. For a family who is creditworthy for a prime loan but receives a subprime loan, the total loss in equity can be easily between $50,000 and $100,000. This amount represents resources that could have been used to send children to college or start a small business. Instead of building family wealth, the equity was transferred from the family to the lender.

Building upon this example, the equity drain from a neighborhood can be tremendous. Suppose 15 percent, or 300 families in a predominantly minority census tract with 2,000 households receive subprime loans, although they were creditworthy for prime loans (15 percent of families that are inappropriately steered into subprime loans is a realistic figure based on existing research). Further, assume that these families pay $50,000 more over the life of the loan than they should (the $50,000 figure is conservative based on the calculations above). In total, the 300 families in the minority census tract have paid lenders $15 million more than they would have if they had received prime loans for which they could have qualified. The $15 million in purchasing power could have supported stores in the neighborhood, economic development in the neighborhood, or other wealth-building endeavors for the families and neighborhood. For even one neighborhood, the magnitude of wealth loss due to pricing disparities and/or discrimination is stark. Across the country, the wealth loss is staggering and tragic.

In a study released in December 2003, "Broken Credit System: Discrimination and Unequal Access to Affordable Loans by Race and Age," NCRC selected ten large metropolitan areas for the analysis: Atlanta, Baltimore, Cleveland, Detroit, Houston, Los Angeles, Milwaukee, New York, St. Louis, and Washington, DC. NCRC obtained creditworthiness data on a one-time basis from a large credit bureau. As expected, the number of subprime loans increased as the number of neighborhood residents in higher credit-risk categories increased. After controlling for risk and housing market conditions, however, the race and age composition of the neighborhood had an independent and strong effect, increasing the amount of high-cost subprime lending. In particular, the

- level of subprime refinance lending increased as the portion of African Americans in a neighborhood increased in nine of the ten metropolitan areas. In the case of home-purchase subprime lending, the African American composition of a neighborhood boosted lending in six metropolitan areas.
- impact of the age of borrowers was strong in refinance lending. In seven metropolitan areas, the portion of subprime refinance lending increased solely when the number of residents over 65 increased in a neighborhood.

In another study, "Homeownership and Wealth Building Impeded: Continuing Lending Disparities for Minorities and Emerging Obstacles for Middle-Income and Female Borrowers of All Races," conducted in 2006, NCRC found that racial disparities in the share of borrowers receiving high-cost loans were greater for upper-income borrowers than for lower-income borrowers across the nation. High-cost loans made up a high 41.9 percent of all refinance loans to LMI African Americans. In contrast, subprime loans were 19.2 percent of refinance loans to LMI whites in 2004. LMI African Americans were 2.2 times more likely than LMI whites to receive high-cost loans. Even for MUI African Americans, high-cost loans made up a large percentage (30.2 percent) of all refinance loans. Moreover, the subprime share of loans to MUI African Americans was 2.7 times larger than the subprime share of loans to MUI whites. The same phenomena of increasing disparities when income increased was observed when comparing high-cost lending in predominantly white and immigrant neighborhoods.

NCRC's findings are consistent with a wide variety of research on subprime lending. A study conducted by Freddie Mac analysts found that two-thirds of subprime borrowers were not satisfied with their loans, while three-quarters of prime borrowers believed they received fair rates and terms (Courchane, Surette, and Zorn 2002). Previously, Freddie Mac and Fannie Mae had often been quoted as stating that between a third to a half of borrowers who qualify for low-cost loans receive subprime loans.[3] The Federal Reserve Board (FRB) also released analyses of the 2004 and 2005 Home Mortgage Disclosure Act (HMDA) data revealing racial disparities even after controlling for income levels, loan types, and geographical areas (Avery, Brevoot, and Canner 2006). Immergluck and Wiles pioneered documenting the "hypersegmentation" of lending by race of neighborhood (Immergluck and Wiles 1999).

Calem, Gillen, and Wachter (2002) also used credit-scoring data to conduct econometric analysis scrutinizing the influence of credit scores, demographic characteristics, and economic conditions on the level of subprime lending. Their study found that after controlling for creditworthiness and housing market conditions, the level of subprime refinance and home-purchase loans increased as the proportion of African Americans increased on a census tract level in Philadelphia and Chicago (Calem, Gillen, and Wachter 2002; Calem, Hershaff, and Wachter 2004). The Center for Responsible Lending (2006) also used 2004 HMDA data with pricing information to reach the same troubling conclusions that racial disparities remain after controlling for creditworthiness.

Research Findings

For this report, NCRC analyzed HMDA data gathered in 2005 for metropolitan areas, the most recent publicly available. NCRC considered loans for traditional single-family homes occupied by the borrowers of the loans (investor-owned properties were not considered). The home loan data considered was home-purchase, refinance, and home-improvement lending (first liens only). HMDA data report pricing information for high-cost loans. NCRC considered loans without pricing information to be market-rate loans and loans with pricing information to be high-cost loans.

NCRC analyzed racial disparities in lending experienced by LMI borrowers considered separately from MUI borrowers. Income level is an important factor in the lending process. While persistent racial disparities across all income levels do not prove discrimination, it would appear that stakeholders could take action to narrow particularly large disparities for MUI minorities and whites. Large disparities at all income levels suggest a lack of competition among lenders and other market barriers that can be reduced by concerted action. Stakeholders and policymakers must consider carefully any differences by race that persists for MUI borrowers.

Largest and Smallest Disparities Experienced by African Americans, Hispanics, and Asians

In a more detailed description of the data analysis used in this chapter, on NCRC's Web page (http://www.ncrc.org/pressandpubs/documents/NCRC%20metro%20stu

dy%20race%20and%20income%20disparity%20July%2007.pdf), we discuss racial disparities in lending on a number of dimensions. Disparities are discussed comparing LMI minorities and LMI whites and then separately for MUI whites and MUI minorities. Disparities are detailed in all metropolitan statistical areas (MSAs) for which there are large enough samples of loans (50 or more) for each racial group to provide statistically meaningful analyses. For more detail on disparities across MSAs, please see www.ncrc.org.

Racial Disparities Increase as Income Level Increases

Racial disparities in high-cost lending increase when income levels increase. When the percentage of high-cost loans received by whites is compared with the percentage of high-cost loans received by minorities, the differences in the percentages is larger for MUI whites and MUI minorities than for LMI whites and LMI minorities.

The percentage of high-cost loans received by MUI borrowers is lower than for LMI borrowers, but the percentage of high-cost loans received by MUI whites drops significantly more than the percentage of high-cost loans received by MUI minorities. For example, in Durham, North Carolina, 48 percent of the loans received by LMI African Americans in 2005 were high-cost, while 16.4 percent of the loans received by LMI whites were high-cost. In other words, LMI African Americans were 2.94 times more likely than LMI whites to receive a high-cost loan (divide 48 percent by 16.4 percent, or the portion of the loans that were high-cost for LMI African Americans by the portion of loans that were high-cost for LMI whites).

When considering MUI borrowers, 38.6 percent of the loans received by MUI African Americans were high-cost, while 8.6 percent of the loans received by MUI whites were high-cost in Durham during 2005. For MUI borrowers, African Americans were 4.50 times more likely than whites to receive loans.

The racial disparity in high-cost lending increased for MUI borrowers in Durham because the incidence of high-cost lending dropped much more for MUI whites than for MUI minorities. The percentage of high-cost loans received by whites dropped by about half when climbing the income scale from LMI to MUI (16.4 percent compared to 8.6 percent). In contrast, the percentage of loans received by African Americans dropped by only one-fifth for MUI African Americans compared to LMI African Americans (38.6 percent compared to 48 percent).

For African Americans, differences in high-cost lending increase significantly as income increases across metropolitan areas. LMI African Americans were three times or more likely than LMI whites to receive high-cost loans in just 1 percent of the MSAs. In contrast, MUI African Americans were three times or more likely to receive high-cost loans than MUI whites in 12.4 percent of the MSAs during 2005. The same trend of MUI African Americans experiencing greater disparities continues when considering the number of MSAs in which African Americans were between 2.5 to 3 times more likely to receive loans. LMI African Americans were 2.5 to 3.0 times more likely than LMI whites to receive high-cost loans in 5.1 percent of the MSAs. In contrast, MUI African Americans were 2.5 to 3.0 times more likely than MUI whites to receive high-cost loans in 28.0 percent of the MSAs.

Shockingly, MUI African Americans were at least twice as likely as MUI whites to receive high-cost loans in 167 MSAs. LMI African Americans were at least twice as likely to receive high-cost loans in 70 MSAs.

Just as for African Americans, the disparity in high-cost lending for Hispanics becomes greater for MUI Hispanics than for LMI Hispanics. LMI Hispanics were between 2.5 to 3 times more likely than LMI whites to receive high-cost loans in 1.2 percent of the MSAs. In contrast, MUI Hispanics were between 2.5 to 3 times more likely than MUI whites to receive high-cost loans in 11.8 percent of the MSAs. Similarly, LMI Hispanics were 2.0 to 2.5 times more likely than LMI whites to receive high-cost loans in 4.8 percent of the MSAs, while MUI Hispanics were 2.0 to 2.5 times more likely than MUI whites to receive high-cost loans in 27.0 percent of the MSAs.

A common expectation is that disparities in lending by race would narrow as income increases. More affluent borrowers should have fewer difficulties paying their bills on time, meaning that more affluent borrowers should have fewer difficulties maintaining good credit histories. Therefore, it would seem that MUI minorities should have creditworthiness similar to that of MUI whites. As a consequence, MUI minorities should have expanded access to market-rate loans and receive fewer high-cost loans. On the other hand, some would say that differences in creditworthiness by race could persist even when income increases. Thus, differences in high-cost lending could be the same for MUI minorities compared to MUI whites as it is for LMI minorities compared to LMI whites.

While this study was not able to attain creditworthiness by race and income, it is startling nonetheless that differences in high-cost lending increases as income levels increase. This suggests that creditworthiness of minorities declines compared to whites as income level increases. Another explanation for this finding, which NCRC finds more plausible, is that discrimination and/or other market imperfections are impeding access to market-rate loans for MUI minorities. Lenders could be overtly steering minorities qualified for prime loans into high-cost loans. Alternatively, lenders specializing in high-cost loans could be working harder than market-rate lenders to make loans to MUI minorities. Both possibilities (discrimination and less effort by market-rate lenders) could be occurring simultaneously. The fact that MUI minorities receive such large percentages of high-cost loans suggests that multiple barriers to equal access are occurring. These disparities suggest that the burden lies on skeptics to disprove the existence of discrimination and other barriers to equal access to market-rate loans.

Programmatic and Policy Responses to Steering and Abusive Lending

When any group of borrowers receives a disproportionate amount of high-cost lending, that group of borrowers is more likely to experience price discrimination and an array of other abuses. Standard antitrust theory suggests that exploitative behavior is more prevalent when relatively few companies dominate a market to a group of consumers. In the case of the lending marketplace, this research concludes, as does other research, that minorities, even MUI minorities, are more likely to receive high-cost lending. Minorities, therefore, are more likely to experience equity stripping and other abuses. A number of programmatic and policy steps are needed to combat the imbalance in the marketplace experienced by minorities.

On the programmatic side, an increase in homeownership and foreclosure prevention counseling is needed. On the front end, homeownership counseling assists borrowers as they are shopping for homes to find loans that are appropriately priced and that they can afford. On the back end, foreclosure prevention counseling assists borrowers who are in danger of defaulting on their loans due to a temporary crisis such as unemployment or due to predatory lending. Because steering and predatory lending practices remain an ugly reality in the marketplace, more resources for counseling are urgently needed. Unfortunately, however, counseling will be unable to reach all the borrowers in need, particularly when abuses are widespread in the market as a whole or to certain groups of borrowers and neighborhoods. Accordingly, policy reforms are also needed to eliminate certain systematic abuses.

NCRC's Consumer Rescue Fund

Mechanics of the CRF Fund

Through the national antipredatory lending Consumer Rescue Fund (CRF), NCRC works with victims of predatory lending so their mortgage payments become more affordable and foreclosures can be avoided. NCRC's member groups and their communities are an integral part of this program. CRF identifies consumers who are in predatory mortgages and fixes the mortgages through mediation with lenders or by arranging for refinance loans.[4] Consumers contact NCRC member organizations participating in CRF. In a number of instances, the NCRC members in CRF are counseling agencies assisting consumers experiencing delinquency and default on their loans. To date, over 5,000 consumers have been helped through the CRF's alternative dispute resolution, mediation, consumer counseling, and financial education.

CRF has a nationwide reach, serving consumers in seventeen states. NCRC member organizations (counseling agencies, community development corporations, and others) identify families facing foreclosure and/or bankruptcy as a result of problematic loans. Fair lending specialists at NCRC then review loan documents, including the Good Faith Estimate, income verification statements, and other forms to determine if the loans are in fact predatory. If NCRC staff conclude that the loans are predatory, NCRC staff pursue a number of options. CRF intervenes in the following manners to turnaround a predatory lending situation:

- *Mediation and Loan Modification:* NCRC will engage in mediation with the lender or servicer to have abusive terms eliminated and to delay or stop foreclosure proceedings. Mediation is an effective means of assisting consumers because it is less time consuming and resource intensive than refinancing a problematic loan.
- *An Affordable Refinance Loan:* NCRC has partnered with HSBC North America, which refinances the loans of predatory lending victims. The predatory loans are replaced with market-rate or below-market-rate loans. The new loans also do not contain prepayment penalties, balloon payments, or credit insurance.
- *Litigation:* If NCRC discovers a pattern and practice of abusive lending or servicing on the part of a financial institution, NCRC will pursue legal redress when necessary. NCRC has filed complaints with the Department of Housing and Urban Development (HUD) arising from systematic abuses uncovered by the CRF program. The complaint process often ends before a formal trial when a lender makes a commitment to change an underwriting or marketing practice.

Another critical component of CRF is financial education and counseling that occurs over a period of several months. NCRC staff and member organizations counsel CRF borrowers through the remediation process and coach them on how to avoid predatory lending situations in the future. The counseling occurs before the loan modification or refinance and continues after an intervention to make sure borrowers can succeed in their new loan.

CRF's Success: At Least $500 Million in Equity Saved

The refinance loans of CRF have saved borrowers and their communities millions of dollars. In a sample of 112 cases, the median principal amount of the loans was approximately $157,000. As Table 8.1 shows, the mortgage rates of the previous predatory loans ranged between 5.5 percent and 17 percent. The median prior mortgage rate was 9.38 percent.

The interest rates of the refinance loans were considerably lower than the rates of the previous predatory loans. The new loans had interest rates ranging between 1 percent and 8 percent. The median rate of the new refinance loans rate was 6 percent. The difference between the median rate of the previous loans (9.38 percent) and the new loan (6 percent) was 3.38 percentage points, which results in a substantial amount of equity saved over the life of a loan.

CRF customers have been able to save millions of dollars of wealth by refinancing out of abusive loans. The average monthly payment was $1,198 for the abusive loans. For the new refinance loans, the average monthly payment was only $922. As a result of the refinancing, the average monthly savings was $276.50, which equates to $3,318 annually. Assuming a thirty-year loan term, the total savings on

Table 8.1

Analysis of Loan Terms Before and After Refinance

	Principal Amount	Prior Mortgage Rate	New Mortgage Rate	% Points Difference	Old Monthly Payment	New Monthly Payment	$ Savings
Average	$156,986.2	9.58%	5.74%	3.84%	$1,198.4	$922.0	$276.5
Median	$161,280.4	9.38%	6.00%	3.38%	$1,165.8	$941.7	$224.1

an average loan would be $100,000. Given that CRF has assisted at least 1,000 victims through either refinancing or loan modifications, the program has saved borrowers approximately $500 million in equity.

Minority and Working-Class Americans Are Targeted with Loans Having Multiple Abuses

An NCRC review of CRF cases indicates that abusive lenders are targeting minority and LMI borrowers and communities with high-cost and exotic mortgages (for more details on CRF, see NCRC and Woodstock Institute 2006). A disproportionate number of CRF customers have modest incomes. About 77 percent of borrowers were African American, 3 percent Hispanic, and 3 percent Caribbean. Almost half (47 percent) resided in LMI neighborhoods, and 83.6 percent of the borrowers had incomes below $45,000.

The finding that CRF customers were mostly minority and LMI earners is consistent with NCRC's research and other studies documenting that a disproportionate amount of high-cost lending is directed toward minority and working-class communities. Traditionally underserved communities suffer from less product choice and consequently are more susceptible to abusive high-cost and exotic mortgage lending.

Multiple Abuses in Exotic and High-Cost Loans in CRF Sample

CRF cases also reveal that predatory loans do not usually contain just one or two abusive terms and conditions. More often, a toxic loan in CRF contains abusive features including adjustable rate mortgage (ARM) loans with lax underwriting considering only the initial rates, exaggerated borrower incomes, payments that borrowers cannot afford, exorbitant fees and yield spread premiums, piggyback lending adding excessive debt, and abusive servicing.

While some abuses, such as prepaid credit insurance, have declined in recent years, most loans in the CRF program have multiple abuses confronting borrowers with loans that they can no longer afford and loan terms they can no longer negotiate. If the loans had just one or two abuses, it would be easier for the borrower to either afford the loan or succeed in modifying the loan with the lender. The multiple nature of the abuses, however, suggests that the predatory lender or broker maximized profit by designing a loan that was destined to fail or to be flipped.

Abuses revealed by CRF are summarized in Table 8.2. The sum total of the abuses equals loans that are considerably beyond borrower repayment ability. A sample of sixty-nine CRF cases included calculations of the monthly housing payment-to-income ratio (front-end ratio) and the monthly total debt-to-income ratio (back-end ratio). The front-end and back-end ratios of the predatory loans in the sample were considerably higher than common limits in standard underwriting guidelines. The median front-end ratio was 35.4 percent. The median back-end ratio was about 50 percent, as shown in Table 8.3. Standard front-end and back-end ratios for prime loans are 28 percent and 36 percent respectively. The considerably higher ratios of the predatory loans in the sample suggest that the loans were beyond the consumers' abilities to repay, leading to financial distress and/or bankruptcy and foreclosure.

Compounding the high front- and back-end ratios, most of the loans in the CRF sample did not have escrows covering property tax payments and hazard insurance. Two-thirds of the borrowers in the CRF sample did not have escrow accounts. On top of housing payments and debt levels that were unsustainable, a number of the CRF borrowers experienced payment shock when they discovered that they had thousands of additional dollars in taxes and hazard insurance payments that were not covered by the loans.

Recommendations

NCRC offers the following recommendations.

Programmatic Partnerships

Banks, community organizations, and public agencies should work together to establish programs for refinancing ARM high-cost loans into lower-cost fixed-rate loans. Counseling organizations can identify borrowers who were steered into high-cost loans when they qualified for lower-cost loans. In addition, counseling organizations and lending institutions must identify borrowers who are having difficulties paying ARM high-cost loans with rates that are adjusting upward. Agencies and Federal Home Loan Banks can provide grants and low-interest-rate loans, when necessary, to assist borrowers with temporary cash shortfalls. In 2007, the federal banking agencies issued a statement encouraging banks to engage in these activities. The statement reiterated that banks can earn points on their Community Reinvestment Act (CRA) examinations when engaging in loan modifications and refinancing borrowers into lower-cost loans (Federal Reserve Board 2007).

Table 8.2

Loan Abuses Summarized

Abuses	Description
Asset-based lending	Lenders evaluate a loan application by looking only at the quality of the security or equity, and not at the ability of the borrower to repay the loan
Forced placed insurance	Servicer assigns hazard insurance to borrower; coverage is usually much more expensive
HOEPA loan	A loan with a very high interest rate and/or fees that is covered by federal consumer protections. Predators violate the legal protections of HOEPA loans.
Mandatory arbitration	Stipulation that a borrower cannot sue a lender in a court of law but must use an arbiter
Prepaid credit insurance	Insurance financed into the loan that would cover mortgage payments in a case of disability, unemployment, death. Much more expensive than paying monthly outside of loan
Abuse of right to cancel	Abusive practices that make it hard for a consumer to cancel a mortgage (i.e., abusing right of rescission)
Abusive collection practices	Aggressive tactics of collecting late payments
Default interest rate	Increasing interest rate in case of delinquency
Excessive prepayment penalty	Excessive fee for paying off a mortgage before its maturity
Insincere co-signers	Adding insincere co-signers to the application in order to inflate the income of the borrowers. Abusive lenders will add children and other insincere co-signers who cannot contribute to loan payments.
Loans made in excess of 100% LTV	When the loan amount exceeds the fair market value of the home
Negative amortization	Loan product that requires a monthly payment that does not fully amortize a mortgage loan, thereby increasing the loan's principal balance
Flipping	Persuading a borrower to refinance a loan repeatedly in order to charge high points and fees each time the loan is refinanced
Fraud	Example: forging signatures on loan documents

(continued)

Table 8.2 (continued)

Abuses	Description
Lack of Tangible net benefits	Lack of TNBs that justify the origination of a new, higher-balance and high-cost loan
Targeting/discrimination	Cases when lenders specifically market predatory loans to customers on basis of race, ethnicity, or age
Predatory appraisal	Overestimating the market value of the house
Balloon payment	A mortgage that has level monthly payments over a stated term but provides for a large lump-sum payment due at the end of a previously specified term
Equity stripping	A case when a homeowner's equity is reduced due to repeatedly refinancing, high fees, and other abuses
Home-improvement scam	Home-improvement costs financed into the mortgage usually paid by a lender to a home-improvement contractor directly
Misrepresentation	Misrepresentation of loan terms to a borrower
Falsified application	Falsifying loan applications (particularly income level or adding insincere co-signers, etc.)
Stated income	Not requiring full documentation of income from tax forms and paystubs. Reduced documentation or stated income loans increase the chances of fraud.
Yield spread premium	Fee paid by lenders to brokers for loans carrying interest rates above a par rate
Abusive servicing practices	Servicers not recording payments, forcing placed insurance, applying high late fees, etc.
Unfair terms	High interest rates and loan terms not justifiable by risk (consumer's credit score)
Fee packing	Charging undisclosed, improper, and high fees

Table 8.3

CRF Predatory Loan Study Rsults

CRF Cases	Unaffordable Loans	
	Debt-to-Income Ratios	
	Front-End Ratio	Back-End Ratio
Average	40.77%	50.28%
Median	35.43%	49.78%

National Foreclosure Prevention

NCRC urges policymakers to adopt a foreclosure prevention bill that provides funding for foreclosure prevention counseling. In the spring of 2007, Senators Charles Schumer (NY) and Jack Reed (RI) introduced foreclosure prevention bills worthy of swift congressional passage.

Senator Schumer proposed that Congress appropriate $300 million to provide funding through HUD to nonprofit counseling agencies to engage in foreclosure prevention counseling. A foreclosure can impose societal costs of $80,000 in contrast to foreclosure prevention counseling, which costs about $1,000 per assisted borrower (Joint Economic Committee 2007). The senator's approach is cost effective and promises to prevent financial and emotional stress inflicted upon families losing their homes.

Senator Reed introduced a similar bill, S. 1386—the Homeownership Protection and Enforcement (HOPE) Act—that would provide $610 million for nonprofit counseling agencies and state agencies to provide forbearance and loan modification services to distressed borrowers. Servicers (entities that handle loan payments on behalf of the companies owning the loans) are required to make reasonable loan mitigation efforts before foreclosing on loans.

Comprehensive Antipredatory Lending Legislation

Since our analysis revealed a disproportionate amount of high-cost lending targeted to vulnerable borrowers and communities, Congress must respond by enacting comprehensive antipredatory lending legislation along the lines of bills introduced by Representatives Watt, Miller, and Frank and Senator Schumer. Comprehensive and strong antipredatory lending legislation would eliminate the profitability of exploitative practices by making them illegal. It could also reduce the amount of price discrimination, since fee packing and other abusive practices would be prohibited. A comprehensive antipredatory law would also strengthen CRA if regulatory agencies severely penalized lenders through failing CRA ratings when the lenders violate antipredatory law.

Senator Schumer has recently introduced S. 1299, or the Borrower's Protection Act of 2007, that would require lenders to assess a borrower's ability to pay a loan at the maximum possible rate during the first seven years of the loan. This procedure eliminates the dangerous practice of qualifying a borrower based on a low "teaser" rate in place during the first two or three years of the loan. The bill would also prohibit steering or price discrimination by making it illegal, based on the loan terms for which borrowers qualify, for lenders to refer borrowers to loans that are not reasonably advantageous for them.

Fair Lending Enforcement Must Be Increased

In 2005, FRB stated that it referred about 200 lending institutions to their primary federal regulatory agency for further investigations based on the FRB's identification of significant pricing disparities in HMDA data (Avery, Canner, and Cook 2005). An industry publication subsequently quoted an FRB official as stating that these lenders accounted for almost 50 percent of the HMDA-reportable loans issued in 2004 (*Inside Regulatory Strategies* 2005). In 2006, FRB referred a larger number of lenders, 270, to their primary regulatory agency for further investigations (Adler 2006).

After the initial excitement, the public has not heard about the outcomes of FRB referrals. Not a single case of discrimination or civil rights violations has arisen from the FRB referrals. Given the large share of lending represented by the financial institutions under investigation, the public should receive an update on the status of these fair lending investigations from all the regulatory agencies. In addition, agencies should annually report to Congress how many fair lending investigations they conducted, the types of fair lending investigations, and the outcomes of these investigations. Since the pricing disparities remain stubborn and persistent, fair lending investigations and enforcement must be intensified, yet the public has received little word regarding the actions of regulatory agencies.

Enhance the Quality of HMDA Data

NCRC believes that Congress and the FRB (which implements the HMDA regulations) must enhance HMDA data so that regular and comprehensive studies can scrutinize fairness in lending. Specifically, are minorities, the elderly, women, and LMI borrowers and communities able to receive loans that are fairly priced? More information on HMDA data is critical to explore the intersection of price, race, gender, and income.

The first area in which HMDA data must be enhanced is pricing information for all loans, not just high-cost loans. The interest rate movements in 2005 demonstrate the confusion associated with classifying the loans that currently have price information reported. Economists as well as the general public do not know whether to call the loans with price reporting "subprime," "high-cost," or some other name. If price was reported for all loans, the classification problems would be lessened. All stakeholders could review the number and percentages of loans in all the price spread categories. The most significant areas of pricing disparities could be identified with more precision.

HMDA data must contain credit scores. For each HMDA reportable loan, a financial institution must indicate whether it used a credit score system and if the system was its own or one of the widely used systems such as FICO (a new data field in HMDA could contain three to five categories with the names of widely used systems). HMDA data also would contain one more field indicating the quintile of risk in which the credit score system placed the borrower.

Another option is to attach credit score information in the form of quintiles to each census tract in the nation. That way, enhanced analyses can be done on a census tract level to see if pricing disparities still remain after controlling for creditworthiness. This was the approach adopted in NCRC's "Broken Credit System" and in studies conducted by FRB economists. Finally, HMDA data must contain information on other key underwriting variables, including the loan-to-value and debt-to-income ratios. Finally, Senator Reed's bill, S. 1386, would create a database on foreclosures and delinquencies that would be linked with HMDA. This important data enhancement would help policymakers understand which loan terms and conditions (such as loan-to-value ratios and fixed or ARM) are more likely to be associated with delinquencies and foreclosures.

Federal Reserve Board Must Step Up Antidiscrimination and Fair Lending Oversight

The Government Accountability Office (GAO) concluded that the FRB has the authority to conduct fair lending reviews of affiliates of bank holding companies. The FRB at first insisted that it lacked this authority but now examines affiliates (GAO 1999). The FRB should clarify how and to what extent it is examining affiliates because comprehensive antidiscrimination examinations of all parts of bank holding companies are critical. Most of the major banks have acquired large subprime lenders that are then considered affiliates. A pressing question is the extent to which the subprime affiliates refer creditworthy customers to the prime parts of the bank so that the customers receive loans at prevailing rates instead of higher subprime rates. Or does the subprime affiliate steer creditworthy borrowers to high-cost loans? These questions remain largely unanswered. Consequently, we do not know the extent of steering by subprime affiliates and/or their parent banks.

Apply CRA to Minority Neighborhoods and All Geographical Areas Lenders Serve

In order to increase prime lending for minority borrowers and reduce lending disparities, CRA examinations must evaluate the banks' records of lending to minority borrowers and neighborhoods as well as scrutinize banks' performance in reaching LMI borrowers and neighborhoods. If CRA examinations covered minority neighborhoods, pricing disparities in these neighborhoods would be reduced. The FRB, in its review of 2004 HMDA data, found that bank lending exhibited fewer disparities in geographical areas covered by their CRA examinations than in areas not covered by them (Avery, Canner, and Cook 2005). CRA's mandate of affirmatively meeting credit needs is currently incomplete because it is now applied only to LMI neighborhoods, not to minority communities.

CRA must also be strengthened so that depository institutions undergo CRA examinations in all geographical areas in which they make a significant number of loans. Currently, CRA examinations assess lending primarily in geographical areas in which banks have their branches. But the overlap between branching and lending is eroding with each passing year as lending via brokers and correspondents continues to increase. NCRC endorses HR 1289, or the CRA Modernization Act of 2007. HR 1289 mandates that banks undergo CRA examinations in geographical areas in which their market share of loans exceeds one-half of one percent in addition to areas in which their branches are located.

CRA Must Be Expanded to Nonbank Lending Institutions

Large credit unions and independent mortgage companies do not abide by CRA requirements. NCRC and GAO research concludes that large credit unions lag CRA-covered banks in their lending and service to minorities and LMI borrowers and communities (NCRC 2005; GAO 2006). Unlike their counterparts, credit unions in Massachusetts are covered by a state CRA law. NCRC has also found that CRA-covered credit unions in Massachusetts issue a higher percentage of their loans to LMI and minority borrowers and communities than do credit unions not covered by CRA. Therefore, NCRC believes that applying CRA to both large credit unions and independent mortgage companies will increase their market-rate lending to LMI and minority borrowers.

CRA Examinations Must Scrutinize Subprime Lending More Rigorously

Currently, CRA examinations do not adequately assess the CRA performance of subprime lenders. For example, the CRA examination of the subprime lender Superior Bank, FSB, called its lending innovative and flexible before that thrift's spectacular collapse (Office of Thrift Supervision 1999). Previous NCRC comment letters to the regulators have documented cursory fair lending reviews for the great majority of banks and thrifts involved in subprime lending (NCRC 2004). If CRA examinations continue to mechanistically consider subprime lending, subprime lenders will earn good ratings, since they usually offer a larger portion of their loans to LMI borrowers and communities than do prime lenders.

Regulatory agencies have amended CRA to penalize banks if their lending violates antipredatory law. NCRC has not seen rigorous action to implement this amended regulation. Fair lending reviews that accompany CRA examinations do not usually scrutinize subprime lending for compliance with antipredatory law, for possible pricing discrimination, or for whether abusive loans are exceeding borrower ability to repay. All CRA examinations of subprime lenders must be accompanied by a comprehensive fair lending and antipredatory lending audit. In addition, CRA examinations must ensure that prime lenders are not financing predatory lending through their secondary market activity or servicing abusive loans.

GSEs Must Abide by Antipredatory Safeguards

The government-sponsored enterprises (GSEs), including Fannie Mae, Freddie Mac, and the Federal Home Loan Banks, purchase more than half of the home loans made annually in this country. It is vitally important, therefore, that the GSEs have adopted adequate protections against purchasing predatory loans. Fannie Mae and Freddie Mac have voluntarily adopted significant protections such as purchasing no loans with fees exceeding 5 percent of the loan amount, no loans involving price discrimination or steering, no loans with prepayment penalties beyond three years, and no loans with mandatory arbitration. HUD has ruled that Fannie Mae and Freddie Mac will not receive credit toward their Affordable Housing Goals for any loans that contain certain abusive features.

HUD's ruling is an important first step, but it needs to be enhanced. HUD's ruling, for example, does not include disqualification from goals consideration of loans with mandatory arbitration. The Federal Housing Finance Board, as the regulator for the Federal Home Loan Banks, has not formally applied protections against abusive loans to the Home Loan Banks. Congress has an opportunity to further bolster the antipredatory protections applied to GSE loan-purchasing activity as Congress considers GSE regulatory reform.

Notes

1. Disparities discussed here reflect a number of factors, including income, wealth, credit rating, and many others. Discrimination, of course, remains a significant factor. Several studies discussed in this chapter have found that even controlling on credit-related factors, disparities persist. Disparities do not necessarily reveal levels of discrimination in the marketplace, but they do reveal the presence of ongoing barriers associated with socioeconomic factors.

2. A nontraditional loan is a loan that does not have a standard, fixed interest rate and/or does not have a traditional thirty-year term. An example of a nontraditional loan is an interest-only loan in which the borrower only has to make interest payments during a specified time period of the loan. An option ARM loan features a number of payment options; under one option, the borrower does not even have to pay the monthly interest that is due. A substantial number of subprime loans are nontraditional loans, but so are a significant number of prime loans. Option ARM loans, for example, are almost always prime loans.

3. "Fannie Mae Vows More Minority Lending," *Washington Post,* 16 March 2000, E01.

See also, Freddie Mac Web page, www.freddiemac.com/corporate/reports/moseley/chap5.
htm.
   4. HSBC North America provides refinance loans for CRF and supports counseling.
Other sponsors include Select Portfolio Servicing, Inc., Ford Foundation, Freddie Mac, Fannie
Mae Foundation, Fannie Mae, JPMorgan Chase Foundation, and Heron Foundation.

References

Adler, Joe. 2006. "Big Increase in Lenders with Suspect HMDA Data." *American Banker,*
   11 September.
Aizcorbe, Ana M., Arthur B. Kennickell, and Kevin B. Moore. 2003. "Recent Changes in
   U.S. Family Finances: Evidence from the 1998 and 2001 Survey of Consumer Finances."
   Federal Reserve Bulletin, January.
Avery, Robert B., Kenneth P. Brevoot, and Glenn B. Canner. 2006. "Higher-Priced Home
   Lending and the 2005 HMDA Data." *Federal Reserve Bulletin,* September.
Avery, Robert B., Glenn B. Canner, and Robert E. Cook. 2005. "New Information Reported
   under HMDA and Its Application in Fair Lending Enforcement." *Federal Reserve Bul-
   letin,* Summer. www.federalreserve.gov/pubs/bulletin/2005/05summerbulletin.htm.
   (Accessed 7 July 2007.)
Bucks, Brian K., Arthur B. Kennickell, and Kevin B. Moore. 2006. "Recent Changes in U.S.
   Family Finances: Evidence from the 2001 and 2004 Survey of Consumer Finances."
   Federal Reserve Bulletin, March.
Calem, Paul S., Kevin Gillen, and Susan Wachter. 2002. "The Neighborhood Distribution
   of Subprime Mortgage Lending." October 30.
Calem, Paul S., Jonathan E. Hershaff, and Susan M. Wachter. 2004. "Neighborhood Pat-
   terns of Subprime Lending: Evidence from Disparate Cities." *Fannie Mae Foundation's
   Housing Policy Debate* 15 (3): 603–622.
Center for Responsible Lending. 2006. *Unfair Lending: The Effect of Race and Ethnicity
   on the Price of Subprime Mortgages.* www.responsiblelending.org/issues/mortgage/re-
   search/page.jsp?itemID=29371010. (Accessed 30 December 2007.)
Courchane, Marsha J., Brian J. Surette, and Peter M. Zorn. 2002. *Subprime Borrowers:
   Mortgage Transitions and Outcomes,* prepared for Credit Research Center, Subprime
   Lending Symposium in McLean, VA, September.
Federal Reserve Board, 2007, "Federal Regulators Encourage Institutions to Work with
   Mortgage Borrowers Who Are Unable to Make Their Payments." Joint press release
   of the Board of Governors of the Federal Reserve System, Federal Deposit Insurance
   Corporation, National Credit Union Administration, Office of the Comptroller of the
   Currency, and Office of Thrift Supervision, 17 April. www.federalreserve.gov/Board-
   Docs/Press/bcreg/2007/20070417/default.htm. (Accessed 30 December 2007.)
Government Accountability Office (GAO). 1999. *Large Bank Mergers: Fair Lending Review
   Could Be Enhanced with Better Coordination.* GAO/GGD-00–16.
———. 2006. *Credit Unions: Greater Transparency Needed on Who Credit Unions Serve
   and on Senior Executive Compensation Arrangements.* GAO.
Immergluck, Dan, and Marti Wiles. 1999. *Two Steps Back: The Dual Mortgage Market,
   Predatory Lending, and the Undoing of Community Development.* Chicago: Woodstock
   Institute.
Joint Economic Committee. 2007. *Sheltering Neighborhoods from the Subprime Foreclosure
   Storm.* 11 April. http://jec.senate.gov/Documents/Reports/subprime11apr2007revised.
   pdf. (Accessed 5 February 2008.)
NCRC. 2003. "Broken Credit System: Discrimination and Unequal Access to Affordable
   Loans by Race and Age." Washington, DC: NCRC.

————. 2004. Comment letter to federal banking agencies on joint CRA proposal, 2 April Washington, DC: NCRC (letter available on request from NCRC).

————. 2005. "Credit Unions: True to Their Mission?" Washington, DC: NCRC.

NCRC and the Woodstock Institute. 2006. "Asset Preservation: Trends and Interventions in Asset Stripping Services and Products." Chicago: Woodstock Institute/NCRC.

————. 2006. Homeownership and Wealth Building Impeded: Continuing Lending Disparities for Minorities and Emerging Obstacles for Middle-Income and Female Borrowers of All Races. Washington, DC: NCRC.

Office of Thrift Supervision. 1999. Central Region's CRA Evaluation of Superior Bank, FSB, Docket # 08566, September. Available via http://www.ots.treas.gov, go to the CRA search engine http://www.ots.treas.gov/crasql/cra-search-form.cfm?catNumber=69&fir stview=1 and select "inactive" for the status of the institution being searched. (Accessed 5 February 2008.)

"Pressure on Lenders to Explain Disparities." *Inside Regulatory Strategies.* 2005. 14 November: 2.

9

The Assets Framework

Moving Toward Transformative Transactions

HANNAH THOMAS

Community Development Financial Institutions (CDFIs) are community-based organizations that provide credit for communities not served by banks or credit unions. CDFIs are diverse in products and mission (Benjamin, Rubin, and Zielenbach 2004). Many offer transforming services—in addition to credit—such as regional business strategies, workforce training, business counseling, and homeownership and financial education. In a tighter funding environment, many CDFIs have been shifting their focus from communities to lines of business where they can break even. This may mean providing credit at the expense of transformational services. This potential shift raises questions about the value CDFI credit brings to a community and whether CDFIs need to refocus their mission and program design.

This chapter explores the value a CDFI can bring to a community through a case study of Coastal Enterprises, Inc. (CEI), a CDFI in Maine (for more information, see "About CEI" at "About CEI." www.ceimaine.org/content/section/3/40/). Recognized as one of the country's leading CDFIs, CEI approaches its work from a holistic perspective, recognizing that financing alone cannot develop a community's wealth. Two projects, the Progressive Alliance for Careers and Training (PACT) and the Working Waterfronts Program, offer examples of CEI's work in this arena. Important in this discussion are the underlying theoretical frameworks that inform community development finance. I propose that the market failure framework, traditionally the theory articulated for CDFI's work, is insufficient to account for the transformational activities of CEI. The assets framework incorporated into CDFI work in limited ways, proposes that holding wealth, whether financial or more intangible such as education or networks, provides a net benefit for individuals and communities. I develop an assets framework for understanding the value of a CDFI and propose the framework as a way to reposition how CDFIs work in communities.

Community Development Finance

CDFIs are community-based organizations that provide access to credit for a variety of needs in communities. The limited or nonexistent access to credit for many communities resulted from banks not serving these communities, historically a result of federal policy (Squires 2003).[1] CDFI predecessors include the minority banks of the 1880s and the credit unions of the 1930s (Benjamin, Rubin, and Zielenbach 2004). However, many of the earlier modern-era CDFIs emerged from community development corporations established in the 1960s. These organizations began to see the potential in leveraging capital for investment in communities to stimulate small business creation and homeownership. Implicit for these organizations was a strategy of poverty alleviation through building a community's assets, though the language of assets was not articulated at that point. During the 1990s, two events institutionalized and grew these organizations: retooling the Community Reinvestment Act (CRA) in 1991[2] and creation of the CDFI Fund in 1994, with an annual appropriation to provide grants and loans to support CDFIs. The Fund and the idea of a CDFI industry was promoted by President Clinton on the basis of the experiences of large CDFIs such as ShoreBank.[3] Seeing an opportunity, practitioners formed trade organizations such as the CDFI Coalition and Opportunity Finance Network, providing additional industry cohesion and branding (CDFI Coalition 2006). A third factor was unprecedented economic growth, which meant success for businesses that CDFIs financed. Raising capital to fund loans and investments was relatively easy (Benjamin, Rubin, and Zielenbach 2004), further stimulating growth.

Today, CDFIs offer diverse programs that address financial, human, and social capital community needs, including small business and microenterprise loan funds and equity investments; mortgages and other consumer banking services; housing development financing; and technical assistance and educational programs that enable customers to successfully use CDFI credit. There are an estimated 800–1,000 CDFIs operating today (CDFI Data Project 2005). Data collected for 496 CDFIs (about 50 percent of total estimated CDFIs) indicated that CDFIs held $20.78 billion in assets and underwrote $4.3 billion in loans and investments in FY2005. This accounted for the financing of 9,074 businesses, creating or maintaining 39,151 jobs, the construction or renovation of 55,242 units of affordable housing, and support for 613 community facilities in economically disadvantaged areas.

CDFIs provide community development services beyond access to capital. For example, a small business loan officer may have a business development counselor work with the potential borrower to develop a business plan. Some organizations also provide other forms of technical assistance, such as environmental or employment reviews, or suggest links to regional programs in workforce development.[4] Indeed, CDFI Fund data from FY2001 CDFI activities for 348 CDFIs responding to the CDFI survey showed that 50 percent of CDFIs provided consumer financial education, 45 percent provided homebuyer education, 41 percent provided business counseling and training, and 32 percent provided other counseling and training.

Figure 9.1   **Litvak and Daniels's Six Kinds of Market Failures**

1. The structure of financial markets doesn't allow effective risk pooling for otherwise attractive investment opportunities.
2. The transaction costs of certain investments may be so high that only very advantageous investment can occur.
3. The costs of acquiring information about certain sectors is too high given the expected rate of return.
4. Monopolistic markets may choose to include only the most financially advantageous trades.
5. Prejudice exists against certain populations.
6. Governmental interventions may have adverse effects of skewing funds away from worthy projects.

Source: Abstracted from Daniels and Litvak (1979).

Over 85,600 clients received group-based training, and another 95,500 received one-on-one counseling.

Since 2000, CDFIs have entered a tougher funding environment with reduced subsidies available for transformational activities such as small business counseling and community development programs.[5] As federal funding is cut, there is a question of how CDFIs can remain faithful to their mission or the elements of their business that distinguish them from a bank. Further, transformational CDFI credit offers a virtuous cycle whereby the CDFI's transformational services decrease the risk of credit provided by the CDFI—that is, the likelihood of a loan going into default is ideally reduced with transforming services such as business counseling. With loss of these transformational services, CDFI's loan portfolios could be at higher risk.

CDFI Theory

The theoretical framework for CDFIs was originally articulated by Daniels and Litvak (1979): the idea of market failure in private markets for capital or credit (see Figure 9.1). Levere, Schweke, and Woo (2006) modified this framework, offering a simpler market-failure–based typology focusing on two barriers in accessing capital: (1) misallocation: despite competitive rates of return, capital is not flowing to certain areas; (2) social/public benefits: although the capital market is operating efficiently, private yield is not high enough to justify the risk, since externalities are not excluded.

CDFIs adopted the market-failure framework, seeing it as logical in explaining their work. The market-failure framework is primarily transaction based. The goal is ensuring individuals have the opportunity to obtain credit and, by default, that access is equitably distributed. Not surprisingly, the CRA[6] embodies the principals of the market-failure framework as a piece of legislation designed to ensure fair and equal access to credit for all communities and individuals. Logically, success criteria of transaction-based community finance are defined as equal distribution in access to credit both spatially and racially. An individual's location and demographics are the criteria for the loan, and the individual is the level of measurement.

There is, however, an inherent tension between the goal of CDFIs to provide access to credit and the often unstated mission of CDFIs to provide community development, particularly alleviating poverty (Dymski 2005), a mission that does not fit well in the market-failure framework. Most of the literature has focused on the credit provided by, or transactional elements of, CDFIs, with less focus and understanding on the poverty alleviating, or transformational elements, of CDFIs (Stevens 2006). The market-failure framework may be missing an important element.

Transformational Assets

The assets framework, articulated originally by Michael Sherraden (1991), argued that we should both look at and attempt to address poverty from a wealth- or assets-based perspective, including (1) financial assets—the money available to a family, whether in the form of savings, stocks or other investments, or physical assets such as a house; (2) human capital—knowledge and skills both formal and informal; (3) social capital—social networks both among community members and organizations and between different communities. Assets are not seen as existing in isolation from income but instead complement and add to flows and holding pools of wealth.

A key principle is that holding assets produces an "asset effect" of increased individual and community empowerment (Bynner and Paxton 2001; Shapiro and Wolff 2001; Sherraden 1991), or "transformation." Policy implications from the asset framework include individual development accounts (IDAs) and children's savings accounts.[7] Most research and policy proposals have focused on personal/individual assets or microlevel assets. A small but influential group has focused on community-level assets-based development. Their intent is to look at community assets rather than community deficits. This body of work focuses less on the individual transformation than on the community transformation. Building on this track, recent academic work from the United Kingdom has incorporated public and common assets (Paxton, White, and Maxwell 2006) into the discussion. Public assets are those held by government. Common assets are those held for society and humanity (Bollier 2006).

CDFIs have applied the assets framework to their work in limited ways, such as by offering IDAs and enabling homeownership, with some individual CDFIs measuring and promoting other forms of asset ownership, such as employee stock ownership, and the Sustainable Jobs Fund. Through the case study of CEI, I argue that the real value of the assets framework is in refocusing CDFI missions, program design, and measurement around individual and community transformation to build not only financial assets but also human and social forms of assets.

Coastal Enterprises, Inc.: A History and Profile

Formed in 1977, CEI has always taken a transformative approach to community development finance. The organization's first program targeted the development of the aquaculture sector in Maine, providing access to credit along with a range of technical assistance for aquaculture management (human capital). In 2008, CEI has 85 staff and $371 million of assets under management (http://www.ceimaine. org/content/section/3/40/). Funding is mostly from loan funds, federal and state grants and investments, individual investors, and earned revenue.

CEI's products include small business and microenterprise loans; small business venture capital investments; new-market tax credit financing;[8] affordable housing loans and development; workforce development linked with small business financial assistance; small business technical assistance in developing business plans; sector programs for fishermen, farmers, small lot foresters, childcare providers, and community facilities; IDAs; housing counseling and homeownership education; a lease–purchase program; and policy development related to organizational programs as well as structural issues affecting the organization's clients.

The next two sections explore two CEI projects, looking at the range of assets developed where credit was the starting point for, or a crucial piece in, the project.

Progressive Alliance for Careers and Training

Between 2002 and 2004, CEI, using Federal Department of Labor earmark funds, led a project, PACT, to form a collaborative partnership with economic development, workforce development, and educational and small business organizations to strategically develop assets for a failing rural area: Maine's Western Mountains. In a single county in this area, there were fifty major layoffs between 1995 and 1999 in response to relocations and closing of manufacturing businesses due to global competition (Dickstein and Thomas 2006). PACT goals were to increase human, social, and financial assets that the region could draw on by training the workforce, financing businesses, and providing assistance with business strategies, and developing new alliances and working relationships (see Figure 9.2).

PACT developed a collaborative board that included key economic and workforce development agency staff (such as career centers and workforce investment boards), educational organization staff (such as community colleges), and business leaders who would guide the project over a two-year period, deciding priority areas for investment and allocating funds to specific projects (see Figure 9.3). The board reviewed the region's potential growth areas and identified health care, wood-product manufacturing, and information technology as sectors that could be focal points for investment and growth and that would offer career ladders and employment opportunities. These three sectors were represented on the board and in subcommittees.

The project targeted human capital development of incumbent and dislocated

Figure 9.2 **PACT Project Goals**

- Train and place dislocated workers in jobs that pay a livable wage, provide access to health insurance, and offer opportunities for advancement (human capital development)
- Improve the skills of incumbent workers and production practices of businesses at risk in order to minimize the likelihood of future layoffs and plant closures (human and indirect financial capital development).
- Build and formalize economic and workforce development partnerships (bridging social capital development).

Figure 9.3 **PACT Board Members**

- Coastal Enterprises, Inc.
- Augusta Career Center
- Central and Western Maine Local Workforce Investment Board
- Kennebec Valley Community College
- Medical Care Development (local business)
- Maine Manufacturing (trade Association)
- Care and Comfort (local business)
- Women Work and Community
- Kennebec Valley Council of Governments
- Common Sense Computing (local business)
- Maine Department of Economic Development

workers. Concurrently, businesses receiving incumbent worker training were provided with technical assistance to prepare for future credit investments. Although businesses applied for loans, only one company received financing. This company, a wood-product manufacturer, stayed in business long enough for an angel investor with expertise in financing and marketing to invest in it. Furthermore, one staff member left the company to start up a complementary manufacturing business.

While credit was available, CEI, board members, and loan staff felt most companies needed to build human capital assets, so they focused on firm-specific training. Staff and business owners benefited from training received. For workers, this translated into financial assets with 49 percent of incumbent workers receiving a wage increase and additional employees receiving improved benefits packages. Additionally, seventy-one new jobs were created in participating companies. Notably, business owners and staff indicated a more empowered and motivated staff body. Postproject interviews revealed these benefits spilled over into staff's personal lives. For example, one incumbent worker described increasing self-confidence, which led him to return to school after the training. In the case of the Maine General Rehabilitation and Nursing at Glenridge, a peer mentor system led to increased wages and developed employees' soft skills, which employees reported being transferable for their personal home lives (Dickstein and Thomas 2006) (see Figure 9.4).

At the community and regional levels, the PACT board established strong relationships, building social capital between critical organizations based in the potential

Figure 9.4   **Building Human Capital in the Nursing Profession**

There were two main strategies to develop workforce career opportunities in the nursing sector: (1) development of a nursing training program; (2) a culture change program in nursing homes. The nursing training program was an eighteen-month program leading to licensed practitioner nurse certification at the local university. Sixteen students graduated, and of these, 60 percent, or ten graduates, were making a livable wage by the end of the project. Local nursing homes participated in a project to alter the social capital and work structure within the institutions with the goal of improving nursing retention rates. The strategy was considered a massive success leading to national recognition for the effectiveness of change.

for financial assets—grants and loans awarded through the project. Companies involved in the trainings were often past recipients of CEI loans. While the board did not continue to meet after the end of the project, the local Workforce Investment Board pulled members of the PACT board into its committees and peripheral structure. In Somerset County, members of the PACT board developed a county-level taskforce to deal with economic and workforce development. In 2006, some members of the PACT board, working together in new regions of Maine, successfully secured a grant for the Maine Marine Trade Association, and a second PACT proposal is awaiting funding to build on work accomplished.

PACT developed capital or assets at different levels: human capital for individual employees of targeted industries as well as more broadly for institutions, especially businesses in the region. Social capital was developed among the organizations that worked collaboratively as well as between these organizations and the businesses and employees who they worked in ongoing partnerships. Groups drew on this social capital after the project's end to develop proposals for further funding, thus leveraging access to other social networks. It is unclear whether PACT businesses developed financial assets, but some businesses did survive longer than anticipated, suggesting at least maintenance of financial assets (Dickstein and Thomas 2004). Development of human and social capital or assets may be the precursor to the future development of financial assets. Financial assets prior to the grant period and the promise of grants and loans were important stimulators of both social and human capital development.

This example points to the role a CDFI can play in developing a combination of different assets. CEI's institutional capacity in developing human and social capital was important.

Working Waterfronts

CEI's fisheries program lends to fishermen. However, access to working waterfronts was becoming a problem. CEI contracted with the Maine State Planning Office to survey the state of working waterfronts. Only 25 miles of working waterfront remained as a result of the privatization of Maine's coast (CEI 2004). This set the stage for the development of CEI's loan fund targeted at preserving working waterfronts. The first project was in conjunction with the York Land Trust to preserve a working dock in York, a coastal community in Southern Maine.

Large prices associated with coastal property present a challenge in preserving working waterfronts. York was no exception. When the Sewall's Bridge Dock originally came on the market in 2002, the community was concerned it would become another condominium development, meaning loss of one of the last remaining access points to the York River for fishermen. Two lobstermen attempted to purchase the property with no success. However, when it came back on the market in 2003, they were determined to find a way to save the dock (Lyman 2007).

Together, CEI, the York Land Trust, and the two local fishermen devised a plan by which the development rights to the land and the actual land costs were bifurcated. CEI provided financing to the York Land Trust, combined with donations from community foundations for the purchase of development rights. The fishermen obtained financing from a local credit union to pay for the remaining portion of the land (Lyman 2007). This innovative financing allowed the preservation of the waterfront use.

Clearly, this deal developed the personal financial assets of the two fishermen involved. But there was a far larger asset created for the community. Fishermen now had permanent access to the York River. Access to the waterfront, crucial for fishermen's ability to work, is a community asset, where the community is defined as local fishermen. The York Land Trust also saw value for the broader community in ensuring there was ongoing access to the waterfront and support for Maine's fishing industry, considered vital to the state. Public access to the river has been maintained, providing another form of community asset, but with a larger community, namely the town of York. The asset building for both the fishermen and York are a form of common asset building (Paxton, White, and Maxwell 2006).

In addition, several other forms of assets were developed. Bridging social capital was created between York Land Trust, the fishermen, and CEI, three groups that had not worked in combination before. Human capital was developed in York Land Trust, CEI, and several community foundations as they learned a new method of financing innovative asset-preservation deals. Important institutional bonds were created. As a result of this innovation, the Working Waterfront Coalition requested money from the state legislature to fund a Working Waterfront Access Pilot Program. This loan fund, currently run by CEI, is in its initial stages, having made loans to eleven groups in the preservation of working waterfronts. Three of these have been cooperative models (Cowperthwaite 2007).

Common Themes

What do these examples from CEI tell us? Both programs highlight how credit can be more than an opportunity or transaction. Credit transforms a community, building both individual and community assets. Both programs show the importance of links among forms of capital or assets. If any one of the assets or capital had been developed or maintained in isolation, impact would have been less. For example, PACT's strength was in developing human, social, and to some degree financial assets for businesses and agencies. Similarly, without recognizing and preserving the community asset inherent in working waterfront access, the partnership that enabled affordable financing of the waterfront for the two fishermen would not have taken place.

These links force us to think about the different roles that various assets play. Social capital has a related but functionally different role in transforming a community from that of financial assets. By articulating the different roles of and links among assets involved in developing any one community or individual, we can illuminate new ways to approach old problems.

Partnerships, a form of social capital, were crucial in both vignettes. For PACT, one of the key reasons for the project was to build partnerships between economic and workforce development agencies to leverage greater impact. The York fishermen partnered with the local Land Trust and CEI to preserve an important asset for fishermen and for the local community. Partnerships offer a way to make credit transformational and to build and preserve assets using financial resources more efficiently, while developing forms of social capital that transcend a specific project. These partnerships can and should be further leveraged by tapping into resources for community self-sufficiency. CDFIs can be part of this effort and will benefit as businesses and consumers become positioned to take out loans, thereby building CDFIs' transactional business model.

The partnership theme develops into a common theme of leveraging impact to a larger scale. In PACT, social capital developed in the Western Mountains region continued to develop after the project. Likewise with the York waterfront project: its success leveraged into a larger statewide initiative resulting in a Working Waterfront Loan Fund funded by the state and managed by CEI (Zezima 2007).

To assess the outcomes of these projects, CEI went beyond just counting the transaction. Knowing that the loan was made to the York fishermen does not allow measurement of the other processes and changes that occurred as a result. So a case study was conducted to capture the depth of the project (Lyman 2007). Similarly, in the PACT project, knowing the numbers of people employed and the numbers of loans made did not capture the rich transformations that took place in the social fabric of the region. An in-depth internal process evaluation took place throughout the duration of the project (Dickstein and Thomas 2006).

Where Next?

There are some key points where this case study and framework development have potential in helping the CDFI industry in the future.

1. *Program Design.* The asset-building framework offers a way to develop more holistic programming, asking questions about what credit is doing

in a community. The asset-based theory articulates areas of asset development that can benefit communities, offering a linking mechanism to bring departments within organizations, or possibly from different organizations, together across sector and specialty silos to create innovative partnerships.

2. *Program Financing.* In a recent speech at a Federal Reserve Board community affairs conference in Washington, D.C., Chairman Ben Bernanke suggested that future changes to the CRA should include incentives for banks to provide transformational services for loans made in low-income communities (Bernanke 2007). He was talking about technical assistance, such as housing counseling and small business counseling. If CRA moves in this direction, it could offer a legislative framework for CDFIs to work with banks, providing the transformational services to the banks for a fee.

3. *Measurement.* Former Federal Reserve Board Chairman Alan Greenspan and current chairman Bernanke have called for increased research in community development finance (Bernanke 2007). As noted, measurement based in the asset framework involves more in-depth data collection focusing on the qualitative, as well as quantitative, elements of credit. While federal funders expect ongoing outcomes measurement, there are limited resources available (Dickstein and Thomas 2006). Funders could build into grants and loans funding to allow more in-depth evaluation of CDFIs, enabling helpful program feedback and useful knowledge about the value of CDFIs to communities.

Notes

1. The Federal Housing Authority established racially restrictive lending policies guaranteeing that houses would be occupied by the same class and race (Squires 2003).

2. This provided a more stringent framework for banks to invest in communities. CDFIs offered a useful vehicle for banks' community investments and for creating partnerships in reinvesting.

3. The 1994 Reigle Community Development/Regulatory Improvement Act created the Fund.

4. CEI has established a workforce development agreement called ETAG, which requires businesses to provide work opportunities for low-income and welfare recipients. ShoreBank Enterprise Cascadia provides Brownfield loans whereby loan recipients get assistance in the technicalities of cleaning up their land.

5. From 2001 to 2005, Fund appropriations dropped from $118 million to $54 million per year.

6. CRA provides a framework for pushing banks to make loans in all communities discontinue redlining, whereby certain communities were excluded from bank lending.

7. IDAs are accounts in which a dollar saved by an eligible low-income person is matched. Children's savings accounts are an innovative policy in Britain, where each child born is provided with a pot of money that can be deposited into an account and matched by others. Low-income families receive double the initial grant with an additional top-up later in the child's life.

8. New Markets Tax Credits are tax credits for investments in low-income qualifying census tracts. See www.cdfifund.gov/impact_we_make/overview.asp.

References

Benjamin, L., J. S. Rubin, and S. Zielenbach. 2004. "Community Development Financial Institutions: Current Issues and Future Prospects." *Journal of Urban Affairs* 26 (2): 177–195.

Bernanke, B. 2007. "The Community Reinvestment Act: Its Evolution and New Challenges." Speech, Federal Reserve Board of Governors Community Affairs Conference. Washington, DC.

Bollier, D. 2006. "Using Stakeholder Trusts to Reclaim Common Assets." In *The Citizen's Stake: Exploring the Future of Universal Asset Policies,* eds. W. Paxton, S. White, and D. Maxwell. Bristol, UK: Policy Press.

Bynner, J., and W. Paxton, eds. 2001. *The Asset Effect.* London: Institute for Public Policy Research.

CDFI Coalition. 2006. "About the CDFI Coalition." http://www.cdfi.org/cdfi-aboutus-1.asp. (Accessed 5 February 2008.)

CDFI Data Project. 2005. *Providing Capital, Building Communities, Creating Impact.* Philadelphia, PA: Opportunity Finance Network.

CEI. 2004. "Tracking Commercial Fishing Access: A Survey of Harbormasters in 25 Maine Coastal Communities." Maine State Planning Office.

———. 2005. *Investing in People, Investing in Places: CEI Annual Report FY 2005.* Wiscasset, ME: CEI.

Daniels, B., and L. Litvak. 1979. "Innovations in Development Finance." In *Financing State and Local Economic Development,* ed. M. Barker. Durham, NC: Duke Press Policy Studies.

Dickstein, C., and H. Thomas. 2006. Measuring Impact in Practice: Reflections and Recommendations. Wiscasset, ME: CEI. http://www.ceimaine.org/images/stories/pdf/measurement.pdf. (Accessed 5 February 2008.)

Dymski, G. 2005. "'New Markets' or Old Constraints? Financing Community Development in the Post–War on Poverty Era." *National Economic Association Conference.* Philadelphia.

Levere, A., B. Schweke and B. Woo. 2006. "Development Finance and Regional Economic Development." Washington, DC: CFED.

Lyman, M. 2007. "An Assessment of the Mt. Agamenticus to the Sea Conservation Initiative October 2002–October 2006." Mt. Agamenticus to the Sea Coalition. http://www.mtatosea.org/MTA-evaluation.pdf.

Shapiro, T. 2004. *The Hidden Cost of Being African-American.* New York: Oxford University Press.

Shapiro, T., and E. Wolff, eds. 2001. *Assets for the Poor: The Benefits of Spreading Asset Ownership.* New York: Russell Sage Foundation.

Sherraden, M. 1991. *Assets and the Poor.* Armonk, NY: M.E. Sharpe.

Squires, G. 2003. "Introduction: The Rough Road to Reinvestment." In *Organizing Access to Capital: Advocacy and the Democratization of Financial Institutions,* ed. G. Squires. Philadelphia: Temple University Press.

Stevens, J. 2006. "Show Me the Money: Promises and Pitfalls of Asset Growth in Community Development Credit Unions and Loan Funds." Department of Urban Studies and Planning, Massachusetts Institute of Technology. Cambridge: MA.

10

Connecting Asset Building and Community Development

W$_{ILLIAM}$ S$_{CHWEKE}$

Assets create opportunity. Assets create mobility. Assets create economic security *and* community renewal. Asset-building strategies hold a key to diminishing poverty for millions of economically disadvantaged Americans. Assets contribute to financial security by providing a hedge against downward fluctuations in income, a fund for extraordinary expenses, savings for a child's college fund, and refuge during retirement.

Assets, like development and freedom in Nobel laureate Amartya Sen's framework, are both ends and means. Asset ownership through expanded savings, educational attainment, home ownership, and entrepreneurship are clear indicators of the level of development for individuals, families, communities, states, and the nation. Less recognized but perhaps even more important, savings and assets provide a platform, inspiration, and investment for economic progress.

More conscious, efficient, and equitable public policies would open up asset ownership to all. The goals of such policies would include (1) helping the working poor to achieve a more comfortable and stable socioeconomic position, (2) strengthening the middle class in a time of greater insecurity and economic turmoil, and (3) helping to transform communities caught in cycles of poverty, middle-class flight, high unemployment, and despair. This chapter makes the case for such policies by

1. Acquainting community and economic development professionals and policymakers with basic knowledge about asset-building research, programs, and policies.
2. Exposing asset experts and policymakers to fundamental community development and economic development strategies.
3. Demonstrating that not only are asset-building policies compatible with job creation and income growth, they are vital parts of the development dynamic.
4. Showing the substantial staying power, political virtues, and resonance of asset-building strategies in American culture.
5. Describing the roles that asset building and protection play in raising

143

economic mobility for the poor, strengthening the middle class, broadening the ownership of wealth, and renewing economically struggling communities.

At the start, the chapter defines assets, asserts why they matter, offers a snapshot of asset policy and history in America, and provides evidence for enlarged asset building and protection policy government. Then the prerequisites of upward mobility and the role of community development in economic renewal are discussed. The chapter explains the practice of community-based economic development and describes its connections to asset-building programs and policies. Finally, a federal and state agenda to broaden asset ownership and renew struggling communities is proposed.[1]

Assets Were a Springboard for Upward Mobility in Yesterday's America

Assets have always been a springboard for achieving the American Dream. Initially, the pivotal asset was land. Millions of immigrants to America, seeking sanctuary from oppression and a higher standard of living, came because land was available. Labor shortages made it easy to get a job at decent wages, while in the Old World, overpopulation and underproduction led to widespread joblessness, beggary, and hunger. America was young and filled with promise and opportunity, while the immigrants' countries of origin were old and undemocratic.

Jefferson's vision of a yeoman democracy is a historical example of asset building. In the Virginia Constitution of 1776, Jefferson set a property qualification for voting of owning twenty-five acres, stating that "every person of full age neither owning nor having owned 50 acres of land shall be entitled to an appropriation of 50 acres" (Boles and Gintis 1998, 361). Jefferson's proposal did not materialize, but other strategies to spur asset ownership were set in place. Examples include the Homestead Act, the GI Bill, the National Defense Education Act, the Morrill Act, and tax deductions and home mortgage secondary markets. Despite a strong belief in individualism and self-reliance, Americans have looked out for the unfortunate and protected assets from loss by creating social security, Medicare, and unemployment insurance.

The Benefits and Costs of Current Federal Assets Policy

For years, lawmakers at the federal level have enacted policies that encourage individuals to accumulate assets. Dozens of programs have helped millions of Americans plan for the future, buy a home, prepare for retirement, send their children to college, and weather unexpected financial storms. Measured conservatively, the federal government provides at least $367 billion to support savings and investments, retirement, homeownership, and small business. A good example is the home mortgage deduction. That's the good news.

Then there is the bad news. Federal assets policy has been an ad hoc enterprise that primarily benefits the affluent with substantial subsidies, principally through the tax code. "The poorest fifth of the population get, on average, $3 from these policies, while the wealthiest 1% enjoy, on average, $57,673. Households with incomes of $1 million or more receive an average benefit of $169,150" (Woo and Buchholz 2006, 7).

Assets holdings have become increasingly skewed toward the rich:

- The rate of asset poverty is about twice the rate of income poverty in the United States.
- The richest tenth of households own 83 percent of assets.
- The richest 1 percent owns 49 percent, while the bottom 80 percent own only 8 percent.
- In 2004, the median net worth of the bottom 25 percent was $13,300, compared to $328,500 for the 25 percent.
- The ratio of median net worth of whites to African Americans is 11 to 1.[2]

This is where new approaches to asset building enter the picture, holding promise as a way to reallocate ineffective and inequitable public subsidies that is productivity enhancing without increasing inequities between the haves, have-nots, and struggling middle class.

Why Do Assets Matter Today?

Since the time of Adam Smith, economists have recognized the important role that assets play in a capitalist economy. More recent scholarship[3] and community practice show that having even a small amount of assets—in the form of savings, home equity, business ownership, human capital—is critical to the well-being and future prospects of lower-income families. In a very real sense, it is assets that allow us to live in and for the future. Assets provide the reason to believe in a future, the confidence that we can shape it, the impetus to plan for it, and the investment to make it real. This is why Michael Sherraden calls assets "hope in concrete form." (1991).

Assets are as important for poor families as for the nonpoor. In fact, recent evaluations of asset-building programs are revealing the powerful effects of assets on low-income children, families, and neighborhoods.[4] These and similar studies show that with budget counseling and financial incentives, the poor can save. Furthermore, assets can

- Provide greater household stability.
- Create long-term thinking and planning.
- Lead to greater effort in maintaining assets.
- Lead to greater development of human capital.
- Provide a foundation for taking prudent risks.

- Increase personal efficacy and a sense of well-being.
- Increase social status and social "connectedness."
- Increase community involvement and civic participation.
- Enhance the well-being and life chances of offspring.

IDAs and the American Dream Demonstration

There is also a growing research literature on asset-based antipoverty strategies. The Down payments on the American Dream Policy Demonstration (ADD) was the first large-scale test of the efficacy of individual development accounts. IDAs are savings accounts that help low-income individuals save for the purchase of life-changing assets—a first home, a college degree, or capital to start a business. IDAs match accountholders' savings contributions toward approved needs and provide savers financial education.

The ADD's successful delivery of IDAs entailed a partnership between a wide range of community organizations and private financial institutions offering a few hundred accounts a year along with basic and asset-specific financial training. Over its six-year course, ADD created 2,364 accounts in fourteen sites, generated extensive documentation of their effects, and stimulated the development of a national movement.[5] ADD demonstrated that assets "change people's heads" by increasing the expectations, work, confidence, and economic engagement of accountholders and their families. Ninety-three percent of accountholders said they were more confident of the future, 84 percent more economically secure, 85 percent more in control of their lives, 85 percent more likely to buy a home, and 57 percent more likely to start a business.[6]

While the evaluation of ADD continues, much has been learned. Indeed, ADD has largely established the hypothesis that it began with: *that poor people can and will save if offered the right combination of incentives, access, and institutional supports.* Low-income people, regardless of race, age, gender, or education and whether employed, unemployed, or receiving welfare, can and will take advantage of the asset-building opportunity provided by IDAs. Neither income, gender, nor participation in the welfare system are good predictors of the likelihood of saving or the level of savings.

Confidence, Competence, Connections, and . . . Capital

In 1987, the Mott Foundation asked the Corporation for Enterprise Development (CFED) to identify the elements of effective economic opportunity strategies. After studying a wide variety of strategies across the nation—housing, business, organizing, training, employment, education—the researchers concluded that all successful initiatives built confidence, competence, and connections (Noftdurth and Dyer 1990; Okagaki 1988). The three C's have great relevance to today's asset-building and community renewal efforts.

Why are *confidence* and *competence* so important? The poor are often caught in a vicious cycle of low wages, little education, bad role models, and weak links to the wider mainstream economy. The savings process initiated through IDAs breaks the cycle and builds confidence step by step—by each expense avoided because it is merely "a want, not a need" and by each deposit rewarded through deposit slips and bank account statements.

After a few months during which savings grow and are matched, there is an unmistakable change in accountholders' self-esteem and self-confidence: even though achieving the asset goal is months or years away, *accountholders know that they can get there simply by continuing to do what they have been doing.* The money they have accumulated provides measurable evidence of their success in controlling their economic lives.

But IDA programs accomplish even more than that. Through basic financial education and asset-specific training, IDA programs provide an opportunity for accountholders to build critical knowledge—skills and practices ranging from savings and debt reduction to credit repair to preparing a budget and balancing a checkbook. IDA accountholders come to know themselves much better too. They become clearer on what they value, want, and need and on the behavior that corresponds to those goals.

Which brings us to *connections:* through IDAs, accountholders establish relationships with financial institutions and become accustomed to making deposits and transacting business. Classes introduce accountholders to bankers, financial planners, investment managers, real estate brokers, entrepreneurs, and counselors. Accountholders may visit home sales, employment fairs, and college expos. In a very concrete way, IDAs invite people to *live in the financial future,* to consider what they most want and need: a house, a business, or an education.

To the three C's we add a fourth: *capital.* IDAs mobilize the savings of working families and, in matching them, create a powerful, though modest, fund for self-investment. Capital anchors the other three C's and measures progress in simple numbers. Therefore, the *most* successful initiatives build confidence, competence, connections, *and* capital.

What Is Community Development? Economic Development?
Community Economic Development?

In shifting from asset building to community and economic development,[7] we begin with a few definitions. Community is "an organization of people in a physical setting with geographic, political, and social boundaries and discernable communication linkages" (Shaffer, Deller, and Marcouiller 2004, 317). *Community development* is less consistently used than assets or economic development. Sometimes it is used as a synonym for all economic development that is not business attraction. Other times it emphasizes housing, amenities, social services, literacy programs, leadership development, and so forth. Community development is also associated with *social capital*—the dynamic process of *community capacity building* that underpins economic development.

Economic development is the process by which a society increases its level of material and social well-being over time. In a developing economy, employment increases, incomes go up, the rate of productivity rises, and innovation occurs. Yet economic development is more than just growth: it also implies changes in technology, management strategies, products, and market-supportive institutions and rules. Economic development includes entrepreneurship, development of skilled labor power, building of modern infrastructure, creation of new financial intermediaries, and accumulation and channeling of savings.

The concept of *community economic development* adds another dimension: the creation and strengthening of economic organizations and capital controlled or owned by the residents of the area where these institutions are located. Community economic development broadly encompasses owner-occupied homes, savings, IDAs, housing development corporations, personal retirement accounts, community land trusts, industrial parks, incubators, banks, credit unions, businesses, cooperatives, and community development corporations (CDCs) and community development financial institutions (CDFIs).

According to Michael Kieschnick, a leading authority in the field, community economic development has four goals:

1. Stimulating self-sustaining processes of economic development.
2. Creating jobs at acceptable wages and with appropriate benefits for area residents.
3. Producing goods and services that meet social criteria (e.g., more affordable housing, farmers' markets, public goods, investments, and public services).
4. Establishing community influence over basic economic decisions such as hiring, investment, and location.[8]

The first goal is shared by other more conventional development strategies. The last three distinguish community economic development from tradition and are especially important for low-income and blue-collar communities.[9] *This is where we see synergies between community-based development strategies and asset-building programs.*

How Does Entrepreneurship Fit Into the Economic Development Process?

Development is a profoundly human process. People who combine resources—natural, capital, and technological—in new ways and to new ends are the dynamic elements in the economic equation. These individuals are usually called entrepreneurs. The classic definition of an entrepreneur is someone who creates value in an economy "by moving resources out of areas of low productivity and into areas of higher productivity and greater yield."[10] Hence, entrepreneurship is one of the major drivers of the structural changes, generating the volatility, benefits, and hardships that characterize capitalism. Economist Joseph Schumpeter called these the "gales of creative destruction." (1942). The popular image of the entrepreneur is that of a white, male engineer in his midthirties, starting a high-tech business backed by venture capital. Yet, this is an accurate picture of only *some* of the hundreds of thousands of Americans who start a business each year, or, more importantly, of those who could start a business.

Despite popular wisdom, most entrepreneurs are made, not born. The extent of "made" entrepreneurs depends on how they are perceived by society—and by themselves—as potential creators of wealth. It equally depends on how much encouragement, education, and access to capital would-be entrepreneurs receive to hone their talents. There is evidence, however, that the entrepreneur who wants to develop new products and services and grow a business exhibits different psychological aptitudes and work styles than the business owner who wants to stay small and balance his or her home and working lives.[11]

Numerous studies have identified the same essential factors of a "climate" conducive to entrepreneurship: venture capital access, bank capital reluctance, experienced entrepreneurs in the area, technically skilled workforce, availability of suppliers, access to customers or new markets, universities, favorable government policies, good local quality of life, transportation access, degree of community's isolation, and so on. An inhospitable environment is characterized by perverse regulatory and tax policies: antiquated and excessive building codes, zoning, land use regulations, local and state business licensing requirements, and business and property taxes.

This means that aiding entrepreneurship involves mainly the creation of a supportive environment rather than a lot of direct assistance, although both are needed:[12]

1. Strategically targeted tax, spending; and regulatory policies to foster economic development and entrepreneurship ("development climate"); and
2. Customized support to encourage new enterprise development and new products, services, markets, and ventures.

The Nexus of Asset Building and Community Economic Development

Let's take a step back and distill what we now know about asset building and community economic development.

Our economy is in constant change. Inevitably, growth and decline occur; some places and people benefit, while others take it on the chin. We can't stop most of these changes. But, through thoughtful asset-building and community economic development policies and programs, we can seize opportunities where they exist and provide humane but efficient transitional help to those being left behind.

Asset policies encourage entrepreneurialism, build confidence and a longer financial perspective, and promote savings, investment, homeownership, additional education and training, and new business start-ups. These are good things that not only are compatible with job creation and income growth but are *vital parts of the development dynamic.* Connecting asset building to community renewal corrects a fatal flaw in many programs and policies: insufficient focus on expanding opportunities for those left behind or falling behind. We need policies and programs that embody the values of entrepreneurial initiative, individual responsibility, and community—policies and programs that spur individual ascension *and* community renewal. We also need programs targeted to people and places that require the most help and that build in ways to bolster resident confidence, competence, connections, and capital.

Promising Ideas, Tools, and Programs to Build Assets and Renew Communities

There are multiple opportunities for action in economically distressed places. Here are several promising practices and policies.

Homeownership has a huge impact on a local economy. Along with good schools and low crime rates, nothing captures the middle-class psyche more than stable home sales. IDA down payment–savings programs, housing counseling, and other affordable housing programs are powerful tools for building assets and revitalizing struggling areas. In places with business closings and downsized firms, *antiforeclosure programs* can protect the foremost asset employees own: their home. This is all the more important when you realize that a person's home assets, once sold, will play a major part in capitalizing some of a household's retirement portfolio. People also use a "second" on their home mortgage to get cash for all sorts of worthy and not-so-worthy goals, ranging from seed capital for a business venture to payment of an emergency expense to financing credit card debt.

Financial literacy and *competence* are the best prevention against being conned. Many Americans get in terrible fixes when contending with monthly payments, credit cards, payday lenders, and debt, debt, debt. Programs that promote awareness of money management and facility with financial tools help people avoid these threats and protect their growing assets.

Credit cleaning is a necessary "start over" step for bankrupt or overly leveraged households. No one can be a positive contributor to the local community economy when drowning in debt. A variety of nonprofit counseling organizations help households to get into the "black" and reenter the mainstream financial system.

Community-based development organizations play a vital role in strengthening local development capacity. They provide leadership development, mediation services, financial literacy courses, affordable housing development and ownership programs, upgrading and professionalizing business-retention programs, foreclosure counseling, emergency loans, and more. As the ADD research demonstrated, community development organizations form partnerships with financial institutions that work.

New markets are another resource. Many poor communities boast larger populations than more affluent areas. This, along with the absence of many retail services, creates unique opportunities for private investment. Active and significantly sized asset programs are another indicator that a community is open for business. Many new market sites are characterized by a large, new immigrant presence. They are ideal places to reach out to the "unbanked" so that newcomers are not caught up by the "debt trap" created by predatory lending and easy credit.

Seed capital is critical for starting any business, but it is very hard to get, even for the entrepreneur with a formidable business concept. Private venture capitalists rarely provide seed capital, and so-called "small business angels" want a respectable rate of return. Nonprofit and governmental funders seldom provide anything but debt capital. What if a business idea does not have a great upside potential for outside equity investors but could give the entrepreneur the kind of autonomy and income she has always wished for? What if a would-be business owner comes from a background devoid of well-heeled friends, family, and associations? This is where IDAs fit in. An IDA could be the vehicle for mobilizing the seed capital an entrepreneur needs.

The *Community Reinvestment Act* is a regulatory tool for getting depository institutions to meet not only the safety and soundness needs of their customers but also their credit needs. Banks and other regulated depository institutions are now experimenting with IDAs and other asset strategies as a strategy for fulfilling the Act's requirements.

Entrepreneurship development is happening in communities, regions, and states across the nation. Regardless of size or sophistication, regions are implementing strategies for growing and sustaining new small businesses. From these experiences, communities are learning to

- Start with youth entrepreneurship programs in the public schools.
- Conduct an audit of the region's entrepreneurial support infrastructure; make it more accessible, seamless, customer-friendly, and effective.
- Create networks for entrepreneurs to get to know each other and discover new contacts.
- Advertise management education, training, and technical-assistance programs.
- Try to attract successful, middle-aged former residents to relocate their businesses.

Employee ownership has become an alternative ownership structure for businesses. Today, about three thousand companies in the United States are majority employee-owned.[13] Employee ownership can be a strategy for saving jobs, increasing productivity, and improving employee pay, benefits, security, and "say" in company decision making. The primary barrier to employee ownership is not financial but informational. Most lenders are wary of nonconventional ownership structures and unfamiliar with incentives. And most workers and employers have little exposure to the concept. This is a ripe area for outreach and education, especially for companies undergoing succession difficulties because of poor planning by business owners.

Promising Federal and State Asset-Building Policies

A number of initiatives at both the federal and state levels have gained broad, bipartisan support. Here is a summary of some notable policy efforts.

The *Assets for Independence Act* was the first dedicated national program for IDAs. It provides support, on a competitive basis, to nonprofit community-based IDA programs in diverse settings throughout the United States. This valuable federal investment has enabled nine thousand low-income people to buy homes, pursue postsecondary education, or start a business. CFED is working to reauthorize the program by expanding its funding and making a series of technical improvements to ease its implementation.

If enacted, the *Savings for Working Families Act* (SWFA) would result in an eighteenfold increase in match funding for IDAs. SWFA would provide a tax credit to financial institutions that match the savings of 900,000 low-income Americans. Other promising strategies include (Boshara, Cramer, and O'Brien 2007, 1)

- Creating universal children's accounts at birth.
- Raising or removing asset limits in public assistance programs.
- Resurrecting savings bonds.
- Requiring employers to use payroll deduction to fund employees' IRAs.
- Expanding state-based 529 college savings plans.
- Improving financial education.
- Reforming laws to protect assets and reduce consumer debt.

States, and some localities, have become increasingly engaged in asset-building initiatives: funding, providing financial education, earmarking public funds for savings matches, outlawing predatory lending, and eliminating policy disincentives to acquiring assets. Some state programs and policies furnish essential financing for a home purchase, business start-up, or postsecondary education required to secure a better job and financial security.

Recently, states have begun to take a more comprehensive approach to ensuring financial security and opportunity for all citizens. Some of these statewide asset policy initiatives are led by government (e.g., Delaware and Pennsylvania); others are led by community-based advocates (e.g., California, Illinois, and Michigan). These initiatives have two things in common: commitment to a broad, state-level policy agenda that expands economic opportunity, asset building, and financial security; and diverse stakeholders, including government agencies, elected officials, community-based organizations, and business.

A recent report by the Fannie Mae Foundation looked at six statewide assets policy initiatives (McCulloch 2005):

- Delaware: Governor's Task Force for Financial Independence (2001)
- California: Asset Policy Initiative of California (2003)
- Illinois: Illinois Asset Building Group (2003)
- Pennsylvania: Governor's Task Force for Working Families (2004)
- Hawai'i: Ho'owaiwai Asset Policy Initiative of Hawai'i (2004)
- Michigan: Michigan IDA Partnership (2004).

These initiatives have produced legislative and administrative policy changes; brought new players, strategies, and resources to the table; added "assets" to the policy dialogue; and built public support for a broad range of economic-opportunity ideas. The following states are also engaged in statewide asset policy initiatives: Arkansas, Connecticut, Florida, Massachusetts, New Mexico, North Carolina, Oregon, and Texas.

In fall 2007, CFED partnered with ten organizations to improve state-level asset-building and protection policies as a means of expanding economic opportunity. The campaign will be linked to the release of the 2007–2008 *Assets and Opportunity Scorecard*. The *Scorecard* uses forty-six outcome measures to report how well the residents of each state and the District of Columbia are able to build and retain wealth. CFED has prioritized twelve core state policies of the twenty-six covered in the *Scorecard*. The collaborative campaign will focus on:

- Asset limits in public benefits programs
- Housing trust funds
- Incentives for college savings
- IDA programs support
- Microenterprise support
- Curbing of predatory lending
- Expanded coverage of Medicaid and SCHIP
- School spending fairness
- Support for community development lenders
- State-earned income tax credit
- State-supported preschool
- Tax expenditure reports

Conclusion

We know that conscious, efficient, and equitable public policies could open up asset ownership to *all* Americans. This is a hard time for advancing such an agenda for public monies. We will have to do more, and better, with less. The fundamental principles presented in this chapter may guide us forward:

1. Long-standing federal assets policy and programs primarily benefit the affluent with substantial subsidies, principally administered through the tax code. Such policies and programs provide almost no help to the nonaffluent.
2. New federal and state policies that aid citizens in augmenting, acquiring, and protecting assets (e.g., unemployment insurance) can help to achieve growth and equity.
3. The keys to economic advancement in today's economy are confidence, competence, connections, and capital.
4. Much research and community practice demonstrates that poor people can and will save if offered the right combination of incentives, access, and institutional supports.
5. When parents have better jobs and building assets, they are better able to meet their children's needs and to prepare the next generation for economic success and civic involvement.
6. Asset strategies reinforce optimistic, future-oriented attitudes and create incentives to earn, save, and invest.
7. The broad-based ownership of assets is good for economic development, creating and sustaining a healthy middle class that boosts consumption.
8. Safety net programs and regulations that protect poor and working families from asset-stripping (e.g., credit card approval processes and penalties for late payments, predatory lending, exploitive insurance products) are essential.
9. New asset policies appear to reallocate ineffective and inequitable public subsidies in a way that enhances productivity without increasing inequities between the haves, the have-nots, and the struggling middle class.
10. Asset-building policies not only are compatible with job creation and income growth—they are vital parts of the development dynamic.

Asset-building strategies and policies hold great promise. They may be *the key* to helping low-income individuals escape from poverty and avoid a return to the bottom due to bad fortune. Asset approaches build on other antipoverty efforts. They leverage the benefits generated by programs focused on expanded employment opportunities, progressive tax reforms, and living/minimum wage hikes. Asset approaches also leverage community economic development. The input of growing financial net worth among residents creates the dynamism and resiliency that characterizes transforming communities.

Asset building and community economic development have great potential in replacing the old development paradigm of business attraction and financial incentives with a better approach—one more appropriate for today's economy built on globalization, rapid technological change, higher skill requirements, and individual initiative.

Notes

1. Even though I may have made a mess out of their work, there is hardly an original thought in this paper: my thanks go to Bob Friedman, Ray Boshara and his team, Alan Okagaki, Bill Noftdurth, Michael Sherraden and his team, Beadsie Woo, Dave Buchholz, Roger Vaughan, Michael Kieschnick, and many others. Thanks also to Nancy, Jerome, Will, Nathan, and Lucy for putting up with me.

2. Ray Boshara, *The U.S. Experience with Asset Building Policies and Programs* (HRSD Roundtable on Asset-Based Policy Options, Government of Canada. Ottawa, Canada, June 19, 2006). Also consult for more detail CFED's "State Assets Development Report Card 2002." http://www.cfed.org/sadrc/, and "Assets and Opportunity Scorecard 2005." http://www.cfed. org/focus.m?parentid=2&siteid=504&id=508 (Both accessed 2–5-08.)

3. For an excellent compilation of the most recent research and thinking on the importance of asset for low-income families, see Thomas M. Shapiro and Edward N. Wolff, eds., *Assets for the Poor* (2001).

4. For a thorough review of the research findings on asset-building initiatives, see Ray Boshara, *Building Assets* (2001).

5. These findings are drawn from CFED, Robert Friedman, *Hope in Concrete Form* (2005), pp. 3–8.

6. Ibid.

7. A succinct definition by economist Kenneth Boulding is "the discovery and implementation of better ways to meet our wants." A more normative, High Road Economic Development goal statement that has guided CFED since 1986 is that economic development should promote more widely shared and sustainable increases in our standard of living. See http://www.cfed.org for metrics that track the goal, "The Development Report Card for the States."

8. From a conversation with Michael Kieschnick over two decades ago.

9. Here are a few synoptic definitions of community economic development that summarize what has been said: "Those strategies in which local development organizations initiate and generate their own solutions to the community's economic problems and thereby encourage long-term community capacity–building and foster the integration of economic, social, and environmental objectives" (*The Dictionary of Community Economic Development*). "Community economic development is sustained progressive change to attain individual and group interests through expanding, intensifying, and adjusting the use of resources; identifying new or expanding markets; altering the rules of economic activity to facilitate adjustment to changing conditions or altering the distribution of rewards; and improving the insights into the choices available" and "Community economic development decision-making capacity is the ability of a community to initiate and sustain activities that promote local economic and social welfare. The overall purpose of community development policy is to reduce and/or abolish the barriers in product and factor markets that prevent the positive culmination of economic development processes" (Shaffer, Deller, and Marcouiller 2004).

10. The ideas on entrepreneurship are highly based on the writings of Roger Vaughan, especially the classic *The Wealth of States* (1985). The thinking of my colleague Bob Friedman is much in evidence here as well.

11. For a contemporary, more conservative view along these lines, see William J. Baumol, Robert E. Litan, and Carl J. Schramm, *Good Capitalism, Bad Capitalism and the Economics of Growth and Prosperity* (New Haven, CT: Yale University Press, 2007).

12. See Baumol, Litan, and Schramm, *Good Capitalism, Bad Capitalism,* and visit CFED's "Development Report Card for the States" for more on these issues.

13. National Center for Employee Ownership. http://www.nceo.org. (Retrieved on May 22, 2007.) As of 2004, there were about 11,500 Employee Stock Ownership Plans covering about 10 million participants.

References

Boshara, R., R. Cramer, and R. O'Brien. 2007. *The Assets Agenda 2007: Policy Options to Promote Savings and Investment for Low- and Moderate-Income Americans.* Washington, DC: New America Foundation.

Bowles, S., and H. Gintis. 1998. *Recasting Egalitarianism.* New York: Verso.

Friedman, Robert. 2005. *Hope in Concrete Form*: The Downpayments on the American Dream Demonstration: Conception, contributions, challenges, and consequences (No. 05-37). St. Louis: Washington University, Center for Social Development.

McCulloch, H. 2005. "Promoting Economic Security for Working Families: State Asset-Building Initiatives." In *Housing Facts and Findings: Policy, News, and Innovations,* vol. 7, no. 2. Washington, DC: Fannie Mae Foundation.

Noftdurth, W., and B. Dyer. 1990. *Out from Under: Policy Lessons from a Quarter Century of Wars on Poverty.* Washington, DC: Council of State Policy and Planning Agencies.

Okagaki, A. 1988. "Windows on the World: Best Practice in Economic Opportunity Strategy." *The Entrepreneurial Economy Review* (November).

Schumpter, Joseph A. 1962. *Capitalism, Socialism and Democracy.* New York: Harper-Collins Publishers.

Shaffer, R., S. Deller, and D. Marcouiller. 2004. *Community Economics: Linking Theory and Practice.* Ames, IA: Blackwell Publishing.

Sherraden, Michael. 1991. *Assets and the Poor: A New American Welfare Policy.* Armonk: M.E. Sharpe, Inc.

Vaughan, Roger J., Robert Pollard, and Barbara Dyer. 1985. *The Wealth of States: The Political Economy of State Development.* Washington, DC: Council of State Planning Agencies.

Woo, B., and D. Buchholz. 2006. *Return on Investment: Getting More from Federal Asset Building Policies.* Washington, DC: Corporation for Enterprise Development.

11

Innovation in State Government

Pennsylvania's Financial Education Office

RENE BRYCE-LAPORTE AND HILARY HUNT

Financial literacy and financial education have been in the public dialogue for two decades. The story takes many forms: woeful student test scores, a housing foreclosure crisis, skyrocketing credit card debt, bankruptcy reform, negative savings rates, working-poor families, and too many others to name—all major community development issues. The chorus of voices calling for increased financial education is diverse: educators, policymakers, activists, civic leaders, and parents. What is less clear, however, is *who* should do *what* to ensure that America becomes more financially literate.

Under Governor Edward G. Rendell, Pennsylvania determined that there is a warranted, significant, and valuable role state government can play to help improve the financial knowledge and skills of its citizens. In addition to elevating the quality of life for Pennsylvanians, the state's leaders believe that an increasingly financially literate citizenry will also result in a more vibrant economy and reduced reliance on costly state-provided services. In April 2004, the Pennsylvania Office of Financial Education (POFE) was created.

The origin and operation of POFE was largely shaped by three factors: a long-standing interest in asset-building issues by an influential legislator from Philadelphia; the appointment of a new, activist banking secretary; and the fact that the same executive order was used to create both the Governor's Task Force for Working Families (TFWF) and POFE.

Origin

Dwight Evans, chairman of Pennsylvania House of Representatives' Appropriations Committee, represents an urban district that includes the West Oak Lane section of northwest Philadelphia, which is 95 percent African American and middle to lower class. Throughout his elected career, Evans has been deeply involved in community and personal asset-building issues. In 2003, Evans worked with the National Conference of State Legislatures, the Annie E. Casey Foundation, and the Corporation for Enterprise Development (CFED)—a national economic development think tank—to develop a framework for a public dialogue to identify realistic ways state government can help working families in tight budget times.

A. William Schenck III was appointed Pennsylvania's Secretary of Banking in 2003. A well-respected career banker, Schenck had no professional government experience prior to assuming this public-sector leadership position. During his first several months in office, however, it became clear to him that state government could and must do a better job of protecting consumers of financial service providers in Pennsylvania's financial marketplace. Stricter oversight and better enforcement was necessary, to be sure. But given the complexity of the financial marketplace and the lag between product innovation and financial regulation, among the best ways to protect consumers, Schenck thought, was to help them gain knowledge and skills so they would have a better shot at protecting themselves.

In October 2003, Schenck participated in a meeting hosted in Philadelphia by Evans to consider asset-building and protection strategies. They discussed ways this work could be valuable on a statewide basis, and they took their ideas to Governor Rendell.

In his February 2004 budget address, Governor Rendell announced the appointment of a Helping Working Families Task Force. On April 29, 2004, the governor made good on that pledge by issuing executive order 2004–7, which established the governor's TFWF and created POFE to be housed in the Pennsylvania Department of Banking. Evans and Schenck were named co-chairs of the TFWF, and Hilary Hunt was hired by Schenck and the Banking Department to develop the state's freestanding POFE. Her first task—which would consume nearly a year—was to assist Schenck in his role as co-manager of the task force.

Sixty-three people (and sixty-two alternates) were invited to sit on the TFWF. Senior-level representatives from state government, financial entities, educational institutions, community groups, business associations, unions, and other organizations invested their time and lent their expertise to the task force. The governor charged members with identifying strategies to build the incomes and assets of working families, promoting financial education, and protecting families from abusive financial services. He was interested in receiving recommendations about how Pennsylvania could help working families in tight budget times without duplicating the state's existing economic stimulus, workforce development, health care reform, manufacturing modernization, or mortgage foreclosure prevention efforts.

The task force organized into four subcommittees and held twenty-four public meetings across the state. The meetings were spirited, and a wide array of topics was brought to the table—everything from mass transit systems to dental health issues to entrepreneurship factors. The one topic discussed at every meeting was financial education.

There was a resounding call for increased financial education in the schools, but despite the passion behind the call, it was widely recognized that—even if Pennsylvania's governance structure could require it and even if schools started teaching personal finance *immediately*—such an investment might well take more than a decade to yield results. Subsequently, much additional discussion centered on ideas and challenges associated with reaching adults. The conversation also included frustrations voiced by community-based financial education providers who acknowledged that their classes were often undersubscribed or empty.

The task force worked for months and submitted a comprehensive analysis to the governor in January 2005 (www.banking.state.pa.us). With regard to financial education, however, recommendations endorsed by consensus of the task force included connecting working families to quality financial education by

- Establishing, maintaining, and marketing a clearinghouse with information about financial education resources, income supports, and savings programs.
- Integrating financial education in the curricula already taught in K–12 schools.
- Expanding community-based financial education and counseling.
- Helping employers provide financial education in the workplace.
- Encouraging financial professionals to volunteer in financial education efforts.
- Conducting a long-term study to find out which education strategies are effective.

When the report was issued, POFE had, structurally, existed for nearly one year. However, rather than working to develop its own programming, the office's sole staff person was largely engrossed by facilitating the financial education subcommittee of TFWF.

Operations

By working with senior-level experts and engaging in wide public discussion over time, clear operating and organizing principles emerged. First, it became clear that—in a state of 12.4 million people—there would be no way for POFE to be successful if it concerned itself with the retail delivery of financial education classes. As one public meeting participant said, "It would be like trying to boil the ocean with a candle." It was determined that the office would be most effective if it focused on developing the systems and tools needed to increase the number, quality, and ability of other trustworthy entities to reach citizens. Second, with gradual growth, POFE would eventually develop expertise and resources to build sustainable capacity in schools, businesses, and community-based organizations to provide financial education across the state.

In February 2005, a second staff person was added to the office. This person's first task was to establish, maintain, and market the recommended financial education clearinghouse. Again, armed with information gleaned from public meetings and deliberation of TFWF, it was determined that the clearinghouse would be most useful if it were created and maintained online. (It is important to note that there was much consideration given to the accessibility of Internet tools for low-income/

low-wealth households, senior citizens, and others; however, these concerns were ultimately outweighed by the cost, updating, and distribution barriers presented by a printed document.)

POFE's online clearinghouse and Web site, *Your Money's Best Friend* (www. moneysbestfriend.com), was launched in April 2006. More than 100,000 unique users visited the site in its first year of operation. The clearinghouse was designed to

- Link Pennsylvanians to financial education resources within their own communities.
- Make it easy for school, community, and workplace financial educators to find low-cost, appropriate tools.
- Provide jargon-free, unbiased information and additional resources for citizens.

The first requirement was met through the development of a ZIP code–searchable database of financial education providers. After an initial screening by POFE and submission of a signed, legally binding posting agreement that affirms the financial education they provide puts the interest of Pennsylvanians above their own commercial interests, an organization is provided with a password allowing it to enter its own organizational data, update events, and more. Within its first year, more than 170 providers were active in the database. The ZIP code–searchable database not only benefited citizens who were looking for help, it also assisted financial education providers in marketing their programs and attracting participants.

The second requirement is still under development as of 2008 but will be met when a "resources for educators" section of the Web site goes live. The section will provide links to curricula, teaching tips, best practices, research, case studies, talking points, and networking.

The third requirement is met through nearly three hundred pages of content and more than a thousand resource-specific links. The site offers something for everyone, from talking with loved ones about money to figuring out the differences between 401(k)s and IRAs. Navigation is organized by topic and life stage, and content is cross-linked. Importantly, it is noncommercial and written in clear, jargon-free language. Additional links are prioritized on each page to offer other Pennsylvania government resources first, federal or other state government resources second, nonprofit resources third, and commercial resources last (if included at all).

Also in 2008, POFE had five staff. Director Hilary Hunt remained, joined by a staff focused on school-based financial education, workplace-based financial education, and community-based financial education.

School-Based Financial Education

Some state governments have required that students take and pass personal finance classes in order to graduate from high school. This is not an option in Pennsylvania, where each of its 501 school districts sets its own graduation requirements. Given today's educational climate of "teaching to the test," it is difficult to convince administrators to add "electives" to courses.

One answer to getting more personal finance content into K–12 schools, then, is to teach teachers how to embed personal finance concepts into the reading, writing, and mathematics they're already teaching. For example, if a first-grade teacher is teaching reading and comprehension, he can use the book *The Berenstain Bears and the Trouble with Money*. If a junior high math teacher is teaching how to calculate percentages, she can use real-life examples such as a household budget or a credit card or bank statement. With this approach, children take part in age-appropriate financial education throughout their schooling—making it more likely that the concepts will seat themselves in the child's basic knowledge. This approach is also attractive to administrators who don't have to buy new textbooks, hire teachers with different skills, and make time in already overcrowded academic schedules.

But one cannot assume that teachers necessarily have the financial education they need to manage their own finances, much less teach students. A journalism teacher, for example, may have chosen his profession precisely because he doesn't like numbers and finances! Thus, POFE has developed various levels of teacher training.

Working through its unique partnership with the Pennsylvania Department of Education (in fact, the school-based financial education professional has an office at both the Banking and the Education Departments), annually they jointly convene the Governor's Institute for Financial Education. Each year, this free, week-long, residential summer program hosts 100 teachers at a college or university. During the day, school district teams of teachers from various grade levels and content areas work together to evaluate their school system's personal finance offerings, develop lesson plans, and more. In the evening, participants work with certified financial planners, credit counselors, and others to more fully understand their own financial situation. Since its creation, several hundred education professionals have been trained.

For school districts that may not be ready to participate in a Governor's Institute or may have participated and are ready to expand their work, POFE provides customized, no-cost presentations and in-service programming and personalized curricula consultation. Through 2007, more than twelve hundred teachers had participated in at least one presentation or in-service session.

Workplace-Based Financial Education

Studies show that a financially stressed employee can cost an employer $1,200 per year in lost productivity and absenteeism. Further, there is a clear "teachable moment" when an employee contacts his or her employer regarding, for example, an advance on wages or to discuss a garnishment issue. Yet, at the beginning of the TFWF, there was an assumption that employers would be resistant to providing financial education to their employees.

Conversations with business leaders on this issue proved that assumption to be absolutely false. Without exception, employers thought it was a great idea and wanted to provide this benefit to their employees. Not only did they think financial education would help their employees personally, they expressed a hunch that—armed with this knowledge—their employees may well be equipped to make better business decisions as well. What employers said, however, is that they did not know *how* to provide it. And small employers said that they were focused on running their businesses and did not have time to figure it out.

Thus, the first order of business for the workplace-based financial education specialist of POFE was to discern and document at least one approach to employer-provided financial education. The best way to do this was to start with the second-largest employer in Pennsylvania—which happened to be the commonwealth's state government. This was an attractive test because of the complexity involved in delivering employee benefits and training in a highly bureaucratic system. The development process included labor relations, communications, employee leave, liability, content, and commercial issues, among others.

In 2006, POFE worked with four Harrisburg-based state agencies to offer a twenty-nine-session financial education pilot program. Four hundred commonwealth employees attended, and time-delayed follow-up research showed that 82 percent of the participants turned classroom knowledge into action and were taking positive steps to improve their finances.

Current work proceeds in two directions: first, working to permanently embed financial education into Pennsylvania's human resource and professional development options for its own staff; and second, taking what was learned from the pilot and helping other of the state's leading employers experiment with and integrate financial education into their own business models through a series of regional events and forums beginning in fall 2007.

Community-Based Financial Education

In addition to conceiving, developing, writing, and maintaining the online clearinghouse and Web site, the community-based financial education professional seeks to increase the quality and connectedness of existing financial education programs throughout the state.

In 2006, POFE partnered with the Penn State Cooperative Extension in support of a three-year pilot program funded by the Heinz Endowments. The program identified three rural areas of the state in which to develop, document, and evaluate library-based financial education for families. Parents and children visited the library together, ate a meal, and read a children's book that incorporated a personal finance concept. Parents and children then separated into different sessions, one hosted by a cooperative extension educator and the other hosted by a local librarian. Parents learned adult-oriented content on the topic covered by the book as well as tips and tools to teach and practice money smarts with their children at home. Children engaged in games, crafts, and other learning activities to reinforce the concept they had just learned. Evaluation is ongoing with results expected in 2008.

Also in 2006, the office partnered with the Pennsylvania Newspaper Publishers Association to develop and deliver training to the state's print journalists. The goal of the program was to increase the quantity, quality, and accuracy of personal finance–related stories read by Pennsylvania's citizens. It was also an opportunity to get newspaper publishers thinking a little differently. A key component of the training, for example, was to help journalists look for financial aspects and local information sources of a story where that might not otherwise be obvious. If the paper publishes a June wedding insert, for example, in addition to the usual feature stories, journalists were encouraged to contact their local nonprofit credit counseling organization to consider writing an article with information about talking with your partner about his or her credit score, where to go to get a free credit report, how to correct errors, and how to build and protect a good credit history.

POFE has also served on advisory or steering committees for emerging and active networks of financial education providers in the state and has worked with "Don't Borrow Trouble" and other social marketing campaigns to promote the dissemination of sound financial information to citizens.

Finally, in June 2007, to emphasize community-based financial education, POFE hosted its first "Common Wealth Symposium" to identify a statewide community of organizations that offer financial education, share information on strategies in delivering financial education, and identify common challenges.

Lessons Learned

POFE is a young organization, still evolving, refining, and seeking to expand and document its impact. Here are some lessons learned.

Blend Your Vision

As it exists today, POFE mixes the visions of three policymakers: Representative Evans, Secretary Schenck, and Governor Rendell. Rather than continue to "go it alone" with pet projects—based on subject, mechanism, jurisdiction, or branch of government, for example—they decided to collaborate. The outcome is better for it.

To some financial education advocates, creating POFE at the same time as TFWF was a setback. To them, it didn't seem financial education was getting the attention it deserved. Worse, for that first year, many felt the task force was unfairly draining POFE's resources. Yet, it is exactly what was learned during that intensive first year of work with the task force that allowed the effective, three-prong operating approach to emerge. It is doubtful that the office, if created on its own, would have had the time and resources to so extensively talk with the wide array of senior-level experts and citizens from whom it gleaned the most valuable information.

To some legislators, creating the office by executive order meant giving the governor "credit" for a positive action they could have taken legislatively. Yet, the executive order allowed for the office to be created instantly and to begin work immediately.

Don't Confuse Leadership with Stewardship

Many organizations and people work for years to achieve the high-profile public policy "win." Yet, after the press coverage and celebratory event, policy wins are often just words on paper—even more often, they are *unfunded* words on paper. Real social change does not take place until the words come to life.

Bringing the words to life takes extraordinary, often unexciting, day-to-day effort. It takes attention paid to issues such as planning and budgeting and staffing and office space and procurement. The list is endless. In addition to working with TFWF during the office's first year, for example, the director also had to work through state government human resources and labor relations processes to create and approve new job descriptions and salary ranges in the state system—a time-consuming process.

Policy proposals most effective at achieving social change are those constructed with sustainable staffing and funding.

Acknowledge That Innovation Takes Time

Because state government operates in the public trust and is the steward of public finances, it is right and appropriate that state programs produce tangible results to report to their citizenry. Innovation, however, takes time to produce tangible results.

A key aspect of its success is that POFE is funded by the Department of Banking. The department is not supported by the commonwealth's general revenue fund but by the assessments, fees, and fines of its regulated community. The office was therefore able to build its foundation without being interrupted (and potentially threatened) by the legislative appropriations. Secretary Schenck included funding for the POFE within the Banking Department's overall budget each year. In this context, it is reviewed, scrutinized, and—ultimately—approved by the legislature. Clearly, both the administration and the legislature are interested in results. However, this scenario provides policymakers with greater comfort in giving POFE the time it needed to get up and running.

The Messenger Matters

Some people believe that financial education is only needed by school students or low-income people. Pennsylvania policymakers disagree. There are scores of times in a person's life when his or her course can be changed by good or bad financial decisions—starting a family, buying a house, and participating in workplace benefits are just a few. No matter how much money we make or how old we are, we all have something to learn about money.

Some financial education programs are tied to state welfare or workforce development efforts. Others are tied closely with departments of education. POFE found that fewer people prejudge its work and a wider number of doors open because it is housed with the state's top financial regulator. For the most part, with regard to financial education, the Department of Banking is regarded as an honest broker of information without its own agenda. School districts feel they can be more open with information and concerns because the office is not the entity that controls their funding. Employers take meetings because they don't have a hidden fear that the conversation will turn to wages and other benefits. Community-based organizations welcome the opportunity to connect with the financial sector.

Don't Go Retail

There are national players that have produced high-quality, effective, and often free curricula. A myriad of statewide and local organizations deliver quality programs. Duplicating their efforts would be a poor use of precious resources. Helping those parties provide the highest quality product possible, however, is worthwhile and sustainable. It is a mistake for a state agency to get in the business of providing long-term financial education as a direct service.

Cultivate Partners

The path to success is much more easily negotiated with engaged allies than with disinterested spectators or competing rivals. Do not proceed without external validation. TFWF provided a process by which interested parties were able to contribute their ideas, hopes, and concerns. POFE has continued to cultivate partners in state and local agencies and networks by emphasizing coordination and communication. The office actively seeks to act as matchmaker, connecting funding partners—public sector and private sector, for-profit and nonprofit—with worthy projects. The office also strives to support the efforts of other agencies that seek to provide financial education information to large numbers of people by publicizing their efforts, speaking at their public events, and serving as an advisor on their projects.

Prioritize

From the day it opened its doors, POFE has been presented with more ideas and been offered more potential work than any hundred people could achieve. Once the office's organizational and operating principles emerged, it became easier to say no to projects that would require an intensive effort and only bear limited fruit. It is essential to keep an eye on the ball of meeting the needs of the community that the office's mission dictates. The strength of the office from the start has been working to help local and statewide organizations and their networks provide services more effectively, not attempting to supplant their role.

POFE has also been asked to speak about or help other groups replicate its approach across the country. It is worthwhile to support similar efforts in other jurisdictions to create a community of allies who can help trumpet the need for financial education efforts. Representatives of the office have done so and will continue to do so. While a balance must be struck that prioritizes efforts to build a successful financial education community at home, the effort to cultivate an audience both at home and across the country is beneficial.

You Don't Have to Be a Benefactor

POFE, as part of the Department of Banking, is not a grant-making office. While in other places, some projects draw authority by distributing funds in their community, the experience of this office shows that grant-making is not always necessary to create respect and authority. With no grant money, approaches to the office by existing and potential partners are couched in a different light. While funding is important, discussions with this office far more often address finding ways to deliver financial education more broadly or effectively than they address finding funding. Furthermore, the absence of the grant-making role again solidifies the office's place as an honest broker, able to work to expand and improve the field, with limited concern that actions will be misread as operating in the interest of itself or existing funding partners.

Closing

In a time where there are many threats to the financial security of American households, an effort to help consumers gain the knowledge necessary to protect their financial interests seems to be a worthwhile use of government resources. A member of a financially healthy household learns better and works better; he or she will contribute to the overall financial strength of a community rather than drain its resources. Pennsylvania has sought to address the need by coordinating and enhancing efforts already being made by members of its community to better the economic lives of its citizens, moving them from a vulnerable state in which they cannot see the options and opportunities in front of them to a more secure place in which they have the tools to make sound decisions to protect the livelihoods of households across the state. The hope is that more jurisdictions will see a financially educated citizenry as a priority too, adapt the lessons learned in earlier efforts, and provide innovation from which we all may benefit.

Part 3

Capacity Building and Citizen Engagement

12

Community Capacity Building Through Strategic Philanthropy at the United Way

Yoel Camayd-Freixas, Gerald Karush, Melissa Nemon, and Richard Koenig

United Ways (UWs) have played an intermediary role among nonprofits, collecting donations through workplace campaigns and disbursing funds to local agencies. Faced with increased competition from single-issue philanthropies, decreasing donations, and diminishing relevance, the United Way of America (UWA) recognized the need to compete in this changing environment. Its guidance has driven local UWs to adopt a business model to show that programs impact communities they serve—a good strategy but difficult to implement and measure, and fraught with sensitivities and unexpected pitfalls. This chapter offers a case study of a research, planning, training, and organizational development program by Heritage United Way (Heritage) of Greater Manchester, New Hampshire, with the support of a local university. This case study serves as a model for other cities and explores implications for community and organizational capacity building, strategic philanthropy, public participation, and civil society in community development.

UWA

UWA has served as an intermediary, linking donors to local nonprofits through workplace campaigns. Historically, UWA chapters used a community chest model—the core annual funding came from local workplace campaigns—and their philanthropic approach consisted of disbursing campaign moneys to local nonprofits. Indeed, the forerunner organization to the UWA was called the *American Community Chest.* UWA, like its forerunner, is not a foundation; it lacks an endowment and relies on an annual fund-raising drive for its philanthropy and operations.

Businesses are UWA partners. Businesses and employees participate in workplace campaigns through payroll deductions, business donations, and the pro bono expertise of CEOs, COOs, and CFOs as "executives on loan" to nonprofits and as UWA board members. Designated "United Way Agencies"—affiliated nonprofit recipients of UWA—are also partners. Agencies participate in workplace campaigns and employee payroll deductions, staff organize workplace campaigns and special fund-raising activities, and senior nonprofit leaders serve on boards. Community

169

volunteers—including business and nonprofit staff—are also UWA partners. UWA volunteers staff community investment activities in which volunteers review applications, attend site visits, and make recommendations to UWA boards to increase, decrease, begin, or end program funding. UWs are bound to community partners in a choreography of fund-raising, decision-making, policy, operational management, philanthropy, and community service; building civil society is an integrative principle.

A hallmark of the UWA, and an important strategic advantage, is the ability of local chapters to connect the community to its fund-raising and charitable decisions. Yet this civil society role and organizational strength can act to its detriment. Partnerships between agencies and local institutions (e.g., businesses, government, schools) influence funding allocations on the basis of the need of single organizations, which may not necessarily fit the host community's need. Political considerations play a role. Nonprofits define community needs in terms of what they do, believe they make a difference, and feel justified in competing for resources. Large nonprofits may be a force to contend with. Activist agencies attract media attention, mobilizing public opinion in their favor, and know the UWA network buttons to push. UWs often tread lightly and face difficulty changing allocations. But change does not come easy to an organization that relies on its donor network and philanthropic clients to raise its funds and manage its grant-making. Understandably, UWs became locked into funding select member agencies, linking revenue growth to annual cost of living increases, thus becoming unresponsive to emerging community needs and losing market share to more nimble single-issue philanthropies. Few UWs determined community needs and targeted philanthropy accordingly.

While UW chapters have operated successfully under a community chest model for over ninety years, they have faced increasing competition for two decades. National workplace campaign contributions fell from $4 billion in 2001 to $3.6 billion in 2003 (Talcott 2005). Moreover, UW is no longer the primary source for nonprofit contributions or distributions in many communities. Increased competition from other philanthropies and decreased donations thrust UWs into a more competitive and aggressive fund-raising environment. These conditions, shrinking revenues and shrinking importance, led UWA to rethink how its local chapters should operate.

Strategic Philanthropy

UWA adopted a business model to show program impacts. UWA encourages, but does not require, local chapters to define community priorities tightly and adjust philanthropic grants to fit these priorities. UWA chapters are implementing community impact models and outcome measurement systems to show *added value* results attributable to their grants. This entails change in philanthropic strategy: from guaranteed funding to a set of designated member agencies year after year to community impact funding, which may add open bidding by nonprofits for funds in designated program areas. This shift is the biggest change for UWA in a century. While this strategy is not unique to UWA, its adoption and the public appeal of deliberate, accountable philanthropy may be the edge UWA needs to restore its standing.

While UWA advises local chapters to adopt a strategic philanthropy model, this shift requires components that may be a challenge to medium and small UWs. First, community needs must be identified. To do so, UW can rely on community needs assessments (CNAs); surveys of priorities, assets, and needs (SPANs); community indicators; and similar strategies. Objective data are available from local planning authorities or analyses of existing data sources (e.g., U.S. Census, Bureau of Labor Statistics). To be of use, data must be expertly analyzed. To that effect, academic centers may assist UWs in objective needs assessment. The second criteria, determining community priorities on the basis of objective needs, is often a strength of UWs. Input of stakeholders—donors, business leaders, agencies, local philanthropies, advocates, researchers, boards—can be secured through strategy meetings. A sensible approach is to use the needs assessment to elicit data-driven discussions and subsequently identify priorities.

The next steps are more difficult and entail, respectively, the UW's capacity to change its strategy and operation, capacity of member agencies to conduct outcome measurement, and UW's capacity to monitor and collect performance data and determine actual community impact. These steps require community and UW capacity building.

Impact of this realignment can be significant. In attempting to implement strategic philanthropy, many UW branches reduced their core areas and defunded partner agencies. In Rhode Island, UW stopped funding twenty-five nonprofits (40 percent of their member agencies), while in Massachusetts, UW of Merrimack Valley (e.g., Lawrence, Lowell) stopped funding twenty-five agencies (50 percent of their member agencies), to fund other nonprofits that better fit their new priorities. Some unfunded agencies, long-term UW partners, in spite of receiving ample notice and one or more years of transition funding, faced service cuts or closed. UW chapters ran into conflict with advocates and eroded their political base.

The UW advisory is a good strategy at risk of failure, yet UW should be able to determine community needs and target philanthropy without disruption, deriving not so much from the strategic realignment but from a drift away from UW core principles. UW is not an endowed foundation, and it relies on an annual fund-raising drive, a drive that depends on and is bound to its partners, member agencies, and volunteers. Partner agencies are not the enemy, even if they do not meet new priorities. Ability of local chapters to connect the community to its fund-raising and charitable decisions is UW's strategic advantage. Actions that undermine this network and political base run counter to UWA's civil society principle. A more reliable path may be to seek the needed realignment within UWA's civil society framework.

Heritage United Way

Manchester, New Hampshire, hosts many nonprofits, ranging from early childhood education to elderly transportation, from affordable housing to public health. Heritage, an important funder, serves fifteen communities. Heritage is representative of UWA chapters generally. Starting in 2000, donations began to decline along with its community influence. Heritage noticed and sought a solution by exploring the UWA guidance regarding strategic funding and community impact.

Yet, with a staff of ten and no experience in outcomes measurement, Heritage leaders felt it needed an experienced partner. Heritage approached the Applied Research Center (ARC) at the School of Community Economic Development in Southern New Hampshire University (SNHU) for help. Heritage entered into a partnership with SNHU, cost-sharing a contract with the ARC. ARC was to design a needs assessment, a prioritizing process, and performance measurement systems to determine impact and show the added value attributable to Heritage donations, all through a broad community planning process.

The Intervention

The intervention consisted of a research, planning, capacity-building, and organizational development program designed by ARC and implemented in a sweat-equity partnership with Heritage. Research examined social and economic indicators in a baseline study. The planning program guided the overall strategy and convened community stakeholders to elicit data-driven discussion of community needs and priorities for Heritage's philanthropic programs. Training built capacity of member agencies in logic models and performance measurement and designed a new management-information system to report and monitor performance outcomes. As part of the organizational development program, Heritage created new strategic grants, shifted to a request for proposal (RFP) model to fund agencies, reorganized its grant-making, and transformed itself into a strategic philanthropy. No agencies were defunded.

In 2005, Heritage agreed to transition to a community impact and performance measurement system to add to its community chest model the features of strategic philanthropy (Heritage United Way 2007). This new initiative was named the *Community Impact Program.* The ARC strategic philanthropy model entailed (1) periodic targeting of resources to address strategic priorities; (2) reflecting these targets in RFPs to community agencies, to be addressed in their ensuing grant proposals; (3) a UW proposal review and grant-making process based on target priorities and available resources; (4) periodic agency reporting (and UW monitoring) of program performance data based on specific program goals set out in their grant proposals; (5) ongoing use of program performance data by UW to realign resources and funding priorities for the following year and by agencies to adjust their program goals on the basis of missed and achieved goals; and (6) periodic redefinition of strategic priorities and targeting of resources by Heritage. ARC and UW anticipated that the model would entail a transition to multiyear funding adjusted (or discontinued) through annual review, seeking to

- Target grants at evolving areas of high and/or strategic community need.
- Make measurable and demonstrable change in those need areas over time.
- Allow Heritage to show donors how their money makes a difference.

Heritage decided to concentrate grant-making in public education, health, and housing/community development. Almost all their partner agencies fit into one of these. This decision realigned the philanthropic strategy with little disruption. Strategic targets were free to shift within a domain (e.g., community development). Agencies faced competition for funds in a domain—a common enough experience—but not a shift in what domains would be funded. Agency grants would be based on need, and denial of funding on relevance or nonperformance.

The intervention was designed to take place over three years and included research, planning, training, and organizational development programs by ARC–UW teams. Heritage staff would later report to the board that community impact invigorates fund-raising by enhancing donor confidence: it highlights needs identified through data and community stakeholder input; links grants to specific program outcomes, showing donors how their money makes a difference; linked to *marketing,* it enhances UW's visibility as a leading, enabling community agent; and sets the stage to leverage other funding sources (e.g., foundation matching grants, municipal management contracts) in support of board priorities.

Research

The strategic philanthropy role required Heritage to conduct analyses of community needs to then target priorities and allocate resources. But UW also needed to reestablish its role in the community. ARC recommended pursuing the role of a more activist philanthropy—convening community discussions and enabling problem-solving planning in its three funding areas. Heritage would shift from an intermediary fund-raiser to an active, leading agent. This shift focused on convener, enabler, partner, and leader roles.

In the first year, ARC examined regional social and economic indicators to identify community conditions. Findings were discussed with municipal and community agencies. This process illuminated issues and brought together groups with similar goals. Data were analyzed and organized into demographic and economic profiles for Greater Manchester and baseline profiles for UW in health, public education, and housing/community development. Results were widely distributed in a *Community Indicators* monograph (Camayd-Freixas et al. 2006).

Community Indicators democratized data and information, fostered informed civic discourse, elicited and prioritized strategies, and tracked progress on a shared civic agenda to (1) provide a baseline against which to measure future progress and assess changing trends in community needs, and (2) identify startup strategic priorities and proportionately target resources to address them. The publication signaled Heritage's return to active relevance.

Planning Program

The planning program guided the overall strategy and designed a public convening process to elicit data-driven discussion of community needs and priorities. In early summer, Heritage convened stakeholders and held public forums in public education, health, and housing/community development. At each forum, ARC presented baseline studies and discussed community needs. The goal of the forums was to discuss the accuracy of data based on its fit with local knowledge and provide a data-driven context to elicit public input and priorities and recommendations. Ideas generated were captured and included in *Community Indicators*. Community stakeholders were invited to the forums using a search conference model to achieve broad representation (Camayd-Freixas, Baker-Smith, and Schon 1984). This approach entails the application of network sampling methods to select a balanced cross section of stakeholders, followed by a strategic planning process applied to entire communities.

The second set of meetings consisted of more specialized planning with UW partners. Heritage played an activist philanthropy role as convener, enabler, and partner. The goal of the meetings was to cross-fertilize ideas generated by the *Community Indicators* research and forums to identify new and innovative strategic funding initiatives. Each area identified problems and interventions designed to use UW funds to leverage existing resources in new ways. For example, research noted a high rate of tooth extractions among school-aged children—deemed a deficit in dental health insurance. The Health Department had operated a large bus equipped with dental chairs for preventive hygiene, but its staff had retired. A plan was proposed to remake the dental hygiene bus into a primary dental care program traveling between local schools; the city would redefine the Health Department open positions to hire a dentist, and UW would fund the program gaps. Leveraging resources to target need with a highly visible bus that offered a school-based direct service was a model approach to community impact and performance measurement. As such, it offered agencies preparing proposals for the 2008 RFPs with a model.

A community impact goal is to reestablish the UW's role in the community to invigorate fund-raising through enhanced donor confidence. Marketing enhances visibility as an active, leading agent—an activist philanthropy engaged in convening community discussions and enabling problem solving. This goal cannot be achieved through dialogue between UW and its network. Yet this was not accomplished by planning even though the three forums addressed key themes and convened in fifteen municipalities. Since community impact entails follow-up convening and public events, Heritage contracted with a firm to implement a marketing plan.

Community Capacity Building

The capacity-building program was designed to train Heritage member agencies, staff, and select volunteers in logic models and performance measurement (Camayd-Freixas 2006). Agencies and Heritage staff were shown how to link programs to strategic performance outcomes and accountability. An additional benefit is it prepares agencies to submit proposals to other funders requiring logic models (e.g., federal agencies).

ARC trained UW staff and member agency staff to (1) target resources to address emerging and strategic priorities (new *Community Impact Committee [CIC]*); (2) prepare member agency RFP submissions outcome/performance measures; (3) review funding awards based on priorities and resources (reorganized *Citizen Review Teams [CRT]* and staff); and (4) use performance data to target resources and funding priorities for the following year. Following are training goals.

Member Agency/Applicant Training

- How to respond to an RFP incorporating community impact measures
- How to construct a logic model
- How to prepare and measure program performance outcome indicators
- How to report on measurement goals—as periodically required

CIC Training

- The RFP, target indicators, and criteria for funding
- How to propose allocation of funds to each target area and determine the funding cycle
- How to interpret and use program performance data

CRT Training

- How to review and evaluate proposals, including site visits and funding recommendations
- How to interpret and use program performance data
- How to evaluate the implementation of the community impact process and identify gaps in service to which a targeted RFP can be developed

An example of how training was conducted is logic modeling. The logic model training was provided free to some fifty Heritage member agencies and to other agencies for a registration fee (grants were made available to these agencies); UW staff were trained along with member agencies. The logic model training module consisted of five training days over five weeks, including two field visits by ARC staff to assist agencies in building logic models for their programs. Through this process, agencies framed their program goals and outcomes to determine their potential impact on the community.

Given the role of logic model training in community impact, it was important to insure that participants built capacity to use it in the RFP. The 2008 RFP will include a second round of the capacity-building program as field-based consultation by ARC and UW staff with community agencies preparing submissions. This support is sufficient if trainees developed familiarity with the model and a positive attitude after exposure to training. Evaluation surveys were conducted before and after training, and focus groups after training, and showed that after training, 87 percent of participants were at a practicing or proficient level, 67 percent had already authored their agency's models, 93 percent felt the model is helpful to community organizations, 93 percent felt they would use the skills with other funders, and 79 percent felt they would use the skills in their work with other agencies.

Outcomes measurement was part of logic model training. UW members have often designed effective programs, but their efforts are not always recognized because the changes achieved by these programs are often not identified and/or measured. Practitioners can readily say what they do and why but are less certain measuring changes in the lives of their clients that result from their work. Difficulty measuring the impact of programs also inhibits the ability to accurately ascertain what activities, strategies, and approaches work best. Agency participants were trained to identify short-term, intermediate, and long-range outcomes on the basis of their program goals and objectives. This task was supported by national sources—UWA's *Outcome Measurement Resource Network* and NeighborWorks America's *Success Measures Guidebook* (NeighborWorks America 2006).

Transition to community impact entails changes that can be expected to generate anxiety among member agencies, even among UW board members. Heritage adopted a transparency policy and, to help assuage undue anxiety, created an FAQ on the process that was widely published, asking and answering the following:

- What happens to funding that agencies are accustomed to receiving?
- What does the CIC do?
- How will the RFPs differ from the current application process?
- How will the new investment process be different?
- How will we show "impact"?

Organizational Plan

The Heritage board agreed to reorganize to accommodate community impact. Like most UWs, Heritage is organized to deliver a workplace campaign but not to manage grant-making strategically like a foundation. It is like an athlete who favors and overdevelops only one well-muscled arm. Since workplace campaign fund-raising and strategic grant-making are seasonal, with loads concentrated over key periods, ARC proposed a reorganization plan that would balance the structure by retraining staff to play both offense and defense—fund-raising and strategic grant-making—as the new program officers. ARC first proposed to align corporate functions under a COO (existing), a CPO (new), and a CDO (redefined) to manage, respectively, operations, programs, and development.

Reorganization focused primarily on the community building division that engages with member agencies. A new programs and community impact division would lead strategic grant-making and the interface with member agencies, but its program officers would play offense and defense—working primarily in strategic grant-making but switching to development to help organize workplace and fund-raising campaigns in their area. When playing that role, they would work under the guidance of the chief development officer, who has overall responsibility for fund-raising and development. This approach would integrate closely the knowledge of community impact and community needs with the development arm of UW. This new division would be headed by a senior program officer experienced in foundation strategic grant-making, who would supervise a department of three program officers each in charge of a program area.

A new CIC of the board would oversee community impact, including staffing changes needed to meet the demands of a new proposal review and approval process. The CIC would also oversee reorganization of a new CRT for each impact area, with a new composition of board co-chairs, stakeholders, domain experts, and traditional UW volunteers. The CRT works with program officers of the programs and community impact division in strategic grant-making (grant allocations), performance outcomes (program review), and strategic philanthropy (strategic priority setting).

Lessons Learned

Sometimes More Is Less

In retrospect, UW branches that implement strategic philanthropy by rapidly reducing their core funding areas and defunding a large share of partner agencies made a tactical mistake that created conflict with long-term partners and eroded their political base. Ample notice and multiyear transition funding is not enough. UW branches must understand that they are not foundations, they lack an endowment, and they rely on the goodwill of their network for annual drives to fund their philanthropy, administration, and operations.

Sometimes Less Is More

UWs are intricately bound to their community partners in a choreography of fund-raising, decision making, philanthropy, and service. This is a strategic advantage and also serves the UW core integrative principle of building civil society. Actions that undermine this network and political base run counter to UWA's civil society principle. ARC's proposition that realignment be operationalized within UWA's enduring civil society framework was sound. Heritage's decision to phase in the strategic grant-making process and buffer its network was consistent with this framework. Heritage's rule to "do no harm" or unnecessarily alienate its network may appear as less change over longer time, but it is more grounded and ultimately faster than other tactics.

Sometimes More Is More

The complexity of realignment should not be understated. It entails an ideological change in philanthropic strategy: from virtually guaranteed funding to designated member agencies to competitive impact funding through open bidding. It requires major changes in organizational function, staffing, and skills, and an adept hand to avoid political conflict. A three-year intervention that involves research, planning, capacity building, and organizational development is not overcautious. UWs that seek this extent of change with less may place themselves at risk of failure.

Innovation and Entrepreneurship

Heritage has proposed to be an intermediary for social program funding for small towns—to manage the grant-making process for these municipalities. This strategy leverages UW community investment and strategic grant-making capacity and enhances its annual funding pool. It is a form of entrepreneurial leadership not anticipated in the community impact planning that opens the door to a more involved relationship with the community and, perhaps, a new hybrid model of UW philanthropy.

Note

This chapter derives from a research, planning, capacity-building, and organizational development program by the Applied Research Center for Heritage United Way. The authors gratefully acknowledge the contribution of all team members from ARC and Heritage.

References

Camayd-Freixas, Y. 2006. "Heritage United Way Logic Model Training." Manchester, NH: Applied Research Center, School of Community Economic Development.
Camayd-Freixas, Y., H. Baker-Smith, and D. Schon. 1984. "Search of Community: A Strategic Planning Conference in Boston's Dudley Street Neighborhood." Roxbury, MA: Alianza Hispana & Nuestra Comunidad Development Corporation.

Camayd-Freixas, Y., G. Karush, B. Iyer, D. Jackson, R. Koenig, N. Mijoba, M. Nemon, and D. Sodnomdarjaa. 2006. *Community Indicators.* Manchester, NH: Community Economic Development Press. www.heritageunitedway.org/community/2006CIEducation.pdf. (Accessed 10 January 2008.)

Heritage United Way. 2007. "Implementation Plan: Heritage United Way's Transition to Community Impact." Heritage United Way.

NeighborWorks America. 2006. *Success Measures Guidebook.* Washington, DC: NeighborWorks America.

Talcott, S. 2005. "United Way Shifts Focus, Some Funds: Dozens of Area Nonprofits Facing Cutoffs." *Boston Globe,* April 17: A1.

13

Building Community Capacity Through Multisector Collaborations

JANE F. MORGAN

This chapter explores the Detroit Local Initiatives Support Corporation's (LISC)—a national community development intermediary—experience with geographically targeted, cross-sector collaboration. This chapter identifies lessons learned from Detroit LISC's shift to targeted Strategic Investment Areas (SIAs), in establishing and supporting collaborations across community development, educational, human service, and other sectors.

Communities continue to struggle with the daunting challenge of revitalizing local neighborhoods, particularly in older cities, like Detroit. Progress in neighborhood redevelopment depends, in part, on a community's ability and willingness to implement new approaches to achieve their goals. Changing strategies can have positive outcomes but rarely come easily. In Detroit, LISC conducted the research, obtained stakeholder input, and implemented the model explored here.

An assessment of Detroit's experience is best accomplished within the framework of neighborhood planning. The chapter begins by providing a brief history of the evolution of neighborhood planning and community development corporations (CDCs). The next section provides a context for understanding community planning in Detroit and the forces that led to the development of the SIAs. Then the chapter addresses the increasingly critical role of multisector collaboration as the cornerstone not only of the SIA model but of any effective neighborhood planning process. Following on this, the chapter identifies key factors that can be used to measure the success of multisector collaborative planning models for SIAs. The chapter summarizes the implications for the field.

Detroit LISC

The Detroit LISC is a local organization within the national LISC network. National LISC, founded in 1980, is the largest community development support organization, partnering with more than 2,400 CDCs in over 300 rural and urban communities. Since its inception in 1990, Detroit LISC has invested over $100 million and leveraged $650 million in funding for revitalization. The organization's mission is to develop strategic relationships that serve as the catalyst to empower neighborhood developers, using financial and technological resources to build economically viable neighborhoods. LISC provides local CDCs access to capacity building, technical assistance (TA), and financial resources to assist them in transforming neighborhoods. By accessing these and other resources, CDCs are better able to develop affordable housing and businesses as well as parks, playgrounds, healthcare facilities, and more.

Detroit LISC's SIAs are one reason it was named one of National LISC's eleven *Sustainable Communities*. Sustainable Communities is a national push propelling community development beyond a traditional focus on affordable housing and toward a more strategic, comprehensive, sustainable approach. There are five core objectives:

- Expanding capital investment in housing and other real estate.
- Building family income and wealth.
- Stimulating local economic activity.
- Improving residents' access to quality education.
- Developing healthy environments and lifestyles.

To be fully realized, each of these objectives must be rooted in neighborhood organizing, participation, and planning, requiring LISC to become more engaged in building relationships among residents, funders, program providers, policymakers, and other stakeholders. As a fiscal intermediary, LISC's historical role has been underwriting and financing real estate development. Within Sustainable Communities, it integrates those efforts with other strategies—within a neighborhood's vision.

Planning at the Neighborhood Level

A Brief History of Neighborhood Planning

Neighborhood planning can be traced back as far as the settlement house movement in the late nineteenth century, an effort to address urban poverty, illiteracy, ill health, and criminal behavior. As time passed, the concept of neighborhood began to shift from a social focus to a geographical one. Like the settlement movement, the neighborhood movement was paternalistic in that there was no place for resident input in the planning process (Rohe and Gates 1985).

The evolving concept of the neighborhood is reflected in the Community Action Program and Model Cities, two federal programs in the 1960s to combat poverty. In the 1970s, the Community Development Block Grant (CDBG) program, a federally funded physical and social development initiative that required local resident participation in planning, implementation, and assessment, was established. Further, planners recognized the limitations of traditional city planning, which too often focused on business districts to the exclusion of neighborhoods. Neighborhood planning has emerged as a means of addressing the equitable distribution of public goods through decentralized, participatory, and action-oriented processes (Rohe and Gates 1985).

CDCs and Intermediaries as Neighborhood Stewards

Beginning in the 1960s, CDCs were established to address the needs of well-defined or *targeted* geographical areas (Twelvetrees 1996). Operating in both rural and urban communities, CDCs are multipurpose nonprofits engaged in a range of activities designed to benefit neighborhoods: improving the physical fabric of a community; focusing on housing and commercial revitalization; and leading to job creation, asset building, and social services, including youth and workforce development. While there is diversity in organizational capacity and effectiveness, CDCs have become key players in rebuilding neighborhoods.

Most CDCs rely on public and private support, including federal CDBG funds, low-income housing tax credits, state and local governments, banks, corporations, and foundations. Securing financial support is an ongoing challenge. Further, intermediary organizations, LISC, the National Community Development Initiative (NCDI), and others pool resources from a variety of public and private sources and distribute them to CDCs and also provide TA and serve as public policy advocates for the industry (Ferguson and Dickens 1999).

The Neighborhood Planning Process

Much of the success of CDCs is due to two core principles of community development: democratic decision making by those whose lives are affected, typically residents, and the community leadership development (Burkholder, Chupp, and Star 2003), including

- Promoting active and representative participation designed to provide all community members an opportunity to meaningfully influence decisions affecting their lives.
- Educating community members on community issues and the assorted economic, social, environmental, and political impacts associated with alternative courses of action.
- Incorporating diverse interests in the planning process and withdrawing support of any effort likely to have an adverse impact on disadvantaged members of the community.
- Enhancing the leadership capacity of residents and community organizations.
- Maintaining a willingness to utilize a broad range of strategies to support the long-term sustainability and community well-being (www.comm-dev. org/principles.htm).

This framework distinguishes between *planning at the neighborhood level* and *neighborhood planning,* a distinction largely a function of who initiates or controls the process. CDCs and other community-based organizations tend to be more concerned with ensuring that the process is resident or community led. While resident participation can be high in both city-initiated and community-based approaches, the community-based approach tends to have more resident control of the decision-making process (Peterman 2000).

LISCs play a unique role as a community development intermediary organization in neighborhood planning. On one hand, they provide financial and technical support to CDCs while supporting the activities of the organizations leading the planning process. Intermediaries do not presume to have the same relationship with residents and stakeholders as CDCs and therefore recognize the appropriateness of supporting a CDC-led process. At the same time, as a TA provider, intermediaries provide leadership.

Strengths and Limitations of Neighborhood Planning

There are advantages in neighborhood planning. One is that implementation is usually more successful, as evidenced by a greater number of physical improvements (Rohe and Gates 1985). Another strength is that neighborhood planning tends to be more responsive than comprehensive planning in terms of local characteristics, issues, and needs. Neighborhood planning can also strengthen communities through increased interaction among residents and others involved in developing the plan. Resident and organizational capacity are developed, and the planning process can generate momentum for creating change (Burkholder, Chupp, and Star 2003). Also, when residents and other stakeholders are truly engaged, neighborhood planning can be empowering, leading to increased stakeholder confidence, skills, and capacity, as well as cooperation. In these neighborhoods, residents and community-based organizations often become more proactive and are better prepared to respond to unwanted development. Long-term outcomes are improved because residents feel more attached to an environment that they helped create, which leads to better maintenance and less vandalism and neglect (Burkholder Chupp, and Star 2003).

Neighborhood planning is not without limitations, including economic, political, and logistical difficulties associated with planning. It may be difficult from an economic standpoint to implement a number of small programs. Economies of scale that can be achieved through citywide programs will be difficult in individual neighborhoods. Poor representation can be the result of low resident participation. Unclear or unrealistic expectations and responsibilities can hinder successful implementation of neighborhood plans (Burkholder, Chupp, and Star 2003).

Strategic Investment Areas: A New Planning and Investment Model

Community Development in Detroit

Neighborhood planning varies from one community to another. In some, comprehensive planning at the community-wide level includes parallel planning at the neighborhood level. Many municipalities have established formal processes for recognizing and adopting plans developed by CDCs. Sometimes local planners are assigned to assist individual CDCs to ensure coordination and the incorporation of their plans into the comprehensive plan. In other communities, municipalities may recognize and support neighborhood planning processes, but the relationship between CDCs and local government is less formal.

In Detroit, CDCs undertake planning and development. CDCs made an effort to obtain local resident input into the planning process. At the local government level, however, it was not until the mid-1990s and the city-sponsored Community Reinvestment Strategy that residents were given an opportunity to become fully engaged—beyond the requisite public hearing—in planning for their communities. Presently, the relationship between CDCs and local government is best described as uneven. Both local officials and CDCs recognize and appreciate that CDCs have a critical role to play in the revitalization of Detroit's neighborhoods.

There are more than ninety CDCs in Detroit, a figure not accurately reflecting the growing presence of faith-based CDCs. Of these, Detroit LISC supported twenty-five in the first two years (2005–2006) of its three-year targeted cross-sector initiative through grants, loans, and TA. LISC also funded bricks-and-mortar activities in eleven social service/social action agencies, but not as their main line of business.

Shifting Gears: The Case for Developing a New Planning Model

Since its establishment in Detroit, LISC has reviewed and approved requests from CDCs for grants, loans, and TA to support revitalization. Applicants for funding were required to be fiscally sound, Detroit-based, with a strong business case. Until recently, Detroit LISC's approach to investment focused on identifying feasible projects throughout the city and supporting them—understanding that the success of these projects, regardless of their location in Detroit, would advance development of viable neighborhoods.

In 2005, as part of a comprehensive organizational assessment, LISC considered its impact in Detroit over the years and contemplated whether or not a change in its investment approach was needed. Between 2002 and 2005, Detroit LISC had invested in neighborhood revitalization at more than $15 million in grants and loans to local CDCs. This investment, in turn, leveraged $280 million in additional investments, resulting in 1,500 new units of housing and 56,000 square feet of commercial space (Detroit LISC 2005). During this time, LISC also continued to provide training and TA to build capacity.

However, while the value of LISC's neighborhood investment is evident, as the organization began to consider whether or not it was *maximizing* its investment or if an alternative planning and investment strategy might not be more effective, the answers were not as clear. The outcomes of LISC's role as an investor for housing and commercial development were visible, but LISC also understood that community revitalization was not limited to bricks and mortar.

Consequently, Detroit LISC started thinking about its role as a change agent on a more comprehensive level. While bricks-and-mortar projects remain the cornerstone, LISC and other key stakeholders agreed that education, health care, public safety, workforce development, business assistance, and other sectors should have a seat at the table.

LISC also recognized that the convergence of the following trends and resources provided an opportunity to move in a different direction.

- Technological advances that create new ways of sharing of data, identifying trends, tracking outcomes, and making informed decisions.
- Increased power at the local level for deciding how money and policies are used.
- Successful sustainability of comprehensive, multisector neighborhood planning initiatives in cities like Chicago, Pittsburgh, and Philadelphia.
- Increased support for collaboration from funders who are collaborating more themselves to ensure the best alignment of resources.
- Increased pressure from residents on public and private funders and service organizations to address challenges in their communities.

Moving forward, LISC was prepared to make a fundamental change in the way it worked with community-based stakeholders, including a willingness to take on the role of *catalyst* by convening meetings, engaging other non-CDC community-based organizations, and supporting cross-organizational and cross-sector efforts. LISC also encouraged CDCs to become change agents and think more broadly about their role in the community. Detroit LISC considered how it might support CDCs in working with organizations across sectors and partnering with new organizations to identify and address community issues and needs. Finally, Detroit LISC understood that moving in a new direction called for inviting and welcoming new stakeholders to the planning process as *equal partners.*

Developing the New Framework

Detroit LISC began the process of exploring alternative approaches to planning and investment by seeking input from a wide range of stakeholders, including CDCs. LISC wanted to balance the twin goals of strategically allocating resources in a way that leverages visible and measurable improvement in the city's neighborhoods and providing continued support to successful CDCs.

The shift to a cross-sector, geographically targeted planning and investment strategy in this instance was initiated by an external convener. That is, Detroit LISC provided the leadership for this effort. However, the cross-sector, targeted model was developed from an inclusive, participatory strategic-planning process that solicited and incorporated input from local CDCs and other key stakeholders. The SIA strategy included

- Three separate CDC focus groups.
- Approximately thirty-five interviews with Detroit-based CDCs.
- Input from LISC's Local Advisory Council, which serves as the board of directors.
- Research on national community planning and investment models.

The participatory strategic-planning process allowed CDCs not only to review but also to offer feedback on the first draft Neighborhoods NOW plan, which was adopted. For example, LISC received strong objections from CDCs to the use of the term "neighborhood developers" to describe LISC's primary stakeholder group. As a result, LISC eliminated references to "neighborhood developers" and used of the term *CDCs*. Later, to further ensure that the shift to a new strategy was undertaken in a supportive and participatory manner, a few CDCs provided input into the SIA Request for Proposals (RFP), later disseminated to all CDCs.

At the time, LISC staff reported that, overall, there was considerable CDC support for the comprehensive, targeted investment vision that was to become the new planning and investment model. LISC also reported that CDCs appeared to be supportive of taking a more comprehensive approach to investing in Detroit—one that moved beyond bricks and mortar. There also appeared to be support for LISC providing other stakeholder groups access to resources.

This integrated strategy was designed to increase both the effectiveness *and* efficiency of revitalization and community-building efforts. Through financial, technical, and capacity-building support, Detroit LISC hoped to provide the resources needed to assist CDCs and other community-based organizations and institutions in developing a sustaining governance structure in each target area, whose role would be to identify and implement programs that help strengthen and repair the physical and social fabric of the community.

The New Model

Ultimately, with stakeholder input, LISC decided not only to take a more comprehensive approach to community development planning and investing but to take a more *targeted* approach as well. Four geographic areas were identified in which LISC would focus the lion's share of its SIA investments (Detroit LISC 2005).

Implicit in this new model is interorganizational, multisector collaboration. While LISC may be the intermediary that invited the stakeholders to the table, the success of the SIA model depends in large part on the ability of these organizations and residents to develop a viable collaborative partnership. Organizations representing the community development, education, human services, health, and other sectors would need to come together to organize their work effectively and efficiently to solve the community's problems.

The new model is expected to lead to the development of a self-governing body of community leaders within each SIA. The new governing body, a unique feature of the model, provides a mechanism for transferring "temporary ownership" of the process from LISC—as convener—to a multisector partnership of community stakeholders. It sets the SIA model apart from many other neighborhood planning models because it hopes to put in place a permanent structure whose role will be to provide the oversight and accountability required to ensure successful implementation of the plan. Further, the new governing body will provide a framework for sustaining revitalization efforts well beyond the end of the LISC initiative, achieved through a strategy that incorporates broad community outreach and engagement, participation in an organizational capacity-mapping process, organizational development technical assistance, and the development and implementation a comprehensive investment strategy for each SIA, including

- Mapping community assets,
- Building relationships across sectors,
- Convening participants and continually inviting other partners to the table,
- Identifying shared issues and areas of concern,
- Developing a shared vision,
- Leveraging resources to support the implementation of the investment strategy, and
- Implementation of the work plans.

The SIA strategies address a range of needs: housing development (affordable, market-rate, rental, etc.); commercial revitalization; neighborhood improvement initiatives (crime/safety, beautification, community outreach, etc.); and institutional improvement initiatives (recreation centers and parks, health centers, schools, etc.).

Transition to a New Model

In launching the new SIA model, LISC knew that the transition would not be entirely problem-free. LISC understood that for some CDCs, the strategic move to focus a good deal of the organization's financial and technical resources on four geographically targeted communities would not be universally well received. Historically, community development funding in Detroit had *not* been geographically based. Perhaps this is why the SIAs were fairly large. In fact, the four selected target areas *combined* accounted for one-half of the city's 139 square miles. However, while the four SIAs represent a significant portion of the city, not everyone ended up on the "right" side of the boundary lines. Understandably, LISC retained the flexibility to support a few promising strategic and/or high-impact projects whether or not they were located in an SIA.

Planning Collaboratively

In recent years, public–private coalition building has grown and is becoming more common in community planning and redevelopment. Researchers point out that this has led to a shift in the planner's role as "expert" to planner as the facilitator of a consensus-building approach to decision making (Peterman 2004). Fortunately, the change has also resulted in increased opportunities for meaningful engagement in policy formation.

Collaborative neighborhood planning requires coordinated and cooperative efforts on the part of a wide range of stakeholders, individuals as well as organizations. These stakeholders come together in a process, bringing their own sometimes disparate interests and issues. The collaborative process is designed to provide a framework for building consensus through the adoption of shared rules, norms, and decision-making structures, as well as acceptance of responsibility for those decisions (Wood and Gray 1991). The collaborative process has multiple layers, but can be divided into three key phases (Margerum 1999):

- *Problem setting,* whereby stakeholders come together and commit to developing a structure and working together to facilitate a collaborative process.
- *Direction setting,* which focuses on working together to identify and develop consensus around issues, goals, and an implementation strategy.
- *Implementation,* whereby a structure is established for implementing and monitoring actions and measuring outcomes.

Collaboration is viewed by some as a "way to mediate the interests of powerful groups, while promoting the interests of less powerful groups" (Julian 1994, 9). Having said that, collaboration appears to work best when certain conditions are in place to support the process. According to the Chandler Center for Community Leadership, it is important that collaboration occurs in a "transparent" environment where stakeholders' intentions and agendas have been made visible to all participants. The collaborative's diversity should be viewed as a strength, and a system for communicating, building trust, and sharing resources should be in place (http://crs.uvm.edu/nnco/collab/wellness.html).

Consistent with the collaborative process, Detroit LISC's SIA model was developed with consensus building and shared decision making in mind. With LISC's support, SIAs have moved through the collaborative process to implementation. Establishing trust, a vital element of collaborative planning, is an ongoing, challenging process.

Multisector Collaboration

Researchers at the Community Tool Box (CTB) define multisector collaboratives as those established to address problems that affect the *whole* community—where public, private, and nonprofit organizations as well as community members work together in partnership toward a shared vision. That is, they are designed to solve *systemic* problems that might involve areas such as the environment, health care, or community-wide economic issues. According to CTB, multisector collaboration (http//ctb.ku.edu):

- *Is based on cooperation, not competition:* Unlike the emphasis that mainstream American culture places on competition to be the best, most profitable, or most effective, collaboration is based on cooperation. Resources are pooled, stakeholders assist each other, and everyone achieves more.
- *Works better because it puts the decision-making process back in the hands of ordinary people:* Those who are the most affected are involved in developing and implementing solutions. Participation is increased when individuals and other stakeholders feel included in the planning and decision-making process. The participatory and power-sharing nature of collaboration is beneficial because a community that operates more democratically promotes a greater sense of unity in addressing its problems.
- *Is messy:* Multiple individuals and organizations representing a variety of interests and sectors require a good deal of flexibility and comfort with a process that is not always tidy and straightforward.
- *Is a long-term enterprise that calls for a significant investment of time and resources but offers significant rewards:* Collaboration should be undertaken with full awareness of the resources (time, energy, financial) needed to support the process.

In shifting from a bricks-and-mortar investment approach to a more comprehensive model, LISC clearly recognized that neighborhood revitalization calls for a coordinated effort designed to address multiple community issues. Redevelopment issues facing neighborhoods are not limited to the built environment, and therefore, the potential for LISC to make a greater impact by addressing *multiple* community issues is in the organization's best interest. No organization possesses the human, financial, and material resources required to meet most urban neighborhood needs. If an effective partnership is developed, collaboration becomes a "win-win" for individual and organizational stakeholders and, ultimately, the community.

Challenges and Limitations

As stated earlier, while the payoff can be significant, the collaborative planning process is not without its challenges and limitations. Although collaborative planning incorporates multiple community viewpoints, too often it appears that this leveling dynamic lasts only as long as stakeholders remain at the table. Once planning is completed, previous power relationships tend to reassert themselves (Peterman 2004). There are other challenges and limitations as well:

- *Difficulty influencing the allocation of resources:* While a partnership may produce results, studies of past collaborative efforts suggest that changes in decision-making patterns are also difficult to achieve (Margerum 1999).
- *"Inside-outside" tension between those connected to the neighborhood and*

those outside of the neighborhood: Individuals and organizations such as funders or sometimes even technical assistance providers can be perceived as "outsiders" by the community, creating a tension that can make collaboration more difficult. When negotiated and balanced, this tension can enhance collaborative partnerships, but it involves a push-and-pull process that can be difficult to work through (The Aspen Institute 1997).

- *Limited community empowerment:* The governance structure within *some* multisector collaboratives allocates agenda-setting authority and decision making to government, business leaders, and nonprofit organizations, with community members as advisors.
- *Inadequate resources:* The lack of adequate resources, particularly funding, to actually implement the neighborhood plan can, understandably, derail the collaboration (http://crs.uvm. edu.nnco/collab/wellness.html). Throughout the planning process, there is an expectation among stakeholders that resources to implement the action plan, once developed, are available or forthcoming. However, without resources in place, there will be no activity to keep the collaborative moving forward.
- *Limited capacity building:* It is clear that a collaborative planning process helps to increase community engagement. Residents and other stakeholders not usually involved can be drawn into the process. It is not clear that participation in a collaborative planning process actually *builds capacity* within those communities. Studies indicate that while local residents may feel engaged by the process, few planning efforts have increased residents' capacity to comfortably discuss planning principles, market dynamics, and approaches to neighborhood development (Burkholder, Chupp, and Star 2003).

LISC's Commitment to the New Model

In exploring alternative planning and investment strategies, Detroit LISC reviewed research on multisector collaboration and best practices in neighborhood planning. LISC wanted to ensure that its new neighborhood revitalization model incorporated all critical elements of a solid multisector, community-based planning approach. Consequently, the SIA strategy is a participatory planning model designed to maximize community involvement with its "always leave an empty chair for new participants" approach (Detroit LISC 2003).

LISC's commitment to capacity building is also evident in the resources the organization has allocated. SIA target areas have access to a wide range of TA in the form of planning, design and organizational development consultants, staff support, and training for building capacity within organizations. Further, the community governance structure is arguably the component that has the greatest opportunity for building capacity because ultimately the "ownership" of the plan and the process rests with community stakeholders.

Measuring Success in Multisector Collaboration—Lessons Learned

The factors or indicators used here as measures of successful multisector collaboratives were taken in part from the Amherst H. Wilder Foundation's indicators in *Collaboration: What Makes It Work?* (Mattessich, Murray-Close, and Monsey 2001), from the National Network for Collaboration (Bergstrom et al. 1995), and from Cleveland State University's Center for Neighborhood Development planning principles (Burkholder, Chupp, and Star 2003), combined in a new ten-point framework for Detroit's LISC's SIA collaborative:

- Committed catalyst(s)
- Stakeholder engagement and buy-in
- Effective leadership
- Cooperative culture
- Democratic decision making
- Supportive communication processes
- Supportive structure and policies
- Favorable social and political climate
- Sufficient resources and capacity
- Sustainability systems

It is premature to draw any conclusions about Detroit's SIAs. But the following is what LISC has been learning thus far.

Committed Catalyst(s)

The development of a collaborative begins with the need to take a different route to address a challenge or achieve results that, in the eyes of the initiating organization(s), cannot be fully realized any other way. Planning collaboratively can have many benefits for the neighborhoods and communities. That discussion also described the challenges and limitations inherent in the collaborative planning process. Consequently, the organization or group of organizations that initiate a collaborative not only must agree on the need for taking a collaborative approach but also should have identified a clear vision that will ultimately resonate with stakeholders. Further, the catalyst organization(s) should bring to the table a high level of commitment to providing leadership and support to a process that will be, at times, both rewarding and difficult.

As the catalyst for the SIA collaborative effort in Detroit, LISC took steps to prepare itself for embarking on this journey by ensuring that there was cross-sector, stakeholder support for moving in this direction. In launching SIA, LISC announced its commitment to provide leadership for a minimum of three years to help establish the new model. The organization then convened a wide range of community-based stakeholders in each SIA and invited them to participate in the new planning process

—knowing that a number of the organizations coming to the process would be sitting at the table with local CDCs for the first time. As the catalyst, LISC provided necessary planning and implementation resources, understanding they would be used to leverage support from other stakeholders.

As is often the case in transitioning from vision to reality, implementing SIAs proved to be more challenging than anticipated. For example, just as Detroit LISC was preparing to make the strategic shift to a new planning and investment model, the organization was facing internal organizational challenges that ultimately led to the decision to take a brief hiatus from implementing the SIA initiative. The three-month interruption provided LISC an opportunity to clarify internal roles and responsibilities and develop processes to ensure that the new planning process would meet the needs of stakeholders. Having taken a temporary but necessary step back, LISC, as catalyst, was prepared to provide leadership and support for collaboration.

Stakeholder Engagement and Buy-In

Critical to the success of any collaborative is its ability to engage a cross section of stakeholders over the long term. In Detroit's multisector collaborative, this requires conducting outreach to engage diverse stakeholders—residents, organizations, businesses, financial, educational and faith-based institutions, and others—and securing their commitment to actively participate. To support this, LISC created a *pre*planning phase to afford CDCs and other stakeholders an opportunity to gain a clear understanding of the SIA strategy, conduct a quality-of-life assessment in each target area, complete a stakeholder analysis, and develop a work plan for the planning phase. The preplanning curriculum was facilitated by consultants provided by LISC.

An assessment of the extent to which SIA stakeholders are engaged and have "bought-in" to the process thus far reveals mixed results. To LISC's credit, the preplanning phase may have helped to promote and strengthen stakeholder engagement and participation. When surveyed on stakeholder support for the collaborative, the overwhelming majority of SIA stakeholders reported that they believe that their organizations will benefit from collaborating. However, despite efforts to encourage broad community involvement, a significant proportion of SIA stakeholders thought that all of the individuals and organizations that *should* be a part of the collaborative had not yet been engaged. Further, although LISC sought input from CDCs and other stakeholders in developing the new strategy, interorganizational dynamics in one of the SIA target areas in particular impeded that area's ability to participate.

Other factors to consider when assessing stakeholder engagement and buy-in include participation levels and the establishment of a shared vision. It is one thing to reach out to stakeholders to get them to collaborate. It is another to sustain high levels of participation as the process moves forward. So far, the SIA stakeholder model appears to be maintaining strong participation among stakeholders, but in some target areas, participation can be inconsistent and uneven. Regarding the establishment of a shared vision, which speaks directly to stakeholder buy-in, survey responses were mixed, perhaps due in part to the early timing of the survey.

Effective Leadership

As catalyst for the SIA strategy, Detroit LISC is clearly in the position of providing leadership for this effort. For purposes of measuring the effectiveness or success of a collaboration, however, leadership is not defined in such narrow terms, but refers to those individuals and organizations that have taken on important roles related to supporting or advancing work collaboratively. This might include residents who reach out to and engage other residents in the process, as well as organizations that build bridges and cultivate relationships.

Effective leadership in this context is also intended to refer to leadership that encourages team building, including the development of coalitions as needed, and promotes consensus building among stakeholders. Effective leadership might also mean that the effort is largely community-led and that stakeholders who are *of* the community are taking an active role in planning. At some point during the planning process, effective leadership will likely involve the willingness to take risks to move in new directions or forge new relationships.

The evaluation of LISC's SIA strategy is still under way and has not yet measured all of these dimensions of effective leadership. However, when stakeholders were asked whether they thought that the "leaders" had the *skills* to work with other stakeholders, survey responses indicate that while a majority agreed or strongly agreed that collaborative leaders possessed the necessary skills, more than 30 percent reported being neutral or having no opinion. Perceptions of leadership likely will be addressed and will improve over time.

Cooperative Culture

The success of a collaboration effort can also depend on whether a community has worked cooperatively before. Communities experienced in working as partners—not as independent, self-contained entities, or worse, as competitors—benefit from higher levels of trust and respect, and greater flexibility. These communities also tend to do well in other areas important to the viability of a collaborative.

Overall, the majority of SIA stakeholders reported having a history of working together collaboratively. However, there was variation among the SIA target areas on this issue. While there was broad agreement within most target areas that there was a history of working together collaboratively in their communities, one target area in particular stood out as not sharing this perception. In terms of respect and flexibility, other indicators of a cooperative culture, the majority of SIA stakeholders agreed that there is mutual respect among members of their collaborative and that collaborative members are flexible in terms of making decisions. Trust is an area from which all SIAs could benefit.

Democratic Decision Making

A democratic process for making decisions during the planning process may be implied but should be expressly stated as one of the core features of collaborative planning. This means that stakeholders should be involved early on, before crucial decisions that influence the balance of the planning process are made. Early in the process, stakeholders should also determine how decisions will be made—that is, whether by majority or consensus. The decision-making process, including guidelines for resolving the inevitable conflicts that may arise along the way, should be clear, communicated to all stakeholders, and adhered to (Burkholder, Chupp, and Star 2003).

One more aspect of a democratic decision-making process worth noting has to do with stakeholders' ability to fully engage in the decision-making process as *informed* participants. In other words, it is not enough to simply provide stakeholders' an opportunity to share in the decision-making process. To ensure that the collaborative's decision-making process is one in which equality and balance of power is maintained, decisions should be made in an environment where all stakeholders are well informed about issues before those decisions are made. If the dynamics of the collaborative are such that neighborhood residents, for example, are asked to help make decisions about issues in which they may have a limited background compared with some of the other stakeholder groups, or vice versa, then care must be taken to ensure that, to the fullest extent possible, stakeholders have a certain threshold of information going in. In prioritizing strategies, for example, some stakeholders may have more information than others. Consequently, some stakeholders may hesitate during the voting process to quickly gauge how others, particularly those they consider to be better informed, will vote. Avoiding this situation might require additional effort in terms of educating members of the collaborative before making key decisions, but it will help ensure that the collaborative make decisions that are made by stakeholders who not only are participants in the process but are *fully informed* participants.

To date, data have not been gathered from Detroit's SIA stakeholders addressing democratic decision making as an indicator of collaborative success. However, when asked whether or not sufficient time was provided to discuss issues within their respective organizations before making decisions, less than one-quarter of SIA stakeholders agreed that there was.

Supportive Communication Processes

For obvious reasons, communications are crucial to the success of any collaborative planning. Open, clear, and frequent communication patterns must be established early on. Formal communication processes within the collaborative—regularly scheduled mailings and e-mails as well as communication to the broader community—must be developed. In addition, the utilization of informal channels of communication, such as allotting time for purely social purposes to promote better communication and, ultimately, stronger links among members of the collaborative.

Overall, preliminary evaluation suggests that a majority of SIA stakeholders believe communication is open and that the collaborative utilizes both formal and informal channels. Even so, there was variation in stakeholders' responses, suggesting that communication can be strengthened. There is room for improvement in the frequency and extent to which SIA leaders communicate with group members.

Supportive Structure and Policies

Another characteristic shared by successful collaborations is the existence of an organizational structure and policies that support and guide the collaborative (Mattessich, Murray-Close, and Monsey 2001). In any collaborative, it is important that its members have a clear understanding of their roles and responsibilities. There is also a need to establish and adhere to a set of operating policies and procedures that guide the collaboration functions. These might include guidelines for resolving conflicts. In addition, some collaboratives find it useful at some point to establish written agreements or memorandums of understanding as well. These agreements can be particularly helpful in clarifying stakeholders' roles and commitments as multisector collaboratives move from planning to the implementation phase.

The development of a supportive organizational structure takes on even greater importance, where stakeholders in each SIA are charged with establishing a governance structure to provide a permanent framework for redeveloping the community. Early data indicate that SIA stakeholders would benefit from greater clarity around their collaboration-related roles and responsibilities. There also appears to be uncertainty among stakeholders that a clear decision-making process is in place.

Favorable Social and Political Climate

Researchers also agree that the success of collaboratives such as the SIA also depends, in part, on the social and political environment in which it is taking place (http://crs.uvm.edu/nnco/). A favorable social and political climate is one where the overall mission of the collaborative is supported by, or at least not opposed by, key community stakeholders such as political leaders, organizations, and institutions who control resources and public policy (Mattessich, Murray-Close, and Monsey 2001). This support tends to have a positive impact on the development of effective collaborations. A favorable social and political climate can also have a positive influence on the sustainability of collaborations.

Fortunately, the overwhelming majority of SIA stakeholders agree that the political and social climate was right for LISC's new multisector planning and investment model. This widespread consensus may be due to factors such as recognition in the broader community that the myriad challenges facing the city's neighborhoods necessitated a coordinated, multisector response. Faced with economic uncertainty, Detroit would need the support of all stakeholders in neighborhood revitalization. Socially and politically, stakeholders appeared to understand and appreciate the mutually beneficial nature of the new SIA collaborative model.

Sufficient Resources and Capacity

Clearly, even if the collaboration is doing well in terms of the success factors or indicators described in this chapter, without sufficient resources and organizational capacity, the model is doomed to fail. The process of developing and working toward a shared vision is one that requires financial, in-kind, and technical support. The need for funding resources to support planning and implementation efforts is obvious. However, the need for in-kind and human resources in community-led collaborations may not always be readily apparent. For example, human resources in the form of technical support might include planners, architects, and organizational development consultants. Training and capacity building can also be part of the technical support package. Additionally, members of the collaborative should be prepared to provide in-kind support, often in the form of meeting space and staff support.

As a major initiative of Detroit LISC, the SIA strategy was launched with significant resources that included $40 million over three years for grants and loans, and TA, including capacity building. In spite of resources LISC brought to the new initiative, SIA stakeholders expressed mixed views about whether they believed sufficient financial and human resources were in place. However, given the depth and breadth of the challenges within each target area, it would not be fair to expect that any one organization would be in a position to immediately provide the level of financial and human resources needed to achieve the outcomes identified by the collaborative. As the catalyst organization, Detroit LISC had always envisioned its role as helping stakeholders leverage additional resources.

Sustainability Systems

Finally, the long-term viability of collaboratives requires that certain systems be put in place to sustain them. The development of strategies for maintaining and/or building membership, for example, is needed to ensure that the collaboration continues to thrive. Resource development is of critical importance, given the ongoing need to maintain the level of financial, in-kind, and human resources required to continue the work of the collaborative. The development of a process to periodically review current strategies and identify new and emerging issues and opportunities is important to the sustainability of the collaborative as well. As new issues arise or circumstances change, it is important that a process be in place to keep abreast of how these changes will affect the collaborative.

Conducting an evaluation of the planning and implementation process can be very useful in helping collaboratives learn more about what is working well, what the challenges and limitations of the collaborative are, and what changes or course corrections should be made to strengthen the collaborative. Evaluations are also critically important to the collaborative process because they can be used to measure the extent to which desired outcomes are being achieved. Additionally, because funders appreciate the value of evaluation—and increasingly require them—the incorporation of evaluation into the collaborative model, as seen in Detroit, can help stakeholders strengthen their case for receiving financial support.

References

The Aspen Institute. 1997. *Voices from the Field: Learning from the Early Work of Comprehensive Community Initiatives.* Washington, DC: The Aspen Institute.

Bergstrom, Arno, et al. 1995. Collaboration Framework: Addressing Community Capacity. Fargo, ND: National Network for Collaboration Framework. http://crs.uvm.edu/nnco/collab/framework.html. (Accessed 28 April 2007.)

Burkholder, Susan H., Mark Chupp, and Phillip Star. 2003. "Principles of Neighborhood Planning for Community Development." Cleveland: Center for Neighborhood Development. http://urban.esuohio.edu, October.

Detroit LISC. 2005. "LISC Guidebook for Strategic Investment Areas," August.

Ferguson, Ronald F., and William T. Dickens, eds. 1999. *Urban Problems and Community Development.* Washington, DC: Brookings Institution Press, p. 208.

Julian, D. 1994. "Planning for Collaborative Neighborhood Problem-Solving: A Review of the Literature." *Journal of Planning and Literature* 9 (1): 3–13.

Margerum, R. D. 1999. "Getting Past Yes: From Capital Creation to Action." *Journal of the American Planning Association* 65, 181–192.

Mattessich, Paul W., Marta Murray-Close, and Barbara Monsey. 2001. *Collaboration: What Makes It Work?* 2nd ed. St. Paul, MN: Amherst H. Wilder Foundation.

Peterman, William. 2000. *Neighborhood Planning and Community-Based Development: The Potential and Limits of Grassroots Action.* Thousand Oaks, CA: Sage.

———. 2004. "Advocacy vs. Collaboration: Comparing Inclusionary Community Planning Models." *Community Development Journal* 39 (3): 266–76.

Rohe, William M., and Lauren B. Gates. 1985. *Planning with Neighborhoods.* Chapel Hill: University of North Carolina Press.

Twelvetrees, Alan C. 1996. *Organizing for Neighbourhood Development: A Comparative Study of Community Based Development Organizations.* 2nd ed. Aldershot, Hants, England: Avebury.

Wood, D. J., and B. Gray. 1991. "Towards a Comprehensive Theory of Collaboration." *The Journal of Applied Behavioral Science* 27 (2): 139–162.

14

Southern Bancorp's Model for Community Economic Development

The Delta Bridge Project

BEN STEINBERG, BEN GOODWIN, AND MICHAEL ROWETT

Since late 2003, Southern Bancorp (Southern) has pioneered a comprehensive and geographically focused community development initiative in one of the most distressed communities in rural America: Phillips County, Arkansas. While it is too early to conclude that Southern's strategy will achieve its goals, there are initial signs of success. The *Delta Bridge Project* has generated over $50 million in investments in Phillips County and created the beginnings of an economic revival. From a practitioner's view, this chapter explores Southern and its theory of change; the status of Phillips County; the components of Southern's new community development strategy; and Southern's innovative financing packages and leverage.

Southern Bancorp

Southern is a development bank holding company committed to transforming rural economies by creating new trends of investment in people, jobs, businesses, and property. Southern's shareholders—foundations, religious institutions, and philanthropically minded individuals—mandated that Southern provide a social return to shareholders, foregoing a financial return. The social return is largely measured by Southern's impact on community development. This model allows Southern to reinvest and leverage a large portion of its net income to support community development investments rather than paying dividends out to private shareholders.

For more than fifteen years, Southern has operated a family of banks and nonprofit development companies that work in concert with one another to promote development in rural Arkansas and the Delta region of Arkansas and Mississippi. With $530 million in assets, forty locations in rural Arkansas and Mississippi, and more than 250 employees, Southern is the largest and most profitable rural development banking organization in the United States. In total, Southern operates three banks, Elk Horn Bank in Arkadelphia, Arkansas; First Bank of the Delta in Helena-West Helena, Arkansas; and Delta Southern Bank in Ruleville, Mississippi.

198

Southern's three affiliated nonprofits play an important role impacting individual, family, and community development in intensively managed ways that go beyond the scope of a community bank. Southern Financial Partners, the first nonprofit affiliate, spearheads comprehensive community development initiatives like the Delta Bridge Project in Phillips County. It also provides loans and technical assistance to small businesses in support of community development initiatives. Southern Good Faith Fund, the second nonprofit affiliate, seeks to increase the income and assets of low-income and low-skilled residents of the Delta in Arkansas and Mississippi through services such as Individual Development Accounts, career pathways, and small business–development technical assistance services. A third nonprofit affiliate is Southern Community Development Corporation, which is its affordable housing subsidiary. Southern CDC's housing units are developed and managed for low- to moderate-income individuals and families. Southern employs the expertise and synergy of its family of companies to produce a results-oriented, comprehensive approach to community development.

Theory of Change

Formed in 1988, Southern's initial theory of change was based on a model that focused on accessibility of credit to stimulate entrepreneurship, develop local economies, and spur regional economic development. Southern's initial service area covered most of Arkansas, an enormous area for development with only limited resources. Southern's theory of change at the time did not include the wider elements shared by vibrant communities—education, health care, housing, and local leadership.

After an honest assessment of its impact to date, the Southern's board reconsidered its theory of change in the late 1990s and developed a new strategy, incorporating the lessons learned from its initial efforts. The new strategy focused on working intensively in a defined and limited geographic region and addressing the complex and integrated set of problems that constrained rural communities from developing.

In its new strategy, Southern determined that effective community development must be locally initiated, planned, and implemented. On the basis of its experience and other research, Southern also determined that development processes inserted into a community by outside organizations generally fail because of a lack of sustained community support. As such, community development is fundamentally a local institution-building process, requiring the emergence of community organizations, processes, and structures.

Since development occurs at a community level, Southern concentrates its efforts in communities where it has a banking presence and is thereby already interwoven into the local community fabric. Southern believes that a hub community's influence can extend out in a fifty-mile radius, thereby serving as an economic engine for other communities in the radius, creating a cluster of growth. As the clusters of growth begin to overlap and to reinforce each other, regional change occurs.

Southern uses its community banks as catalysts for local development activities. As long-term and essential financial participants in a community, Southern's community banks are able to provide significant degrees of institutional influence in local financial, business, and political environments. Southern's banks operate with a local board of directors, local management, and local employees who hold positions of community leadership. Southern's banking staff and directors, consequently, are able to influence both public and private policy initiatives and to provide local support for Southern's community development initiatives. Southern also is able to access the community leadership base of professional, civic, and governmental institutions that traditional nonprofit organizations are unable to reach and to organize all of the above in a manner that promotes action and creates core institutional change.

To effect local community development, Southern works with community organizations to

- Develop a long-term and comprehensive community development plan.
- Increase the capacity of local community organizations to enable sustained community development work. In order to increase local organizational capacity, Southern personnel have daily involvement with community leadership and assist local leadership in developing and executing a vision that produces real community change. Southern provides financial support for local organizational development.
- Work on a daily basis with community organizations to ensure that development initiatives progress according to a defined timeline.
- Provide the full range of Southern's development programs, including development banking, nontraditional lending, business assistance, technical assistance to local groups, housing, individual development account programs, bank-the-unbanked initiatives, financial skills training, and workforce development.

Southern recognizes that a significant amount of time is required to achieve results. Given its long-term banking presence in local communities and the complexity of the challenge, Southern views its development efforts as twenty-year commitments, allowing the possibility for change to come at generational intervals.

Phillips County, Arkansas

Because of the enormous need in this Delta community, Southern selected Phillips County, Arkansas, to pioneer its new development approach. Phillips County has extensive social and economic needs, including but not limited to harsh poverty, dysfunctional leadership, economic decline, and racial tensions:

- It has the highest poverty rate in Arkansas (33 percent) (2000 Census).
- It has the highest child poverty rate in Arkansas (46 percent, which is the

thirty-sixth highest child poverty rate among the nation's 3,140 counties) (2000 Census).
- It has the lowest homeownership rate in Arkansas (56 percent, which is lower than all but 93 of the nation's 3,140 counties) (2000 Census).
- It consistently has one of the highest unemployment rates in Arkansas—8.7 percent in September 2006, the second highest among the state's seventy-five counties and much higher than the overall state unemployment rate of 5.3 percent.
- Its population declined by 49 percent between 1960 and 2000.

The crisis extends far beyond statisticals. The county's two largest cities—Helena and West Helena—historically competed for individual shares of an ever-shrinking economic development pie. Both cities had financial management problems, with budget information in some cases consisting of handwritten records on scraps of paper.

In West Helena, the larger of the two cities, city government was described in a February 2005 newspaper article as a "circus." The racially divided West Helena City Council did not meet at all during in 2004 because not enough aldermen would show up for a quorum. In 2005, a group of five aldermen attempted to unseat the other three aldermen, abolish all city boards and commissions, reinstate a fired police chief, hire and fire new department heads without the mayor's approval, derail passage of the city budget, reduce the salaries of certain city employees, and award themselves $1,000 bonuses.

Financial problems at the county's 3,000-student school district resulted in the state's taking over administration of the district in August 2005. The district had a projected deficit of $2.26 million for the 2005–2006 school year. Additionally, the district in recent years has reported student test scores well below the state average. In 2005, the district had a graduation rate of just 54 percent and a college remediation rate of 95 percent. Of the district's 3,113 students, 99 percent are eligible for free- and reduced-price lunches. Approximately 38 percent of the population in Phillips County has less than a high school degree.

These daunting challenges were complicated by constant infighting. Past attempts at planning and constructive cooperation were stymied by racial tensions that resulted in more than one meeting ending in shouting matches. The culmination of these issues, magnified by continued economic decline, made Phillips County residents cynical of any planning efforts to revive the dying community.

Aside from the enormous need, the second major reason for Southern to select Phillips County was the headquarters location of First Bank of the Delta (FBD) in West Helena. The location provided Southern with the physical presence, access to local leadership, and the credibility to launch its development programs consistent with its theory of change.

The ability to form partnerships served as the third reason for Southern to launch the program in Phillips County. Southern's new geographically targeted approach appealed to the Walton Family Foundation, which provided a substantial grant over three years to support both operations and funding for community-based initiatives. Finally, some key local institutions and individuals from the Phillips County community signaled a desire to partner with Southern to attempt community revitalization.

The Delta Bridge Project

Southern created the Delta Bridge Project to effectuate locally led community development consistent with the theory of change outlined earlier. The Delta Bridge Project refers to the process of establishing a common community vision, the development of both a structure and community-led process for creating a strategic community plan, and the implementation of the plan. While the process is managed by Southern, it is a separate community entity requiring real and substantial involvement on the part of residents of these rural communities. As part of its comprehensive approach, the Delta Bridge Project seeks improvements in education, health, housing, leadership, and economic development.

The first step in the Delta Bridge process in Phillips County was to establish a baseline study of the area economy; evaluate past development efforts; asset-map the social, civic, and economic infrastructure of the region; and formulate a county-specific development strategy. More than 8,000 person hours were expended in this effort, and the result was a determination that Phillips County maintains a sufficient critical mass of community assets and population to achieve real development success both for itself and for the surrounding region within fifty miles.

The next step was to initiate a community strategic planning process. Southern hired a facilitator and began the difficult work of engaging the community, which has seen many well-intentioned but ultimately unsuccessful revitalization efforts come and go, in yet another round of discussions about the future of their county. Southern's on-the-ground community development staff, consisting of five full-time employees, was a critical factor in overcoming this inertia and getting a broad cross-section of the community to participate.

The development of the Phillips County Strategic Community Plan (PCSCP) required an extensive effort (see www.deltabridgeproject.com/strategicplan.html). Over an eighteen-month period, 300 residents participated in more than 500 meetings to develop the PCSCP, a document that provides a unified vision and a blueprint for community development with forty-six strategic goals and nearly 200 action steps.

The approximately fifty-member PSCSCP Planning Steering Committee unanimously ratified the proposed strategic plan in January 2005. After the vote, one steering committee member commented, "Nothing ever happens unanimously in Phillips County. This is no small accomplishment." After its adoption by the local community, Southern's task was to support the efforts of the community to see the plan implemented.

After its ratification in January 2005, the PCSCP was endorsed by a long list of community organizations, politicians, businesses, and other actors, which served to make the PCSCP the official development plan for the county. This group remains an important set of stakeholders for the project. Endorsements came from every municipality in the county, every school district, every educational institution, each of the largest ten employers in the county, the Phillips County Chamber of Commerce, every major nonprofit organization in the county, Phillips County Ministerial Alliance, and civic organizations such as Kiwanis, Lions Club, Rotary, Alpha Kappa Alpha, Delta Sigma Theta, and others. Other endorsements came from both of Arkansas' U.S. senators, two of Arkansas' congressmen, and state officials including the governor, the attorney general, and the county's state senator and state representative.

The strategic goals discussion around the PCSCP and the fora that the Delta Bridge Project provided to the younger generation in the community helped to create the belief in the community that positive change was possible. Participants from the PCSCP launched a separate effort to merge the cities of Helena and West Helena to realize efficiencies. Although past efforts to merge the two cities had failed over the previous fifty years, voters in each city voted by a two-to-one margin to merge Helena and West Helena in January 2006. The vote provided solid evidence to the community that by working together, significant change could be realized.

The goals in the PCSCP are divided into five categories, which together represent the five pillars of community development in Southern's model: economic development (subdivided into traditional economic development and tourism), education, leadership, housing, and health care. In vibrant communities, each of these pillars is strong and active. Southern has also facilitated the creation of a local infrastructure for implementing the plan, including a Steering Committee, a Local Development Council (LDC), and six pillar-specific goal teams, which are charged with developing plans for achieving the PCSCP's goals. Southern works with community groups to build their capacity for implementing these plans.

Southern responded to the political gridlock and divisiveness in Phillips County by creating a new infrastructure that allowed for the emergence of new local leadership, particularly allowing a younger generation of leaders to step forward. The creation of new fora with structured processes and rules provided the community with a critical new tool to break the logjam that has paralyzed past efforts at social action in Phillips County.

The Delta Bridge Project components include the Steering Committee, goal teams, objective teams, and the LDC. Participants are informed about the standardized procedures, including the funding process, application forms, and support documentation for community-based organizations and resource partners to develop funding proposals in support of the PCSCP.

Overseeing the entire Delta Bridge Project, the Steering Committee functions like a board of directors whose purpose is to provide overall governance. The Steering Committee is the keeper of the vision and must approve any changes to the

PCSCP. It ensures that both the civic infrastructure and individual projects receive sufficient oversight and management—essential components to sustainability. The purpose of the Steering Committee is to provide overall governance for the Delta Bridge Project.

The Steering Committee has twelve seats, with members representing the racial, professional, gender, age, and geographic diversity of Phillips County. The committee is designed to be self-perpetuating, with membership changes by a majority vote of the committee members. Southern staff do not serve on the committee. The committee meets monthly.

Goal teams are focused around a single general interest area (e.g., housing) in the comprehensive approach and report to the Steering Committee. Goal teams are responsible for identifying overarching goals and action steps for the strategic plan. Since goal team participation is always open to any interested resident, the goal teams bring together residents who share a common interest in an issue, providing a forum for dialogue and collective action.

Under each of the Delta Bridge Project goal teams, objective teams organize in order to develop a specific proposal and then to implement the specific project. One goal team may have multiple objective teams serving under it. The objective team develops the proposal, submits it, and then, if funded, implements the project. For instance, residents formed an objective team to construct an affordable housing complex for low to moderate income individuals.

Once a proposal is developed, it is submitted to the LDC, which represents a key element of the civic infrastructure in the Delta Bridge Project. LDC's specific function is to review funding applications, vetting them at the local level. In essence, LDC serves as an important check to ensure that projects or activities for which monies are being requested are viable, there is no self-dealing among local entities, the need exists in the local community for such a project, and the proposal will not duplicate existing resources already available in the community. LDC also ensures that all project proposal and funding requests accomplish an action item in the plan. Project proposals and funding requests not contained in the plan are not considered for funding. LDC functions independently of the Steering Committee.

LDC is one of the keys to the Delta Bridge Project's success because of its thorough screening of proposals. In 2006, more than half of the proposals submitted to the LDC were returned to the applicants for further work. Once it is revised, LDC reconsiders the proposal. If not satisfied with the revisions, LDC may request that the applicant further refine the proposal. LDC is currently composed of seven diverse professionals with backgrounds in law, banking and finance, education, grant writing, and philanthropy. At least one member on the LDC has had in-depth field expertise for every proposal that has been submitted. LDC meets on an as-needed basis, calling meetings when proposals are due.

Southern's staff in Phillips County continues to play an important role in the process, essentially serving as staff to the Steering Committee and LDC and continuing to work with the goal teams. After LDC's approval of the proposal, Southern's board reviews the proposal, and it is then submitted to the Walton Family Foundation or other potential funders.

Results from the Delta Bridge Project

The Delta Bridge Project has already achieved results, including the following highlights.

Economic Impacts

- A $30,000 feasibility study for a 40-million-gallon-per-year biodiesel manufacturing plant that will create a sustainable industry in Phillips County and a market for soybean farmers—construction of the plant began in early 2007.
- A $2 million sweet potato processing facility that will benefit a group of extremely low-income African American farmers.
- The funding of a $1 million feasibility study for a proposed four-lane corridor connecting Interstates 55 and 40 through Phillips County.
- $400,000 to perform six EPA Brownfield audits and clean up of abandoned commercial sites.
- Development of a "greenspace corridor" along a primary entrance into the city, with $165,000 expended thus far for acquisition of property in order to promote the tourism industry.
- More than 200 matched-savings account participants who saved more than $100,000 (matched by more than $300,000). Asset purchases include thirteen homes, leveraging more than $500,000 in mortgage loans.
- Business counseling and training services provided to more than 1,300 people. Southern Financial Partners provided more than $2 million in loans to businesses in Phillips County.
- $356,000 to raze condemned buildings (including 125 houses), clear vacant lots, and remove more than 300 junk cars.
- $50,000 to help fund a regional labor survey to promote industrial recruitment.

Social Impacts

- A $4.2 million health and wellness center (the county's largest building project in decades).
- $2.3 million in financing and grants to support the KIPP charter school. The 95 percent African American middle school has been astonishingly successful—the first cohort of students has gone from a mean 20th to 90th percentile on standardized tests in four years.
- A $116,000 project to create a fixed-route public transportation system linking areas of the community where private vehicle ownership is lowest.

- A $1.5 million, twenty-unit low-income housing development.
- $300,000 to help restore the Centennial Baptist Church in downtown Helena–West Helena. The National Parks Service made the award to the E.C. Morris Foundation to help restore this national historic landmark designed and built by African American architect Henry James Price in 1905.
- A $240,000 grant to fund the start-up of the Boys and Girls Club of Phillips County, which will expand its capacity to serve over a thousand members.
- A $64,000 grant to enable secondary school students in Phillips County to attend vocational and technical training at the local community college.
- Support for new leaders in government, business, and nonprofit groups, including $15,000 for training elected officials of the newly merged city government of Helena–West Helena.
- More than 150 adult students in the two years of the Career Pathways program. Thus far, Phillips County students have a 100 percent graduation rate and an 85 percent job placement rate.

One of the greatest successes of the Delta Bridge Project to date is the leveraging of project resources. The Delta Bridge Project has generated over $50 million in grants and loans invested in Phillips County. From its own internal resources, Southern has awarded over $800,000 in grants and loaned over $6.8 million for projects directly tied to the PCSCP. Southern's funding has leveraged additional funds from private foundations (including the Walton Family Foundation), state and national governments, and the private sector.

As a community in the rural Delta, Phillips County is relatively isolated, and it often lacks both the local expertise and the community resources to attract funding. Southern staff, including its development office, have helped to mitigate this weakness. By using the community-developed PCSCP, Southern's staff are able to match local priorities with external funding from state, federal, and private sources. Southern staff include professional fundraisers and grant writers who have access to grant-making databases, varied networking opportunities, and technical expertise on a broad range of issues. Through these methods, Southern has the ability to supplement existing local fundraising capacity.

After identifying a funding opportunity, Southern personnel often provide technical grant-writing assistance to local Phillips County–based organizations. In one example, Southern staff assisted the E.C. Morris Foundation to draft a proposal to the National Park Service that resulted in a $300,000 grant. As local groups continue to submit applications to the Delta Bridge Project funding process, Southern's staff will continue to work with local participants to provide one-on-one training and to develop their fund-raising capacity.

The targeted and comprehensive community development approach also appeals to donors. When Phillips County–based organizations submit proposals referencing both the community developed strategic plan and the resources that are available to support development efforts, funders have been generous. In one example, according to the grant writer for a $5.7 million multicounty education grant, the resources available to the Phillips County community were critical to the successful evaluation of the proposal, particularly when the proposal was weighed against other communities without an active program like the Delta Bridge Project.

On several occasions, local organizations that have secured partial funding for a community project have contacted Southern's staff for assistance in securing the remaining funding. In one economic development example, a local nonprofit stated that it required a $400,000 matching grant for a $2 million value-added agriculture project primarily funded by the federal government. To complicate matters further, the local nonprofit stated that it was up against a tight deadline and needed the funding within days or it would lose its other funding commitments. Expediting its approval process, Southern was able to abbreviate the traditional funding process and awarded the funding. By preserving the ability to respond quickly with its resources, Southern has helped local groups to capitalize on funding opportunities.

Funding from the Delta Bridge Project has also been used to develop the long-term capacity of local institutions. From its internal resources, Southern has awarded grants to two local institutions to hire grant writers to fuel the future local institutional growth. In both these cases, Southern determined that the local institution already had a high level of management capacity and an excellent track record delivering outputs, but without a grant writer faced future funding constraints and deprived the community of other services.

Significant community change projects require substantial investments to effect revitalization. With $530 million in assets, Southern can internally provide the combination of financing resources required for key projects, including grants, development loans, bank loans, credit enhancements, and technical expertise. If additional resources are required, Southern has the external public and private financing to assist in project funding. By making financing possible, many strategic goals in the PCSCP become realistic and achievable.

To illustrate how Southern supports the growth of community institutions, an analysis of the KIPP Delta College Preparatory School, a charter school in Phillips County, is instructive. The KIPP program currently enrolls students from grades five to nine. Every year, the KIPP School adds two new fifth-grade classes, requiring an expansion of its physical facilities. To meet this need, Southern and other partners have provided a mix of grants, development loans, bank loans, credit enhancements, and technical expertise.

For the expansion into its new building located on Cherry Street in Helena, Arkansas, the KIPP school required a $2.3 million loan to renovate an abandoned historic building. Southern provided a $1.169 million loan in KIPP's second year of operations, roughly dividing it equally between the First Bank of the Delta and its nonprofit affiliate, Southern Financial Partners. The local Southern Financial Partners' loan officer arranged for the U.S. Department of Agriculture's Community Facilities program to provide the remaining $1.169 million in financing. Southern's lending staff had the expertise to ensure that USDA program requirements were met. The USDA also provided a 90 percent guarantee on Southern's portion of the loan.

A traditional bank would have been unlikely to lend to KIPP for several reasons. First, the school was still relatively new and had not established a three-year operational track record. Second, school buildings are specialized structures. In the event of foreclosure, it would have been difficult to sell a special-use building on a street largely occupied by abandoned, boarded up buildings. Third, a traditional bank is less likely to have the expertise and to commit the staff time to pursue the USDA loan and guarantee. Understanding that public education is a key economic driver, Southern was willing to commit the resources and to assume more risk. Southern Financial Partners later provided an additional $300,000 working-capital loan to the KIPP School. In addition to its lending, Southern has provided grant support to develop the KIPP program in Phillips County. Through the Delta Bridge Project, KIPP received a $400,000 grant to add on portable, temporary classrooms for the upcoming tenth- and eleventh-grade classes. Southern has also provided several other grants for the KIPP program, including a $250,000 grant to purchase land options for the creation of a high school and a middle school campus. Southern then provided a $50,000 grant to clean up the blighted area where the campuses will be located. Other large Delta Bridge Projects have also received multiple forms of financing from Southern. Southern provided $2.1 million in permanent financing for the health and wellness center. For the biodiesel manufacturing plant, Southern provided a $30,000 grant for the feasibility study as well as partial financing for the project.

Conclusion

The Delta Bridge Project is a targeted and comprehensive community-led development initiative. Creation of a local infrastructure and a defined process enabled the community to establish a unified vision and to establish a blueprint for change detailed in the PCSCP. Southern's staff are working closely with the community to implement key priorities from the strategic plan, serving as a resource to match identified priorities with funding opportunities. Southern has funded community projects largely with its own internal resources and, where needed, with external financing partners. While change will come only gradually in a complex rural community like Phillips County, beset with a myriad of deep social and economic problems, Delta Bridge Project has made some initial substantial strides to revitalize the economy and reengage residents to cooperate to realize a better future of their community.

15

Effective Civic Engagement

Lessons from the Seattle School District—A Memoir

NORMAN RICE AND LYNDA PETERSEN

Norman B. Rice, former mayor of Seattle from 1990 to 1998, has learned the value of civic engagement. A foundation of the Rice administration was the strategic involvement of the citizenry in policy development. Having gained a reputation for uniting opponents during his tenure on the Seattle City Council, Rice faced the most divisive of issues during his first few months as mayor. The faith of the community in the Seattle schools was all but lost prior to the 1990 mayoral election. Race, economic status, and disputes over financing disillusioned citizens as the special interest groups and political players remained irresolute. What was missing from the debate was quality education for Seattle's children, without which the community would not grow and develop. After campaigning a platform of unity and promised solutions for the struggling school district, Rice convened the Seattle Education Summit to counter those divisions and use community values and priorities to craft proposed solutions.

The Education Summit of 1990 was never promised as a permanent solution for the Seattle schools. Indeed, engaging the public to determine community values and priorities should be a continuing process. This strategy requires a strong political will for elected officials who will implement recommendations the process produces. While there are no guarantees, garnering community support is an advantage few elected officials or community leaders could deny. What follows in this chapter is a memoir about the efforts to restore confidence in the Seattle schools in 1990 and offer a possible blueprint for new efforts.

Anti-Busing Initiative on the November 1989 Ballot

In 1989, a year before the Seattle Education Summit, the Seattle schools faced many of the same problems that plague schools in nearly every other American city. School officials were grappling with declining enrollment, inadequate state funding, poor academic performance, and growing frustration by parents, students, and teachers. Tensions around race and class were exacerbated. Initiative 34, also known as the Anti-Busing Initiative, was slated for the November 1989 ballot. This initiative was supported by a group called Save Our Schools (SOS) and was led by Seattle City

Attorney Doug Jewett, a Republican and a candidate in the Seattle mayoral race. Proponents of the initiative wanted to end mandatory busing intended to desegregate Seattle schools. The initiative provided that the Seattle School District would receive 6 percent of all city revenue to be used to improve neighborhood schools and implement an open enrollment system. Rice entered the mayoral race just minutes before the filing deadline and stated his frustration with the busing initiative, divisive language, and isolating politics as his prime motivators. Campaigning on efforts to unify the city and improve schools, Rice faced Jewett, an outspoken supporter of the initiative.

In November 1989, Seattle voters sent a mixed message with their ballots narrowly passing Initiative 34 with less than a 1 percent margin of victory, while electing Rice over Jewett with 58 percent of the votes. Six weeks later, the school board turned down the extra money, in effect ending the initiative (HistoryLink 2007). Pressure was exerted on newly elected Mayor Rice to fulfill his campaign promise of addressing the declining standards of the Seattle schools. However, he would have to work within the politics of the school board and special interest groups and with skepticism of the community to do it.

Citizen Involvement Mission

As mayor, Rice promulgated a citizen involvement mission to guide all actions conducted by the mayor's office (Tupper 1993):

> To provide honest, accessible leadership and outstanding service to the citizens, employees, and regional neighbors of the City of Seattle, and further develop a clear collective sense of vision, empowerment, and responsibility, in order to make our diverse City and the surrounding region an even better place to live, learn, work, and play.

Upholding his campaign promise, Rice went to work organizing a Seattle Education Summit, an event he hoped would utilize the input of the Seattle community on implementing real change for the ailing Seattle School District. Mayoral intervention in urban education reform was a bold move for a first major initiative. Mayors are often hesitant to spend their political capital on public education, since they do not appoint school board members and have no control over the district's fiscal policy. However, as others have affirmed, mayoral leadership is needed to bring full engagement of the community to public education and to ensure school system accountability. Further, mayors often see an improving public school system as a key social indicator for urban livability and indeed community development. This was Rice's motivation for undertaking the Seattle Education Summit in 1990.

Seattle Education Summit

To begin the planning process, Rice appointed Constance Rice and Ancil Payne as co-chairs of the agenda committee. Payne, a beloved community steward with a long political and broadcasting career, and Rice, a community leader with a doctorate in education, were charged with developing the summit. Many leaders supported the idea of hosting an event that would garner community-wide support and work toward the goal of improving the schools. However, outlining the detailed plan of the event was a more complex task that took months. A planning mission statement was created to guide all of the subsequent planning: "The purpose of the Summit is to move all segments of Seattle toward a comprehensive solution to problems facing our schools and community" (Education Summit Planning Mission Statement 1990).

A committee of sixty stakeholders, widely representative of the community, was created to oversee the planning of the summit and to ensure the different components of the event remained aligned with the larger issues. Long-term strategies were developed to work toward the renewal of "educational equality, safety, and parental confidence in our schools" (Rice 1990). Rice included representatives from every sector in the planning process because he felt they would all be critical players in the implementation of the action plan for improving the schools. And, while he intended to be present and participate in the event, he understood he could not be a part of everything and instead associated himself with a respected group of professionals.

Underlying Theory

From the inception, Rice and summit organizers intended the event to be accessible to every citizen. Just as every person in the public, private, and nonprofit sectors stood to benefit from high-performing local schools, so the responsibility for improving them falls on every citizen. The goal was to engage not only principals, teachers, students, and parents but also citizens from the larger community. Further, effort was made to promote the summit as worth the time necessary for full participation.

At the heart of the summit was the belief that results of community engagement were in no way predetermined. Indeed, if priorities were already known, resources used to plan and implement the summit would have been wasted. The election of a new mayor created hope for change and opportunity for consensus among disparate stakeholders.

To guide the summit planning process, a list of values and preferred outcomes was developed. Many of the statements in this list focused on the inclusion of all citizens and an intention to bring in groups or individuals who typically did not participate in community debates (Education Summit Implementation Plan 1990). Further, no one was to dominate the summit. The summit provided for future engagements. Success was defined as the creation of "a positive environment for similar cooperative community processes organized around other issues." School-related outcomes were encapsulated as "the summit should end in general agreement that the groups and individuals who participated will commit resources and work together to achieve progress on three to five major education issues" and that both short-term and long-term achievable action steps will be identified. A final value was that the summit would not be a "quick fix" for the schools (Education Summit Implementation Plan 1990).

Community Summit Meetings

The summit convened community meetings intended to identify the priorities of the community for improving schools that would lead to the discussion at a citywide summit. Summit organizers understood the importance placed on including all segments of the community. Recruiting an extensive and diverse participation from *all neighborhoods* was a formidable task in recruitment and cooperation.

As locations around the city were considered, several critical components were assessed: available parking, proximity to public transit, handicap accessibility, a separate room suitable for child care, the capability for wired technology, and a space large enough that groups could be separated for smaller discussions. By fulfilling these criteria and providing food, summit organizers hoped to eliminate any barriers preventing an average citizen from participating. Further, organizers included meetings on Sunday to accommodate those who could not come to Saturday meetings. Thirty-two locations meeting the criteria were chosen throughout the city and included community centers, high schools, and elementary schools.

After the locations were confirmed, the plan for recruiting diverse stakeholder participant groups was put into action. The Rice mayoral campaign had a significant number of grassroots organizations and volunteers that aided in its success; they were subsequently called upon to assist in outreach for the summit. Sue Tupper, lead community organizer for the summit, figured that going door-to-door in every neighborhood to advertise the event was not feasible. Thus, she and her team obtained the list of Seattle voters who consistently vote in local elections. At the very least, this list provided a large pool of participants who were informed about the schools. Outreach teams were sent throughout the neighborhoods armed with invitations personally signed by Mayor Rice to attend the community meetings. Tupper believes the invitation from Rice was a powerful tool, symbolizing an opportunity to ease conflict and promote solutions to school crisis. Houses that were "door-belled" also received subsequent mailings and phone calls prior to the community meeting. To ensure that every citizen heard about the summit, a multipronged media campaign was launched. Press releases and public service announcements were widely distributed.

While a major mayoral initiative, resources to plan and implement the summit were not exclusively city funds. Bob Watt, then deputy mayor, remembers participating in significant fund-raising for the event. Also, there were considerable in-kind resources from stakeholders: computers were donated, much of the facilitation was accomplished with donated labor, and there was no cost associated with the use of the sites selected. Even with this support, Watt estimated the cost of the summit to be around $100,000, a cost yielding much more in benefits.

Community Summit Meetings

In April 1990, over 1,950 people gathered at thirty-two sites around the city to discuss and prioritize the issues facing the schools and the ways in which to improve them (Summary of Community Meetings 1990). Tupper remembers the relentless rain during the days leading up to the April meeting and the fears they all had that nobody was going to show. Instead, the sun came out and so did the community. Site managers, included in the training and organization of the event, organized the participants into groups of ten at the different sites. Participants were welcomed and informed of the agenda and process for the day's discussions. Every group selected a timekeeper, a recorder, and a leader, who was given the task of reading the instructions at every table and beginning the discussion. There were few planned speeches. Posturing was not allowed, but people were afforded the opportunity to speak their mind. Community meeting organizers wanted to ensure the day began positively, so each group was instructed on how to participate in a visionary exercise. People were encouraged to imagine the results of the summit five years down the road. Participants were then asked to share what they saw and what they believe would need to be accomplished at the summit to produce those outcomes. This exercise was not meant to take more than twenty minutes to complete, and from there participants were told to begin a list of current problems. The visioning exercise created a positive start for all participants and prevented any negative agenda from dominating the discussions.

When problem lists were complete, participants prioritized them by selecting the top five most distressing issues. This exercise, repeated at all of the sites, produced a community-initiated comprehensive list of the schools' most pressing problems or issues. Organized community groups who had a specific motive or stake in the summit were encouraged to meet before the community meetings to plan which issues they would include as a priority. These groups were interspersed with the average citizens attending the community meetings, preventing any special interest group from promoting their agenda.

Soon after the community meetings, summit organizers and Rice and his staff gathered in a room where the walls were covered by the prioritized lists developed at the meetings. Very quickly, patterns and reoccurring themes emerged and evolved into the most frequently stated priorities. The reports from the thirty-two sites were compiled into a final report that was prepared for the citywide summit meeting in May 1990. At the core of this report were the five priorities determined at the community summit meetings (Summary of Community Meetings 1990):

1. Enhance the learning environment for students and teachers.
2. Involve the community in school-based decision making and make schools community focal points.
3. Make sure every child is safe, healthy, and ready to learn.
4. Recognize and celebrate cultural diversity in the schools.
5. Enhance basic education funding.

To the surprise of some and to delight of others, busing was not a common response and thus not included among priorities. Perhaps participants felt they had addressed busing with their vote in the election five months earlier, or perhaps they believed there were larger issues at the root of busing or related issues. Success of the community meetings was evident in the number of participants and in the robustness of the reoccurring priorities. Organizers were pleased with the quality of discussion and effort put forth in the community meetings and were confident outcomes would lead discussions at the summit. Tupper remembers the renewed energy organizers felt after the community meetings: "Everyone was excited to get back to work to make the [citywide] summit equally successful."

Citywide Summit

Summit organizers were not the only ones energized by the successful community meetings. A number of positive newspaper articles and editorials portrayed the city's collective hope that the summit was genuine in its attempt to reverse the recent negative discourse surrounding Seattle schools and to listen to the community for change. One editorialist for the *Seattle Times* who attended the community meeting at a local high school wrote there was "enough [hope] to make you nervous, because hope is such a fragile thing. Now that so much of it has been generated, the next steps are critical" (Cameron 1990). In other articles, Rice was quoted as hopeful but cautious: "Some of the changes identified at the community meetings are things we can do right away. But many of these changes will take time" (Flores 1990a).

The citywide Summit was held in May 1990 in the centrally located Seattle Center. On the first day, the public attended or joined small group discussions on issue priorities. On the second day, meetings included only preappointed task forces composed of representatives from the community meetings. Each group at the community meetings selected one representative to act as spokesperson at the summit. Additionally, there were representatives from the school board, city council, county council, and other public officials, who increased the level of political discourse at the summit. Undoubtedly, this was the reality in which any proposed solution would have to be considered.

Even though not all of the almost 2,000 participants of the community summit meetings could attend the citywide summit, organizers were diligent to keep them engaged. After having worked hard to gain the trust of the public, considerable effort was made to keep everyone abreast of the progress of the summit. Further, a larger goal of the summit was to foster trust and belief in the utility of civic engagement for sustained participation. All community meeting participants were sent a copy of the citywide priorities that were to be used as the focus of the summit discussions and contact information if the individual had any questions or concerns. In order to sustain legitimacy, organizers wanted to ensure that all future discussions and actions steps implemented could be directly traced back to the community meetings. As one of his administration's first events, Rice was adamant that the summit be a positive experience for the community participants.

The first day of the summit was devoted to discussions of the priorities outlined in the reports from the community meetings. The day began by viewing a professionally made video that welcomed the participants, provided background information, and explained the purpose of the summit. It summarized the results of the community meetings and presented a balanced account of the issues to be discussed. In addition to outlining current school problems, the video highlighted successful efforts the school district and other players were helping implement (Education Summit Implementation Plan 1990). Participants were separated into working groups and charged with the task of further discussing the given priorities and potential action steps required for each and perfecting the priority statements by the end of the day. While increased state funding, higher salaries for teachers, and other large-ticket items were often included, organizers encouraged participants to keep centered on solutions community members could implement. Rice and other leaders assured participants they understood the need for additional resources and would lobby state lawmakers to bolster education funding (Flores 1990a).

The second day was devoted to determining the action steps that would help achieve those goals. Additionally, all of the discussions from the first day of meetings were entered into a central computer system. When the participants returned on the second day, they were asked to confirm that what was recorded was indeed what was said. This step is crucial in any implementation of effective citizen engagement, as participants want to know they have been heard and heard accurately. A community leader from different sectors was assigned to chair five working groups, each addressing a priority identified by the community summit meetings. Attaining additional education funding from the state, perhaps the hardest priority to achieve, was given to Dan Evans, former Washington State governor and U.S. senator. Other leaders included business leaders and a librarian. These groups were to identify specific action steps and spend the next month beginning to implement these steps or working to build commitments from community and business leaders that could be unveiled at the community celebration scheduled for June 1990.

Many of the summit's critics voiced concern that the city did not need another report that would gather dust and provide few tangible results for the schools. Rice was aware of this criticism and placed great importance on working to create real results for the schools. A summit implementation group was established to provide an ongoing mechanism to monitor and coordinate initiatives the working groups created ("Are We Sustaining . . ." 1990). This group had very similar membership to the planning committee, including leaders from the public and private sectors, schools, and community. It was developed to assume responsibility for the short-term and long-range implementation plans and was a visible commitment to action by those involved in the summit. Significant community participation made the summit successful, but without the commitment from public leaders to turn participation into action, the summit could have resulted in another dust-gathering report.

The summit implementation group vowed to support implementing the initiatives in "Are We Sustaining Commitment and Accountability?" (1990). Within this report, vital players in the schools—such as Rice, the city council, Superintendent William Kendrick, members of the school board, Seattle community colleges, the Seattle Business Alliance, and representatives from the teachers' labor union—all pledged their support. Indeed, by the middle of May 1990, even the most staunch cynics and critics had to publicly associate themselves with the summit's positive results, given such widespread community support.

With the backing of major political, business, and community leaders and a number of confirmed short-term victories, Rice and summit organizers were ready to unveil the results and celebrate the success of the summit with the entire Seattle community.

A Celebration and Commitment to the Seattle Schools

June 16, 1990, had been selected as a day for celebrating the end of the Education Summit and the beginning of the implementation of the resulting recommendations. The day had been designated, but what would be celebrated and by how many people were larger unknowns that left many organizers anxious. As the day grew near, and the successes from the summit were counted, the anxiousness morphed into excitement. The day began with a culmination breakfast at Garfield High School. Among the attendees were summit organizers and political and education leaders. Members of the media were also on hand to capture these leaders signing agreements and pledges to continue their cooperation and support of the developed initiatives, all while standing behind a banner proclaiming JUST THE BEGINNING in large bold type. The afternoon was spent at the Seattle Woodland Park Zoo, where the public was invited to a rally celebrating the summit's achievements. Three hundred parents, educators, and children gathered for entertainment, carnival-style food, and an update on the summit progress.

In just two months, the summit brought in $1 million of new resources to the Seattle Schools. Following are a few of the successes noted (McCloud 1990):

- The region's Metro Transit Authority agreed to provide up to $200,000 or more in free bus passes for school field trips to enhance learning opportunities outside the classroom.
- The Seattle business community agreed to finance and develop a training institute for school district personnel, principals, and teachers.
- The Seattle-King County Health Department and several local healthcare providers agreed to develop a comprehensive student healthcare system.
- The State of Washington agreed to provide additional early childhood education funding.
- The Seattle Public Library agreed to work with school libraries to coordinate information, making textbooks and assigned reading available at city branch libraries.

While these smaller victories would not be the catalyst for broad systemic change the district needed, there were vitally important victories for keeping the support for the Education Summit high. Furthermore, they bolstered the efforts to attain the larger victories.

The working group charged with researching new funding options, led by former Governor Dan Evans, addressed the dropping enrollment in the Seattle schools, as the number of students enrolled is linked to state funds the district receives. They also explored other avenues for increased funding, including private foundations and efforts to strategically lobby the state legislature to lift the "levy lid" that limits local financing of school districts (Flores 1990b). Mayor Rice pledged to give updates every six months regarding Summit Implementation Group progress and other task forces working to implement more change for the Seattle schools. Less than six months after that community celebration, Mayor Rice gave a very positive update with the passing of a voter-approved levy guaranteeing additional funds for Seattle's students.

The Family and Education Levy

In November 1990, just one year after the divisive busing initiative threatened to cause irreparable damage to the Seattle Schools, the Families and Education Levy passed and stood as a statement of the city's support for the schools and the biggest financial contribution to come out of the summit. Making children "safe, healthy, and ready to learn" was not only a priority of the levy but was also used as the motto by which the levy was promoted throughout the city. The levy guaranteed $69.2 million at about $8.5 million annually for seven years, paid through increased property taxes. The levy passed with 57 percent support from those who voted. However, according to the *Seattle Times,* in 1990, 86 percent of Seattle voters did not have children (Seattle Times Editorial Board 1990). Support of this levy by so many voters who did not have school-age children illustrates the extent to which the summit gained the trust of the larger community and successfully portrayed the importance in leaving the whole community vested in the success of the schools.

The city aimed to address multiple issues outside the classroom that can affect the ability of a student to learn or remain in school through graduation (Bock 1990). Additionally, the levy freed up $2.1 million in the district's budget that could be redirected to classroom education. The following goals undergirded the Family and Education Levy as Proposition 1 on the November 1990 ballot (Street 1990):

- Implement community priorities established through the Education Summit.
- Make children safe, healthy, and ready to learn.
- Support families and strengthen parent effectiveness as educational partners.
- Develop community schools.
- Build stronger partnerships between schools and community-based agencies.
- Celebrate cultural diversity and promote equal learning opportunities.
- Free school district resources to improve classroom learning environments.

The programs funded by the levy included expanding latchkey programs, dropout prevention, and adding school counselors, nurses, and family resource centers (Bock 1990). As can often happen when a city government works to improve the state of a school district, there was opposition from a school board fearing their power being usurped. However, this levy was savvy in its efforts to relieve some of the financial burden on the school district and, in essence, assist the school board in its mission. This effort confirmed the role of the city to assist in the well-being of its youngest constituents.

The levy was reauthorized by Seattle voters in 1997 and again in 2004, when it was expanded to contribute $116 million over seven years (City of Seattle 2008). A sharper focus was placed on preparing children for school, improving academic achievement, and reducing disproportional results in the schools. Further, an emphasis was placed on serving students and schools that have traditionally underperformed and on improving early learning in the first three years based on current research identifying this crucial time in a student's development.

Conclusion

Just five months into his first term as mayor, Norman Rice embarked on the Seattle Education Summit. While divisive issues surrounding the Seattle schools prompted him to join the race for mayor and promise a summit during his campaign, the process of the summit and the eventual outcomes were widely unknown. Rice gathered professionals from the public and private sectors to assist in the planning and implementation of the summit, while intentionally not allowing the political powerhouses of the issue to dominate the discourse. The Families and Education Levy was passed as a way to address the issues identified in the summit and deliver a real outcome just a few months after the community engagement. However, a less tangible but equally important outcome of the summit was the trust that was built within the community by the process. Rice and summit organizers were adamant that the process be rooted in fidelity, and that it be transparent, ethical, and without predetermined outcome. The result of this diligence was a developed trust in city government.

This early success in the Rice administration guided other major accomplishments and the use of citizen engagement within those. Then–Deputy Mayor Watt does not believe the downtown development that was later achieved by Mayor Rice would have been possible without the trust and respect that he developed early in his administration. Other major accomplishments from the Rice administration include the city's revised Comprehensive Plan and the Welfare to Work policy. Rice's legacy in Seattle includes the ability to bring consensus to an issue ripe with conflict and to gather the various players together for the public good.

He is bringing these lessons to a new generation of public leaders. Norman Rice is heading up the *Civic Engagement in the 21st Century Project* at the Evans School of Public Affairs at the University of Washington, his alma mater (then called the Graduate School of Public Affairs). It is not by luck or chance that Rice's major accomplishments used effective citizen engagement and a developed trust from the community. His most recent project aims to convey the vital elements of best practices such as the summit and others from his administration. He is also emphasizing the efforts he has worked on since leaving office, such as community and economic development and improved transportation planning in the Puget Sound region. Indeed, the necessity and value of utilizing effective citizen engagement in policymaking knows no boundary of generation or jurisdiction.

References

"Are We Sustaining Commitment and Accountability?" 1990. Education Summit and Related Materials. 4601–02 47/8. Seattle Municipal Archives.

Bock, Paula. 1990. "Many Who OK'd Levy Don't Have Children—Most Supporters Don't Use the Public Schools." *Seattle Times* (November 14).

Cameron, Mindy. 1990. "Education Summit's Hopeful Start." *Seattle Times,* April 22.

City of Seattle Department of Neighborhoods. 2008. "Families and Education Levy." http://www.seattle.gov/neighborhoods/education/edlevy.htm. (Accessed 14 January 2008.)

Education Summit Implementation Plan. 1990. Education Summit and Related Materials. 4601–02. 47/8. Seattle Municipal Archives.

Education Summit Planning Mission Statement. 1990. Seattle Education Summit. Briefings and Planning Papers. 4583–02. 3/1. Seattle Municipal Archives.

Flores, Michele Matassa. 1990a. "Education Summit Starts Acquiring a Rice Focus." *Seattle Times* (May 2).

———. 1990b. "Education Summit Scores Success—Even Among Critics." *Seattle Times* (June 17).

HistoryLink. 2007. "Anti-Busing Initiative Campaign Launched on June 16, 1989." HistoryLink: The Online Encyclopedia of Washington State History. http://historylink.org/essays/output.cfm?file_id=3943. (Accessed 2 April 2007.)

McCloud, Thom. 1990. "The Seattle Education Summit: Grassroots Effort Restoring Quality, Confidence in Schools." *Nation's Cities Weekly* (August 6): 3.

Rice, Norman. 1990. *Mayor's Letter to Education Planning Committee Members.* Seattle Education Summit Briefings and Planning Papers. 4583–02. 3/1. Seattle Municipal Archives. (March 2).

Seattle Times Editorial Board. 1990. "Without a Vested Interest—Seattle Voters Are Strong Building Block for Schools." *Seattle Times,* November 18.

Street, Jim. Legislative Department. 1990. 4683–02. Box 2/11. Seattle Municipal Archives.

Summary of Community Meeting Reports Prepared for the Citywide Summit Meeting. 1990. D-202 Item No. 3084. Seattle Municipal Archives, May.

Tupper, Suzanne. 1993. Your City: Seattle Works in the 1990s. D-172. Item No. 2603. Seattle Municipal Archives.

Part 4

Federal Policy

16

Reforming CDBG

An Illusive Quest

Terry F. Buss

The U.S. Department of Housing and Urban Development's (HUD) Community Development Block Grant (CDBG)—$4 billion in funding distributed to 1,128 entitlement communities and fifty states in FY2006—in operation since 1974, is the largest federal community development program. Until 2001 or so, CDBG management gave little concern to whether the program actually produced results for communities, citizens, and businesses. Although there had always been considerable anecdotal evidence that CDBG did good things, there was little objective data to substantiate its results. Communities and states—grantees—also showed little interest in demonstrating results (at least to the federal government, many viewing funding as a kind of revenue sharing whereby they could do mostly what they wanted within the broad confines of law). Under the second term of the George W. Bush administration, five separate reengineering initiatives were undertaken to improve CDBG's performance, some successful, others perhaps not so:

- Strengthening America's Communities Initiative (SACI).
- Reengineering the performance measurement system.
- Reforming the CDBG allocation formula.
- Developing a new management information system (IDIS—Integrated Disbursement and Information System).
- Streamlining the Consolidated Plan.

In this chapter, I look closely at each of these initiatives, laying out possible future directions or alternatives not necessarily on the HUD agenda.

The CDBG Program

The CDBG program, administered by HUD's Community Planning and Development (CPD) office, funds entitlement communities and states[1] with annual grants to develop viable urban communities by funding decent housing, a suitable living environment, and economic opportunities for low- and moderate-income persons.

223

Grantees carry out a wide range of community development activities targeted at revitalizing neighborhoods, stimulating economic development, and improving community facilities and services, against grantee program and funding priorities. CDBG funds may be used for acquisition of real property; relocation and demolition; rehabilitation of residential and nonresidential structures; construction of public facilities and improvements, such as water and sewer facilities, streets, neighborhood centers, and the conversion of school buildings for eligible purposes; public services, within certain limits; activities relating to energy conservation and renewable energy resources; and provision of assistance to profit-motivated businesses to carry out economic development and job creation/retention activities. HUD allocates grants through a statutory dual formula, using objective measures of community need: extent of poverty, population, housing overcrowding, age of housing, and population growth lag in relationship to other metropolitan areas.

Because grantees have discretion in how and on what they invest funding, CDBG presents challenges to performance-based management at all levels of government (GAO 2006b).

Strengthening America's Communities Initiative

The SACI initiative was intended to be results oriented, flexible, and targeted toward greatest need. SACI would achieve this by merging eighteen disparate programs into one, then consolidating it in the Department of Commerce (DoC), with strict accountability and performance standards. Many of the programs to be merged were adjudged by the U.S. Office of Management and Budget (OMB) in its Program Assessment Rating Tool (PART) assessments as ineffective, unable to demonstrate results, or duplicative of other programs (Boyd et al. 2005). In the case of CDBG, its PART ostensibly found it to be "ineffective," scoring badly on program purpose and design, strategic planning, program results and accountability, and only somewhat better on program management.[2] So CDBG was high on the target list for reform.

But, for many insiders, not only was the program a poor performer on the PART, it also was widely held to be mismanaged and resistant to any attempts at reform. At one point, HUD had fallen so low that an outside inspector general had to be appointed to proctor HUD operations. In nearly every budget cycle for years, OMB unsuccessfully proposed eliminating CDBG altogether. The Government Accountability Agency (GAO)—a watchdog agency of Congress—reflected the tenure of management criticisms in its reports:

> [HUD] has been repeatedly criticized for management and oversight weaknesses that have made the agency vulnerable to waste, fraud, abuse, and mismanagement. In 1994, GAO included HUD in its list of high-risk programs because of four long-standing deficiencies: weak internal controls, poor information and financial management systems, an ineffective organizational structure, and an insufficient mix of staff with the proper skills. In June 1997, HUD announced its

"HUD 2020 Management Reform Plan," a sweeping set of proposals intended to, among other things, address management weaknesses and downsize the agency (GAO 1998).

In what many believe to be a last-ditch effort at reform, the lame-duck Bush administration believed that the only way to achieve reform was to move CDBG out of HUD to DoC, where they believed it would have much stronger management oversight.

SACI was never authorized by Congress. Congress loves CDBG because its members are able to take credit for millions of dollars spent on their constituencies, as are mayors and governors. SACI pitted the administration against powerful lobby groups, representing states and communities receiving grants, but also individuals, nonprofits, churches, and numerous other organizations, ranging from social services to housing to economic development, which received funding. Cutting off federal funding to entities that have received it since 1974, needless to say, was very unpopular, although perhaps politically courageous. Even senior HUD management—part of the executive branch—gave limited public support for SACI, while actively undermining it in private. Inexplicably, though, SACI may have failed because of the way it was managed through Congress. Rather than consulting congressional leadership and gaining their support, the Bush administration sent SACI to Congress cold.

One thing SACI did do for federal community development programs, especially CDBG, was send a message that they needed to reform or risk continued assaults by the Bush administration. Many grantees worried about CDBG prospects, as did HUD senior management. Performance took center stage at CDBG.[3] With the loss of control of Congress by Republicans to Democrats in 2007, it is yet to be determined whether the CDBG reform movement can be sustained.

Performance Measurement System Reform

Negotiated Performance Partnership—Joint Working Group

A joint working group comprising representatives from the Council of State Community Development Agencies (COSCDA), National Community Development Association (NCDA), National Association for County Community Economic Development (NACCED), National Association of Housing and Redevelopment Officials (NAHRO), National Council of State Housing Agencies (NCSHA), CPD and HUD's Office of Policy Development and Research (PD&R), and OMB met regularly for well over a year in formal and informal meetings to negotiate and develop a performance measurement system for CDBG, along with HUD's other block grants—HOME Investment Partnerships Program (HOME), Emergency Shelter Grants (ESG), and Housing Opportunities for Persons with AIDS (HOPWA). Interestingly, this working group was already achieving results long before the administration initiated SACI. The Bush administration lost a lot of credibility with community development groups, having kept them in the dark about SACI while at the same time promoting collaboration in the working group.

COSCDA took the initiative in addressing the performance measurement issue, then in spawning the working group and seeing it through to its successful conclusion. This initiative could serve as a model for intra-agency (HUD), interagency (OMB–HUD), intergovernmental, and advocacy group cooperation.

Paraphrasing from COSCDA's performance initiative documents:[4] Over the past eighteen months, COSCDA engaged its members and outcome framework experts in the development of an "integrated outcome framework" for CDBG, HOME, ESG, and HOPWA. COSCDA took a proactive design approach. COSCDA believed those who deliver programs at the community level are better suited than HUD to determine appropriate outcome indicators and measures for their projects and activities. One of COSCDA's basic tenets was that any outcome system must serve the management interests of programs. CDBG's strength is its flexibility, tailored to meet state and local needs; therefore, outcome measures must also be flexible enough that grantees can use them, thereby ensuring that the system is meaningful, relevant, and useful at the service level and that information gathered is valid and reliable. A key COSCDA objective of an outcome system is that it must add value for grantees without causing undue burdens.

Any nationwide outcome system must be developed in accordance with CDBG statutory purposes and objectives. The system must distinguish between direct program outcomes on those being served in accordance with statutory requirements and indirect longer term impacts that might be accomplished for programs. The system must be comprehensive, including objectives, outcomes, and indicators of program activities such as housing rehabilitation, water and sewer programs, and shelter for the homeless. Every activity and project currently funded by CDBG—including HOME, ESG, and HOPWA—must be covered.

COSCDA argued that CDBG must include three overarching objectives: creating suitable living environments; providing decent, affordable housing; and creating economic opportunities.

After reaching agreement among state grantees, a process that took months to accomplish, COSCDA worked with other group representatives to reach agreement on the measurement system's design. The final set of indicators appeared in the *Federal Register* (see Figure 16.1).[5]

Although the working group made great strides in developing and implementing an effective performance system based on consensus, the initiative glossed over four critical issues: agreeing on CDBG's purpose, creating "viable" communities, establishing program impacts, and targeting places in need.

Program Purpose

There is little consensus on CDBG's purpose. Some see it as a kind of revenue sharing with few strings attached, while others see it as a program intended to fund

Figure 16.1   **Initial Negotiated Performance Measures for CDBG**

Number of households assisted (i.e., with water/sewer, community centers, etc.)
Number of community-wide assistance activities
Number of new businesses assisted
Number of existing businesses assisted
Number of persons served (e.g., in shelters, in public services, etc).
Number of jobs created
Number of jobs retained
Number of new homeowners assisted
Number of rental housing units produced
Number of new home ownership units produced
Number of housing units rehabilitated (to code)
Number of housing units repaired (for emergency)
Number of affordable housing units preserved
Number of years of unit affordability
Number of dollars of investment leveraged

pressing needs not met by states and communities. The Housing Act of 1974 lists twenty-five eligible community development activities that CDBG might fund; HUD expanded these to over eighty (see NAPA 2005a). CDBG overlaps with other programs in other agencies, making it anything but unique. The bottom line is that CDBG's purpose is whatever more than a thousand communities and fifty states, not to mention Congress, HUD, and OMB, say it is.

The working group, seeing no possibility of reaching agreement on purpose, prudently chose not to address the issue. Among stakeholders, with the exception of OMB, there is no momentum to formally clarify CDBG's purpose. As a result, CDBG's efforts to achieve results will inevitably fall short, because without a single purpose, there can be no agreement on whether the program has been or will be successful.

Viable Communities

OMB asked CDBG to incorporate the "viable community" concept—drawn from the Housing Act of 1974—into the performance measurement system: specifically, a definition of viable community against which entitlement communities and perhaps states can report progress. The working group resisted doing so: the implication was that were a community to become viable, it would likely no longer be eligible for CDBG funding. No jurisdiction willingly gives up federal funding. Additionally, even if the working group had agreed in principle to include community viability, they never figured out how to measure it: they believed that communities vary too significantly in character, structure, and need to allow for uniform measurement.

The National Academy of Public Administration (Academy) proposed an approach that was not adopted by the working group but nonetheless is useful in helping policymakers think about what CDBG is supposed to do. CDBG could

Figure 16.2   **Community Viability Analysis**

Neighborhood	Viability score	Viability target	Score/target	Annual $ estimate to achieve viability
#1				
. . .				
#5				
Viability indicators: [specified]				

designate a menu of approved indicators from which entitlement communities and states might craft their own definitions of viability. Communities would select at least five indicators from a list of agreed-upon metrics and use these to propose alternative definitions that could be utilized with CDBG approval. For each indicator, CDBG policymakers would suggest, or communities designate, some level constituting a viable community. For example, a viable community might be one in which median housing values meet or exceed a certain dollar amount. Individual indicators would receive a score on a range from most to least viable, and specific indicators could be weighted. Each indicator would be summed to yield a *community viability score.*

In addition to viability, CDBG might allow variation when defining "community," which may represent census blocks or tracts, political jurisdictions, designated neighborhood strategy areas, informal neighborhoods, zip codes, and the like. Because CDBG makes expenditures in different communities in different amounts, it could require communities to designate a reasonable number—five may be appropriate—of most distressed neighborhoods to assess viability. Communities with fewer neighborhoods would report what they have.

The Consolidated Plan or its annual update should be the reporting vehicle for community viability measurements. A new table in the performance measurement system might resemble Figure 16.2. Based on the sum of the indicators, each neighborhood would receive a viability score constituting a viable community. The score could be divided by the viable community score to yield a ratio or, if multiplied by 100, a percentage.

This approach allows communities to estimate how much funding—CDBG and/or federal and private funding—would be required to make America's most distressed communities "viable" over an extended period, say twenty years. CDBG might offer communities a series of options to calculate revitalization costs. This quantifies community viability using a flexible approach amenable to CDBG and the grantee. It also provides a cost estimate to achieve viability to show OMB and HUD how much federal investment might be required.

Alternative Performance Measurement Systems

CDBG grantees, thanks to the working group, use commonly available performance indicators—mostly outputs and occasionally outcome measures—gathered from administrative data, surveys, client records, and the like. But output and outcome indicators do not measure CDBG program impacts (see Chapter 6 for the distinction), although these indicators do help the administration and citizenry hold CDBG accountable for how funding is spent. If CDBG impacts were to be established, an alternative set of methodological approaches might be required.[6] The Academy proposed several alternatives that would complement or supplement parts of the traditional approach pursued by the working group (NAPA 2005a).

- *Social Science Attribution.* Take social science research that demonstrates—with high credability—CDBG program impact on one city or neighborhood, and then extrapolate the impact to all similar programs across the nation using econometric modeling.
- *Shift-Share.* Produce performance data allowing planners to estimate impacts by approximating the share a neighborhood contributes to the city on the whole, an already widely used method in urban economics—shift-share analysis.
- *Best- and Worst-Case Scenarios.* Take indicator data from those communities reporting, calculate the range of impacts from high to low, and then attribute them to nonrespondents.
- *Simulation.* Commission computer simulations of impacts in those CDBG expenditure areas where it is difficult to acquire primary data from grantees.
- *Opportunity Costs.* Ask communities to report opportunity costs—what investments were foregone in order to make the investment being assessed—as a measure of CDBG's importance.
- *Oversight and Accountability.* Create an independent board of practitioners, researchers, policymakers, and advocates to certify that the performance information produced is objective, satisfies social science research criteria, and is consistent with laws, regulations, and policies. An analog—consensus conference—for this is found in other fields—medicine and science, for example.[7]
- *Demonstration Projects.* Fund demonstrations for which performance data are gathered traditionally and compared with data gathered through the supplemental methods.

Targeting

To target or not to target is a major unresolved issue in CDBG (see next section, "CDBG Formula"). The Bush administration opposes spreading funding widely across communities to meet a variety of disparate needs and investing in areas that are not particularly in need or have become so distressed that they cannot be restored—or where the magnitude of needed funding is so great that investment would be infeasible. The administration prefers for grantees to target funds in selected areas in need where they believe investments will make a difference.

Others argue that the Housing Act of 1974 explicitly leaves it to communities (and later to states) to decide according to their priorities where investments will be made. Many are opposed to any HUD mandate to target, even when that might be a viable approach in their interests. Many communities that actually target oppose any targeting mandates. SACI was an attempt to compel some targeting mandates on communities. Opponents also suggest that the scant literature on CDBG impacts does not conclusively establish the efficacy of targeting.

Trying to force communities and states to target was probably the wrong approach to take given such strong resistance. HUD regulations have few teeth in this domain, and Congress likely will never pass legislation to compel targeting. What has not been tried by the administration is offering incentives within HUD's program to reward those that target.[8] Communities that target could receive advantages on HUD's competitive grant programs or waivers that would allow communities to pursue projects they might not otherwise be able to undertake.

CDBG Formula

A common complaint about CDBG is that the dual formula[9] often allocates funding to communities not in need, in the process reducing funding available for those most in need. OMB, in criticizing the formula in its FY2003 PART assessment, found, for example, that the "200 communities with the highest poverty rates received 35% less CDBG funds for each poor resident than 200 communities with the lowest poverty rates."[10]

There appears to be little impetus to radically change the formula. HUD's PD&R recently prepared an analysis—*CDBG Formula Targeting to Community Development Need*—exploring possible revisions to the existing CDBG formula. GAO also explored several options in its report *CDBG Formula* (GAO 2006a, 2006c). Although the revisions posed some interesting options that address some of the current formula's deficiencies—investing funding in well-off communities who are able to fend for themselves—PD&R and GAO basically tinkered with the existing ranking data without exploring more innovative possibilities. GAO has also explored the formula in a working group of experts under the auspices of the National Academies of Science but did not consider any innovations. Every interest group representing CDBG grantees—nine or so—opposed anything but minor tinkering with the formula (see Ramirez 2005).

Following is a summary of several major formula issues and possible alternatives that merit further exploration to assess their feasibility.[11] None of the issues and alternatives presupposes a coherent definition of what community development is and how it should be achieved by communities and states using federal money. Again, some see the CDBG program as being everything to everyone rather than focused on a tight set of needs. Some see CDBG as an antipoverty program, others as an infrastructure initiative. Still others believe it duplicates numerous other federal programs or displaces state and community investments. None are right or wrong, but they can greatly affect how funding is allocated and for what purpose.

1. Allocating Funding Based on Need and Fiscal Capacity

The current CDBG formula and PD&R's revisions reward entitlement communities on the basis of demographics such as numbers of poor people, poverty rates, income levels, and the like that measure need. However, communities that, by these measures, have needs may in some cases also have the fiscal capacity to meet those needs with their own resources. In these cases, the formula directs federal government resources both to places that can and places that cannot meet needs from their own resources. A proposed alternative: If the policy goal is to channel CDBG funds to poor communities, one alternative is to base the formula ranking of entitlement communities on a combination of poverty indicators and fiscal capacity. To receive CDBG funding, communities would need to score high on need and low on fiscal capacity. The portion of the formula ranking communities on need—measured by numbers of poor people, poverty rates, average incomes, and the like—has been demonstrated under PD&R proposals. The other portion on fiscal capacity is more difficult to measure, because there is limited experience in ranking communities this way, and federal data are less frequently gathered for this purpose. One way would be to create measures of fiscal capacity from the *Census of Government survey* (http://www.census.gov/govs/www/cog2002.html):

- *Census of Government Finance:* Revenues [taxes], debt, intergovernmental transfers from all sources, as proxy measures of capacity.
- *Census of Business:* Industries [sales receipts, payroll, etc.] as proxy measures of local economies' ability to pay.
- *Per capita income:* The average incomes of residents are likely to be highly correlated with fiscal capacity. Income may serve as a proxy for fiscal capacity.

Or, HUD could require entitlement communities to report local government fiscal information as part of the CDBG applications, through the annual Consolidated Planning process (see the section, "Reforming the Consolidated Plan"). If Congress wanted to increase funding to distressed communities that have fiscal capacity, it might legislate a matching fund requirement for wealthier places.

2. Targeting Funding Geographically Within Communities

Some believe that targeting relatively scarce CDBG resources into distressed communities will benefit poor people more than will the scattered investment approaches. It should be noted that there is no large body of scientific research supporting or refuting the viability of this investment strategy. At present, many communities target, others do not, but there is no targeting requirement in CDBG legislation. A proposed alternative: If the policy objective is to target CDBG funding to America's most distressed communities, then one approach under the formula would be to take all U.S. Census tracts in the country and rank them according to absolute distress and distress with growth potential—this measure is potentially complex and would need careful development and refinement. Set an appropriate cutoff in the rankings, and provide CDBG funding for these tracts. Funding could be provided outside tracts when it is determined to be critical to the successful investment and performance of the eligible tract. Another approach would be to rank tracts within states or communities, and fund those that meet a minimum threshold of need. This approach can be combined with the fiscal capacity ranking option suggested in the previous section (first bulleted item).

3. Reducing Administrative Burden on Smaller Communities

Small entitlement communities—with populations of at least 50,000 people—are perceived by some to be burdened with planning and reporting requirements—Consolidated Plans—that divert funding into planning for which they may lack sufficient capacity. The objection is that small communities do not receive much funding, but they are nonetheless required to prepare the same plans and reports as larger communities. A proposed alternative: If the policy objective is to relieve smaller communities of planning and administrative burdens that limit availability of funding for projects, then one option is to raise the statutory minimum population required for eligibility as an entitlement community to a threshold population greater than 50,000. The precise threshold at which a community becomes entitled to direct CDBG funding would have to be systematically assessed. Communities not making the threshold as an entitlement would become eligible for funding under the state CDBG program, which has no planning and minimal administrative requirements.

4. Rewarding Communities That Stress Economic Development Activities

Some observers say that although economic development (ED) activities are eligible expenditures under CDBG, few entitlement communities invest much funding in them. They also say economic development spurs community development by creating new fiscal resources the community can use to address its other development needs. Extensive research does not exist to support of refute this contention. A proposed alternative: If the policy goal for CDBG is to encourage ED investments, then the CDBG formula might be altered to encourage such investment by moving communities that have economic development deficits—a precise measure would need to be defined—up in the rankings to receive funding. To do this, the formula might include numbers of unemployed and/or unemployment rate, numbers of discouraged workers and rate, numbers of workers affected by mass layoffs, and small business job creation as components. But entitlement communities could, under CDBG, still invest funding in community development. To channel investment into economic development, HUD would likely have to establish performance goals in economic development that communities would have to achieve in order to qualify for funding in future years.

5. Assisting Communities Impacted by Immigration

Some have raised the issue of the burden that large-scale immigration—especially when it includes a high proportion of undocumented aliens—places on some communities. Because they are undocumented, some immigrants may not appear in Census counts or other federal data, yet communities still bear the cost of providing services. HUD recognized needs of those living along the U.S.–Mexican border by requiring states to set aside CDBG funding for "colonias" along the border.[12] A proposed alternative: If communities affected by heavy immigration—undocumented or otherwise—are to be assisted, the CDBG formula could be revised to include an immigration component based on census data.

Upgrading IDIS

IDIS allows grantees to apply for funding, submit strategic plans, provide performance data, report on project status, and disburse payments. IDIS was not viewed by practitioners in the field nor by HUD staff as a particularly user-friendly system. Extensive training was required to operate the system. The system was not Internet-based. Reports were difficult to produce and read. Planning documents required by law did not necessarily interface. Data had to be entered multiple times. The system was not used by HUD headquarters or field office staff to monitor grantees: another independent system—Grants Management Process (GMP)—served that function. Some performance and budgeting systems operated by communities and states for their own purposes were incompatible with IDIS. For years, HUD IT staff and contractors tried to patch the system up when parts of it failed.

In 1997–1998, HUD began development work on a replacement system for IDIS, the Departmental Grants Management System (DGMS).[13] DGMS was a failed system even as its development began. Original specifications for DGMS were not followed, end users were not consulted, management was not engaged, extensive delays were encountered or created, and no project manager was in place. Outside contractors became so dissatisfied with work on the system that they walked away from a multimillion dollar project, unfinished. Inexplicably, HUD tried to develop DGMS as a competing system to IDIS rather than a unified one. By 2000, HUD abandoned work on the new system and continued to jerry rig IDIS.

Eventually, HUD management decided to substantially upgrade IDIS, in part to accommodate the new performance system.[14] In the new IDIS, the Consolidated Plan, Annual Action Plan, Consolidated Annual Performance and Evaluation Report (CAPER), and Performance Evaluation Reports (PER)—are integrated into a single performance system. Interestingly, HUD elected not to formally consult its forty-three field offices, which work with and monitor grantees. The reason IDIS is important for reforms is that were the system to be inefficient and ineffective, the performance system would also fail because it is contained within it. Only time will tell whether the system will enhance performance.

Reforming the Consolidated Plan

In 2002, the Bush administration published the President's Management Agenda (PMA), an analysis of program management issues that required immediate attention. HUD's Consolidated Plan process was highlighted. According to PMA, HUD must work to remove meaningless compliance burdens on states and communities. Specifically, "By 2003, HUD will work with local stakeholders to streamline the Consolidated Plan, making it more results-oriented and useful to communities in assessing their own progress toward addressing the problems of low-income areas" (OMB 2002, 51). In response in 2003, CPD launched the Consolidated Plan Improvement Initiative, which would[15]

- Reduce meaningless compliance burdens.
- Streamline the plan into a meaningful, readable document.
- Link the plan to performance.
- Incorporate technology to a greater extent in plan preparation and dissemination.
- Promote the plan as a tool for tracking performance results.

CPD pilot-tested eight Consolidated Plan options with several dozen volunteer grantees. CPD never revised the Consolidated Plan process to reflect best practices of volunteers, although CPD did offer grantees software options to assist them in developing and submitting their completed Consolidated Plans. Many observers consider this a lost opportunity to improve the planning process, a large portion of which has to do with CDBG.

Notes

The author, working for the National Academy of Public Administration, directed a project offering technical assistance to HUD to reengineer its performance management system. Final reports are available at NAPA (2005a, 2005b).

1. www.hud.gov/offices/cpd/communitydevelopment/programs/. (Accessed 3 July 2007.)
2. www.whitehouse.gov/omb/expectmore/detai1.10001161.2005.html. (Accessed 3 July 2007.)
3. www.hud.gov/offices/cpd/about/performance/. (Accessed 3 July 2007.)
4. See COSCDA. 2004. *COSCDA's Outcome Framework System.* Washington, DC: Council of State Community Development Agencies, March.
5. www.hud.gov/offices/cpd/about/performance/index.cfm. (Accessed 3 July 2007.)
6. Few CDBG impact studies exist. The most widely known study found virtually no impacts. See Chris Walker, Chris Hayes, George Galster, Patrick Boxall, and Jennifer Johnson, *The Impact of CDBG Spending on Urban Neighborhoods* (Washington, DC: Urban Institute, 2000).
7. Consensus conferences bring together experts having a wide variety of opinions on an issue, then in a formal group process, they work to develop a consensus opinion on an issue. Conferences are widely used in the medical field.
8. Ironically, SACI, were it implemented, would have offered targeting incentives.
9. *CDBG Formula Targeting.* Washington, DC: Policy Development and Research, HUD, February 2005, www.huduser.org; see also *Statement for the Record, Community Development Block Grant Formula,* May 26, 2005, before the U.S. House of Representatives, Committee on Government Reforms, Subcommittee on Federalism.
10. See the FY2003 CDBG PART, Section 1.5, note 3.
11. See note 10.
12. www.hud.gov/offices/cpd/communitydevelopment/programs/colonias/cdbgcolonias.cfm. (Accessed 3-26-08.)
13. Office of Inspector General (OIG). *Initial Development Efforts—DGMS.* Washington, DC: OIG, HUD. http://www.hud.gov/offices/oig/reports/internal/ig0d0002.pdf. (Accessed 6 February 2008.)
14. www.hud.gov/offices/cpd/systems/idis/index.cfm. (Accessed 3 July 2007.)
15. www.hud.gov/offices/cpd/about/conplan/improvement/index.cfm. (Accessed 3 July 2007.)

References

Boyd, Eugene, Bruce Mulock, Pauline Smale, Tadlock Cowan, Garrine Laney, and Bruce Foote. 2005. "An Overview of the Administration's Strengthen America's Communities Initiative." Washington, DC: Congressional Research Service, CRS Report, RL.
Government Accountability Office (GAO). 2006a. *CDBG Formula: Targeting Assistance to High-Need Communities Could be Enhanced.* Washington, DC: GAO-05–622T.
———. 2006b. *CDBG: Program Offers Recipients Flexibility but Oversight Can Be Improved.* Washington, DC: GAO-06–732.
———. 2006c. *CDBG Formula: Options for Improving the Targeting of Funds.* Washington, DC: GAO-06–904T.
———. 1998. *HUD Management.* Washington, DC: T-RCED-98–222.
NAPA. 2005a. *Developing Performance Measures for the CDBG Program.* Washington, DC: National Academy of Public Administration.
———. 2005b. *Integrating CDBG Performance Measures into IDIS.* Washington, DC: National Academy of Public Administration.
Office of Management and Budget (OMB). 2002. *President's Management Agenda.* Washington, DC: OMB. http://www.whitehouse.gov/omb/budget/fy2002/mgmt.pdf. (Accessed 6 February 2008.)
Ramirez, Saul. 2005. "Testimony of Saul Ramirez." Before the House Government Reform Committee, Subcommittee on Federalism and the Census, April 26.

17

Rethinking Federal Low-Income Housing Policies

F. Stevens Redburn

Federal community development assistance takes many forms. Amounts provided in the federal budget are much smaller than those provided through programs that subsidize investors in and operators of low-income housing, and in other cases, directly to low-income households to help them pay rent. These include major programs of the Department of Housing and Urban Development (HUD), the U.S. Department of Agriculture (USDA), and the Federal Low-Income Housing Tax Credit. Together, these programs each year spend over $30 billion, aid over 5 million low-income renting households, and support development of close to 100,000 new apartments. Their scale alone ensures that these funds will have important implications for community development. However, these resources could be used more effectively and purposively. The development of opportunity in low-income communities is just one example of goals that would be better served by wiser use of these resources. Achieving this improvement will require a basic rethinking and restructuring of the major federal low-income housing programs, as described in this chapter.

On one level, public policies are supported by theories and evidence; on another, by coalitions of economic and group interests. In its heyday, the federal government's commitment to low-income housing expanded behind a pragmatic coalition combining those who believed housing assistance would improve the lives of the poor with organized interests—such as builders, lenders, and local governments—who benefited directly from this spending. The expansion was fueled as well by a belief that improving housing conditions was an effective way to ameliorate and reduce poverty in America. The goal of reducing and eventually ending poverty at one time had broad support, and housing policy was seen as integral to that effort.

The combination of interests and intellect that powered expansion of federal housing assistance for more than fifty years beginning in the 1930s has weakened. Other priorities—from health care to education to homeland security—have pressed competing claims on limited budgets. The intellectual case for subsidized housing as a social strategy—never very solid—has fallen apart. Rationales offered for these policies are not as compelling or convincing as the theories or stories—some of them backed by solid evaluation research—that support competing social investments: No Child Left Behind, the policies and programs that constitute welfare reform, investments in children's health, programs to control drug use and crime.

Today, federal housing programs are sustained more by inertia and the difficulty of unwinding financial obligations than by a consensus that these policies are effective in helping people. Established rationales have been weakened both by changes in the nature of the housing problems faced by low-income households and by a failure on the part of those responsible for evaluating those programs to demonstrate that they are as cost-effective as alternative means of helping improve the lives of the poor. Not surprisingly, there is disagreement—even among advocates for those programs—about what they are expected to accomplish.

What should be done in these circumstances? Staying the course seems increasingly likely to result in declining resources and an unwinding of current commitments. At the margin, new resources would be redirected to programs with clearer goals and demonstrated efficacy. Setting a new course requires us to rethink housing policy—from its premises on up.

Such fundamental reexamination may produce a new agreement on what this spending is intended to accomplish, and that goal, clearly defined, could support and steer efforts to alter the way federal housing policies are designed and administered in order to increase their effectiveness.

It is also possible that a closer, systematic examination of low-income housing policy would lead to the conclusion that much of this spending should be directed to other social needs and more effective uses. While some may fear a fundamental reconsideration of federal low-income housing policies, in the end, rethinking these policies may prove less wrenching than the alternative.

Policy Stalemate

Congress has not passed significant low-income housing legislation since 1998. The amount of federal low-income housing subsidies—which help pay the rent for over 5 million poor households—has hardly been increased by the administration and Congress in the past five years. Efforts to establish an affordable housing trust fund have foundered. Other urgent problems get priority for new spending. Why is this?

Low-income housing advocates routinely proclaim an affordable housing crisis. They count the millions who at any one time use more than one-half of their income for housing costs, live in severely inadequate units, or are homeless, and they cry out for more attention and resources. This is the conventional wisdom, but it ignores some inconvenient realities.

Doubts About the Effectiveness of Housing Assistance

Housing advocates must recognize that despite the urgency they feel, they face an uphill struggle convincing policymakers and the public that a larger proportion of the nation's resources should be devoted to housing subsidies. One big reason for this reluctance to increase resources is the perceived failure of the large federal programs to improve the lives of those who receive assistance. The image of public housing—partly accurate—is of a shabby, overly dense complex located in an area of crime and bad schools, concentrating and often trapping families in intergenerational poverty. In some cases, poor families are, in effect, paid substantial sums—the average subsidy for a family of four is around $7,000 a year and much higher in high-cost cities—to live in the worst neighborhoods, where their lives are threatened and their efforts to progress needlessly stunted. Let's be blunt: the federal government routinely subsidizes substandard housing and offers subsidies to families tied to locations where they are in constant fear of violent assault, where their children attend the worst schools, and where they are isolated from economic opportunity.

The Office of Management and Budget (OMB) has rated most of the major housing aid programs either as "ineffective" or "results not demonstrated"; anyone can read these detailed public critiques of the programs and understand why they are at a disadvantage when budget priorities are being set. Some may doubt the objectivity or fairness of OMB program assessments. Strong, verifiable, scientific evidence that the programs were effective in improving the lives of those assisted would trump subjective program ratings. Unfortunately, there is uncertainty and little objective evidence regarding the benefits of housing assistance. Although evaluations have been conducted of innovative uses of housing subsidies, none of today's major housing assistance programs has been the subject of a broad, rigorous, independent evaluation employing experimental controls to isolate and measure its impacts. There is little solid evidence establishing who benefits, in what circumstances, and in combination with what other forms of assistance. Does housing aid, more often than not, lead to increased economic self-sufficiency, better school outcomes for children, increased safety, improved health for the elderly, and increased independence for the disabled? In fact, we have almost no evidence with which to confidently answer these basic questions about benefits. Would a housing subsidy—for a specified family type in specified circumstances—yield greater benefits than similar spending on education, job training, health care, food assistance, child care, or other programs? Who can say?

Because housing assistance is not an entitlement, it is mostly awarded to income-eligible applicants on a first-come, first-served basis modified by priorities set by local public housing agencies (PHAs) or local managers of privately owned subsidized projects. Absent evidence about who is more likely to benefit, project managers have no way to effectively prioritize the large but limited pool of subsidies. Once awarded, subsidies are generally open-ended and conditional only on continued income eligibility. As incomes rise, subsidy levels are reduced, possibly discouraging work effort. The probable effect of the inability to effectively prioritize or condition assistance is to dilute any benefits of this spending. Other examples could be given of subsidies, in the absence of well-tested models showing how the effects of housing assistance vary with circumstances, terms and conditions, and context, being distributed willy-nilly and used less effectively than they could be.

Crumbling Intellectual Foundations for Housing Assistance

Support for federal housing assistance is limited by lack of agreement about what it is intended to accomplish. Historically, public housing was supported by reformers as a way to help poor families escape the hardship and threats to physical and moral well-being posed by slum life and seriously deficient housing. On a practical level, it also gained support as a means of moving the poor and minorities out of the way so that land could be redeveloped. The coalition of social reformers and development interests powered the expansion of public housing over four decades, and later, the federal government financed and subsidized construction of privately owned apartments for low-income households.

Gradually, the rationale for federal low-income housing subsidies shifted. In the last few decades, a further major expansion of housing assistance was justified largely as a response to shortages of affordable housing, partly resulting from the clearance of poor-quality but cheap housing and the resulting gap between the incomes of the poor and what it cost to rent adequate housing. A new form of assistance—housing vouchers—emerged that allowed recipients more choice of location and was attractive to appropriators because it required smaller initial appropriations. Implicitly, and again on a more practical level, expansion of federal housing subsidies compensated for the effects of local and national policies—such as highway construction and urban renewal—that reduced the supply of affordable housing.

By 2001, over five million federal low-income housing subsidies were in use—including over two million vouchers. Research shows that portable housing vouchers provide greater benefits (or greater choice) at a smaller long-term cost than do project-based subsidies. However, the number of portable housing vouchers has been frozen, while expansion of federally assisted project-based housing has continued at a pace approaching 100,000 units annually—funded by new low-income housing tax credits, HOME block grants, and construction subsidies through smaller programs for the elderly and disabled, including the chronically homeless. These construction programs continue expanding the number of federally subsidized affordable units, although access to them by the poorest households requires an additional rent subsidy.

Even as the incremental expansion of subsidized housing continues through federal support for new construction, what agreement there was in the past on the need for expanded federal efforts to provide assistance has crumbled. Federal cash assistance to families with children—welfare payments—and related policies to support work went through a major intellectual reformulation in the 1990s, resulting in a new consensus that led to reform of those programs. The new view is that federal aid to poor families should be designed to move them as quickly as possible into the workforce and toward self-sufficiency. Following much debate, building on a substantial body of research, and following the overthrow of established premises, a new clarity of purpose emerged, at least provisionally. This consensus on the rationale for cash assistance to families with children has supported agreement on reforms and a shift in the terms of assistance, the way it is administered, and the way it is used by families.

Some thought the momentum for welfare reform would carry over to the largely separate world of housing policy. In 1996, when Temporary Assistance for Needy Families (TANF) replaced Aid for Families with Dependent Children, about one million families who received welfare payments also held a HUD housing subsidy. In fact, the logic of welfare reform helped motivate the Quality Housing and Work Responsibility Act of 1998. However, the Act as passed applied only minor elements of TANF reform model and did little to reduce the gap—both administrative and intellectual—between these two major streams of federal aid to poor families.

Rebuilding the Intellectual Foundations of Housing Policy

What will it take to attract new attention and priority to low-income housing assistance? A necessary, although perhaps insufficient, condition for regaining forward motion and rebuilding support for housing assistance programs is the development of broad agreement about the aims of that policy. A second intellectual building block would be the identification of a set of cost-effective policies for achieving those aims. And finally, building on those new foundations, consensus would be needed on a clearly defined, achievable goal or goals commensurate with the likely availability of federal and other budgetary resources.

A Possible Model

In the midst of the current intellectual disarray, there is a promising, instructive example of how a rethinking of low-income housing policy might proceed and how it could attract new resources and energy. The model is the federal government's commitment to end chronic homelessness. What is distinctive about this policy? First, there is broad, if not universal, agreement on a national goal set by the federal government. Second, there is a sound research base and growing practical experience suggesting that it is cost-effective to invest public resources in the effort.

Why was it possible to get agreement on this goal? We can speculate on this. First, the target is of manageable proportions: a population estimated to be no more than 200,000 individuals. Second, there is a methodology—assisted housing linked to appropriate supportive services—for which there is reasonably strong research evidence showing that in most cases it gets people permanently off the streets. Moreover, there are studies indicating that it does so at a cost to the public sector hardly greater than that incurred by allowing them to remain on the streets or cycling through emergency rooms, jails, institutions, and shelters. Given this information, it is possible to calculate quickly the additional or redeployed resources needed to reduce or end chronic homelessness and to calculate the marginal public cost to do so. All in all, it seems the goal is not just meritorious but within reach.

What has been the result of setting this policy goal? New resources have been committed, not only in the federal budget—appropriations for HUD homeless assistance increased by 30 percent from FY2001 to FY2006, for example—but in the form of plans and matching commitments by mayors, governors, foundations, and others. The goal has focused energy and mobilized political support sufficient to sustain the initial effort for five years so far. And, preliminary evidence suggests it is producing, in many places, measurable reductions in the numbers remaining homeless for long periods. Real success sustains and feeds the effort, resulting in continued progress toward the goal.

The central lesson? In one instance, many have come to believe that housing assistance can be used in a particular way to achieve an important outcome with a feasible investment of additional resources. Seeing this success, politicians have rallied to the effort. Budgets have increased.

Could this be the model for a general reshaping of low-income housing policies? What other desirable, achievable social goals can be identified for which there is or conceivably could be a demonstrated cost-effective link between provision of assistance and progress toward the goal? Before attempting to answer these questions, it will help to clear away some of the intellectual scrub brush that has grown up around low-income housing policy. We must adjust some of our standard ways of thinking about housing needs and housing assistance.

Gutting the Old Place and Getting False Ideas Out of the Way

What are low-income housing needs? For over twenty years, the federal government's standard measure of the need for low-income housing assistance has been HUD's estimate from census data of "worst-case needs." By this conventional measure, over five million very low-income renter households have severe housing needs, that is, use over one-half of their income for rent and utilities or, in far fewer cases, occupy severely inadequate units. Contrary to repeated reporting of an "affordable housing crisis," the estimated number of households in "worst-case need" has hardly moved over the last twenty years.

Is this a meaningful measure of need for housing aid? It is absolutely true that millions of households struggle to afford decent housing in a decent neighborhood. At the same time, it is absolutely wrong to infer that the current standard needs estimate—or any number like it—represents a shortfall in the number of government housing subsidies. Apart from methodological issues, the measure has three problems as an estimate of need:

- It is largely a count of those with excessively high rent burdens, which is not a measure of housing need—the housing may be quite adequate—but rather

of the numbers who are required (or in some cases to some degree choose) to use most of their income for housing.
- Most people solve their housing cost problems without receiving a federal housing subsidy—within a year, roughly one-half of those using over one-half of their income for housing will no longer do so, usually because of a change in their income.
- Providing a subsidy to a household in this category may not solve its housing problem; that is, providing a subsidy in the wrong circumstances or in the wrong form may not solve a housing problem or convey any benefit at all. Many who receive assistance continue to live in dangerous housing or bad locations. In fact, some are induced to do so with aid.

A better way to estimate housing assistance needs would be to identify the group of households for whom housing assistance is likely to yield a benefit, for example, by improving opportunities and living conditions. This approach does not look at reduced housing cost burdens as a benefit in and of itself, although reduced housing costs will in many cases free income for other uses and may yield direct benefits if it supports a move to a superior location or unit.

A measure of housing need must identify the portion of the population at risk of having long-term severe housing needs without continuing housing assistance. Using the American Housing Survey or other census data, it is possible to estimate the number of households that currently experience the most severe housing needs and cannot afford housing that is not severely substandard and in a safe location.

- Those with the most severe housing needs are those who are either homeless, living in severely substandard housing, or living in an unhealthy location (e.g., high rate of violent crime; dangerous environmental exposures). Certainly, for families with children, the indicators of unhealthy location could include failing neighborhood schools.
- In determining whether a household can afford better housing, it is important to estimate all financial resources and needs, including wages and cash income from all sources, food stamps, and other major in-kind resources.
- To determine whether households with a given level of resources can afford adequate, safe housing, it is necessary to consider the availability of such housing in the local market that is affordable to them (e.g., costs no more than 30 percent of total resources or 50 percent of cash income). Some portion of this supply should be subtracted from the initial estimate of subsidy needs because it can be accessed by providing information and relocation aid rather than a continuing housing subsidy.
- Finally, within the group who have housing needs that cannot be met with their current resources from the local affordable stock, it is necessary to estimate the proportion in need who were in a similar situation for a long period, say two years prior. This is the approximate number of households likely to require

long-term rental assistance to meet their housing needs because they will not find the resources on their own.

Calculations using such information can produce a reasonable estimate of how many households may benefit from a long-term housing subsidy. This is not to say, necessarily, that a form of assistance other than a housing subsidy—perhaps a subsidy for child care or transportation—would not better serve the needs of many people in this group. And, there are some in this group for whom a housing subsidy will not provide a benefit; a subsidy may be a disincentive for work or other self-improvement, or it may be used in a dangerous location, for example.

Within the group who could benefit from a subsidy, there will be a high proportion whose incomes are limited by disability or lack of preparation for employment. For many people, help that directly addresses limits on their earning power, possibly offered in conjunction with a housing subsidy, may prove more cost effective than housing assistance alone.

Some households may face an immediate, severe housing problem—perhaps precipitated by a family crisis or disaster—that does not require long-term assistance but may require short-term housing assistance (or another form of aid). Correctly identifying the groups needing various kinds of help, including either long- or short-term housing subsidy, will help us think about when and how housing subsidies should be offered and about which combinations or sequences of housing aid and services are appropriate to a given set of personal circumstances.

Current Programs Have Flaws in Their Design

Existing federal housing programs share common flaws that reduce their effectiveness and damage their chances for regaining broad political and budgetary support. For example,

- Who thinks that unconditional, open-ended housing subsidies encourage families to go to work or otherwise take new steps to improve their lives? Yet, that is the promise offered to virtually anyone who gets to the top of their local waiting list for housing assistance, regardless of their circumstances or desires.
- Who thinks it is a good idea to subsidize the poor to live in places where they are in physical danger, with bad schools and poor services, and isolated from the social mainstream? Yet, some recent research and a substantial body of anecdotal evidence suggests that these are the places where a great many, if not most, housing subsidies are used; and too often the subsidy is only offered on the condition it be used in such a place.
- Who thinks that the most cost-effective strategy to address shortages of affordable housing is to continuously build new subsidized housing in nearly every housing market in every state? Federal tax credits and grants

add close to 100,000 new apartments to the affordable housing supply each year—approaching one-third of all U.S. multifamily production. Reason and research suggest that these increases are substantially offset by, and contribute to, continuing losses of marginal private affordable stock. In most markets, an oversupply of apartments for rent virtually guarantees that for every new subsidized unit built, an older unit will be abandoned. Generally, decisions about where to build new subsidized apartments are too often made without regard to an overall community development plan or strategy, where these exist.

- Who thinks that the terms and conditions for housing aid should be the same for the elderly or the severely disabled as for families with children? Yet, most analyses of housing needs don't recognize the varied ways that housing assistance can be used by people in different circumstances and at different stages of life.
- Who believes that it is wise policy to separate the administration of low-income housing assistance—at all levels of government—from the administration of other benefit programs for low-income households and individuals and from the administration of programs for the development of low-income communities? It is reasonable to ask whether progress in addressing poverty depends first on reorganizing delivery so that it is possible to provide integrated packages of assistance under unified supervision and with clear accountability at each level for their effective use to achieve locally established public policy objectives.

Rebuilding with Ideas That Could Shape a New Low-Income Housing Policy

A new, stronger intellectual base for low-income housing policy will require a lot of learning, both through more systematic testing and evaluation of new approaches and by designing programs in such a way that they promote and reward local success and facilitate replication of successful models.

Housing assistance is not, as those who talk about a shortfall of subsidies often imply, an end in itself. It can only be justified if it improves lives for those who receive it and if dollars spent in this fashion provide greater social benefits than the same dollars spent for other forms of assistance (e.g., child care or health insurance for similar households).

Advocates of low-income housing must recognize the place that these programs hold in relation to major social goals such as improving economic opportunity and upward mobility; building safe, viable, socially diverse communities; and providing access to health and safety. By its nature, housing assistance is subordinate to and supportive of broader social strategies to achieve these social goals; it is part of the tool box and is not always the most appropriate or cost-effective tool to use to aid a given household at a particular time or over time. Moreover, it appears that, to be effective, housing assistance often must be combined with other sources of support to families and those with special needs.

Recognizing that knowledge of when and how housing assistance is likely to be applicable is inadequate, we can nevertheless begin its reconsideration with certain premises:

- The benefits of housing assistance vary greatly in different circumstances and depend on the contractual terms on which it is offered.
- Using housing assistance to expand location choice and mobility can benefit some groups (e.g., by making them safer or improving their access to good schools), but more must be learned about the circumstances and conditions under which it yields such benefits.
- Given the physical nature of housing and its interaction with its surroundings, the rationale for housing assistance will be strengthened or weakened depending on whether a given approach supports other local community development goals, including providing affordable housing close to employment centers, reducing concentrations of poverty that contribute to crime and inhibit neighborhood development, and building assets and homeownership opportunity for younger households.

Based on these very general insights and what we know to date about the conditions under which housing assistance is likely to be beneficial, here in outline is a multipart strategy for a new federal housing policy built on more solid foundations:

Reforming Housing Policy

Part One: Focus Housing Assistance on Specific Social Objectives

Although we don't know nearly enough about who will benefit from housing assistance, under what conditions, offered on what terms, there are some promising targets for its use. It is important, as noted, to start by focusing where economic returns and budget offsets can help justify this particular form of investment. The ongoing effort to end chronic homelessness is the model. Here are three candidate uses of housing assistance combined with other tools in circumstances where there is reason to believe that this use of housing assistance is likely to produce benefits commensurate with its cost:

1. Community-Based Employment Support and Rent Incentives

This approach combines employment-related services, conditional rent reductions for residents of subsidized housing (allowing them to keep more of their earnings as an incentive to work and earn more), and the promotion of social ties among participants to create community support for work to improve the employment prospects of the hardest-to-employ residents of high-poverty neighborhoods. There is at least the potential for offsetting reductions in public costs and gains in productivity and taxes. The Manpower Demonstration Research Corporation (MDRC)'s 2005 evaluation of the Jobs-Plus public housing demonstration found it substantially boosted earnings for people in high-poverty housing developments, particularly when the program was skillfully implemented (Bloom, Riccio, Verma, and Walter 2005). It offered the first hard evidence that a work-focused intervention based in a public housing environment can effectively promote residents' self-sufficiency. Its effects were particularly striking for men.

2. Asset Building for Working Families

This strategy uses housing assistance as part of a longer-term asset-building/homeownership strategy for young working families on the model of HUD's Family Self-Sufficiency (FSS) program. This model, although different in several ways from Jobs-Plus and targeted at working rather than unemployed people, also uses rent subsidies and incentives built on those subsidies to help sustain work effort and to give people the means to achieve other goals. An analysis of the experiences of FSS participants from 1996 through 2000 found that the program met basic expectations for increasing earned income and helping build assets (Ficke and Piesse 2004); however, a more rigorous evaluation of benefits and costs has not yet been performed. Its relatively low cost helps lower the bar for expected benefits; it is representative of a broader class of asset-building strategies for low-income families that would help move them from dependence on rental assistance and other subsidies to owning their own homes.

3. Helping Avoid Unnecessary Institutionalization

A third strategy uses housing assistance to prevent premature institutionalization of the frail low-income elderly and others with severe disabilities. Intuitively, avoiding or postponing institutional care in favor of properly supported home care both benefits the individual and saves public dollars. Although the evaluation research to support a claim of cost effectiveness is thin, there is enough anecdotal evidence to suggest that housing assistance—well targeted by income and need—deserves systematic testing as an alternative to institutionalization. It is plausible—by analogy to the strategy for chronic homelessness—that carefully designed use of housing assistance linked to appropriate supportive services may not only improve and extend the lives of low-income elderly persons but produce offsetting savings, especially in the federal Medicaid program.

A first step in constructing a new approach to low-income housing assistance is to find and test other strategies for its effective use in achieving objectives. It can be used, for example, to increase the probability that released prisoners and probationers will successfully reintegrate into their home communities or to increase the probability that children aging out of foster care will become economically independent and successful adults. Strategies for the effective use of low-income housing assistance to support local community development objectives also can be imagined. All of these strategies, however, must be subject to systematic testing and evaluation to provide the necessary intellectual and experiential foundation to justify their wider use.

How, in general, do we assure that such uses of housing assistance are well managed and well targeted so that the benefits are maximized and the costs justified relative to alternative uses of the public's resources? This requires rethinking the administrative systems that support delivery of low-income housing aid and provide incentives for managers at all levels.

Part Two: Reengineer the Administrative System

It is time to consider replacing the existing administrative systems for federal low-income housing assistance with a unified performance-driven system under the control of general-purpose local and state governments committed to specific numerical performance targets consistent with national priority uses of housing assistance. Moving to an effective system for low-income housing administration will require three big structural changes:

1. Integrate Administration of Housing Subsidies with Administration of Other Social Services

Decisions about the best use of housing subsidies should be made in the context of plans to help particular low-income households achieve their goals. The insight and expertise necessary to decide who will benefit from housing aid more than another form of aid or to monitor and condition continued assistance do not lie with administratively isolated local housing authorities and private landlords, who currently set priorities for assistance. Their expertise has mostly to do with real estate, and their administrative isolation from the agencies responsible for helping low-income people escape poverty or avoid its worst effects makes it difficult for them to make the right choices. If housing assistance is to be part of a package of services tailored to the situation, needs, and commitments of the recipients, then it must be administered by agencies with a continuing, comprehensive involvement with the recipients. Housing authorities and private landlords cannot play this role effectively.

2. Separate Decisions About Low-Income Housing Development from Decisions About Households

Much confusion about the role and best use of housing dollars arises from a blurring of the difference between subsidizing the production of affordable housing and subsidizing the housing costs of individuals. Regardless of one's views of the merits of subsidizing construction or rehabilitation of low-rent housing, much waste and mischief have arisen from policies that combine decisions about how and where to subsidize housing development with decisions about who will receive assistance and on what terms. In general, decisions about the former should be made as part of broader community development strategies under the control of general-purpose local and state governments. Decisions about the latter, as noted, are best made by public and private agencies—or networks of agencies—whose mission is to help low-income households or individuals with particular needs. Breaking apart these two sets of decisions will not only improve the chances of housing assistance being administered effectively but have a healthy effect on real estate development decisions. To separate these two, it will be necessary going forward to permit households to use their subsidies in a broad range of housing and not permit landlords or housing authorities to "capture" subsidies for housing that cannot compete in the marketplace.

3. Replace Current Systems for Control and Reporting with Streamlined Accountability, Both Locally and Nationally, for Results

Obsolete program designs that demand compliance with complex prescriptive regulations but fail to ensure that the housing services provided meet minimum standards, much less that they are properly targeted and administered to achieve greater benefits, must be replaced. Accountability for results can best be achieved by shifting from a traditional formula grant model to a performance-contracting model in which compensation and career decisions are based on results promised and achieved. These would be defined in terms of the mission of the administering agency at each level of government. Locally, this would be the non-housing agency that would distribute and monitor housing subsidies along with other services as part of a program to improve prospects for low-income households.

At the federal level, it is unclear whether a single agency should continue to have primary responsibility for administering housing assistance. In principle, there is no reason that HUD could not administer housing aid to solve problems using a performance-based model; indeed, the administration of HUD's homeless assistance comes close to fitting this model today. However, because of its history and limitations, HUD may not be the best choice to administer federal low-income housing assistance. HUD's capacity to lead the nation in addressing the needs of low-income communities and people has diminished almost to the vanishing point, and leadership has shifted elsewhere: to national foundations and networks and to local communities. Administration of federal housing assistance also has fragmented. The largest source of federal assistance for the construction of low-income apartments, the Low-Income Housing Tax Credit, is outside HUD's domain and in the hands of the states. Shifting federal leadership to the Department of Health and Human

Services (HHS), for instance, would not necessarily improve focus or coordination of federal efforts. Transferring responsibility to HHS would, however, allow better integration of housing aid with other policy tools to address problems of poverty; and it would allow HUD to focus on problems of community development and finance, where it has a comparative advantage of expertise and institutional capacity. It is worth considering whether a reduced and more focused role for HUD would provide national leadership for the development of low-income communities.

Two other changes are needed to correct flaws in the way the federal government approaches its responsibilities for low-income housing assistance. These changes will be accomplished in part as a consequence of the reengineering of the administrative system outlined above but will require additional legislation:

1. Develop a timetable and transition strategy to retire all federal public housing and privately owned subsidized properties that cannot ensure residents' minimum safety, access to good schools, and employment opportunity; and relocate residents using housing vouchers. It should go without saying that the federal government must not subsidize poor families to live in places where they face danger and are denied opportunity. A strategy to retire unsuitable housing units from the federal inventory would be facilitated by breaking the link between subsidy and real estate—that is, making subsidies portable, thereby giving all recipients the option to move to what they consider better housing and applying a market test to determine which units can be sustained at market rents (Olsen 2006). Using the federal block grant funds, mayors and governors should have a say in which units are retained at what level of subsidy.

2. Reallocate federal production subsidies, including low-income housing tax credits, to markets where affordable housing is in short supply, require recipient jurisdictions to take regulatory and other actions and commit to specific targets to increase their supply of affordable housing, and at the same time give them adequate discretion to integrate affordable housing into their own community development strategies. Paralleling the shift of housing subsidy administration to a performance-contracting model, federal housing production subsidies should be subject to a performance test. These subsidies—including Low-Income Housing Tax Credits and HUD's HOME Investment Partnerships program and Community Development Block Grants (CDBGs)—should be used to support national as well as community objectives, including the transformation of poor neighborhoods into places where residents have the opportunity to work and build personal assets. Jurisdictions should be asked to make strategic investments that provide a demonstrable return. This will require, among other changes, the transformation of the CDBG program into one that requires and rewards its strategic use to achieve specified national objectives and holds communities accountable for results to which they have

committed in advance. Principally, these results will be measured by gains in economic opportunity that improve lives of low-income residents of those communities and make those communities eventually self-sustaining. The federal role will include rigorous evaluations of promising strategies for using low-income housing subsidies in combination with other tools as part of a community development strategy. At present, we have little idea of what works and therefore little to go on in designing an effective use of federal resources.

How Can We Learn What Works?

It is ambitious to ask that the federal government rethink housing policies that have been wasteful and often counterproductive. Governments have trouble learning from experience. They underinvest in program evaluation. They also fail to capture, sustain, and transfer actual successes. Given how much we do not know about how to design and deliver cost-effective low-income housing assistance, both a research agenda and a redesign of the program model to support knowledge building and transfer are called for. Any housing assistance program should not be undertaken without a built-in, rigorous, controlled evaluation plan; and future funding should be made a function of evidence about what works and is cost effective.

To begin learning what works, it is not practical or necessary to wait for the results of evaluation research—and based on experience, the wait could be long. What is needed is a national learning process built into the design of federal housing policies and led by the federal government: a national performance-driven administrative model that encourages local innovation through flexibility, rewards success with financial incentives and documentation of results, and communicates and transfers successes by keeping score and promoting peer-to-peer technical assistance.

A new system of performance accountability and learning would

- Provide everyone with a guiding framework of national goals and performance targets.
- Require communities and states to set comparable goals and targets.
- Publish report cards on community progress.
- Increase funding flexibility (including the ability of states to "cash out" their low-income housing tax credits and use dollars under the HOME block grant authority).
- Offer challenge funds or bonuses to reward progress.

Conclusion

Support for federal low-income housing subsidies depends on finding a convincing rationale for their use in achieving social goals, reforming their administration to promote policy learning and accountability for results, and demonstrating that housing assistance is the best use of scarce resources in particular situations. Intellectual foundations of federal low-income housing policy must be rebuilt; and political leaders at all levels of government must be convinced that this spending can help them achieve important social goals. Only by acknowledging that the case for continuing support of the present program structure is weak and fundamental reform is needed can believers in housing assistance begin to reclaim ground they have lost.

Note

This chapter is an earlier version of a working paper for the New America Foundation.

References

Bloom, Howard S., James A. Riccio, Nandita Verma, and Johanna Walter. 2005. *Promoting Work in Public Housing.* New York: Manpower Demonstration Research Corporation.
Ficke, Robert C., and Andrea Piesse. 2004. *Evaluation of the Family Self-Sufficiency Program.* Washington, DC: U.S. Department of Housing and Urban Development.
Olsen, Edgar O. 2006. "Achieving Fundamental Housing Policy Reform." In *American Democracy and the Political Economy of Government Performance,* ed. Alan Gerber and Eric Patashnik. Washington, DC: Brookings Institution.

Part 5

Smart Growth and Land Use

18

Smart Growth and Community Investment

Confronting Suburban Decline in Baltimore

Thomas J. Vicino

Scholars and practitioners have increasingly paid attention to the changing nature of American suburbs, with an emphasis on the decline of the nation's older suburbs located near central cities. Commonly know as "first-tier" or "inner-ring" suburbs, these communities were once the icons of the American Dream.[1] After World War II, they allowed returning veterans to escape overcrowded central cities and to purchase a spacious home with a garage and yard. Scores of city residents became suburbanites in just one generation. From the late 1940s to the early 1970s, this period became known as the Great American Century as mass suburbanization gave way to the creation of the nation's large middle class. Yet, this prosperity was short lived. What followed were a series of social and economic transformations that changed the character and quality of life in first-tier suburbs. The last three decades of the twentieth century brought massive deindustrialization, coupled with an aging population, an obsolete housing stock, and a more diverse population. Furthermore, unfettered growth of metropolitan areas and decentralization of people and jobs meant the suburbs were no longer places of destination by 2000. These suburbs—like so many others—had reached a crossroads by the beginning of the twenty-first century. The fate of these first-tier suburbs rested in government's ability to confront suburban decline and reengineer communities to again be places for people to live, work, and play.

The Baltimore metropolitan area is illustrative. Maryland was one of the early recognizers of the challenges of suburban decline and uneven patterns of growth. During the 1990s, the state reengineered its urban and suburban communities through the Smart Growth and Neighborhood Conservation Initiative, known simply as "smart growth." Maryland's policymakers and planners reinvested in already-established suburban communities near the urban core, hoping to alter the pattern of persistent decentralization and grow in a smarter, more sustainable manner. Despite having been lauded as the cure for urban sprawl, there have been few systematic inquiries into the diverse patterns of different types of suburban development. Thus, upon the tenth anniversary of smart growth in Maryland, it is important to reflect on the state's experience, particularly in suburban decline and community development. What have been the patterns of suburban decline in Baltimore, and how has smart growth impacted suburban decline? What lessons can be drawn from the experience of using smart growth to confront suburban decline and develop communities? And what are the future prospects for first-tier suburbs in metropolitan America?

In this chapter, I attempt to answer these questions by considering how Maryland engaged the revitalization and community development of Baltimore's first-tier suburbs. First, I chart the emergence of patterns of social and economic decline of suburban Baltimore through a spatial analysis of change from 1970 to 2000. Second, I examine the smart growth policies Maryland, and specifically Baltimore County, employed to confront this problem. Last, I reflect on the political realities and economic imperatives of using smart growth for community development. Based on the lessons from Maryland's experience, I offer a set of strategies for revitalizing and developing stronger first-tier suburban communities.

The Emergence of Suburban Decline

The decline of suburban areas is hardly new. In fact, during the early 1980s, scholars noted that older suburban neighborhoods around central cities demonstrated some of the very characteristics of social and economic decline that urban neighborhoods had long experienced. Listokin and Beaton (1983) conducted one of the earliest in-depth studies of "mature" suburbs of New York. Focusing on Englewood, New Jersey, they demonstrated a clear pattern of socioeconomic decline in this suburb whose heyday was a memory among older residents. Englewood no longer attracted as many new residents as the growing outer suburbs did during the 1970s. Moreover, by 1980, household income had stagnated, and racial residential segregation was prevalent. Englewood's residents also began losing manufacturing jobs due to technological and global advances (Bluestone and Harrison 1982). As a result, Englewood developed a higher crime rate than most other suburbs, and its retail and employment sectors grew increasingly fragile. In another study, Culver (1982) found that suburban decline, highlighted by the Englewood example, was not an isolated case. Suburbs of many large U.S. cities were "distressed," in part because of fragmented local government. According to Culver, such a political structure inhibited the ability of an incorporated suburban community to effectively combat forces of socioeconomic decline. Essentially, political fragmentation of suburbs allowed these communities to maintain greater control over fiscal resources (through property taxes) and to create landscapes of racial and economic segregation (Teaford 1979). In consequence, early suburban communities began to suffer as competition with other newer suburbs grew.

Despite this evidence of suburban decline, there were few studies during this period that investigated the decline of suburbs aside from these cases. Some two decades later, the socioeconomic condition of these suburban communities—and many more—continued to deteriorate. By the late 1990s and early 2000s, literature

Table 18.1

Definition of Baltimore's First-Tier Suburbs

Census Designated Place	Temporal Criterion (%)	Spatial Criterion
Arbutus	79	Central City
Brooklyn Park	84	Adjacent
Catonsville	65	Central City
Dundalk	91	Central City
Edgemere	70	Adjacent
Essex	66	Adjacent
Ferndale	56	Adjacent
Glen Burnie	63	Central City
Hampton	70	Adjacent
Lansdowne	81	Central City
Linthicum	70	Adjacent
Lochearn	70	Central City
Lutherville	79	Adjacent
Middle River	59	Adjacent
Overlea	70	Central City
Parkville	84	Central City
Pikesville	44	Central City
Pumphrey	61	Adjacent
Rosedale	67	Central City
Towson	75	Central City
Woodlawn	55	Central City

Source: Author's calculation of U.S. Census tract data.

on suburban decline was burgeoning (Hanlon, Vicino, and Short 2006; Hudnut 2003; Leigh and Lee, 2005; Lucy and Phillips 2000, 2006; Orfield 2002; Smith, Caris, and Wyly 2001). Continuing in the pioneering work of Lucy and Phillips (2000, 2006), this study charts the decline of Baltimore's first-tier suburbs and then reflects on the implications for smart growth.

The study area is the Baltimore primary metropolitan statistical area (PMSA), including five counties: Anne Arundel, Baltimore, Carroll, Harford, and Howard, as well as the City of Baltimore and encompassing twenty-one first-tier suburbs that surround the central city. First-tier suburbs are located near the central city and tend to be the oldest suburban areas of a metropolitan area. Table 18.1 shows that first-tier suburbs were identified using spatial and temporal criteria.[2] First, suburbs that shared a boundary with the central city were automatically classified in the first-tier. Second, the median age of the housing development was used as a proxy for the age of a suburb. If half of the suburb's housing stock was older than 1970 and it shared a spatial boundary with other first-tier suburbs, it was also classified in the first tier. In summary, twenty-one first-tier suburbs were identified.

Based on these definitions, it was possible to conduct a change-over-time spatial analysis of the socioeconomic transformations from 1970 to 2000. Specifically, using Geolytics' Neighborhood Change Database provided an opportunity to collect census tract data and aggregate them to the census place level. Employing this method proved robust because the data were calibrated for spatial boundary changes each decade. Thus, it facilitated accurate comparisons among and between suburban areas over time. The analysis illuminates a unique perspective because it compares how Baltimore's first-tier suburbs changed *relative* to the central city, outer suburbs, and metropolitan area. The key transformations in the population, poverty and income, housing, and labor force of metropolitan Baltimore are summarized next.

Population

Metropolitan Baltimore witnessed moderate population growth since the 1970s (see Table 18.2). Overall, the region grew by 23 percent, from approximately 2 million to 2.5 million. The region's central city, Baltimore, continued to lose population since its peak in 1950 of nearly 1 million. Since 1970, the city lost about one-third of its residents to the suburbs. Suburban Baltimore grew by 1 million from 1970 to 2000, doubling its population. Despite these suburban growth patterns, the distribution of the growth was uneven. Outer suburbs experienced overwhelming growth; in contrast, the population of the first-tier suburbs stagnated. A more detailed examination of the spatial distribution of population change over time reveals several distinct patterns.

The population of the first-tier suburbs and the outer suburbs mirrored one another in 1970. The population size of both the first-tier and outer suburbs stood at approximately 500,000 each. But since then, a diverging pattern of slow growth, no growth, and population loss occurred, as Table 18.2 reveals. In the aggregate, suburbs in the first-tier shrank by 11 percent; 65,615 persons left between 1970 and 2000. In contrast, the outer suburbs grew significantly during the same time period. The population soared by 138 percent in three decades, and just over 800,000 persons moved to the outer suburbs.

The population trend among the first-tier suburbs was a pattern of slow growth or loss. Table 18.2 demonstrates that the majority of first-tier suburbs lost population since 1970. The loss was dramatic in four of these suburbs. Catonsville, Dundalk, Lutherville, and Towson each lost almost one-third of its population. Only six of the first-tier suburbs experienced population growth since 1970, but the growth in Essex, Glen Burnie, and Hampton was negligible. Ferndale and Woodlawn were two exceptions. Located to the west and south of the city, they grew substantially by 62 and 37 percent respectively. In addition, two population trends were apparent among the majority of these places between 1970 and 2000. First, they failed to attract residents, and when they did, the growth was small relative to the growth in the outer suburbs. Second, many of these communities could not maintain their population base, and they lost a significant number of residents. Changes in the spatial distribution of the population during the 1970s, 1980s, and 1990s in Baltimore's

Table 18.2

Distribution of Population in Metropolitan Baltimore, 1970 to 2000

Place	1970	1980	1990	2000	Total Change Percent	Net
Arbutus	22,724	20,163	19,750	20,116	−11	−2,608
Brooklyn Park	13,847	11,508	10,987	10,938	−21	−2,909
Catonsville	54,983	33,208	35,233	39,820	−28	−15,163
Dundalk	85,267	71,293	65,800	62,306	−27	−22,961
Edgemere	10,346	9,078	9,226	9,248	−11	−1,098
Essex	38,112	39,614	40,872	39,078	3	966
Ferndale	9,886	14,314	16,355	16,056	62	6,170
Glen Burnie	38,547	37,263	37,305	38,922	1	375
Hampton	4,358	5,220	4,926	5,004	15	646
Lansdowne	16,922	16,759	15,509	15,724	−7	−1,198
Linthicum	9,878	7,457	7,547	7,539	−24	−2,339
Lochearn	29,056	26,908	25,240	25,269	−13	−3,787
Lutherville	24,042	17,854	16,442	15,814	−34	−8,228
Middle River	19,917	26,756	24,616	23,958	20	4,041
Overlea	13,186	12,965	12,137	12,148	−8	−1,038
Parkville	33,935	35,159	31,617	31,118	−8	−2,817
Pikesville	25,252	22,555	24,815	29,123	15	3,871
Pumphrey	6,387	5,666	5,483	5,317	−17	−1,070
Rosedale	19,430	19,956	18,703	19,199	−1	−231
Towson	77,825	51,083	49,445	51,793	−33	−26,032
Woodlawn	26,284	29,453	32,907	36,079	37	9,795
First-Tier Suburbs	580,184	514,232	504,915	514,569	−11	−65,615
Outer Suburbs	583,652	871,844	1,141,579	1,387,271	138	803,619
Baltimore City	905,759	786,775	736,014	651,154	−28	−254,605
Region	2,069,595	2,172,851	2,382,508	2,552,994	23	483,399

Source: Author's calculation of U.S. Census tract data from Neighborhood Change Database.

first-tier suburbs indicated that these places lagged behind the explosive population boom of the outer suburbs.

Baltimore's suburban racial landscape changed between 1970 and 2000. Overall, there were large increases in racial diversity in the first-tier suburbs. These changes did not occur uniformly: some suburbs witnessed significant diversification of race and ethnicity while others experienced very little change. The greatest changes occurred between the white and black population. In 1970, the first-tier suburbs were 96 percent white, 3 percent black, and less than 1 percent Hispanic and other races and ethnicities. By 2000, these places diversified. The white population dropped to 76 percent while the black population increased to 18 percent.

Further analysis of the changes in the racial composition among the first-tier suburbs reveals two important trends: increased racial diversity and persistent segregation. The region's northern and eastern first-tier suburbs remained primarily white, while the western first-tier suburbs witnessed dramatic racial change. The outmigration of the white population was quite marked. Two suburbs located on the western fringe of the city, Woodlawn and Lochearn, were cases in point. Both suburbs were majority white places in 1970, and by 2000, they both were majority black places. In Woodlawn, the white population declined from 97 percent in 1970 to only 38 percent in 2000. There was a similar trend in neighboring Lochearn. The suburb was 91 percent white and 8 percent black in 1970. By 2000, Lochearn's white population declined to 18 percent, and the black population climbed to 78 percent. Changes in the racial composition of these two suburbs are significant because together Lochearn and Woodlawn represent two very large suburban communities containing some 61,000 residents.

These dramatic racial changes in the western first-tier suburbs provide evidence of resegregation in first-tier suburbs like Woodlawn and Lochearn. This process had begun as early as the 1950s in the western neighborhoods of Baltimore City, bordering the suburbs. By 1970, these places had high levels of white segregation. During the 1980s and 1990s, they integrated to an extent as the black population grew in the first tier. Yet, in 2000, the majority of the white population had left, and a black population became the majority. The result was a racial resegregation. In 2000, these places now had high levels of black segregation. The black population moved into the western first-tier suburbs and succeeded the white population from 1970 to 2000. White flight from the first-tier suburbs fueled growth of the outer suburbs.

Poverty and Income

One of the most revealing changes in the economic status of first-tier suburban residents was the increase of the poverty level since 1970. Overall, the number of persons living in poverty in the first-tier suburbs *doubled* between 1970 and 2000. Figure 18.1 shows that the poverty level stood at 4 percent in 1970, and by 2000, over 8 percent of the population was living in poverty. In contrast, there was a slight decline in poverty in the outer suburbs during the same period. The outer suburbs had a higher poverty level in 1970 than the first-tier suburbs, attributable to the rural character of these areas. In 1980, poverty levels in both the first-tier and outer suburbs converged at 6 percent. During the 1980s, poverty increased in the first-tier suburbs and simultaneously decreased in the outer suburbs. The gap continued to widen in the 1990s as poverty leveled off in the outer suburbs and continued to increase in the first-tier suburbs.

A comparison of poverty status among Baltimore's first-tier suburbs demonstrates considerable variation. Nineteen of the twenty-one first-tier experienced increases in the poverty level since 1970. Several suburbs had much larger increases in poverty than others. For example, Dundalk and Middle River, each located on the waterfront to the east of the central city, reached a 10 percent poverty level by

Figure 18.1   **Poverty Population in Metropolitan Baltimore, 1970 to 2000**

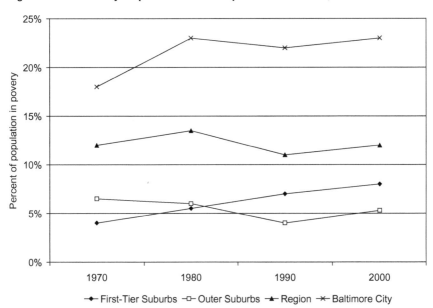

—◆— First-Tier Suburbs   —□— Outer Suburbs   —▲— Region   —✕— Baltimore City

2000. Similarly, Essex and Lansdowne experienced a large increase in poverty and approached 15 percent by 2000. Unlike the overall poverty trend, three suburbs stand out as remarkably stable. Hampton, Linthicum, and Lutherville maintained a low poverty population. Thus, while a few wealthy enclaves were protected from poverty, the majority of first-tier suburbs experienced increases in residents living in poverty.

Examining changes in the median household income shows a similar pattern to the analysis of poverty status. In the Baltimore metropolitan area, median household income consistently rose each decade, and it stood at $49,938 in 2000 (see Table 18.3). In contrast, median household income essentially stagnated at $35,000 in Baltimore City. In suburban Baltimore, there was a diverging trend among first-tier suburbs and outer suburbs. The median household income in Baltimore's first-tier suburbs was $49,669 in 2000, a decline from $4,861 since 1970. In comparison, household income in the outer suburbs consistently rose each decade from $46,721 in 1970 to $57,558 in 2000. This income deviation shows that first-tier suburbs were better off in 1970 than all other suburbs in the region. By 1980, household income was, for the most part, equally distributed between the suburbs. Both the first-tier suburbs and outer suburbs had a median household income of approximately $50,000. During the 1980s, first-tier suburbs began to lose income relative to the outer suburbs. In the 1990s, income in the first-tier suburbs deteriorated even more as the income in the outer suburbs continued to climb.

Table 18.3

Distribution of Median Household Income in Metropolitan Baltimore, 1970 to 2000

					Total Change	
Place	1970	1980	1990	2000	Percent	Net
Arbutus	$45,141	$43,676	$47,412	$47,792	5.87	$2,651
Brooklyn Park	$45,986	$44,494	$42,740	$42,207	−8.22	−$3,779
Catonsville	$50,250	$48,039	$52,948	$53,061	5.59	$2,811
Dundalk	$45,450	$46,740	$41,884	$39,789	−12.46	−$5,661
Edgemere	$43,418	$48,786	$48,381	$46,928	8.08	$3,510
Essex	$41,473	$40,687	$36,993	$34,978	−15.66	−$6,495
Ferndale	$49,595	$47,862	$50,394	$45,816	−7.62	−$3,779
Glen Burnie	$46,550	$47,122	$48,495	$45,281	−2.73	−$1,269
Hampton	$129,917	$98,660	$91,222	$95,546	−26.46	−$34,371
Lansdowne	$42,223	$38,880	$41,326	$37,160	−11.99	−$5,063
Linthicum	$55,800	$61,775	$63,817	$61,479	10.18	$5,679
Lochearn	$64,716	$52,444	$53,323	$49,517	−23.49	−$15,199
Lutherville	$68,473	$70,547	$68,997	$61,573	−10.08	−$6,900
Middle River	$43,618	$42,163	$41,382	$37,900	−13.11	−$5,718
Overlea	$48,405	$49,469	$48,833	$48,242	−0.34	−$163
Parkville	$51,550	$44,131	$44,740	$41,410	−19.67	−$10,140
Pikesville	$67,605	$62,005	$65,175	$58,598	−13.32	−$9,007
Pumphrey	$44,241	$49,637	$49,047	$45,321	2.44	$1,080
Rosedale	$50,668	$51,398	$53,026	$47,801	−5.66	−$2,867
Towson	$51,236	$56,377	$56,036	$53,775	4.95	$2,539
Woodlawn	$58,822	$50,646	$55,102	$48,878	−16.91	−$9,944
First-Tier Suburbs	**$54,530**	**$52,168**	**$52,442**	**$49,669**	**−8.91**	**−$4,861**
All Suburbs	**$46,721**	**$50,620**	**$56,946**	**$57,558**	**23.20**	**$10,837**
Baltimore City	**$40,016**	**$36,076**	**$37,911**	**$35,438**	**−11.44**	**−$4,578**
Region	**$39,289**	**$42,949**	**$49,107**	**$49,938**	**27.10**	**$10,649**

Source: Author's calculation of U.S. Census tract data from Neighborhood Change Database. Adjusted to 1999 dollars.

To further illustrate the income disparity between suburbs, the income ratio is a useful method for measuring income levels of individual first-tier suburbs to the income level for all suburbs. Table 18.4 shows that the average income ratio for the first-tier suburbs steadily declined over thirty years. In 1970, the first-tier income ratio was 1.17, indicating that the first-tier had 17 percent more income that the suburban median income. In 1980, the income ratio was 1.03, which suggests that household income was evenly distributed between the first-tier and other suburbs. During the 1990s, the ratio continued to decline, and by 2000, the income ratio was 0.86, which demonstrates that the first-tier suburbs as a whole had 14 percent *less* income than other suburbs. Income ratios fell in *every* first-tier suburb since 1970, and in many cases, change in the income

Table 18.4

Ratio of First-Tier Suburban Median Household Income to Suburban Median Household Income in Metropolitan Baltimore, 1970 to 2000

Place	1970	1980	1990	2000	Net Change
Arbutus	0.97	0.86	0.83	0.83	−0.14
Brooklyn Park	0.98	0.88	0.75	0.73	−0.25
Catonsville	1.08	0.95	0.93	0.92	−0.15
Dundalk	0.97	0.92	0.74	0.69	−0.28
Edgemere	0.93	0.96	0.85	0.82	−0.11
Essex	0.89	0.80	0.65	0.61	−0.28
Ferndale	1.06	0.95	0.89	0.80	−0.27
Glen Burnie	1.00	0.93	0.85	0.79	−0.21
Hampton	2.78	1.95	1.60	1.66	−1.12
Lansdowne	0.90	0.77	0.73	0.65	−0.26
Linthicum	1.19	1.22	1.12	1.07	−0.13
Lochearn	1.39	1.04	0.94	0.86	−0.52
Lutherville	1.47	1.39	1.21	1.07	−0.40
Middle River	0.93	0.83	0.73	0.66	−0.28
Overlea	1.04	0.98	0.86	0.84	−0.20
Parkville	1.10	0.87	0.79	0.72	−0.38
Pikesville	1.45	1.22	1.14	1.02	−0.43
Pumphrey	0.95	0.98	0.86	0.79	−0.16
Rosedale	1.08	1.02	0.93	0.83	−0.25
Towson	1.10	1.11	0.98	0.93	−0.16
Woodlawn	1.26	1.00	0.97	0.85	−0.41
First-Tier Suburbs	1.17	1.03	0.92	0.86	−0.31

Source: Author's calculation of U.S. Census tract data from Neighborhood Change Database.

ratio from 1970 to 2000 was dramatic. As economic status of first-tier suburban residents eroded, these places fell behind their suburban counterparts in the metropolitan area.

Housing

Age of the housing stock is a factor for charting suburban changes in the first tier. Most of the housing stock in the first-tier suburbs was older than the stock in the outer suburbs. By 2000, the first-tier suburbs were fully built. In Baltimore, over half of the housing stock was constructed prior to 1970, and about one-third was built during the 1950s and 1960s. Over 85 percent of the housing stock in Baltimore City was built before 1970. In contrast, there were marked differences in the age of the housing stock in suburban Baltimore. Housing units in first-tier suburbs were older than other suburbs. The housing stock in the outer suburbs was substantially younger than the stock in the first-tier suburbs. Just under one-third of the housing

Figure 18.2   **Age of Housing Stock in Metropolitan Baltimore, 2000**

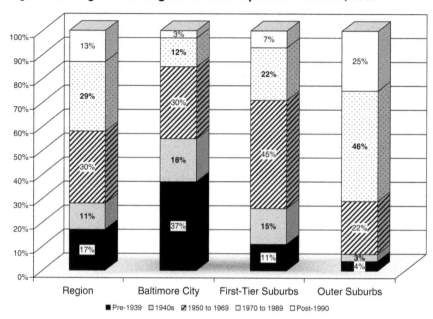

stock in the outer suburbs was built before 1970, compared to over two-thirds of the housing stock in the first tier. Plus, over a quarter of the stock in the outer suburbs was built in the 1990s alone. About one-third of the housing stock in the first-tier suburbs was very old—built prior to 1950, whereas the number of pre-1950 housing in the outer suburbs was negligible (see Figure 18.2).

Throughout metropolitan Baltimore, there were also many differences in the size of housing units (see Figure 18.3). In 2000, approximately half of all housing units in the region had between four and six rooms, while just over one-third of the houses had seven rooms or more. Housing units in the first tier were smaller than those in the outer suburbs. Two-thirds of the houses in first-tier suburbs had six or fewer rooms. Conversely, 91 percent of the housing units in the outer suburbs had more than six rooms. First-tier suburbs contained the majority of the suburbs' smallest housing units. They were small by today's standards. The overall trend was that larger houses were located further away from the urban core while smaller houses were located in the first-tier suburbs near the urban core.

Labor Force

The regional economy of Baltimore transformed during the period from 1970 to 2000. Typical of the Rustbelt, a considerable portion of residents in the Baltimore

Figure 18.3 **Size of Housing Units in Metropolitan Baltimore, 2000**

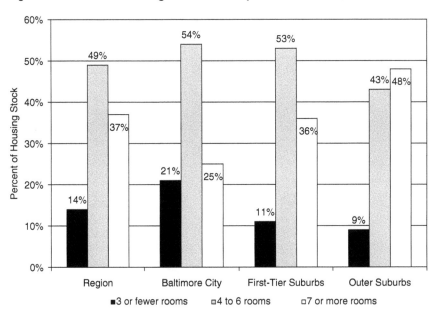

region held manufacturing jobs in 1970. Yet, with each decade since then, the number of manufacturing jobs declined. At the same time, employment in the service sector increased continuously between 1970 and 2000. There was evidence of this transformation throughout suburban Baltimore. Approximately one-third of the labor force in the first-tier suburbs and Baltimore City was employed in the manufacturing industry in 1970 (see Figure 18.4). In the outer suburbs, the portion of residents employed in the manufacturing industry was considerably less; 18 percent of residents held manufacturing jobs in 1970. Over three decades, the entire region witnessed striking declines in the number of residents employed in manufacturing. For instance, by 2000, only 7 percent of central city residents and 8 percent of outer suburban residents held manufacturing jobs. In the first-tier suburbs, 11 percent of the labor force worked in the manufacturing industry by 2000. While this was the highest in the region, it is important to note that the first-tier suburbs lost a disproportionate number of manufacturing jobs among all suburbs. Baltimore's first-tier suburbs experienced a 200 percent *loss* in the number of residents who worked in the manufacturing industry, which amounted to some 45,000 jobs over thirty years.

Amid the losses in the manufacturing industry, employment in service industries became increasingly more prevalent throughout metropolitan Baltimore. Every first-tier suburb experienced growth in the number of residents with jobs in service industries. In 1970, services jobs comprised between 10 and 20 percent of

Figure 18.4   **Manufacturing Employment in Metropolitan Baltimore, 2000**

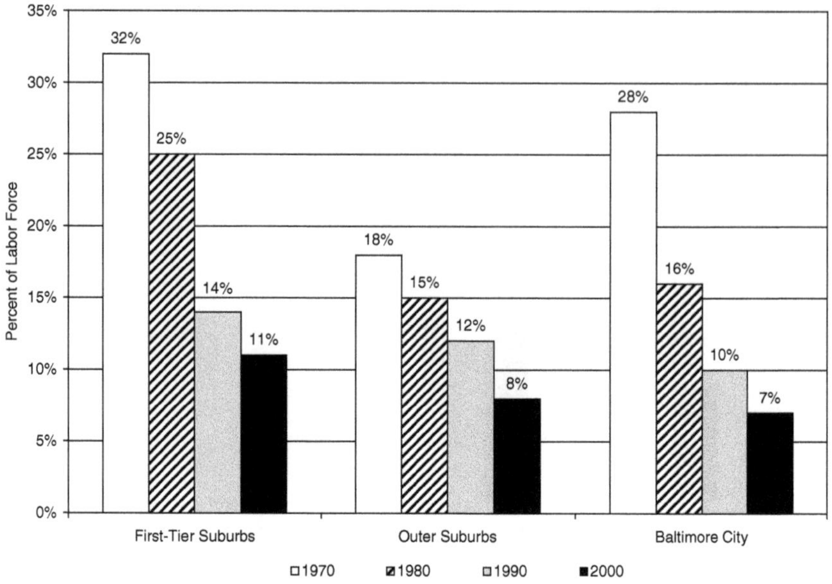

the labor force. By 2000, the percentage of residents with service jobs was at least 30 percent in every first-tier suburb. In comparison, residents in the outer suburbs disproportionately held the majority of all service jobs.

In summary, the onset of the 1970s ushered in a new era for America's suburban landscape. The Baltimore case illustrates that by 2000, a social and economic dichotomy emerged between the first-tier and outer suburbs. The first-tier suburbs were no longer nascent and bucolic; rather, they transformed into mature places and exhibited indicators of distress during this period (Hanlon and Vicino 2005). Analysis of census data demonstrated a pattern of decline on a number of measures between 1970 and 2000. Decline, relative to the outer suburbs, related to the characteristics of the population, the income dynamics, the nature of housing stock, and the labor structure of the first tier. Patterns of urban decay that afflicted the nation's central cities during the 1960s and 1970s are now prevalent in first-tier suburbs. Sternlieb (as quoted in Listokin and Beaton, 1983, xiii) captures the essence of this phenomenon:

> The older suburb is the forgotten frontier of America. It is coupled with its near relative, the free-standing smaller city, as elements of our society largely overlooked by academics and planners as well. On the one hand, the trauma of the central city has dominated the scene. On the other, there is the issue of coping with the growth of the outer suburbs. Lost in the middle are the older suburbs.

Indeed, older suburbs were neglected during the 1970s and 1980s. But during the 1990s, local and state political actors in Maryland woke up to the need to address this problem.

Baltimore County Confronts Suburban Decline

Baltimore County, Maryland, stands out as a national leader among local governments in confronting suburban decline (Outen 2005). Beginning in the mid-1990s, Baltimore County pursued a strategy to confront suburban decline. Using principles of smart growth, the county invested in its older suburbs rather than fund new growth. Baltimore County Executive "Dutch" Ruppersberger created the Office of Community Conservation (OCC) in 1995. During his eight years in office, the Ruppersberger administration focused on four strategic goals: education, crime, economic development, and community conservation. The idea was to build human capital throughout this maturing jurisdiction by investing in areas that were already built and had existing infrastructure. Thus, the OCC was charged with stabilizing and revitalizing the county's older neighborhoods and commercial areas in first-tier suburbs. The county's mandate to address this problem continued into the 2000s when the next county executive, James "Jim" Smith, following Ruppersberger, also made first-tier suburban renewal a platform issue for his administration. Following in the spirit of former County Executive Ruppersberger, Smith acknowledged the importance of revitalization: "The role of government is to protect the individual character of our neighborhoods and safeguard our resources and adjust to the changing development needs of our communities" (Smith 2003).

Thus, Baltimore County's (2000) OCC was charged "to preserve, stabilize, and enhance the human, physical, and economic conditions of the County's urban communities." The OCC developed the Renaissance Development Initiative, a countywide revitalization plan. It sought to create a "renaissance"—or a new beginning—for Baltimore's aging suburban communities. When it began in 1995, the plan called for redevelopment projects that addressed a dilapidated housing stock and struggling commercial strips in first-tier suburbs. OCC used this map to guide its planning process and public investments. Funding for revitalization projects was directed exclusively to these areas. All of the county's first-tier suburbs were located within the conservation boundaries. The county's public mandate from the county executive allowed the OCC to focus its resources on community development in these first-tier suburbs.

The OCC carried out a variety of projects to address the problem of an aging housing stock and struggling commercial areas from 1995 to 2005. While the OCC focused attention on the western and eastern declining suburban neighborhoods, perhaps the case of Dundalk, Maryland, provides a nice illustration of the overall strategy for reengineering this declining community. This first-tier suburb, located on the eastern fringe of the central city, is one of the largest and oldest suburbs of Baltimore. Since 1970, Dundalk transitioned from a stable, working-class community to a place of dramatic decline. The home of various large industrial plants, including the behemoth Bethlehem Steel Corporation and General Motors, massive deindustrialization hit the local economy hard. Two out of three manufacturing jobs disappeared between 1970 and 2000. Plus, the poverty rate nearly doubled, from 5 percent to 10 percent; household income declined by 12 percent, falling from $45,000 to $39,000 in 2000 (in constant 1999 dollars). In consequence, the population declined by one-third; approximately 22,000 residents left. Dundalk became an aging community, and the number of residents over sixty-five tripled since 1970. By the end of the 1990s, Dundalk faced especially challenging issues. Dundalk's legacy became a familiar history for Baltimore's other first-tier suburbs (Hanlon and Vicino 2005). This historical account of decline suggested that Dundalk would continue to deteriorate unless something was done to thwart the decay of this suburb.

Ruppersberger and Smith thus took a special interest in the revitalization of Dundalk. Since 2002, the OCC has invested $70 million into Dundalk. These investments were aimed at demolishing rundown apartment complexes, renovating older housing units, and refurbishing the suburb's town square. At a press conference, Smith continued his pledge to give Dundalk a suburban makeover. On March 27, 2006, Smith announced the $5.5 million purchase of the York Park Apartments. The housing complex, located in the center of Dundalk, was decrepit and an eyesore. It became a magnet for criminal activity—there were more reported crimes in this area than in any other part of the county (Smith 2006). The county worked for several years to condemn the property for demolition, and plans to raze the property are imminent. Smith declared, "The wait is over . . . today Dundalk's renaissance shines like never before, and I promise you that as the York Park complex comes down, a wonderful new community will be born" (1). Other projects included the renovation of the Dundalk Village Center; streetscaping of Dundalk Avenue; large-scale renovations of the Dundalk Village Apartments; and expanding the Heritage Trail to neighborhoods and various parks. Dundalk residents, including the suburb's community development corporation, the Dundalk Renaissance Corporation (DRC), rallied behind county planners and Smith for this milestone. Residents felt that the demolition of York Park would help Dundalk confront its challenges, including fighting crime and providing attractive, quality housing. DRC President Scott Holupka commented that "the creation of desirable housing options for families in the area is critical for Dundalk's continued renaissance. The county's commitment to changing the landscape along Yorkway is a major step forward in that effort" (Smith 2006, 1).

It is important to note that the process of redevelopment of Dundalk and other first-tier suburbs has not received homogeneous community support. In 2000, the Maryland General Assembly, with the endorsement of Baltimore County's OCC, Department of Planning, and Office of the County Executive, passed S.B. 509, which was a bill to permit the county to use eminent domain for economic development purposes. With this power, Ruppersberger and planners sought to condemn approximately 300 properties in the eastern first-tier suburbs for a new waterfront mixed-use development. Residents strongly opposed the county's attempts to seize private property for private redevelopment. On November 7, 2000, residents mobilized 70 percent of the electorate to vote to remove the county's right to use eminent domain for economic revitalization purposes.[3] In the aftermath of the community's opposition to S.B. 509, the OCC developed a participatory planning process for the redevelopment of its other first-tier suburbs. For instance, the county funded and gave logistical support for the development of the DRC. This community development corporation served as the suburb's community liaison and voice. A planning charrette process also provided additional community voice and feedback on projects. In consequence, subsequent efforts to revitalize the county's suburbs proceeded with the support of the community.

Although the revitalization of eastern suburban Baltimore was a slow and lengthy process, spanning over a decade, these projects offer evidence of progress. Baltimore County focused on the renewal of physical infrastructure rather than the development of human capital throughout its older suburbs. While revitalization occurred in the built environment, it remains to be seen whether these projects will raise the economic standing for residents of first-tier suburbs. Still, this approach was one of the most comprehensive local approaches to decline.

Political Realities and Economic Imperatives of Smart Growth

Maryland has been heralded as a national leader in managing the growth of its urbanized areas (Burchell, Listokin, and Galley 2000; Cohen 2002; Downs 2001). In 1997, then Governor Parris Glendening developed a state program to combat urban sprawl. The Smart Growth Areas Act of 1997 sought to encourage the investment and revitalization of cites and established suburbs. This legislation provided state funding for transportation, housing, economic development, and environmental projects to "priority funding areas" (PFAs). In Baltimore County, the PFAs were strictly located in only the first-tier suburbs. These were areas that already had existing development, and they covered all of the first-tier suburbs of Baltimore. To enforce the smart growth policies, the legislation allowed the governor to deny state funding for projects that demonstrated the potential to exacerbate sprawl (Cohen 2002).

Despite the national recognition that Maryland received, various scholars have noted that Maryland's smart growth policies are severely limited in what they can realistically do. Cohen (2002) points out two critical limitations in Maryland's smart growth program: (1) it preserves local autonomy; and (2) it favors incentives over regulations. Similarly, Knaap (2001) argues that smart growth will continue to be largely ineffective as long as local governments maintain exclusive zoning and planning powers. Indeed, smart growth policies are only as strong as the willingness of Maryland's counties and municipalities to support them. For example, if a jurisdiction does not want to embrace smart growth's plan for mixed-use, high-density communities, then it can simply prohibit that type of development through its own zoning laws (Gainsborough 2001). In effect, this diminishes the state's role in smart growth. Given the political reality of popular support for control over local zoning, it is unlikely that county governments will relinquish these coveted powers any time soon.

Furthermore, smart growth policies in Maryland do not regulate land use; they only provide incentives by making funds available for projects. According to Porter (1999), without the state explicitly regulating the use of land, smart growth policies are too weak to alter the pattern of development. If the state withholds funding to a local government for a project that it deems as a stimulus for sprawl, then little can be done to stop the local government from pursuing alternative sources of revenue to fund the project. Therefore, the economic imperative is that financial incentives alone are not strong enough to slow urban sprawl. Because of these two limitations, Maryland's first-tier suburbs have not benefited as much from smart growth policies at the state level as they have at the local level. As a result, leap-frog growth has occurred between counties. In short, Maryland's version of smart growth can only effectively confront suburban decline *if* substantial changes are made to overcome these limitations.

Maryland's smart growth initiatives have also not been immune to politics. While former Governor Glendening voiced significant support and provided substantial funding for smart growth initiatives from 1995 to 2003, his Republican predecessor did not. Under the Republican Governor Robert Ehrlich administration from 2003 to 2007, support and funding for smart growth dramatically waned. In 2003, Ehrlich authorized the Governor's Office of Smart Growth to be dismantled. Plus, in the wake of a recession and a reallocation of the state's resources based on the governor's priorities, Maryland's Departments of Housing and Community Development and Planning suffered from large budget cuts during the early 2000s (Wheeler 2005). By 2007, the state's newly elected Democratic Governor Martin O'Malley reinstituted the Governor's Office of Smart Growth and provided additional funding for such programs with the support of a Democrat-controlled state house (Green 2007).

This highlights the political fights and philosophical divides between Maryland Republicans and Democrats. It also demonstrates that support for smart growth, in part, is a function of state's economic climate and the political will of the state's leaders to use the program as a tool for suburban revitalization. Without increases in state funding, explicitly for first-tier suburbs, and a strong commitment from the state's leaders, the impact of smart growth on first-tier suburban revitalization is tenuous at best. As a result of the lack of land use regulation and a regional zoning authority, the political reality is that Maryland's smart growth initiative remains a futile tool for revitalizing first-tier suburbs. To date, the state has been unable to prevent the decline of first-tier suburbs because it has not provided zoning powers necessary to seriously alter the patterns of urban development, and political leaders throughout the state have not maintained a continuous commitment to these programs.

Future Prospects

The question about whether Baltimore's decade-long quest to confront suburban decline will work effectively still remains unanswered. Baltimore may well be in a marginally better position than other metropolitan areas to confront its problems of suburban decline given the structure of local government and its political culture. Baltimore County has a strong government that does not have any incorporated municipalities. As such, the county maintained jurisdiction over all of its first-tier suburbs. The county was able to redistribute funds and create zoning tools to facilitate revitalization. In addition, the county benefited from three consecutive county administrations over twelve years that had the political will to support suburban renewal as platform issues. These characteristics made it possible for Baltimore County to do *something* about decline, but a systematic and comprehensive approach that was regional in nature was still lacking nearly twelve years later after the county set out to confront suburban decline.

To reengineer communities, it is necessary to not only embrace smart growth principles but to expand local, regional, and state policies. Local governments are not fully equipped—if at all—to engage in the revitalization necessary to reverse decades of socioeconomic decline. In the case of Baltimore, a large population base that resided in both the first-tier and outer suburbs allowed the county to generate public funds to begin suburban renewal. Yet, for regions without such a political environment, it will be even more difficult to raise revitalization funding. Therefore, it is essential for Maryland, as well as others, to realize that the decline of first-tier suburbs will continue in the absence of meaningful growth-management policies. A growth boundary that is truly regional in nature would limit leapfrog development and uneven growth that contributes to the demise of first-tier suburbs. Without a true regional growth-management policy, this pattern will continue. It is plausible that greater public investments will benefit growing outer suburbs rather than declining first-tier suburbs. The economic imperative is that market-driven development will continue to move outward as the aging process in first-tier suburbs continues. Political reality is that policies are unlikely to garner support they need to be adopted. In the absence of such regional tools, governments need to provide substantial funding for the reinvestment of established communities in the first-tier suburbs.

Despite the challenges of confronting suburban decline, two lessons prevail about how to effectively deal with this problem. First, a federal government role is needed to overcome institutional barriers, political and economic, confronting suburban decline. A federal role would overcome the political impediments of regionalism and local government fragmentation. It would also be in a position to provide economic support directly to localities for suburban revitalization. This is what Senator Hillary Clinton attempted to do during the previous legislative session in Congress. She co-sponsored the Suburban Core Opportunity Restoration and Enhancement (SCORE) Act (S.1024) to create a federal block grant program for revitalizing older suburban communities. Even though the bill failed, it represents a step in the right direction for achieving suburban renewal. Second, the Baltimore case informs us about the importance of a housing-focused revitalization strategy to overcome the challenges of an outdated and unmarketable housing stock. Baltimore's first-tier suburbs lacked both the charm and character of the nineteenth-century Baltimore City rowhouse and the amenities and newness of larger houses in the outer suburbs. Stuck in the middle of the region was the first-tier suburban postwar housing stock built from 1950 to 1970. A strategy that tore down dilapidated properties, funded improvement projects to provide houses with new amenities, and provided funds for first-time homebuyers proved successful in Baltimore.

The older suburb is no longer the forgotten frontier, as Sternlieb (as cited in Listokin and Beaton, 1983) once observed. As a group, the first-tier suburbs have systematically declined in recent decades relative to their respective outer suburbs, and scholars and practitioners have finally paid more attention to this often-neglected area of study. As the first generation of suburbs for the masses, first-tier suburban communities have reached a crossroads. They have not decayed as much as their counterparts in the central city. Yet without immediate and sustained intervention, this analysis shows that the pattern of decay has the potential to become a down-ward spiral. The time for change has arrived for the first-tier suburbs. Whether that change occurs—and makes a difference—is a question of public policy, politics, and planning, and future research should examine the impacts of those three processes on first-tier suburbs in America.

Notes

An earlier version of this chapter was presented at the 37th Annual Meeting of the Urban Affairs Association, Seattle, April 26–28, 2007. The author thanks Donald F. Norris, John Rennie Short, Todd Swanstrom, Cheryl Miller, George Wagner, Bernadette Hanlon, and Amy Glorioso Rynes for their valuable insights. Research here was partially funded by the U.S. Environmental Protection Agency (EPA). It has not been subjected to EPA peer and policy review; therefore, no official endorsement should be inferred.

1. Numerous terms have been used to describe older suburban communities located on the fringe of central cities (Lee and Leigh 2005). Here, I adopt the term *first-tier suburbs* because it addresses a period of time when these suburban communities developed ("first") without presuming a specific geographic pattern of development (such as "rings").

2. The census designed place (CDP) geography was used in this analysis. CDPs de-lineate unincorporated areas with concentrations of population, housing, and commercial sites and a degree of local identity. Baltimore's first-tier suburbs are unincorporated, as are the majority of its outer suburbs.

3. The U.S. Supreme Court subsequently reaffirmed the right to use eminent domain for economic development in *Kelo v. City of New London* 545 U.S. 469.

References

Baltimore County. 2000. *Master Plan 2010.* Towson, MD.
Bluestone, B. P., and B. Harrison. 1982. *The Deindustrialization of America.* New York: Basic Books.

Burchell, R. W., D. Listokin, and C. C. Galley. 2000. "Smart Growth: More Than a Ghost of Urban Policy Past, Less Than a Bold New Horizon." *Housing Policy Debate* 11 (4): 821–880.

Cohen, J. 2002. "Maryland's Smart Growth: Using Incentives to Combat Sprawl." In *Urban Sprawl: Causes, Consequences and Policy Responses,* ed. G. Squires. Washington, DC: Urban Institute Press, 293–324.

Culver, L. W. 1982. "The Politics of Suburban Distress." *Journal of Urban Affairs* 4 (1): 1–18.

Downs, A. 2001. "What Does 'Smart Growth' Really Mean?" *Planning,* April.

Gainsborough, J. 2001. "Smart Growth and Urban Sprawl: Support for a New Regional Agenda?" *Urban Affairs Review* 37 (5): 728–744.

Green, A. A. 2007. "O'Malley Pledges to Fund Preservation Effort." *Baltimore Sun,* January 12: B5.

Hanlon, B., and T. J. Vicino. 2005. "The State of the Inner Suburbs: An Examination of Suburban Baltimore, 1980 to 2000." Baltimore, MD: Center for Urban Environmental Research and Education, Report #2, April.

Hanlon, B., T. J. Vicino, and J. R. Short. 2006. "The New Metropolitan Reality in the US: Rethinking the Traditional Model." *Urban Studies* 43 (12): 2129–2143.

Hudnut III, W. H. 2003. *Halfway to Everywhere: A Portrait of America's First-Tier Suburbs.* Washington, DC: Urban Land Institute.

Knaap, G. J. 2001. *Land Market Monitoring for Smart Urban Growth.* Cambridge, MA: Lincoln Institute of Land Policy.

Lee, S., and N. G. Leigh. 2005. "The Role of Inner Ring Suburbs in Metropolitan Smart Growth Strategies." *Journal of Planning Literature* 19: 330–346.

Leigh, N. G., and S. Lee. 2005. "Philadelphia's Space in Between: Inner-Ring Suburb Evolution." *Opolis* 1 (1): 13–32.

Listokin, D. and W.P. Beaton. 1983. "Revitalizing the Older Suburb." New Brunswick, NJ: State University of New Jersey, Center for Urban Policy Research.

Lucy, W. H., and D. L. Phillips. 2000. *Confronting Suburban Decline: Strategic Planning for Metropolitan Renewal.* Washington, DC: Island Press.

———. 2006. *Tomorrow's Cities, Tomorrow's Suburbs.* Chicago: APA Planner's Press.

Orfield, M. 2002. *American Metropolitics: The New Suburban Reality.* Washington, DC: Brookings Institution.

Outen, D. 2005. "Baltimore County, Maryland: Using the Entire Toolkit for Habitat Protection." In *Nature-Friendly Communities: Habitat Protection and Land Use Planning,* ed. C. Duerksen and C. Snyder. Washington, DC: Island Press, 152–173.

Porter, D. R. 1999. "Will 'Smart Growth' Produce 'Smart Growth'?" *The Abell Report* 12 (January): 1–8.

Smith, N., P. Caris, and E. Wyly. 2001. "The 'Camden Syndrome' and the Menace of Suburban Decline: Residential Disinvestment and Its Discontents in Camden County, New Jersey." *Urban Affairs Review* 36 (4): 497–531.

Smith, J. T. 2003. Renaissance Redevelopment Press Release, December 15. Towson, MD: Office of the County Executive.

———. 2006. Smith Seeks Council Approval to Purchase York Park Apartments Press Release, March 27. Towson, MD: Office of the County Executive.

Teaford, J. C. 1979. *City and Suburb: The Political Fragmentation of Metropolitan America, 1850–1970.* Baltimore: Johns Hopkins University Press.

Wheeler, T. 2005. "Smart Growth Pace Slower in Maryland." *Baltimore Sun,* March 6: 1C.

19

Positive Cycling

Riding Our Bicycles Down the Path to Community Development Success

David W. Sears and Colin D. Sears

Let's spend a day in the Netherlands! You will notice many people going about their daily lives using their bicycles. You will see children riding their bicycles to school. And you'll encounter workers riding to their jobs, or to the train station where they will continue the journey to work. You will see mothers and fathers taking the kids to day care on their bicycles. And you will see lots of folks with their bicycle baskets brimming with the purchases from shopping trips.

Bicycling is woven into the fabric of life in the Netherlands. This is especially true in Amsterdam and other high-density regions, but also holds in rural districts. Very interesting, you might respond, and certainly spending a day wandering around the Netherlands can be fun; but what does this have to do with community development?

The Theory of Positive Cycling

The thesis of this chapter is that *increasing the per-capita use of bicycling for daily transportation will produce community development and economic development gains* for most U.S. regions (see Table 19.1). We call this our *theory of positive cycling.*

For most regions in the United States, the *rush-to-the-top strategy* for economic development is much more attractive and viable than the *low-tax-low-wage rush-to-the-bottom strategy.* A region that is selling itself using the *rush-to-the-top strategy* is generally offering a *development package* of highly qualified workers, excellent infrastructure, and first-class public services, along with an overall high quality of life for both workers and managers.

In the *rush-to-the-top strategy,* economic development (e.g., high median household income) and community development objectives (e.g., good health of residents, good air, and water quality) are intertwined; that is, generally, economic development success (strong prosperity) enhances community development success (high quality of life) and vice versa.

Table 19.1

How Increased Bicycling Will Promote Community Development Success

Increased transportation bicycling will lead to

1. Improvement in per-capita health status
2. Improvement in air quality
3. Reduction in greenhouse emissions
4. Reduction in noise
5. Increase in per-capita smart growth development*
6. Decrease in per-capita transportation expenditures (both private and public)
7. Increase in open-space opportunities
8. Decrease in travel time (in some situations)
9. Increase in mobility options
10. Increase in recreational bicycling
11. Increase in tourism bicycling
12. Benefits to nonbicyclists
13. Increase in community friendliness

Note: More smart growth, in turn, leads to increases in per-capita transportation bicycling as well as to other quality-of-life increases via improvement in per-capita health status, improvement in air quality, reduction in greenhouse emissions, and more time for family and recreation activities (due to less time per-capita spent on commuting).

We argue that any steps a region can take to increase per-capita use of *transportation bicycling*[1] will make the region's *development package* stronger and lead to greater economic and community development.

As we stated, increased per-capita transportation bicycling will produce several quality-of-life improvements. Taken together, these improvements will enhance both economic and community development. The following quality-of-life improvements assume that increased transportation bicycling will come almost entirely at the expense of automobile driving.

- Each mile for which bicycling is substituted for driving will result in increased exercise for the participant. Thus, one of the quality-of-life benefits of increased bicycling will be the improved per-capita health of the community.
- Increased transportation bicycling will result in decreased air pollution and greenhouse gases.[2] Since bicycles are quieter than cars, noise in the community will also be reduced. So another quality-of-life benefit of increased bicycling will be the improved environmental quality of the community.[3]
- Increased transportation bicycling will lead to a stronger constituency for smart growth policies and practices.[4] The logic here is that as people switch from driving their automobiles to riding their bicycles, they will increasingly appreciate the benefits of the shorter trips made possible by the smart growth approach and will be encouraged to use their bikes even more.
- Per-capita transportation costs will be lower, since both the capital cost and

per-mile operational cost of a bicycle is a tiny fraction of the cost of driving a car.[5]

- Costs will be lower for infrastructure needed to support vehicles (compare the cost of providing parking for a car with that for a bicycle; likewise, compare the number of square feet of pavement required to travel in a car with that required for a bicycle). In addition, new open-space opportunities may appear as need for automobile space on roads and parking lots is replaced by much less space to accommodate bicycles.
- People will have more time for family, recreation, and other activities. Bicycling will often, especially for shorter trips and in higher density communities, take less time than driving.
- Some people do not have cars because they are too young or too poor. Improving the bicycle infrastructure can vastly increase the realistic mobility options for them.

The focus of this chapter is not on recreational bicycling. Nonetheless, many of the following infrastructure improvements suggested for encouraging more transportation bicycling will have the side benefit of making recreational bicycling more attractive.

- Increases in transportation bicycling will likely lead to increases in exercise (assuming at least some of the additional bicycling hours were previously spent on more sedentary activities), thus leading to health improvements for the community.
- Improving the bicycling infrastructure of a community will increase quality of life. That is, even beyond any health benefits, the bicyclists who can enjoy more and higher quality bicycle routes will find living in this community more attractive than before.

Tourists can also enter into the equation. Some tourists may be attracted to a community or region partly because of its strong infrastructure for bicycling. Simply by drawing more tourists to the area, the enhanced bicycle infrastructure will directly contribute to local economic development. In addition, a strong bicycle infrastructure may induce some tourists to choose to do some of their internal transportation (e.g., from hotel to museum, from park to restaurant) using rental bicycles. Assuming this transportation bicycling by tourists is, at least partially, substituting for automobile travel, then again, the result is an increase in the community's quality of life thanks to improvements in environmental quality.

It is noteworthy that even those who never bicycle at all will benefit in some ways from increased per-capita bicycling in the community. For instance, drivers will enjoy improved air quality and lower traffic congestion that results from getting others onto bicycles.

Finally, there is the intangible positive "feel" that a community with lots of bicycling creates. Visitors and residents can read a community dense with bicycling activity as a friendly and safe place. It's much easier to wave a friendly greeting from your bicycle than from your car.

Using the latest figures available, looking across an array of costs and benefits, including most of those mentioned previously, one researcher has estimated that the net benefit of shifting a trip from automobile to bicycle is at least $5.72 in urban settings (rising to $11.20 in peak periods) and is $3.04 in rural areas. He adds that these estimates are likely quite low, since he did not include some of the more difficult-to-quantity benefits, such as improved health and increased smart growth (Littman 2004, 25).

The Ultimate Bicycle-Friendly Community

Let's shift gears for a moment (yes, pun intended). Positive bicycling requires *the ultimate bicycle-friendly community*. Let's get specific about what this ultimate bicycle-friendly community would look like.

The psychology of this community is one in which the very first thought about almost any trip is to use a bicycle. It is not weird or unusual to use a bicycle for a trip to work or to shop or for other daily business; such trips are so commonplace that they are totally unremarkable. In fact, for many such daily trips, no thinking is needed; the use of the bicycle is simply a part of the rhythm of life (similar to brushing your teeth every morning). To reach this state of commonplace daily bicycling, the community must have in place a strong physical and social infrastructure to support bicycling.

The bicycle-friendly community is one in which bicycling is easy and safe and pleasant. All major daily destinations are located within easy bicycling distance for most of the population, including schoolchildren and elderly riders, not just athletes. Routes would be well paved, well marked, and well maintained. The route network must be very dense, coming up to the front doors of many common destinations (such as jobs and schools), within a few hundred feet of other such common destinations, and within half a mile of most residences.

In the ultimate bicycle-friendly community, bicycling is safe. All bicycling is well separated from speeding automobiles, trucks, and buses. Any bicycling on the same route as cars and trucks involves only vehicles traveling at 20 miles per hour or slower. This separation of bicycles from high-speed automobile traffic contributes to safety and, as a fringe benefit, makes the bicycling experience much more pleasant.

Eventually, strict segregation of bicycling from other uses will not necessarily be important or even always desirable. Part of what must happen in the ultimate bicycle-friendly community is that all citizens recognize that bicycling is a critical and positive part of the community fabric. Thus, automobile drivers understand that keeping bicyclists safe is a civic duty, not an option; once bicycling has "caught on," for most drivers, consideration of bicyclists will be

Table 19.2

Characteristics of the Ultimate Bike-Friendly Community

1. Transportation bicycling is commonplace
2. Bicycling is easy
   - Dense route network
   - Most common destinations served
3. Bicycling is safe
   - Segregation from automobile traffic
   - All citizens considerate of bicyclists
   - Routes well paved, well maintained
4. Bicycling is pleasant
   - Many common routes are short (in time and distance)
   - Bike parking convenient
   - Routes well marked
5. Bicycling is encouraged via economic incentives

easy because the same person who drives an automobile at one point in the day may ride a bicycle later on.

The ultimate bicycle-friendly community is a smart growth community. A higher density, integrated-multiuse, smart growth development is, all else equal, more conducive to bicycling than a lower density, segregated-use, and dumb growth development. The reason? When thinking of transportation bicycling, for most riders in most situations, a shorter ride is more appealing than a longer ride.

The ultimate bicycle-friendly community has facilities in place at all common destinations to make the bicycling experience as easy, safe, and pleasant as possible. Thus, the bicycle parking at work (or at home or school or shopping) is not in a dirty, dark basement or alley but in a clean, well-lighted, covered space near the front door.

Finally, the ultimate bicycle-friendly community has a system of market incentives and subsidies in place to encourage transportation bicycling and, on the flip side, to discourage automobile usage (see Table 19.2). Even though many communities will not reach the ultimate in bicycle-friendliness, movement in that direction will improve the local quality of life.[6]

How to Create the Ultimate Bicycle-Friendly Community

If you were convinced that creating the ultimate bicycle-friendly environment in your region is a terrific idea, how would you go about making that happen?

First, you would want to frame the matter as a transportation bicycling issue, not as a recreational bicycling issue because transportation is serious business, deserving serious thought and serious resources. On the other hand, recreation is far less serious; it's just fluff and fun and nice to have, but deserving neither serious thought nor serious resources. In America, unfortunately, the knee-jerk reaction to the term *bicycling* is a bunch of guys on slick, thousand-dollar bicycles wearing bright spandex shirts and riding in bunches on sunny weekends—oh, and perhaps school kids riding aimlessly around their neighborhoods under the not-so-watchful eyes of their parents. With that as your starting point, no one is going to engage you in a serious conversation about bicycling as a key community development ingredient. You must work hard to change that initial first (and wrong) impression. You must explain how bicycling can, if properly supported, be a true daily transportation option for many people in many situations.

Second, you would want to frame the issue under the broader heading of "community development" or "economic development" rather than under the more limiting "transportation." Transportation bicycling is, of course, a mode of transportation; and what you are advocating is creating an environment in which people will be enticed to get out of their cars and onto their bicycles for many daily trips. But you don't want to set yourself a trap in which the only people you can talk to about policies and practices are in the transportation arena. By framing this as a "community development" or "economic development" issue, you allow yourself the freedom to talk with those well beyond the state department of transportation.

Third, "you" would want to be a broad coalition of interested institutions, not just an interested citizen, and not even just the local economic development agency.

Fourth, you would want to have a large number of specific potential actions in your toolbox. You would want to work on several of these simultaneously, expecting that some would produce good results while others would be dead-ends, at least in the short run. Let's go through some candidates.

Potential Action 1: Create and Maintain a First-Class Bicycle Route Network

The creation—and strong maintenance—of a truly first-class bicycle route network will do wonders for encouraging transportation bicycling.[7] This network should have several key characteristics, including routes that are well paved (e.g., no slipping or sliding on loose gravel or drainage grates), well maintained (e.g., snow, ice, litter, and leaf removal are thorough and timely; potholes are repaired regularly), and well marked (e.g., directional signs pointing toward common destinations and frequent maps with "you are here" indicators). Routes need not be designed for bicycle racing, but safe riding at moderate speeds (about 12 miles per hour) should be possible; this means foliage should be pruned to allow good sightlines ahead, and sharp turns should be eliminated or well marked. Creating an excellent bicycling network is important, but maintenance is equally critical. In Albuquerque, for instance, a street sweeper works exclusively on the city's bicycle trails.

The route network must be high density, going to almost all important destinations in the community, including transit hubs, workplaces, schools, homes, shopping, medical offices, libraries, cafes, sports fields/gymnasiums, and so on.

To be first class, this network must be a true continuous system, with all individual components clearly and rationally linked together, preferably at the regional level: when the Mill Creek bicycle path meets 22nd Street, for instance, the bicyclist must understand immediately which way to continue on her or his journey to work. The network must never unceremoniously disappear, for instance, upon entering a tunnel or crossing a bridge.

The route network should also be safe, especially in terms of separating bicycles from high-speed automobile traffic. When the bicycle route network sends riders onto streets, intersections are an issue in terms of convenience and safety. Thus, the community should redesign major intersections and recalibrate traffic signals to give cyclists early and safe passage. When the bicycle route is a dedicated lane on a street, traffic-calming measures are needed to slow down automobiles.

To the extent possible, the route network should include attractive features, perhaps offering vistas of ponds, lakes, streams, cityscapes, bridges, attractive fencing, murals, sculptures, and other outdoor art. Routing the network through parkland and supplying occasional benches for stops can add ambience to the trip.

In communities with public transit, the buses, trains, and ferries should all be seamlessly woven into the overall bicycling network. For instance, putting bicycles on the bus or the train should be easy and a well-accepted practice.

Potential Action 2: Create and Maintain Convenient and Safe Bicycle Parking

For many potential transportation bicyclists, a major impediment is not so much the journey as what to do with the bicycle at the destination. Either there's no place to park the bicycle or the available parking is highly unattractive—for example, requiring the rider to carry her or his bicycle down two flights of a dark stairway into the subbasement to put the bicycle in a puddle of water surrounded by abandoned second-hand furniture.

Bicycling can be made more attractive by providing safe and convenient parking at most major destinations. These parking spaces should be in clean, well-lighted locations, preferably with protection from the weather and bicycle thieves. The location should be extremely convenient, such as right at the front door.

Destinations with convenient and safe parking spaces should include transit hubs to encourage and enable riders to combine transportation bicycling with bus or train or other public transit. Bikestation, a nonprofit organization, has developed bicycle parking centers at several transit hubs in California; beyond secure 24-hour parking, these centers offer auxiliary facilities and services, including bicycle repairs, rentals, lockers, showers, and even cafes.

Good bicycle parking should be provided at schools, work, shopping, and home. Home builders and redevelopers should be encouraged to include a conveniently located bicycle mini-garage, or similar facility, for each housing unit.

Potential Action 3: Create and Maintain a Fleet of On-Demand Rental Bicycles

Many bicyclists will want to ride their own bicycles. Some riders, however, will want (or need) an accessible rental bicycle occasionally. For instance, a worker may want to take the bus or carpool to work, and then ride home on a rental bicycle that can be picked up at work and dropped off at or near home.

Other riders will not want to own a bicycle but will want to depend on rental bicycles. For instance, those living in small third-floor walk-up apartments may not want the hassle of owning a bicycle. In addition, tourists will generally not bring their bicycles with them to town.

An institution—public, private, or nonprofit—should be set up to create and maintain a fleet of rental bicycles. Such systems have been created in two French cities: Paris and Lyon. In Lyon, the first half hour is free, which encourages bicycle usage for quick errands.

For a bicycle rental fleet to have substantial impact on building a bicycle-friendly region, it should offer inexpensive, convenient, and reliable service. Some subsidization of the rental cost may be necessary if renting is to be inexpensive.

Convenience will require hundreds of locations (or more) scattered around a large area. The larger the area covered by the rental fleet, the more likely an individual rider will find rental locations at both ends of her or his proposed trip. And, within the covered area, the higher the density of rental locations, the more likely the customer will find a nearby location and therefore use the service.[8]

Convenience will also require minimal time spent checking out the rental bicycle and checking it back in upon return. The details probably include a one-time, online easy "membership" process, use of a credit card for checking in and out, and a look at the Zip Car and Flex Car in-town rental car operations for ideas on workable processes.

Reliability means that the bicycles must be sturdy and well maintained. Also, the operating institution must have in place a system to accurately forecast the demand level at each rental location and to move the bicycles as needed, perhaps on an hourly basis, to the locations where they will best meet forecasted demand. The rental fleet will not be widely used if it has a reputation for not delivering on a consistent basis.

This rental fleet should not appear to be just a middle-class program; both the perception and the reality should be that the rental bicycles serve low-income households as well as the middle and upper classes. Special provisions (e.g., cost structure, advertising, rental locations) may be needed to assure the rental fleet successfully serves the region's lower-income population.

Potential Action 4: Get High-Profile Actors to Model Good Bicycling

Strong public support for the creation of the ultimate bicycle-friendly community requires, among other prerequisites, strong public awareness of bicycling as a potential mode of daily transportation. One way to build such public awareness is to enlist media stars to model good transportation bicycling behavior. Candidates could include local or international film, television, sports, or music celebrities; local or national elected officials; or other high-profile individuals or groups. Even Sammy the Slug, the mascot of the local baseball team, might work. Whoever this person is, get her or him to bicycle where and when maximum exposure is possible. Seeing the mayor riding to work every day, rain or shine, would be a fantastic way to encourage others to begin bicycling to work.

Bicycling at work can also encourage more bicycling in the community. For instance, police officers on bicycles contribute to effective policing and simultaneously provide an additional visible role model of daily bicycling. Building inspectors and other municipal employees can go about their daily business on bicycles. All such role models should demonstrate safe and courteous riding.

Potential Action 5: Hold Bicycle Encouragement Events

Public events can be created to encourage bicycle riding. A Bike-to-Work Day, for example, could involve dozens (or hundreds or thousands) of persons commuting on major thoroughfares on their bicycles, serving as a visual message to those in cars that they too could be riding their bicycles to work. In Brooklyn, there's an annual Bicycle Fetish Day in the Williamsburg neighborhood. The main point of these events would be to remind the public that bicycle riding is a legitimate and viable form of daily transportation.

Potential Action 6: Offer Subsidies or Tax Credits for Bicycle
Purchases and Usage

A local government (or several local governments, or the state government) could offer subsidies or tax credits for bicycle purchases; likewise, a local employer (or several) could offer such subsidies (for instance, for its employees). So that the subsidy or credit is not used primarily to underwrite the purchase of extremely high-end bicycles, it must be capped at a certain level, applying, for example, only to the first $400 of the consumer's price.

Alternatively, the state government, or a consortium of local governments, might negotiate with several bicycle manufacturers for quantity discounts, and then pass these lower prices on to the bicycle-riding public.

Subsidies for bicycle usage might produce an even greater impact. For instance, just as employers subsidize bus riders, bicyclists too could be subsidized. Merchants, for example, could offer them small discounts ("Ride your bike to our shop, get a 2 percent discount").

Potential Action 7: Create and Deliver a Pro-Bicycle Message in Public Schools

Increasing per-capita transportation bicycling is not a one-shot deal, nor is it an overnight deal. Patience is needed, as is continued attention.

To achieve long-term success, strong support in the next generation is necessary. One straightforward approach is simply to give a pro-bicycle message to schoolchildren. In regular courses, the curriculum could incorporate positive references to bicycling (in the story in reading class, the parents ride their bicycles to work; in math, a bicyclist leaves the bus station at 8 miles an hour heading north on the bicycle route toward the library, and so on). In high school driver's education, teaching respect for bicycles could be built into the course. In addition, the local Safe Routes to School program should highlight bicycling options.

Potential Action 8: Provide Bicycle Maintenance and Bicycle Safety and Courtesy Classes

One way to make the bicycle environment attractive is to provide riders with tools to ensure their bicycle riding is a positive experience. Bicycle maintenance classes, provided frequently and in convenient locations, perhaps free or at least low cost, will enable bicyclists to change their punctured tires and make minor repairs (and can encourage them to do the same occasionally for stranded fellow riders). Classes on bicycle safety and courtesy will make the region's bicycling environment safer and more attractive for all, including the bicyclists and those they encounter as they move about (pedestrians, automobiles). Such classes can also deliver hints on how to dress appropriately to stay warm and dry when it rains or a cold wind is blowing.

Potential Action 9: Encourage Smart Growth–Certified Bicycle Shops

As transportation bicycling becomes more accepted and popular in the region, market forces of course will respond with increases in the availability of bicycles, associated equipment (lights, bells, tire repair kits, helmets, and so on), and bicycle maintenance and repair services. The local or state government may, however, wish to help push the market a little to maximize the support for key aspects of the bicycle infrastructure.

One approach would be to offer bicycle shops "smart growth certification." To be so certified, the shop might be required, for example, (1) to be located in a smart growth neighborhood; (2) to offer free (or very cheap) bicycle maintenance classes; (3) to sponsor a bicycle encouragement event at least once a year; and (4) to provide loaner bicycles for patrons whose bicycles are under repair.

There might be several advantages for a bicycle shop that is smart growth certified. First, there would be the public relations value; the shop could tout its "certified" status. Second, some public incentives might be available exclusively (or at a higher level) only for smart growth–certified shops. For instance, certain advertising venues (e.g., municipal bus shelters) might be available only for the certified shops. Another possibility is that customers purchasing subsidized bicycles might receive more substantial subsidies when purchasing from these shops than from noncertified shops. Third, private-sector institutions might also offer certain benefits to the certified shops. The local newspaper, for instance, might offer them lower advertising rates.

Potential Action 10: Include Bicycling as a Prominent Feature in All Smart Growth Thinking

Over the past several years, the smart growth approach to community develop-ment has become increasingly accepted as rational. Bicycling is often a part of the conversation when talking smart growth, but it is often only a small part of the equation. Perhaps it can gain a more prominent position. Let's take the Green Building Code (Code) as an example.

Some states and localities have adopted the Code; some have not. In your region, for any jurisdictions with the Code in place, you will probably need to draw attention to its provisions for the creation of facilities to serve bicyclists. These provisions are generally not as well known as other features of the Code, such as those requir-ing energy efficiency and judicious use of water. In addition, these provisions are not very extensive, but this is a good place to start, since any jurisdiction that has already adopted the Code is likely to be amenable to a proposal for the creation of a more bicycle-friendly community.

Even where the public sector is not taking a lead on smart growth, some ac-tors in the private sector will want to promote smart growth, including perhaps bicycling. Various motivations can drive this behavior, often including the desire to present the business to its customers and shareholders as environmentally and community friendly.

One practice that could make a big difference is requiring all new construction and major upgrading of roads and buildings to include features of the ultimate bicycle-friendly community (e.g., safe and dense bicycle routes, sufficient and well-located parking). In addition, drawing a lesson from the approach some com-munities use for funding schools, fees paid by developers could support enhance-ment of the bicycle infrastructure.

Bicycle planning should not be relegated to the sidelines in an isolated process; rather, bicycling must be a key consideration in all transportation, land use, and development planning.

Potential Action 11: Make Driving the Car Less Attractive

To create the ultimate bicycle-friendly community, the main focus should, of course, be on expanding and enhancing the positive attributes of bicycling. Nonetheless, since the main competitor of transportation bicycling is driving, it is not unreasonable to work on ways to decrease the attractiveness of the automobile as a means of transportation.

A short list of some of the mechanisms that might make the automobile less attractive includes the following: increase the gas tax; increase automobile registration fees; increase the cost of automobile parking (think of all the shopping centers and suburban office parks with acres of free parking); decrease the convenience of parking the car by moving the parking spaces to more remote locations (look at the way airports locate parking miles away from the terminal); decrease the convenience of parking by dramatically reducing the number of parking spaces; slow down automobile traffic by allowing other forms of traffic (buses, bicycles, motorscooters, pedestrians) to proceed first at intersections.

Potential Action 12: Build Courtesy Toward Bicyclists into Driver Licensing Process

Bicycle riders must be courteous to each other and to pedestrians and automobile drivers. In addition, automobile drivers must learn to be courteous to bicyclists. In the state test for driver licenses, courtesy toward bicyclists should be built in as a component both in the original examination and the renewal process.

Potential Action 13: Run Several Pilot Programs

It's possible to design a comprehensive, regionwide bicycling program that would have sufficient political and economic support to be implemented as a successful component of community and economic development. But it's unlikely that things would unfold so beautifully.

Thus, a more realistic approach might involve an early stage of some less grand pilot programs. The pilot approach can be used to build support for a later, fuller program by demonstrating that bicycling really can work as a development tool. In addition, a set of several pilot programs can be useful in learning what types of approaches to promoting transportation bicycling work best, what combinations of elements are especially useful, what specific environments require certain features or emphases, and so on.

A Final Note on Building the Ultimate Bicycle-Friendly Community

Many bicyclists can and will cope with a community less bicycle-friendly than the ultimate. This means that some success in encouraging increases in transportation bicycling can be expected even in communities less advanced. Greater success, however, should be achieved as communities ultimately become bicycle-friendly. Potential bicyclists will be coaxed out of their cars only when most of the components of the ultimate bicycle-friendly community are in place.

Key Institutions

Positive bicycling is not a one-shot deal; it's also not an all-or-nothing deal. Success in moving forward in establishing bicycling as a significant component of the economic development strategy in your community will require patience and persistence. But one major factor in success is partnership. Several key institutions must be brought together to support building the infrastructure that can effectively increase transportation bicycling.

Here our intention is to provide only a few examples of the types of institutions that might be brought into that partnership. In your specific community and region, you should use these ideas as a starting point only. In addition to local and regional institutions, you may want to consider national and statewide organizations.

Think of the reasons that increasing per-capita transportation bicycling makes sense (some enumerated previously); that should give you some hints on the institutions most likely to want to join this partnership. For instance, contact health advocates (e.g., the Heart Association), smart growth advocates (e.g., American Institute of Architects or American Planning Association), environmental organizations (e.g., Sierra Club). Your community may have an elected official who has made these "signature" issues. Likewise, a local or regional foundation may be interested; perhaps a large corporation would want to join the partnership.

An obvious target, of course, would be local bicycle clubs and/or national bicycle associations (such as Rails-to-Trails Conservancy). Just bear in mind that these groups are often focused on recreational biking, where the objectives may be somewhat different from the objectives of transportation biking.

What Some Communities Have Achieved—Three Case Studies

Portland, Oregon

Since the 1980s, the City of Portland has invested heavily in infrastructure improvements to support bicycle commuting. These investments have paid off in the creation of a visible bicycle-friendly culture with a large number of bicycle commuters and advocates. Because of this success, Portland has been named the best overall cycling city in the United States by *Bicycling Magazine* consistently since the mid-1990s. Portland has an extensive network of bicycle corridors and lanes. This network is publicized through well-placed signage as well as detailed route maps that can be obtained in Portland's numerous bicycle shops.

Tri-Met, the regional public transportation agency, has simplified the process for bringing bicycles on the region's bus and light rail network. All buses have front-end racks that carry two bicycles, and light rail cars have designated areas where bicycles can be stowed during commutes. The ease of bringing along your bicycle for part of your commute makes this a very attractive option for commuters residing in this temperate yet rainy climate. Sufficient bicycle lockers at light rail stations and bicycle racks in the central city at all major office buildings add to the ease of bicycle commuting. Additionally, it is commonplace in much of the region for employers to provide showers, lockers, and safe indoor storage facilities.

Manufacturing of bicycles and components has flourished in part because of the City's reputation as a bicycle-friendly environment. Portland is home to a number of independent, small-scale, high-end bicycle frame and parts manufacturers, such as Chris King Precision Components, Vanilla Bicycles, and Ira Ryan Cycles. Although these businesses comprise a relatively small part of Portland's vibrant manufacturing economy, the sector is rapidly growing in size and influence. Without the strong public investment in bicycling infrastructure, it is doubtful that Portland would be such a desirable location for these manufacturers.

Portland is currently exploring the adoption of a subsidized bicycle rental system modeled on the successful approach in Lyon, France. If this system is as effective as it has been in Lyon, Portland will continue to be at the forefront of American bicycle-friendly cities.

Chicago, Illinois

Chicago has been designated the best large bicycle city in the United States by *Bicycling Magazine*. The City of Chicago *Bike 2015 Plan* is a strategic document outlining the roadmap for elevating bicycling to become an integral part of Chicago's transportation options. Mayor Richard Daley championed the plan adopted in January 2006. The plan focuses on two goals over the next ten years: to increase bicycle use so that 5 percent of all trips less than five miles are by bicycle; and to reduce bicycle-related injuries by 50 percent.

A 500-mile bikeway network is the centerpiece of the plan, aiming to have all Chicago residents living within a half mile of a bicycle path by 2015. Bikeways to priority destinations, including schools, universities, and transit stations, are proposed. Street planning will include bicyclists' needs.

While Chicago's roads are congested with automobile traffic and high parking costs make car commuting expensive, bicycle commuting offers clear advantages if easy, inexpensive parking options are made available. The 2015 plan includes several strategies to emphasize this advantage. Among these are plans to install at least 5,000 new bicycle racks and 1,000 long-term bicycle parking spaces, to promote bicycle parking inside office and commercial properties, and to require bicycle parking at new and rehabilitated commercial and office buildings.

The 2015 plan also includes a number of strategies to improve bicyclists' access to public transportation: integrating bicycle commuters' needs in the design and operation of rail commuter trains and stations; developing commuter bikeways to popular rail stations; and providing safe and secure bicycle parking inside and outside rail stations.

Davis, California

The city of Davis, California, is a university town with a long-established bicycle commuting culture. Since the 1960s, Davis has invested in infrastructure to support bicycling for both recreation and commuting. While the bicycle culture in Davis has its origins in the large student population at the University of California at Davis, a moderate year-round climate, a generally flat topography, and adoption of bicycling by the population at large have made bicycle travel an extremely popular option in this city, where there are more bicycles than cars.

It should be noted that Davis was the first city in the United States to designate separate bicycle lanes on public roads. The city has bicycle lanes on 95 percent of its non-highway street grid. Over the past half century, Davis's population has grown from 6,000 to 63,000, with bicycling at the core of the city's comprehensive plan. Today, 17 percent of commuter trips are by bicycle. The city continues to invest in bicycle infrastructure, with expenditures of nearly $15 million over the past decade. In addition, the city of Davis and the university together have two full-time bicycle coordinators and two bicycle advisory committees.

The Future

The current level of transportation bicycling is miniscule compared to the potential. Only 12 percent of adult Americans ride a bicycle for transportation purposes at least once a month.[9] Since about 40 percent of all trips are only two miles or less, one can realistically imagine a United States where half of the population uses a bicycle at least once a day for transportation, and another 25 percent, say, does so at least once a week. So there is a huge gap between current practice and the potential.

We are cautiously optimistic that the gap will be closed, but we are unwilling to predict a date. We see uneven progress over the next few years, with plenty of stops and starts, with some sprinting and also some very tough hill climbing in most communities. It is difficult to get something new going; the cultural inertia in many communities favors not treating the bicycle as a serious quality-of-life player.

The ultimate in bicycle-friendliness may be achieved simply by moving forward slowly but surely with several of the actions spelled out in this chapter. In others, a particular event (e.g., a huge rush-hour traffic jam) may spark dramatic shifts; success in such a case, however, will require that the community has done its homework and is ready to act when the opportunity arises. Some events might impact the possibilities of increasing bicycling in many communities; for instance, if gas hits $10 a gallon, that could have a nationwide effect.

In any case, the details will differ from one community to the next in terms of what is possible and what is achieved. Despite such differences, each community will want to see what others are doing and learn from their successes and setbacks. Sharing information and experience with other communities can, and should, go beyond the U.S. borders.

Over the coming years, many communities will embrace increased transportation bicycling as a key item in the community development toolbox, leading to stronger and more vibrant communities across the country. Thus, we see positive bicycling in our future.

Notes

1. *Transportation bicycling* is any bicycling trip that replaces a trip, or part of a trip, that would otherwise have taken place using some other means of transportation. For instance, it is likely that any bicycle trip to work, school, or shopping would, absent the bicycle trip, have been made anyway—using an automobile or a bus or walking. *Recreational bicycling* is any bicycling trip with the purpose of having fun or exercising rather than going to a destination for a purpose. The vast majority of bicycle trips fall into one of these two categories.

2. In fact, one study estimates that each new mile spent bicycling is accompanied by a reduction of seven miles spent driving a car (Littman 2004, 3).

3. Less driving per capita will also have the positive foreign-policy impact of reducing the U.S. reliance on oil imports from various unsavory petrol-laden regimes.

4. *Smart growth* is the collection of policies and practices that lead to an increase in the percentage of the region's development occurring in higher-density, multiuse neighborhoods.

5. One study by Interface Cycling Expertise (2000) estimates a 1:100 ratio for bicycle cost–automobile cost; both capital costs and annual operating costs are factored into this estimate.

6. The League of American Bicyclists has an audit process to be used for determining the degree of bicycle friendliness for any community: www.bicyclefriendlycommunity.org.

7. A Canadian survey found that 70 percent of respondents would bicycle to work if it could be done in thirty minutes "at a comfortable pace" on a bicycle lane (Littman 2004, 6).

8. While the definition of *convenient* varies from person to person, we know that, for anyone, a distance of x to the nearest bicycle rental location is more convenient than a distance of $2x$.

9. This is computed using data collected in the 2002 National Survey of Pedestrian and Bicyclist Attitudes and Behaviors: www.bikewalk.com.

References

Interface Cycling Expertise (ICE). 2000. *The Economic Significance of Cycling: A Study to Illustrate the Costs and Benefits of Cycling Policy.* Den Haag, Netherlands: VNG uitgeverij.

Littman, Todd. 2004. *Quantifying the Benefits of Nonmotorized Transportation for Achieving Mobility Management Objectives.* Victoria, BC: Victoria Transport Policy Institute.

Part 6

Affordable Housing

20

Aging-Out and Foster Care

Housing Policy

JAMES O. BATES

While state- and national-level data on housing and employment outcomes for youth exiting foster care are scant, several state-level studies estimate that less than 50 percent of the youth "aging-out" of foster care are employed at the time of exit, and of those, most earn a wage below the poverty level (Goerge et al. 2002; Dunne 2004). If we extend this estimate to the U.S. aging-out population at large, only 10,000 of the nearly 20,000 youth exiting foster care annually are gainfully employed, albeit in low-wage jobs. Accordingly, many of these youth also lack housing permanency, likely because of (1) a lack of employment history, credit history, and lease co-signors; (2) limited availability of housing subsidies to offset expenses to meet basic needs; (3) restrictive housing subsidy rules; (4) lack of affordable housing in high-cost urban areas; and (5) a service gap in rural areas (GAO 2004).

Child Welfare and Poor Housing Outcomes for Aging-Out Youth

A basic belief pervasive throughout the U.S. child welfare system is that youth achievement, and by extension overall well-being, is predicated on a child having a permanent, stable household with an adult role model with whom the child can interact (Altshuler and Poertner 2001). As a result, child welfare programs focus on identifying and providing legally permanent families for children by first attempting to preserve the existing family structure to prevent placements outside of the child's home, and second, when the child must be removed from the home, returning the child home as soon as possible or placing the child in another "permanent" family such as with an adoptive family, guardian, or relative who can obtain legal custody (HHS AFCARS n.d.). This family-centered approach results in children being reunited with biological families or placed in nurturing family environments. From 118,000 to 127,000 children are adopted annually (HHS 2004). This practice, while outwardly positive, also highlights the absence of youth self-sufficiency and independence as a primary goal of the child welfare system. In a three-state study of employment outcomes for youth not placed with a family—lacking permanen-

Figure 20.1 **Foster Care Youth Emancipations Trends**

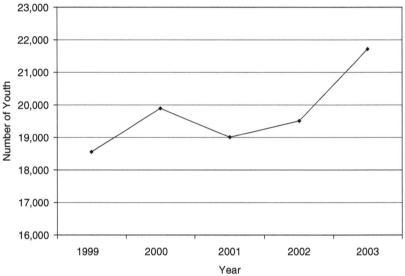

cy—but aged out of foster care, Goerge and colleagues (2002) found that "fewer than half of youth aging out of foster care have earnings in any quarter, many have no earnings at all during the three-year study period, and those who are employed earn very little." This condition appears endemic as children with limited to no skills, assets, social resources, or ongoing social service or family supports enter society as emancipated adults, annually (Kessler 2004)(see Figure 20.1).

Although the Foster Care Independence Act (FCIA) of 1999, known as the Chafee Act, contains administrative provisions for aiding youth to transition from foster care to independence, the full potential of this tool appears to be unrealized as empirical studies reveal a mixed assessment, at best, about youth outcomes (Kessler 2004). Aging-out youth will likely have to contend with protracted episodes of poverty and high rates of unemployment, despite earlier social interventions. Additionally, between 12 and 36 percent will go on to experience homelessness (Child Welfare League of America 2006). As unemployed, underemployed, or low-wage earners, this growing segment of the youth population will find few housing options and experience high-cost burdens in the open housing market.

The Chafee Act affords states the opportunity to use up to 30 percent of their entitlement allocation for room and board for youths ages 18 to 21. The program, a state entitlement, is capped at $140 million. Authorized annual Chafee allotments from 2002 through 2006 were $137,900,000 (National Child Welfare Resource Center n.d.). This means that if states so determined, aging-out youth would be eligible for per-capita annual room and board subsidies that range from approximately $400 to $1,200. That stated, youth who are aging out of the system would

Figure 20.2   **Median Gross Rent Trend by Central City, Suburb, and MSA**

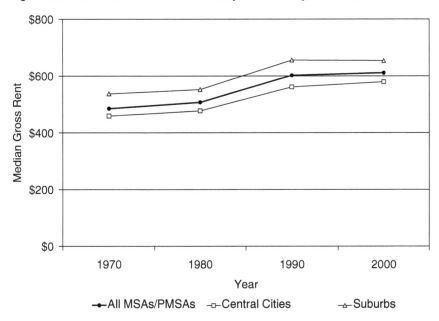

likely be significantly affected by declines in funding for government-subsidized rental and transitional housing, given the meager Chafee room and board subsidies and youth need for deep subsidies for housing.

In addition to housing programs like Section 8, public housing, and the Low-Income Housing Tax Credit (LIHTC), used to ameliorate the housing conditions of low-income people, new rental subsidies and nontraditional housing programs are needed, as merely increasing nonhousing subsidies to this population will not increase available housing or income for housing consumption. For example, a healthcare subsidy to a nonwage earner will not increase funding for housing consumption, since the individual does not have resources for housing.

While median rents for urban and suburban areas appear to have increased by a small percentage between 1990 and 2000, the U.S. Department of Housing and Urban Development (HUD 2003) states in its annual report to Congress that "in 2003, 5.18 million households, comprising 11.4 million individuals, have worst-case housing needs" (see Figure 20.2). These are renter households whose incomes are no greater than 50 percent of area median income—that is, "very low income" or VLI—and who do not receive housing assistance, and who have a severe housing problem known as a "priority problem" (11). The report also states that VLI households with worst-case housing needs reported incomes averaging $10,600 per year ($883 per month) and average gross rents of $669 per month, suggesting a rent burden of 76 percent. From that perspective, the annual addition of 20,000 youth who have aged out of foster care to the U.S. renter market is likely to be reflected in the 91.4 percent figure that represents the bulk of worst-case needs, severe rent burden.

Reconceiving Child Welfare as Community Development

Although child well-being is the goal of foster care, in light of the stop-gap measures supported by the Chafee Act to provide housing, employment, education, and other supports to 18- to 21-year-old former foster care youth, additional emphasis should be placed on capacity and asset building of these youth—even though the Chafee Act itself does not view independent living activities as an alternative to being placed with a family (i.e., permanence). Chafee Act assistance may be used with adoption planning and other permanency services, thereby allowing states to employ the same practices used on younger children on 18 to 21 year olds.

In order for programs that serve older youth to be reconceived as asset-building programs, state child welfare agencies must prioritize human capital development, housing, and work as a performance outcome. Older youth should be expected to have a high-school education or general equivalency diploma, a formal connection to work and the labor market, financial literacy, and access to safe and affordable housing. The ultimate goal of this "shift" would be to increase the likelihood that older youth can be independent and self-sufficient as a result of obtaining assets (e.g., an education and a job) that can generate long-term benefits. While multiple home placements of an individual in foster care can impact educational attainment, as within-grade disruptions and moves can cause youth to fall behind and/or drop out of school, the system goal should be to minimize these disruptions and promote high school graduation.

Although the Chafee Act contains allowances for education and training vouchers, work and housing do not appear to be central service goals. One of the principal housing tools that can be used to bridge the gap between safety and self-sufficiency are Supported Independent Living Programs (SILPs). A SILP is a form of service-enriched housing that assists semi-independent clients who are able to live on their own to become fully independent by teaching skills such as budgeting, meal preparation, problem solving, and housekeeping. In most instances, SILP case managers meet on site with residents on a regular basis to counsel them and review client progress in overcoming barriers to independence. SILPS can be shelters, single-room occupancies (SROs), group homes, and apartments. SILPs are frequently used by the disability community but appear to have garnered national attention as a tool for assisting the homeless. HUD annually issues a Notice of Fund Availability (NOFA) for SILPs under the Stewart B. McKinney Homeless Assistance Act's Supportive Housing Program. Under the Supportive Housing Program NOFA, HUD funds several SILP housing and service approaches. These approaches range from transitional housing that provide childcare and job training to homeless families to permanent service-enriched housing for homeless persons with disabilities who require transportation and onsite healthcare options. Youth in foster care are not an eligible group for assistance under HUD's Supportive Housing Program (HUD n.d.).

To further the goal of self-sufficiency, youth-oriented housing-to-work SILPs could be developed for the aging-out population. The primary goal of these SILPs would be to assist clients in finding jobs while providing stable housing. Newly created SILPs that contain community space could adapt these spaces to support group meetings and open-air technology labs, so that youth have access to technology-based skill-building opportunities—workplace computer applications, online job banks, resume writing programs, and so forth—and to adults who can provide regular on site assistance with problem-solving and job search skills. The adults who assist youth on site with problem-solving and job search skill could be required to assist residents to develop individual housing and vocational development plans (IHVDPs) that outline housing and employment goals, establish milestones, and create progress incentives. This tool would be similar to the treatment and independent-living plans currently used by social workers but would differ in that "sustained housing and employment" are the intended client outcomes of this effort. The IHVDP would also act as an "anchoring" tool for youth who may not have previously considered or mapped out a course of action for employment and self-sufficiency. Housing-to-work SILPs may also serve as mini one-stop career centers in which nonprofit workforce development agencies collocate job training programs. This would insure that residents have access to a full array of employment-related services that are likely lacking, given welfare agency priorities and the limited networks most youth possess for gaining employment information. SILPs that are scattered apartments can be established as "step-up" housing for those who have demonstrated a heightened level of independence but still require some level of support. Youth in these apartments should likely pay a prorated portion of the rent and be employed because this housing would be the last step before the youth moves on to full independence—as a renter and a gainfully employed adult.

In addition to SILPs, a short-term federal housing-to-work rental housing assistance program that provides full rental assistance at the one-bedroom fair market rent (FMR), for the three-year Chafee assistance term, could help this population to become independent. Youth receiving this form of assistance would only be able to maintain the rental voucher for three years. At that point, the voucher would be recycled into the program in order to assist other aging-out youth. The federal government could require states to provide a one-to-one job assistance, education, and case-management match that is to be documented at the individual level, thus reducing "service leakages" that could result from allowing states to aggregate the match. This requirement should ensure that each youth receive some minimum level of education and job search assistance. As a result of this assistance, youth would not be burdened to maintain housing while completing a GED or job-training program and/or working an entry-level job. As youth in this housing program would receive Chafee assistance like counseling and an education and training voucher, it would have elements that are similar to SILPs. In this housing-to-work voucher program, youth could also be compelled to establish an individual development account (IDA) or savings account to stockpile the small percentage of rent offset that is normally collected, under a federal Section 8 tenant-based rental assistance voucher model, as the tenant payment. Section 8 tenants are responsible for paying a portion of their rent, not to exceed 30 percent of their gross adjusted income. These savings could later be used as a security deposit or regular savings as the youth move into the open housing market. The Chafee Act allows youth to maintain assets while receiving government assistance.

Assisted youth would be required and helped to achieve their housing and employment goals six month to a year ahead of Chafee assistance termination in order to ensure that minimum performance thresholds are met. State welfare agencies would be rated by the national government on this accomplishment and required to document the achievement in order to continue receiving federal welfare and housing assistance (without additional federal oversight) for this population. Agencies would use the remaining Chafee assistance period to provide aftercare and perform client evaluations. In instances where youth were unable to meet their housing and employment goals, state welfare agencies would have to demonstrate their efforts to insure the continuity of housing and service provision to these youth prior to assistance termination and program discharge. This might entail the welfare agency linking and documenting the youth referral to and receipt of public assistance, public housing, and a job apprenticeship. Since most SILPs and workforce development programs are operated by community development corporations (CDCs) and nonprofit community-based organizations (CBOs), states may compel contracting CDCs and CBOs to link aging-out youth to neighborhood-based employment programs in local development zones or federally sponsored Empowerment Zones/Renewal Communities and Section 3 programs. Empowerment Zones/Renewal Communities are placed-based economic development initiatives that attempt to revitalize areas by encouraging business start-up and expansion in areas of "pervasive poverty." The intent of the zone designation is to increase the economic prosperity of the target area by placing idle real estate into service and increasing employment opportunities for unemployed and underemployed zone residents. Zone resident employment opportunities are allegedly catalyzed through worker and wage tax credits, education and training programs, and bridging programs that connect residents to real-time information about work. The federal Section 3 regulations are presumed to increase resident employment opportunities by requiring contractors and developers receiving federal funds to give hiring preference to local residents when additional employees are needed to complete a job. In these instances, contracting CDCs and CBOs should be able to verify employment assistance to and job referrals of aging-out youth to prospective employers vis-à-vis the neighborhood-based employment program—in accordance with federal, state, and local government program requirements.

As illustrated in Figure 20.3, federally subsidized multifamily housing production is minuscule. In fact, most of the multifamily housing production over the past two decades has not been federally subsidized, and much of it does not appear to be geared toward low-income households (Census 2001). A voucher-based

Figure 20.3 **Multifamily Housing Permits**

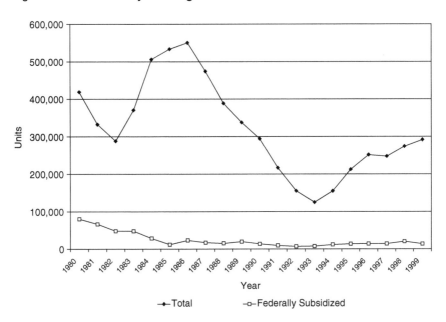

rental assistance housing strategy is therefore paramount if we are to assist youth to overcome the housing affordability barriers that may exist in the open market. Other strategies states and localities may adopt to assist this population to access affordable housing are to promote inclusive zoning practices, enforce fair housing laws and prosecute landlords who engage in housing discrimination on the basis of age and income, transfer InRem/tax-foreclosed properties to nonprofits as "developable" low-income rental housing, and convert state and local grant funds like CDBG and HOME into short-term tenant-based rental assistance vouchers for youth aging-out of foster care. All of these efforts could be wrapped around mandated Chafee assistance and local workforce development goals.

Conclusion

Our well-intentioned but clinically oriented approach to preparing youth aging out of foster care for adulthood has failed to produce the results we as a society value. While it does not make sense to throw the metaphorical "baby out with the bath water," we should challenge our existing system to create better outcomes for the children we deem to be able to better rear than their biological parents. Doing so may require reinventing not only how we deliver housing options but the child welfare system itself. In light of the national Government Performance and Results Act of 1993, we should expect better integration between the child welfare system and education, housing, and employment services. We should also expect federal government to require states to better track and uniformly report on the activities of aging-out youth. This might entail requiring states to engage in performance contracting with not-for-profit and private-sector providers and the state itself to be evaluated by the government on its overall performance: from data collection to service integration to outcomes and follow-up.

Although there is no sure-fire method for reducing the poor housing and employment outcomes of youth aging out of foster care or hard and fast evidence that a crisis is imminent (given the paucity of national and state-level data), it is incumbent upon our society to address the struggle our youth appear to be engaged in and make good on our promise to protect their interests and intervene when parents fail to provide proper care. Housing stability and the promise of work should be our litmus test for the youth in our care who are entering adulthood.

References

Altshuler, S., and J. Poertner. 2001. "Assessment of the Well-Being of Adolescents in Three Substitute Care Placement Types." http://cfrcwww.social.uiuc.edu/pubs/Pdf.files/adolesassess.pdf#search='sandra%2. (Accessed 9 May 2007.)

Child Welfare League of America. 2006 "Programs and Resources for Youth Aging Out of Foster Care." www.cwla.org/programs/fostercare/agingoutresources.htm. (Accessed 29 November 2006.)

Dunne, L. 2004. *Voices for America's Children Issue Brief.* Washington, DC: Voices for America's Children.

Goerge, R., L. Bilaver, B. Lee, B. Needell, A. Brookhart, and W. Jackman. 2002. "Employment Outcomes for Youth Aging Out of Foster Care." University of Chicago Chapin Hall Center for Children. http://aspe.hhs.gov/hsp/fostercare-agingout02/. (Accessed 29 November 2006.)

Kessler, M. 2004. "The Transition Years: Serving Current and Former Foster Youth Ages Eighteen to Twenty-one." Tulsa: University of Oklahoma, National Resource. Center for Youth Services.

National Child Welfare Resource Center. n.d. Chafee Allotments. www.nrcys.ou.edu/nrcyd/programs/chafee.shtml. (Accessed 29 November 2006.)

U.S. Census Bureau. 2001. *Market Absorption of Apartments Annual 2000 Absorptions.* Washington: U.S. Department of Commerce (Current Housing Report no. H130/05-A), April.

U.S. Department of Health and Human Services (HHS). 2006, June 19. [Overview Page]. www.childwelfare.gov/permanency/overview/. (Accessed 9 May 2007.)

———. n.d. *Adoption and Foster Care Reporting and Analysis System (AFCARS).* www.acf.hhs.gov/programs/cb/stats_research/index.htm#cw. (Accessed 9 May 2007.)

———. 2004. *How Many Children Were Adopted in 2000 and 2001.* www.childwelfare.gov/pubs/s_adopted/s_adopted.pdf. (Accessed 9 May 2007.)

U.S. Department of Housing and Urban Development (HUD). 2003. *Affordable Housing Needs: A Report to Congress on the Significant Need for Housing.* www.huduser.org/publications/pdf/AffHsgNeedsRpt2003.pdf. (Accessed 9 May 2007.)

———. n.d. *SHP Deskguide Section B Eligible Participants.* www.hud.gov/offices/cpd/homeless/library/shp/shpdeskguide/dgb.cfm. (Accessed 9 May 2007.)

U.S. Government Accountability Office (GAO). 2004. *Foster Youth: HHS Actions Could Improve Coordination of Services and Monitoring of States' Independent Living Programs.* Washington: GAO # GAO-05-25.

21

Would the Adoption of Land Value Taxation Drive Down the Price of Land and Increase Housing Affordability?

Edward J. Dodson

An important theoretical assertion suggested by Henry George's writings on the subject is whether, as communities approach the full collection of location rental values, the selling price of land will fall toward zero. George predicted this outcome will result because location rental values are no longer privatized and therefore cannot be capitalized into selling price. He concluded that "by compelling those who hold land on speculation to sell or let for what they can get, a tax on land values tends to increase the competition between owners, and thus to reduce the price of land" (George 1879, 416).

The cautious supporter of George's analysis can point to his actual wording and his inference of *tendency*. More generally, George developed his own version of what political economists identified as *the laws of production and distribution of wealth,* which he observed were not absolute in the same way as the laws of the physical universe, but instead or *laws of tendency.* He was well aware of the many variables, or externalities, at play in any society and in local regions.

Even more relevant for the future is the expected change in how people behave in response to the financial incentives resulting from liberation from taxation labor and investment in capital goods—and the simultaneous removal of the financial rewards of hoarding land for speculation. Once the process begins, the dominoes will begin to fall at an accelerated pace in the right direction. As Henry George explained : "[T]his simple device of placing all taxes on the value of land would be in effect putting up the land at auction to whosoever would pay the highest rent to the state. The demand for land fixes its value, and hence, if taxes were placed so as very nearly to consume that value, the man who wished to hold land without using it would have to pay very nearly what it would be worth to any one who wanted to use it" (1879, 437). What full land value taxation accomplishes is eliminating actual or imputed income derived from landownership, which is essentially a static activity. Landownership, by itself, contributes nothing to the community. Low effective rates of annual taxation on location rent allow landowners to hold land vacant, essentially denying these vacant locations to the community for development or the creation of employment and commerce, and driving up land prices by artificially reducing the supply of land.

Externalities Abound

Today, externalities affecting land markets are even more numerous than in George's time. In every regional market there are both natural and societally imposed limits on the quantity of land available for development. Our experience with sprawling development surrounding large cities and even relatively small towns shows that these limits are not fixed in any absolute sense. Land that was once outside the ring of reasonable commuting distance is made accessible by limited-access highways or high-speed rail systems. At the same time, land is also set aside for these and other public purposes. As we move away from the high-density development patterns of our older cities and towns, we press our public officials to keep huge tracts of land open for recreation or (more recently) as wildlife habitat preserves. Zoning and other planning tools can result either in more sprawl (e.g., because of large lot zoning) or, as is now more frequently advocated, in the development of walking communities (e.g., because of provisions for mixed-use development or transit-oriented development).

Height restrictions for buildings also play an important role in the efficient use of land, with the added complexity that even in the central cities, higher buildings tend to create more automobile use and land allocated for automobile parking. Parking lots absorb over 10 percent of the land in U.S. cities, but a much higher percentage in our central business districts. As much as 80 to 90 percent of the total is developed as surface parking lots. The amount of land used for automobile parking around the typical suburban shopping center or mall is several times greater than the actual land area developed with stores. A regional mall will include as much as sixty acres of land paved over for automobile parking (Wolf 2004).

These are important characteristics of every regional market, operating in conjunction with other key factors—all of which are then influenced by state, national, and global economic dynamics. If we were to attempt to construct a regional market model for purposes of forecasting land prices, we would need to know a good deal more information, including the following:

- Population movement, most importantly whether inmigration exceeds outmigration, and whether those entering have greater or lesser household incomes than those departing.
- Population demographics showing to what extent the population is aging and how many households are forecasted to have children attending area schools.
- Landownership statistics to identify who owns the most developable but undeveloped land and whether they reside in the community or are absentee owners.

- Scheduled or contemplated infrastructure projects that will take land out of the market and increase (or decrease) the value of contiguous land parcels.
- The effective age and condition of existing housing units, as well as the number vacant because of condition, abandonment, or other reasons.
- The number of new housing units and type constructed annually.

This is only a partial list of the information required to be compiled and analyzed. And, even with all of this detail put into a computer model, other factors may prove to be more powerful than local or regional dynamics. General patterns do exist with some consistency, however. One safe observation we can make is that where economic activity is vigorous, land values are high (and as a result, the supply of decent, affordable housing is heavily dependent on deep public subsidies).

Where We Are Today

A recent study (Davis and Heathcote 2004), funded by the Federal Reserve examined residential land prices across the United States, came to the following conclusions:

- Since 1970, residential land prices have grown faster but also been twice as volatile as existing home prices.
- Averaged from 1970 to 2003, the nominal stock of residential land under one to four unit structures accounted for 38 percent of the market value of the housing stock and was equal to 50 percent of nominal annual GDP.
- The real stock of residential land under one to four unit structures has increased an average of 0.6 percent per year since 1970.
- Residential investment leads the price of residential land by three quarters.
- In the third quarter of 2003 the nominal value of the entire stock of residential land was the same as annual GDP.

Even before these statistics were published, anyone involved in community development understood that land, and therefore housing prices, have been climbing year after year for more than a decade. What is less well appreciated is that land prices have been climbing with periodic "adjustments" almost from the day the colonists set foot on land at Jamestown. For the first century and a half, what made the experience of life in colonial North America so remarkable was the widespread access to enough land to support one's family at little or no cost. Some poverty existed, but the opportunity was widespread for most families to be largely self-sufficient. Today, there are comparatively few families making their living as farm owners. Yet, for the bottom two-thirds of households in the United States, net worth in a home and the land underneath represents most of their personal wealth. Our economic system has failed to provide the opportunity for most people to accumulate sufficient savings from working to take care of expenses once their working lives have ended. The nation's landed interests have effectively resisted the adoption of full land value taxation as the primary source of revenue for public goods and services, so that most of the revenue comes from the taxation of incomes earned from producing goods or providing services, from commerce, and from property improvements. For those concerned with the development of diverse, prosperous, and stable communities, moving to full land value taxation ought to be adopted as an immediate public policy objective.

As indicated earlier, land value until very recently was approaching 40 percent of the total value[1] of residential property. In many areas of our cities, the percentage remains much higher. The current downturn in the price of newly constructed homes is occurring because there are not enough potential homebuyers with the household income and savings required to afford the financing on the high-priced homes being constructed by developers on land acquired recently at the top of the land market cycle. Of course, prices for newly constructed homes are more volatile than for existing homes, for the simple reason that to a developer a housing unit is inventory that comes with significant holding costs, while for the existing homeowner a house is shelter. Unless a homeowner is pressed by personal circumstances (such as loss of employment, the need to relocate, illness or death, or divorce), the decision to put a property on the market is easily reversed when market conditions are not considered favorable.

There are no reliable statistics on the amount of vacant but developable land parcels in residential communities. Estimates run up to 15 to 30 percent of total land area in many cities and towns. To get a rough idea of the current total residential land value in the United States, we can use the median housing price (see note 1) and the 40 percent land value figure as follows:

- Median residential land value = $91,000 ($227,500 × 40%)
- Total developed residential land value = $11 trillion (120,834,000 housing units × $91,000)

This figure is based on median residential land value. Using average housing and land prices would likely produce a much higher figure. Moreover, none of the vacant but developable residential land is included. We can roughly estimate an aggregate value of somewhere between $11 trillion and $14 trillion for residential land across the United States. Land zoned for commercial development in downtowns and edge cities is some multiple of this estimate for residential land.

High land prices (which translate into high leasing costs for office space) drive out existing businesses, particularly those producing goods the prices of which are determined by global competition. The drive to protect targeted profit margins—and share prices—dictates that businesses must reduce the number of people employed in regions where prospective employees demand higher salaries to compensate for high living costs. When greater automation does not generate higher profits, businesses move to regions (or other countries) where overall production costs are reduced. In many cases today, the land they own is abandoned, the buildings left to decay as a blight on the community. Owners are often successful in having the assessed value of these abandoned properties reduced so that the annual tax bill is so low they are able to ignore the property for decades without any concerns of financial stress. Others simply do not pay the property taxes, and the communities take no action to foreclose (not having the resources to clear the site of derelict buildings or remove toxic chemicals from the ground). Although large cities have gradually cleaned up many of these sites using federal and state subsidies, thousands of smaller communities continue to experience this type of disinvestment and abandonment.

The Future Under a Land Value Taxation Regime

The economic and social stresses associated with spiraling land prices is clear to many but not so clear to others. Numerous analysts discounted predictions of the now evident downturn in the housing sector. Even those who have been forecasting the bursting of "the housing bubble" did not make clear the connections provided more than a century ago in the writings of Henry George. One notable exception is the British economics analyst Fred Harrison. With George's methodology to guide him (Harrison 2005), he forecasted that the year 2010 would see the collapse of the land market. Harrison's research identifies a consistent eighteen-year land market cycle going back hundreds of years. For reasons beyond the scope of this chapter, I am inclined to expect the crash to come before then. After this crash, we will have the next decade or so to achieve significant progress toward a land value taxation regime and thereby avoid yet one more recession or depression.

Whether and how far land prices will fall in response to higher and higher taxation of location rental values is more difficult to predict. As a community imposes higher costs on landowners for holding land out of use, we can expect that some owners will put their land on the market or initiate development plans sooner than they otherwise might have. The lower costs imposed on property improvements will work in conjunction with the higher carrying cost on land to stimulate development to bring land to its "highest and best use" as determined by local market conditions. The tendency of land prices to come down—due to the increased competition between landowners for purchasers—may be offset by increased demand. The key variable will be how quickly investors begin to recognize the opportunity to profitably develop locations in the community and the competition to purchase the most advantageously positioned locations. Another variable is the ability and willingness of owners of land parcels to absorb higher annual taxes without feeling any pressure to act. Wealthy individuals or entities may not bring their land to development even at the point where they are paying the full location rental value in taxes. And, of course, a considerable amount of land is owned by government agencies, schools and colleges, religious organizations, and other tax-exempt entities. This could keep the supply of land offered below that sought by investors for development, causing land prices to fall more slowly over time.

Conclusion

Proponents of land value taxation must stress when attempting to convince elected officials and others of the merits of the case that every regional market is affected by distinct qualities. Thus, while it is theoretically possible for the selling price of land to fall to a very low level, this is not likely to occur in the short run. More likely, land prices will stabilize as supply more closely matches demand. This means that government expenditure and private philanthropy will continue to be needed to increase the supply of decent, affordable housing to people whose household incomes continue to fall in real terms. Additional tools, such as the use of "inclusionary zoning" requiring developers to price a certain percentage of the total units constructed to be affordable—and subject to resale restrictions—remain important components to a comprehensive program of community development.

The extent to which communities have already moved toward land value taxation has been too limited to stimulate the type of expansion in economic activity that those accepting Henry George's analysis of political economy predict will occur when the taxation of location rental values replaces most or all other local taxes. What can be said is this: cities such as Harrisburg, Pennsylvania, which over the last twenty-five years gradually raised more of its revenue by increasing the tax rate on land values, are no longer as hindered by the destructive nature of the traditional form of property taxation. Harrisburg's revitalization over this period has been ongoing and has reached the point that the city's revenue base is strong enough to channel funds into its more distressed neighborhoods, where housing needs are great and housing costs surpass the financial capacity of many residents. The city's turnaround has occurred despite that neither the county nor the school district has adopted a higher rate of taxation on land than on property improvements. The long-time mayor of Harrisburg, Stephen R. Reed, has stated: "The City of Harrisburg continues in the view that a land value taxation system, which places a much higher tax rate on land than on improvements, is an important incentive for the highest and best use of land . . . and continues to be one of the key local policies that has been factored into this initial economic success here" (1994).

There is no other change in public policy with the same potential to stabilize and eventually lower the cost of housing or stimulate the revitalization of our communities in a manner that welcomes a diverse population.

Note

1. "Appreciation in existing single-family home prices cooled to single-digit rates in most metropolitan areas during the second quarter [of 2006], while metro area condo prices were essentially flat in comparison with a year ago, according to the latest survey by National Association of Realtors. The association's second-quarter metro area single-family home price report, covering changes in 151 metropolitan statistical areas, shows 37 areas with double-digit annual increases and 26 metros experiencing generally minor price declines—many of the areas with declines are showing weakness in the local labor market.

The national median existing single-family home price was $227,500 in the second quarter, up 3.7 percent from a year earlier when the median price was $219,400." (Source: "Metro Home Prices Transition in Second Quarter," National Association of Realtors news release, August 15, 2006.)

References

Davis, Morris A., and Jonathan Heathcote. 2004. "The Price and Quantity of Residential Land in the United States." *Finance and Economics Discussion Series 2004–37.* Board of Governors of the Federal Reserve System, July.

George, Henry. 1879. *Progress and Poverty.* New York: Robert Schalkenbach Foundation (1975 edition; originally published 1879).

Harrison, Fred. 2005. *Boom Bust: House Prices, Banking and the Depression of 2010.* London: Shepheard-Walwyn Publishers Ltd.

Wolf, Kathleen L. 2004. "Trees, Parking and Green Law: Legal Tools for Sustainability." *Human Dimensions of the Urban Forest,* Fact Sheet No.15. University of Washington, College of Forest Resources, March. www.cfr.washington.edu/research.envmind/Roadside/Parking_Trees_FS15.pdf. (Accessed 10 January 2008.)

Part 7

Crime and Development

22

Crime's Impact on the Viability of Young Urban Small Businesses

TIMOTHY BATES AND ALICIA ROBB

High prevailing levels of crime impact the viability of urban small businesses, and the resulting impacts are not uniformly negative. It is the negative impacts, however, that are most often noted. Conventional wisdom suggests that business activity levels in inner-city minority communities are held back by high levels of crime. People seeking to establish new businesses therefore tend to avoid these communities: the risk of failure is presumably heightened, while the likely degree of success is lowered.

On the specific issue of crime's impact on urban businesses, our search of the social science literature suggests that no empirical link has yet been established between crime levels and firm viability. Evidence supporting the prevailing conventional wisdom consists primarily of assertions without empirical grounding. Our analyses of crime's impact on urban small businesses are based on large, representative samples of firms, drawn from the U.S. Bureau of the Census Characteristics of Business Owners (CBO) database.

Our findings do not coincide with the conventional wisdom. Crime's impact, properly understood, tends to shape the very nature of area businesses, particularly those in fields where face-to-face customer contact is most frequent. In high-crime niches, for example, nonminority white owners are severely underrepresented, while minority and/or immigrant owners are present in abundant numbers. High-crime niches appear to scare away potential business owners, leaving behind firms that are not necessarily disadvantaged by crime, all factors considered.

Crime's impact may certainly be harmful, other factors constant, but the crux of our findings suggest that other factors do not stay constant in high-crime niches of the small business community. Firms operating in this environment are not found to be less viable than otherwise identical owners and firms reporting that crime has no impact on their business viability. High-crime niches, in fact, may be rational choices for some business owners, present and potential, in the narrow sense that firm survival prospects may be superior relative to other urban opportunities.

311

The Controversy and the Evidence

Studies of crime in the context of business development tend to equate inner-city minority communities with high levels of criminal activity that, in turn, depress business development. Gittell and Thompson (1999) spell out the case against investing in America's inner cities: "High crime rates, social disintegration, lack of developed internal and external business networks, inadequate skills and work habits of potential employees, limited access to equity capital, and a relatively small consumption base because of inner-city residents' low incomes . . ." (488) are factors discouraging business formation and expansion. "The main liabilities for inner cities are mirror images of what makes other areas attractive . . ." (488).

Porter (1995) observes serious impediments to inner-city economic development rooted in the reality and perception of abundant criminal activity. Crime against property raises costs of doing business in the inner city. Crime against employees and customers "creates an unwillingness to work and patronize inner city establishments . . ." (63). It is noteworthy that Porter mentioned "the perception of abundant criminal activity"; in the same article, he opines that the perception is indeed greater than the reality.

Other disadvantages prevail. High crime rates make it difficult to obtain casualty insurance and raise the cost of such insurance (Squires 1999; Yoon 1997). Financial institutions are hesitant to lend to small businesses in this environment; commercial investment is thus hindered (Immergluck 1999; Craig, Jackson, and Thomson 2007).

Scaring away customers, potential employees, lending institutions, even casualty insurance underwriters, however, is only a partial listing of crime's potential impacts. Competitors may also be driven away; underutilized facilities might be available at modest rents; underemployed neighborhood residents may provide a readily available labor pool (Porter 1997; Yoon 1997). Operating in a high-crime area may be advantageous, on balance, for some firms. All of these speculations are discussed in the applicable social science literature, yet testable hypotheses have been missing because the empirical evidence that would allow them to be spelled out and investigated has been in short supply.

Our search for empirical evidence concerning crime's impact on urban business viability took us beyond academic research. The consultant reports generated by Michael Porter's Initiative for a Competitive Inner City (ICIC) offer some insight. A survey of thirty-six retail business owners revealed that shoplifting, vandalism, and the general perception of crime, in that order, were cited as "challenges of the inner-city market" (Boston Consulting Group 1998, 15). Although making no claims about the representativeness of this business sample or its applicability to small business viability more broadly, the report did suggest that crime's magnitude may be exaggerated and that its manifestations were manageable if business managers dealt pragmatically with prevention strategies.

Immergluck has documented that commercial investment in Chicago neighborhoods has declined as percentages of African American and Hispanic residents grow, "even after controlling for income and population changes" (1999, 15). He identifies crime as an unmeasured factor not controlled for in his analysis. One possibility is that increased numbers of minority residents are viewed as a proxy for rising crime, hence discouraging commercial investment. This rising crime may be real or perceived: if it causes bank hesitancy to lend and owner aversion to firm creation and expansion, then it matters little whether the problem is one of reality or perception. Business is discouraged either way.

Is crime's impact a major impediment to business viability in urban America? Is this impact properly thought of primarily as an inner-city phenomenon? How much of crime's impact is rooted in perception as opposed to reality? Absent sophisticated data capable of controlling for crime's impact, we are left with a literature full of speculations.

Buried in a little-known Census Bureau small business database (the CBO database) lie overlooked responses of thousands of individual small business owners to the question, "What was the impact of crime on the profitability of this business?" We utilize these data to examine small businesses that began operations from 1986 to 1992 in urban America. We focus on the subset of business owners who responded "strong negative impact" to the question. How do these firms and owners differ from urban small businesses less or unaffected by crime?

The CBO database is a powerful small business microdata source, providing a wealth of information on firm and owner traits of individual businesses, including owner demographics, education and experience, firm financing, firm operating-environment variables, and numerous others. The CBO microdata are unavailable in public-use format; access is restricted to researchers willing to go through an extensive, highly uncertain, and expensive process of obtaining special permission from the Census Bureau to conduct analyses. We applied for such permission in November 2000 and were given access to the CBO data in October 2006.

We utilize these data to explore crime's impact on young urban firms, delineating those actively operating in 1992 into two groups—those still operating and those shutting down and going out of business by late 1996. Further, we compare the traits of those most impacted by crime to the broader universe of young small firms doing business in urban America in 1992. The former stand out as being heavily concentrated in retailing, and they are overrepresented in the minority-neighborhood market niche.

Indeed, among all of the young urban small firms, 3.3 percent reported a strong negative impact of crime on business profits; in the minority-neighborhood segment, a higher 9.6 percent of the firms were impacted (see Table 22.1). Most firm owners—in minority markets or otherwise—attribute no impact to crime as a determinant of profitability. It is noteworthy how dramatically Table 22.1's three small business groupings—(1) all young urban firms, (2) firms reporting strong, negative impact of crime, and (3) neighborhood firms serving a minority clientele—differ from each other in both firm and owner characteristics. Firm size

Table 22.1

Firm and Owner Traits: Young Small Businesses Located in Metropolitan Areas

	All Urban Small Businesses	Firms Reporting Strong Negative Impact of Crime	Neighborhood Firms Serving Predominantly Minority Clients
A. Owner Characteristics			
1. Demographic Traits:			
% minority	14.6%	36.1%	57.6%
% immigrant	14.1%	30.5%	42.3%
2. Human-Capital Traits:			
% high school or less	29.1%	44.6%	37.3%
% college, 1–3 years	32.5%	34.1%	25.1%
% college graduate	22.6%	14.8%	23.6%
% with grad/professional ed	15.8%	6.2%	14.0%
Hours worked in the firm in 1992 (mean)	1,868	2,285	1,732
B. Firm Characteristics			
Total sales revenues, 1992 (mean)	$117,681	$184,064	$76,276
% discontinued operations by late 1996	23.2%	16.5%	29.0%
Start-up capitalization (mean)	$28,922	$70,877	$30,302
% with paid employees	25.5%	38.6%	23.8%
% started in 1990, 1991, or 1992	47.8%	39.6%	66.1%
% serving neighborhood market	23.5%	39.4%	100.0%
% serving minority clientele	13.9%	30.6%	100.0%
% crime major negative impact	3.3%	100.0%	9.6%

Source: Characteristics of Business Owners database; base year 1992; year of owner survey, 1996; this version of the CBO database was released by census in 1998.

measured by annual sales, firm capitalization, owner race, ethnicity traits, owner education levels, and other factors exhibit widely varying mean values. Firms in the high-crime-impact group stand out as the larger, more established, better capitalized firms, on average, and their rates of closure through yearend 1996 (16.5 percent) are lower than those of either young urban firms (23.2 percent) or minority-oriented neighborhood firms specifically (29.0 percent). Note that comparing urban firm subgroups to young firms was somewhat arbitrary. Other useful comparisons are examined later in the chapter.

In considering the investment potential of small-firm start-ups in stigmatized niches—such as high-crime subfields—mainstream microeconomic theory offers a provocative, rarely considered hypothesis: profit-seeking firms achieve returns in high-crime fields that are neither higher nor lower than the returns available to business investments throughout all segments of urban America. Why should investment opportunities available in high-crime urban areas differ from those accessible in low-crime niches? If systematic differentials in actual or expected returns typified high- and low-crime urban submarkets (or particular industry subgroups), then firms in the low-return areas (or industries), microeconomic theory predicts, would choose to contract and invest their resources in alternatives offering superior returns. This is the crux of rational profit-maximizing firm behavior.

Microeconomic theory predicts that the dynamic of businesses seeking to maximize returns on their production inputs will continue until net yields on investment alternatives equalize across alternatives. If low-crime sectors offer higher returns to small business start-ups, then investments will be directed toward realizing those higher returns. The process of firm creation and expansion in attractive opportunities, combined with disinvestment in "unattractive" niches, will continue until returns have equalized across alternatives.

An extension of this textbook prediction of microeconomic theory suggests that, at equilibrium, returns may actually be higher, on average, in the unattractive (high-crime) niches. Assume that individuals contemplating creating new businesses in high-crime urban subfields anticipate, on average, that in the course of operating their firm, they face a 2.1 percent risk of being shot or stabbed. Low-crime alternative opportunities, in contrast, are expected to offer a 0.1 percent prospect of being shot or stabbed. Perfect equality in expected firm profitability across high-crime and low-crime alternatives would not induce owner entry into high-crime niches because greater owner fear of being shot or stabbed negates this attraction. Rather, a premium would have to be offered to offset the negative utility that potential owners attach to the 2.1 percent probability of being shot or stabbed. In equilibrium, expected returns in the high-crime niches would therefore exceed those in low-crime areas, and the magnitude of those higher returns reflects the premium demanded by owners to compensate them for their greater fear of serious bodily harm in high-crime (as opposed to low-crime) small business niches.

The CBO Database and Specification of Submarkets in Urban Areas

Terms like *inner-city areas* and *minority communities* require clarification as a prerequisite to analyzing the urban submarkets served by small businesses. Such terms often seem to be used interchangeably in the social science literature. When defined, inner-city areas refer commonly to economically depressed sections (either zip codes or census tracts) of urban America where median household incomes are lower, unemployment rates are higher, and/or poverty rates are decisively higher than in the balance of the metropolitan area. Utilizing such criteria, an Initiative for a Competitive Inner City (ICIC) study in 2004 documented that 82 percent of the inner-city residents in the nation's one hundred largest urban areas were minorities). This very large overlap perhaps justifies the common assumption that inner-city areas are predominantly minority residential areas.

The traditional practice of assuming that depressed inner-city areas lie largely

Figure 22.1 **Analysis Matrix**

	Neighborhood Clientele	City/County/Regional or Broader Clientele
Minority Clientele	Cell 1	Cell 2
Nonminority Clientele	Cell 3	Cell 4

within central cities appears to be going out of fashion, and rightly so. Between 1990 and 2000, poverty rates actually increased in the inner-ring suburbs of many metropolitan areas (Jargowsky 2006) while declining in many central cities (Berube and Frey 2005). Concentrated poverty, in particular, dropped overall in the nation's large central cities during this decade.

We have chosen not to constrain the geographic scope of our econometric analyses of urban small-firm survival patterns to central cities; our geographic scope is the metropolitan area. All small firms located in urban areas that are classified by the Census Bureau as metropolitan areas are included in our CBO database sampling frame; all firms located outside of metropolitan areas are excluded from our analyses. Our precise specification of small business market segments has been heavily shaped, as well, by the nature of the questions posed by census to the small business owners who responded to the CBO questionnaire back in late 1996.

The owner responses to the CBO survey describe urban firms along three target-market dimensions: (1) clientele served—household vs. nonhousehold, (2) clientele served—minority vs. nonminority, (3) geographic scope of market served—local/neighborhood vs. city/county/national. Our analysis files of CBO data are structured along geographic-scope-of-market and target-clientele dimensions, as described by the two-by-two matrix in Figure 22.1.

Cells 1 and 3, by design, place the sampled small firms into minority neighborhoods and nonminority neighborhoods, respectively. Firms in cells 2 and 4, in contrast, cannot be identified by location (other than metro/nonmetro or central city/not central city); because their target market is, at a minimum, citywide or countywide, the need for identifying the demographic profile of the neighborhood where the firm is located was judged by the census bureau not to be a priority.

Next, this study utilizes "negatively impacted by crime" as an explanatory variable in the context of a logistic regression exercise investigating survival patterns among the universe of young urban small businesses. Controlling for relevant firm and owner characteristics, as well as target-market identifiers, young firms actively operating in metropolitan areas in both 1992 and 1996 are distinguished from firms active in 1992 but closed down and out of business in 1996. Firms changing ownership during the 1992 to 1996 period were tracked and counted as active firms as long as they were still active in 1996.

Existing studies utilizing CBO data to delineate firm survival patterns through

1996 have shown that abundant owner human capital, in conjunction with abundant firm financial capitalization, typifies those most likely to survive (Fairlie and Robb 2007b). Furthermore, it is the larger scale, more established businesses that tend to remain active, while the very youngest firms are vulnerable to closure and discontinuance of business operations (Bates 1997).

Our analysis of small-firm survival patterns utilizes CBO data describing urban firms that began operations between 1986 and 1992: logistic regression analysis is utilized to delineate the active from the discontinued business ventures. These small-firm CBO data were constrained to include only those firms with owners actively involved in running the business in 1992. Attempting to weed out "casual" businesses, we excluded those reporting sales revenues under $5,000 in 1992, a step that reduced the sample size dramatically. Remaining young urban firms were tracked through 1996, and those shutting down or halting operations were labeled "discontinued"; firms still operating in 1996 with either the 1992 owner of record or a new owner were "active." To delineate small firms still active in 1996 from those that discontinued during the 1992 to 1996 period, we utilize firm, owner, and environmental traits as explanatory variables.

A large, growing body of literature predicts increased survival odds for well-capitalized small firms run by owners having the human capital (expertise, experience) appropriate for operating a viable venture. Owner human capital is described in the CBO data by multiple qualitative and quantitative measures of education and experience. Two types of work experience strongly predict improved firm survival prospects. First, prior work experience in a business whose products were similar to those provided by the owner's current venture is important (Fairlie and Robb 2007a). Second, prior experience working in a family-owned business increases the likelihood of young firm success and survival (Fairlie and Robb 2007b). Furthermore, previous findings indicate that highly educated owners are more likely than poorly educated ones to operate firms that remain active (Bates 1989). Quantity of owner effort, furthermore, shapes business outcomes: part-time businesses exhibit higher discontinuance rates than full-time operations (Bates 1997).

Small-firm survival dynamics depend on factors beyond owner human capital, hours of work, and financial investment in the firm. Very young firms are more volatile and failure-prone than ventures that have built up customer goodwill and an established client base (Bates 1997; Jovanovic 1982). A possible short-cut to successful firm creation entails entering business by purchasing an ongoing firm that already has an established customer base.

Few studies have examined any sort of explanatory variables that describe the operating environment of small firms, including the client subgroups that firms target; data constraints are perhaps the reason for this exclusion. Bates (1989) found that firms serving predominantly minority clienteles were more likely to go out of business than firms targeting nonminorities, holding other factors constant. His 2006 study investigated the types of black-owned firms most likely to develop and grow in urban African American communities.

All of the above explanations of firm viability and survival are essentially hypotheses, which we examine in this study to explain closure patterns among young firms doing business in metropolitan America. Once firm, owner, and environmental traits are controlled for statistically, owner demographic traits—race and gender—are expected to have little impact on firm closure patterns. We undertake our logistic regression analysis of isolating crime's possible impacts by first controlling for impacts of the applicable characteristics discussed earlier.

Recall that firms reporting strong negative impacts of crime on profitability (Table 22.1) were considerably less likely (16.5 percent closure) than young urban firms generally (23.2 percent closure) to go out of business by late 1996. Summary statistics alone, however, do not demonstrate that high-crime-impacted firms are less prone to go out of business than young urban small firms generally. Relative to their urban counterparts, the high-crime-impacted firms are older, larger, better capitalized small businesses, and each of these characteristics is associated with heightened survival prospects. To isolate possible consequences of crime's impact, we proceed by controlling econometrically for differences in firm, owner, and environmental traits. This is undertaken in Table 22.2's logistic regression exercise: firms active in late 1996 are assigned a dependent value of one; discontinued firms are zeros.

Table 22.2's logit exercise delineates firms discontinuing operations in 1992 to 1996 from those still active at the end of 1996. Our CBO sample of nearly 5,000 small firms includes all that meet the selection criteria—young, urban, and active in 1992. The underlying CBO data (and regression results) are weighted to be nationally representative of small firms.

A geographic-scope-of-market variable identifying the market served by the individual CBO small businesses distinguished two market orientations: (1) those catering to a specific neighborhood market, and (2) those serving city-, county-, region-, or nationwide clients. This variable was defined using owner responses to the CBO survey instrument (see the detailed definitions for this variable and all other explanatory variables in Appendix 22.1, "The CBO Data"). Similarly, the "minority market" variable separated the firms into subgroups of those selling to clients who are either (1) predominantly minority or (2) predominantly nonminority. These two binary variables were combined into a "minority neighborhood" variable.

Findings of Table 22.2's logistic regression exercise include a highly positive (0.692), statistically significant high-crime-impact variable coefficient, unambiguously indicating that owners citing crime as a major problem experienced heightened firm survival prospects, other things equal. This counterintuitive finding stands in contradiction to the previously discussed conventional wisdom found in public policy and urban planning studies, but it is consistent with the predictions of microeconomic theory. The actual positive net impact of crime is consistent with the hypothesis that owners entering high-crime niches are lured, at equilibrium, by opportunities sufficiently attractive to compensate for the disutility of operating in a high-crime environment. Crime itself is not a plus; rather, attractive opportunities that lure entrepreneurs into high-crime fields must be sufficiently appealing to overcome disadvantages posed by crime.

Table 22.2

Logistic Regression Analysis—Delineating Young Urban Firms Active in 1996 from Those Discontinuing Operations and Closing Down Between 1992 and 1996

Explanatory Variables	Regression Coefficient	
	Coefficient	Standard Error
Constant	−2.849*	0.566
Education:		
College: 1–3 years	−0.091	0.090
College graduate	0.147	0.103
Graduate school	0.806*	0.144
Prior work experience in a similar firm	0.214*	0.076
Prior work experience in a family member's business	0.226*	0.098
Owner age in years	0.172*	0.025
Owner age squared	−0.002*	0.000
Financial capital at start-up ($000)	0.001	0.001
Firm started de novo	−0.198	0.109
Year entered, 1990, 1991 or 1992	−0.432*	0.077
Owner labor input in hours (00)	−0.002	0.004
Minority-owned firm	0.038	0.140
Immigrant-owned firm	0.726*	0.147
Female-owned firm	−0.260*	0.078
Employer firm	0.722*	0.112
Minority market orientation	−0.041	0.149
Geographic scope of market: neighborhood	0.272*	0.104
Minority market neighborhood interaction	−0.937*	0.234
Crime: a major problem	0.646*	0.275
Crime: a minor problem	0.510*	0.127

N 4,676; −2 Log L4,585.2; and Chi square 437.9
*Statistically significant, .05 significance level.

Heightened likelihood of firm survival (see Table 22.2) is positively associated with a neighborhood orientation per se; indeed, the neighborhood-market coefficient was positive and statistically significant in the logistic regression exercise. This is noteworthy because firms serving neighborhood (as opposed to city- or countywide) customer markets are shown to be more prone to problems rooted in high crime levels. Small-firm closure, furthermore, was not associated with the minority-market coefficient (which was small and insignificant statistically). It was only the interaction of these two factors (minority and neighborhood) that powerfully predicted small-firm discontinuance of business operations.

The factors that predict firm survival through 1996 largely mirror those highlighted by previous studies of small business discontinuance patterns. The most highly educated owners and the entrepreneurs with prior experience in a similar line of business and/or a family member's business are the owners whose firms were most likely to be active at the end of 1996. The very youngest firms and the smaller firms lacking paid employees, in contrast, were the ones most prone to discontinue operations. Explanatory variables measuring firm start-up capitalization and employees are actually highly correlated; dropping either variable causes the statistical significance of the other to rise.

Minority owners, although heavily overrepresented in the high-crime niche, were neither more nor less likely to experience firm closure than were nonminority owners, controlling for firm, environmental, and owner traits. The firms of immigrant owners, surprisingly, were in fact more likely to remain in operation, other things equal. Two unconventional outcomes from Table 22.2's logit exercise were (1) the positive association of serving neighborhood markets with increased small business survival prospects, and (2) the higher survival typifying immigrant-owned firms. The geographic-scope-of-market variable (neighborhood) has not, to our knowledge, been utilized previously as an explanatory factor in econometric analyses of small business viability.

Although serious crime afflicts a small subset of urban businesses and is not a major determinant of small-firm viability in urban America, it surprisingly appears to provide a net benefit—improved survival prospects—to the firm subgroup reporting that it is most heavily shaped by its impact. The crime factor may be providing something of a protected market to those not fearing to operate in the lines of business and neighborhoods where its impact is greatest (Yoon 1997). Market niches where crime's impact is most often high are explored next.

Market Segments in Which Serious Crime Most Directly Impacts Young Firms

Our objective is to isolate the market sectors in which firm owners most often identify crime's "strong negative impact" on their business operations. Table 22.3 breaks young urban firms into two groups: (1) firms serving a neighborhood clientele made up almost entirely of individuals/households; (2) firms serving a clientele that is broader in geographic scope—citywide, countywide, regional, and so on. The neighborhood-oriented firms are primarily retail businesses (including restaurants) and consumer-service businesses that deal face to face with their customers. Firms catering to broader markets, in contrast, serve clients that are most often other businesses; many do, however, sell their products to government and household clients. Numerous in this sector are business service-oriented firms, trucking, construction, wholesale, and manufacturing concerns. Retailing, most often focusing on neighborhood markets, does have a presence as well in the broad-market subsector.

Owner demographics differ noticeably in these two broad subsectors (Table 22.3). In the markets geographically defined as broader in scope, owners are overwhelmingly nonimmigrant as well as nonminority. Minorities own 25.1 percent of all young urban firms serving a neighborhood client base, but their ownership share

Table 22.3

Traits of Urban Firms and Owners in Geographically Defined Market Segments

	All	Neighborhood Market	Broad Market
Owner demographics			
% minority	14.6%	25.1%	11.3%
% immigrant	14.1%	23.2%	11.4%
Firm characteristics			
Total sales revenues, 1992 (mean)	$117,681	$113,503	$119,300
% closing down by 1996	23.1%	22.1%	23.5%
% serving neighborhood markets	23.5%	100%	0%
Crime's impact:			
None	82.8%	77.9%	84.6%
Minor	13.9%	16.5%	12.8%
Major	3.3%	5.6%	2.6%

Source: CBO database.

in the broader market segment is just 11.3 percent. Immigrant owners mirror this pattern: their relative ownership share is over twice as high in the neighborhood-market sector than in the broader marketplace.

The incidence of owners reporting crime's serious negative impact on their operations differs sharply across the neighborhood- and broad-market sectors. Crime thusly defined afflicts 5.6 percent of the neighborhood-oriented firms, which is over twice as high as the corresponding incidence typifying the broad-market small businesses (2.6 percent; see Table 22.3).

Our final disaggregation includes neighborhood firms only, subdivided into (1) those selling to minority clients predominantly and (2) those selling largely to nonminorities. Thusly subdivided, an enormous demographic difference emerges: minority and immigrant owners are overwhelmingly concentrated in the neighborhood minority clientele subsector (Table 22.4). Minority owners are four times more numerous in this sector (owning 57.6 percent of the businesses), relative to their presence in the nonminority neighborhood business sector (they own 15.1 percent of those firms). Immigrant owner concentrations are similarly skewed: they own 42.3 percent of the minority-sector firms but only 17.4 percent of those that cater to nonminority clients. The strong pattern is one of nonminority-owned firms serving nonminority clients while immigrant- and minority-owned firms serve the minority neighborhood market.

Not surprisingly, serious crime's major impact is noted disproportionately by owners of neighborhood firms serving minority clients: 9.6 percent of them report that crime seriously impacts the profitability of their businesses. Only 4.4 percent of firm owners catering to nonminority clients are similarly impacted (Table 22.4). While crime's negative impact is clearly greatest among the minority-oriented

Table 22.4

Traits of Firms and Owners and the Impact of Crime (Firms Serving Neighborhood Markets Only)

	Minority Clientele	Non-minority Clientele
Owner demographics		
% minority	57.6%	15.1%
% immigrant	42.3%	17.4%
Firm characteristics		
Total sales revenues, 1992 (mean)	$76,276	$124,199
% closing down by 1996	29.0%	21.2%
Crime's impact:		
None	60.1%	83.0%
Minor	30.3%	12.6%
Major	9.6%	4.4%

Source: CBO database.

neighborhood firms, it is noteworthy that their firm characteristics are quite unlike those describing the subgroup of all firms experiencing major negative impacts of crime (Table 22.1). While these subgroups overlap, their mean firm traits are certainly dissimilar. The subgroup made up entirely of firms facing major crime-related problems reports mean firm sales revenues, rate of discontinuance, and mean start-up capitalization figures of $184,064 (sales), 16.5 percent (closure), and $70,877 (capital); corresponding figures for the minority-oriented neighborhood firms are $76,276, 29.0 percent, and $30,302. The minority neighborhood firms as a subgroup are nearly 80 percent more likely to go out of business, while reporting less than half the mean sales revenues and start-up capitalization, relative to the subgroup of all firms being seriously harmed by crime. The high-crime and minority neighborhood small business subgroups, in fact, differ dramatically in terms of firm and owner traits, with two exceptions—very large minority- and immigrant-owner overrepresentation typified both subgroups.

Concluding Remarks

If this study is criticized for raising more questions than answers, we plead guilty. A summary of our conclusions is offered here, as well as a list of issues that require further clarification to illuminate relationships between small-firm viability and urban crime. Michael Porter's observation that crime's negative impact on inner-city business viability may be overstated is broadly supported by the evidence put forth in this chapter. Among the small-firm subgroups examined in this study, most of the owners—whether serving regional or neighborhood markets, minority or nonminority clients—report that crime has no impact whatsoever upon the profitability of their business operations.

Among the young urban small businesses analyzed, 3.3 percent reported negative impacts of crime; the firm subgroup serving broadly defined markets was less impacted, with only 2.6 percent of the owners identifying crime as having a significant negative impact on firm profits. The neighborhood market segment, where retail and consumer-service firms deal face to face with their clientele, emerges as the high-crime niche: the minority neighborhood–oriented niche reports a 9.6 percent major negative impact incidence for crime, while their counterparts serving predominantly nonminority clients report a corresponding 4.4 percent rate. Yet, even in the highest crime niche identified by geographic scope or clientele demographics, most owners report that crime has no impact on business profitability (Table 22.4).

When owners do report that crime is having a major negative impact on the profitability of their business, can we infer that firm viability is likely to be undermined? The unambiguous answer is no. In the urban firm subset most hurt by crime, mean business traits include above-average annual revenues, high initial financial capitalization, and low rates of business discontinuance and closure, relative to firms not reporting serious crime issues.

On the narrow issue of crime and small-firm survival prospects, should we stop worrying and embrace crime? Is this an appropriate policy implication for banks and casualty insurance companies contemplating how best to target their loans and insurance policies? Table 22.2's logistic regression, after all, powerfully demonstrates the positive association of crime's impact with small-business survival prospects, holding firm, owner, and environmental traits constant.

We cannot embrace this conclusion. First, crime's negative impact most likely depresses the rate of new-firm formation in high-crime niches of the small business community. Thus, the positive association of crime's severity with firm survival prospects most likely reflects the benefits existing firms derive when concerns over crime scare away most of their potential competitors. Our findings must be extended by empirically examining crime's impact upon new-firm creation in urban America; only then can we begin to comprehend the overall impact of crime on the size and composition of the urban small-business community.

Furthermore, the firm owners operating in high-crime-impacted businesses may select into this sector on the basis of unobservable characteristics. They may be more knowledgeable than the broader population of potential and actual business owners regarding the nature and likelihood of the types of crime that afflict these businesses. Alternatively, they may match owner traits and clientele characteristics in ways that lessen the costs of crime. Owners speaking Spanish and operating in markets where they serve Spanish-speaking co-ethnics, for example, may be able to deal with crime in less costly ways than owners lacking empathy with this particular clientele. How relevant are these unobservable traits? We have no idea, largely because they are unobservable. They come into play in the context of Table 22.2's logistic regression exercise findings, however, in potentially powerful ways. Other factors constant, this exercise indicates that firms most seriously impacted by crime are more likely to remain in operation than firms reporting no impact. Are other factors really constant, or are unobservable characteristics varying systematically such that the seeming positive utility of serious crime is properly understood as correlated to unobserved owner traits that shape the ability of firms to achieve viability in a high-crime environment? A more complete specification of the logit regression delineating firms closing down from those remaining active (Table 22.2) ideally would measure applicable owner traits that are presently unobserved. This is easier said than done.

Appendix 22.1. The CBO Data

Variable Definitions, Table 22.2 Logistic Regression

- Regression analysis dependent variable: Active (or survive)—Firm stayed in business over the period 1992 to 1996, irrespective of presence or absence of ownership changes, then active = 1; otherwise, active = 0.
- Female-owned firm: Firm owner is female, then female-owned firm = 1; otherwise, female-owned firm = 0.
- Minority-owned firm: Firm owner is Hispanic, Black, Asian, or Native American. In multiowner firms, the minority-owned share is 51% or higher, then minority-owned firm = 1; otherwise, minority-owned firm = 0.
- Immigrant-owned firm—Firm owner is an immigrant (not born in the United States), then immigrant-owned firm = 1; otherwise, immigrant-owned firm = 0.
- Owner age in years: Self-explanatory.
- Owner age squared: Self-explanatory.
- High school (excluded variable): Education level of owner, has high school degree only or less, then high school = 1; otherwise, high school = 0.
- College, 1–3 years: Education level of owner, has some college, then college 1–3 years = 1; otherwise, college 1–3 years = 0.
- College graduate: Education level of owner, has a college (bachelor's) degree, then college graduate = 1; otherwise, college graduate = 0.
- Graduate school: Education level of owner, has some postgraduate education (masters, Ph.D., etc.), then graduate school = 1; otherwise, graduate school = 0.
- Prior work experience in a similar business: Previously worked in a business similar to the one now owned, then this variable = 1; otherwise, = 0.
- Prior work experience in a family member's business: Has worked in the past for a parent or relative who owned a business, then this variable = 1; otherwise = 0.
- Financial capital at start-up: Amount of financial capital invested to start the firm.
- Minority market orientation: Firm serve primarily minority clientele (more than 50%)
- Geographic scope of market: % serving neighborhood.
- Minority market: % serving neighborhood.
- Crime: a major problem: Crime had a significant negative impact on firm profits.

- Crime: a minor problem: Crime had a somewhat negative impact on firm profits.

Note

Research results and conclusions expressed are those of the authors and do not necessarily reflect the views of the Census Bureau. This chapter has been screened to insure that no confidential data are revealed. Data can be obtained at a Census Research Data Center or at the Center for Economic Studies (CES) only after approval by the CES and IRS. See www. ces.census.gov for details on the application and approval process.

References

Bates, Timothy. 1989. "Small Business Viability in the Urban Ghetto." *Journal of Regional Science* 29 (4).
———. 1997. *Race, Self-Employment and Upward Mobility.* Baltimore: Johns Hopkins University Press.
———. 2006. "The Urban Development Potential of Black-Owned Businesses." *Journal of the American Planning Association* 72 (2).
Berube, A., and D. Frey. 2005. "A Decade of Mixed Blessings: Urban and Suburban Poverty in Census 2000." In *Redefining Urban and Suburban America: Volume II,* ed. A. Berube, B. Katz, and R. Lang. Washington, DC: The Brookings Institution.
The Boston Consulting Group. 1998. "The Business Case for Pursuing Retail Opportunities in the Inner City." Initiative for a Competitive Inner City (ICIC) working paper, June.
Craig, Ben, William Jackson, and James Thomson. 2007. "Small Firm Credit Market Discrimination, SBA Guaranteed Lending, and Local Market Economic Performance." *Annals of the American Academy of Political and Social Science* 613 (Sept.): 73–94.
Fairlie, Robert, and Alicia Robb. 2007a. "Why Are Black-Owned Businesses Less Successful than White-Owned Businesses: The Role of Families, Inheritances, and Business Human Capital." *Journal of Labor Economics* 25 (2): 289–323.
———. 2007b. "Families, Human Capital, and Small Businesses: Evidence from the Characteristics of Business Owners Survey." *Industrial and Labor Relations Review* 60 (2): 225–245.
Gittell, Ross, and J. Phillip Thompson. 1999. "Inner City Business Development and Entrepreneurship: New Directions for Policy and Research." In *Urban Problems and Community Development,* ed. Ronald Ferguson and William T. Dickens. Washington, DC: Brookings Institution Press.
Immergluck, Daniel. 1999. "Neighborhood, Race, and Capital." *Urban Affairs Review* 34 (2): 397–411.
Jargowsky, Paul. 2006. "Concentrated Poverty: A Primer." *Perspectives.* (Federal Reserve Bank of Dallas): 3–8.
Jovanovic, Boyan. 1982. "Selection and Evolution of Industry." *Econometrica* 50 (2): 649–670.
Porter, Michael. 1995. "The Competitive Advantage of the Inner City." *Harvard Business Review* 73 (3): 15–20.
———. 1997. "New Strategies for Inner-City Economic Development." *Economic Development Quarterly* 11 (1): 11–27.
Squires, Gregory. 2003. "Racial Profiling, Insurance Style: Insurance Redlining and the Uneven Development of Metropolitan Areas." *Journal of Urban Affairs* 25 (4): 347–372.
Yoon, In-Jin. 1997. *On My Own.* Chicago: University of Chicago Press.

23

Courts, Equity, and Community Development

BRENDA BRATTON BLOM, KATE TITFORD, AND ELISABETH WALDEN

Crime as a Deterrent to Successful Community Redevelopment

Neither the people-based nor the place-based redevelopment strategies really anticipated the difficulty that entrenched centers of crime would pose for redevelopment efforts. Tough anticrime and mandatory sentencing policies implemented in the 1980s had enormous social by-products in communities with illegal drug markets—often those same communities where Committee for Economic Development (CED) efforts were under way. The drug trade brought violence into the neighborhoods, soaring arrest rates destabilized the communities, and the number of people returning from prison to the community was growing exponentially. New laws created additional barriers to employment, housing, and education for ex-offenders, so that benefits that might have been available in 1975 for those formerly incarcerated were no longer. The consequence was a near-inevitable return to crime and a growing entrenchment of violence in the communities that were "home."

Several anticrime strategies emerged. In Boston, there was an effort to target violent offenders through parole and probation initiatives (Kennedy 2002). In New York City, then Mayor Rudy Giuliani instituted a "zero tolerance" policy, arresting and incarcerating for violation of minor quality-of-life offenses. This initiative was touted as a success for New York, but it also contributed to long-term problems, including more severe consequences for more of the population and an atmosphere of criminalization of poverty.

While prior community redevelopment efforts have all had their failings, they have also taught valuable lessons. A community cannot be expected to thrive while it suffers either from entrenched crime or from the deleterious collateral effects of hard-nosed enforcement efforts. The role of the justice system in communities is critical. To understand that role or provide constructive suggestions for reform, we must first understand how the structures inherent in the criminal justice system work and how we arrived at this critical juncture.

Communities and Crime: Historical Underpinnings on the British Isles

The American judicial experience has been unique both in its process and its end product. And yet, even as we appreciate our nation's history, it is interesting and instructive to reflect on the earliest influences on our tradition of justice: those that existed on the British Isles around the time of the Norman Conquest in A.D. 1066. A snapshot of life and governance before and after the Norman Conquest presents different relationships between communities and crime. What can we learn, nearly a millennium later, from Saxon localism and Norman nationalism?

William the Conqueror is sometimes portrayed as a great civilizing influence—as the formidable figure of continental culture who boldly imposed order on the British Isles. And yet, in truth, he arrived on English soil in A.D. 1066 to discover a sophisticated and highly functional legal system already in place. Saxon England was prosperous and settled in the centuries preceding the Norman Conquest. Its population operated an agrarian system, engaged in some intervillage commerce, and participated locally in the administration of justice. This localism was a matter of both temperament and convenience (Keeton 1966). Regardless, for Saxon England, the result was the use of small, cohesive groups to decide and implement equitable remedies when conflict arose in communities.

While the Saxon model of governance and justice relied on local administration, it was neither random nor disorganized. Instead, there was an established infrastructure for making and enforcing laws, and that system was heavily oriented toward three specific local levels. There was no strict allocation of functions among these bodies; each was able to deal with administrative, fiscal, or judicial functions as needed.

The basic unit in Saxon England was the township. Consisting of about a dozen agrarian households, the township would work together to resolve interfamily conflicts and tackle projects on the farmland surrounding their homes. At their regular meetings, townships would gather all the households to discuss issues and decide remedies. A more regional approach to governance in Saxon England was through the Hundred. Made up of representatives from adjoining townships, the Hundred acted as both police force and court system. The main governing body of the late Saxon period was the Shire Moot. This administrative body was composed of respected leaders like the bishop and the alderman, as well as representatives of the Hundred. In its capacity as a judicial body, the Shire Moot made decisions by first declaring, and then applying, local custom.

Conflict resolution in the Saxon period is perhaps best exemplified by *wergild*, literally interpreted as "man price." In instances of wrongdoing, wergild was the sum of money paid to the injured person or his family by the wrongdoer or his family. The use of wergild was unique in that it legally required a peaceful solution to the conflict—that is, a family who accepted the money was required under law to renounce a blood feud. The amount of the wergild was determined by an elaborate formula that took into account the nature of the injury and the parties' status (Keeton 1966). Some modern scholars describe Saxon England as being "addicted" to compromise—from its simple complaint-and-reply procedures to its decision making by an impartial official to its use of remedies as dictated by local custom.

The Saxon kingship, which had existed for many years, enjoyed greater reverence and increased powers in the later Saxon period. The king was selected by the Witan, a national assembly, and could seek Witan counsel as he saw fit. Through writs, the king would state a preference for one custom over another. However, the ultimate decision among a choice of laws was left to the local government units.

Norman Legal Systems on the British Isles

Recognizing the virtues of Saxon law and eager to maintain an air of legitimacy, William the Conqueror maintained certain components of the Saxon jurisprudence. However, his coming also brought some feudal customs from the European continent, as dictated by the need for security and loyalty to the king. In England, Norman rule incorporated the blood feud tradition under which land disputes were resolved with trial by battle. While the wergild system of the Saxons survived the Conquest, the criminal law administered in the king's courts after 1066 was mostly inspired by these more primitive Norman customs (Keeton 1966).

The manorial system of post-Conquest England led to isolation of law. Each lord had a court to process agricultural disagreements, petty crime, and more serious crimes. The king would interfere only if there was a significant or salacious dispute between lord and serf.

The king's courts and the manorial courts both struggled to assert jurisdiction over freehold tenants who lived outside the boundaries of manors. By the end of the Middle Ages, freehold litigation was monopolized by the king's court, representing a significant step toward nationalization of the justice system (Fifoot 1993). The usual court for freehold tenants since Saxon times had been the county court, which was maintained after the Norman invasion as a balance to the rising manorial power. In fact, the county court was the center of local justice until around A.D. 1300, when a new law confined jurisdiction of the county court to low-level cases. The ensuing decay of the county court led to the rise of the modern, nationalized English justice system, which provided the framework for the early American court system.

Historical Underpinnings of the Relationship Between Communities and Crime

The modern American justice system is the product of centuries of our own unique tradition added to the rich institution borrowed from the English at the nation's founding. The fair, consistent, and principled administration of justice has always been a central concern both because of the significant impact the justice system has on communities and the importance of public confidence to its successful functioning. However, the meaning and appearance of just courts has changed throughout history, reflecting changes in the prevailing legal philosophy, popular social and political attitudes, and increased experience.

The English Tradition: Judicial Authority Delegated by the King

Lacking any independent history or experience, the early American judicial system was based largely on the English traditions familiar to our founding fathers. Accordingly, an understanding of English judicial history is integral to appreciating the background and basis of our own court system. As discussed previously, by the close of the Norman era, administration of justice had trended away from being a local matter and become a function of the nationalized government.

The Role of Writs in the Courts of Law

Under the English monarchical structure, all governmental functions, including the operation of a justice system to resolve disputes and respond to crime, were fundamentally within the prerogative of the king (Hohfield 1913). Because all authority to administer justice was derived from the king, he enjoyed the option of either exercising that power directly or delegating it to representatives. By the mid-thirteenth century, the monarchy had adopted a system of making delegations of judicial authority to the judges of three courts on a case-by-case basis.

The device by which the king transferred power was the writ, which gave a detailed, fact-specific description of the case being referred. Accordingly, the court's jurisdiction and authority to act was merely "on loan" from the king and circumscribed by the terms of the writ (Hohfield citing Pollock and Maitland, 1913). Litigants would often have to contort their claims to fit within the writ's description to avoid having their claims dismissed and, over time, the writ system gave rise to exacting and rigid procedural requirements (Main 2003). As society and its conflicts grew more complex, limitations of the writ system became clear. Many litigants were denied relief because of their inability to conform to the strictures of the writ.

Development of the Courts of Equity

As the writ system that dominated the courts of law proved unable to provide either procedural or substantive justice in many cases, the courts of equity emerged. When citizens were unable to make use of the law courts, they frequently requested the king's personal intervention in their disputes (Main 2003). Initially the monarchy, assisted by close advisors, handled these appeals, but they were soon overwhelmed. The king relied on the chancellor to intervene in these quarrels when justice required. Indeed, by the end of the thirteenth century, citizens were instructed to bring complaints that were not amenable to resolution in the law courts directly to the chancellor. The large volume of appeals soon overwhelmed the chancellor's office and required the creation of the court of chancery (or court of equity), empowered with broad authority to act in the interests of justice (Main 2003).

Law Versus Equity: The Struggle for Supremacy

After the development of the court of equity with its broad jurisdictional grant, the English justice system essentially operated through two parallel court systems, maintaining the duality of systems that treated entities in either a restorative or punitive manner. However, the law–equity distinction was not a perfectly clear line, and the question soon arose: When law and equity require different results in the same case, which system prevails? Periodic conflicts between the court of law and the court of equity began in the late fourteenth century and continued until a controversy between two prominent jurists required a clear resolution in 1616. In that case, the king issued a decree upholding the judgment of the court of equity where it conflicted with the ruling of the court of law, thereby solidifying the supremacy of the equity court (Hohfield citing Kerley, Holdsworth, et al. 1913).

Different Substantive Rights and Procedural Requirements in a Bifurcated System of Justice

Based on the historical background of the development of the law and equity courts, it is perhaps unsurprising that the courts differed in their substantive rights and technical mechanisms. Equity took a broader approach to the substantive claims for which relief was available. While law courts were generally equipped only to compensate litigants for loss, courts of equity were designed to make an injured party whole and, in addition to compensating parties, could prevent harm with remedies such as injunctive relief (Hohfield 1913). Equity courts, unlike law courts, were also able to give relief on a conditional basis, requiring the recipient to make concessions to reach a fair result.

With respect to the manner of proceeding in court, law courts were notoriously strict in their procedural and pleading requirements because of the formalisms of the writ system. By comparison, courts of equity were more litigant-friendly, allowing flexibility to accommodate the goal of providing justice. However, one significant limitation of equity courts was the general unavailability of a jury trial (Main 2003).

Northern and Southern Attitudes Toward Early American Courts

When the structure of the English system was adopted in the early days of the American judicial tradition, it was received differently by the divergent cultures in the Northern and Southern states. In colonial America, the Northern colonies were settled predominantly by Puritans seeking increased opportunities to better their lives. The South was settled principally by aristocratic Englishmen. Because of this demographic difference, judges were unpopular in the North, being perceived as part of the elite class. The people favored juries. Because juries were not available in the courts of equity, courts of law were preferred in the North. Furthermore, mistrust of the highly educated brought the democratic society to favor laypeople with little or no legal training as elected judges. Southern aristocrats who shared similar backgrounds to trained judges were comfortable with the loose justice administered by equity courts and were untroubled by the unavailability of a jury (Beale 1921).

The Merger of the Courts of Law and Equity

The merger of the law and equity traditions in American courts was a gradual process occurring around the turn of the twentieth century. Initially, equity and law courts occupied separate physical courthouses and were staffed by separate judges. As the merger began to take place, individual states generally followed one of two models (Ingersoll 1911). Some states, most notably New York, went directly to some version of the fully integrated system we have today. This model brought law and equity into the same court, before the same judge, with the same rules of procedure (Ingersoll 1911; Main 2003). Litigants were even permitted to combine legal and equitable claims and defenses in the same action (Ingersoll 1911). Other states took an intermediate step by partially merging the law and equity functions, bringing both types of action under the same courthouse roof, but keeping the two separated (Ingersoll 1911). While all litigants would go to the same courthouse, they would use different procedural mechanisms depending on whether the case was in law or in equity (Ingersoll 1911). They could not mix claims in the same case. Although these states eventually continued to a full merger, during this partially integrated phase, judges were required to sit either in law or in equity and to wear different "hats" according to the nature of the action.

As the merger of law and equity was picking up speed on the state level, many commentators initially viewed the language of Article III of the U.S. Constitution as a barrier to a similar merger in the federal courts. This confusion was eventually resolved when Congress passed a statute giving federal courts the freedom to merge their law and equity functions; the federal courts promptly obliged (Main 2003).

The result of the law and equity merger is our current system of justice. In virtually every American jurisdiction, on both the federal and state levels, litigants appear in one court before one judge to present all the claims arising from the same factual situation. While the merged legal system has adopted some of the more favorable characteristics of the equitable tradition, such as simplified pleading requirements and many of the equitable claims and defenses, many believe that our merged system still falls short (Main 2003). Modern courts are constrained by procedural requirements that were essentially nonexistent in the courts of equity, and many feel that the merger has come at the cost of no longer having any court operating with the flexibility exercised by the equity courts. With the increasingly prominent role the legal system plays in the life of poor communities, the inability to simply respond to a problem with whatever means appropriate has proven especially problematic.

Restorative Justice Initiatives in the United States

Community development lawyers today are working in communities that are overwhelmed by crime and the justice system. According to the ABA's Kennedy Commission Report, in 1970 there were 250,000 people incarcerated in the United States (ABA 2006). By 2003, that number had risen to 2.3 million. The United States currently incarcerates more people than any country in the world, including China, whose population is 4.3 times greater than ours (Geohive 2006). All communities are not affected equally. Statistics confirm the confluence of race and class at a rate unparalleled in the history of the United States (Cashin 2004). Poor communities of all races are experiencing unprecedented and permanent effects due to the justice system's meting out longer sentences as required by mandatory minimum-sentencing legislation. It is in this context that the community development lawyer and the community in which she works approach the fundamental questions of restoration. She is likely to find that crime and the justice system's response to disorder in the public space is now the major impediment to creating a healthy community. Success in the new era of community development may very well require the legal task of our English ancestors: sorting issues of law from issues of equity.

Howard Zehr, who has long been working in the area of restorative justice, has articulated the basic tenets of the field. Under the traditional criminal justice model, crime is a violation of law and an offense against state. Violations of the law create guilt, and justice requires the state to both determine blame and impose punishment. The central driving idea is that offenders get what they deserve. On the other hand, a restorative justice framework shifts much of this foundational thinking: crime becomes a violation of people and relationships. Violations create obligations, and justice involves the victims, the offenders, *and* the community in an effort to put things right. The central focus is on the needs of the victim, and the offender assumes responsibility for repairing that harm (Zehr 2002).

Considering the historical development of the courts of law and equity, there appear to be some threads that perhaps we should pull to understand if we are committed to reweaving a community fabric. First, in the earliest courts on the British Isles, the Saxons used the system of wergild, assuming that the community would mediate the offense appropriately and determine an appropriate restoration price that would be paid by the offender and his family. The victim was compensated, and the community was responsible for holding the offender accountable. This system was effective for resolving disputes, maintaining the primacy of the community's role in the dispute resolution, and ultimately reducing and prohibiting blood feuds.

The Normans incorporated much of this system but brought with them the stronger crown-based system that later developed the system of writs. The law-based courts operated with authority delegated by the king to deal with crimes, but only within the narrow parameters of the writ, which framed both the definition of the crime and the delegation of authority. Clearly this was an inadequate system, and there remained an avenue to appeal to the king for mercy and to deal with matters in a more holistic manner. Out of this pressure valve emerged the court of equity: a system in which the judge had the power to design remedies that fit the circumstances.

Now that the pendulum has swung fully to the systematized justice represented by the courts of law, even judges themselves are questioning the effectiveness of treating violations of people and relationships as violations against the state. The result is bad for individuals and impossible for communities. As Judge Alex Calabrese, the sitting judge at the Red Hook Justice Center in Brooklyn, New York, stated, "I got tired of giving out life sentences 30 days at a time. I was ready to start asking 'Why are you here?' instead of 'What is the charged crime?'" (Calabrese 2007). The simple shift in question takes the inquiry in different directions. When the question is "Why are you here?" it may bring information into the discussion that could change the outcome. In a case brought against a mother for abuse, Judge Calabrese describes a mother with her fifteen-year-old son; the mother said, "I hit him because he refused to go to school. What else could I do?" Rather than punish the mother, Calabrese was able to refer the family for counseling and the child to a resource center to develop a life plan, including an assessment of educational needs and identification of resources. The family was required to report back to the judge regularly, and resources were put in place to support the mother's desire to have her child get an education. This outcome is restorative and equitable in nature. It is not punitive, because this problem is not about blame and punishment, it is about victim needs, offender responsibility, and community support for a successful outcome.

Finding a way for the community to participate in the justice conversation is a more challenging and more important long term goal. When communities are small, there is an element of equity present, even in the jury and law system, because the "jury of your peers" literally is that. The jury will inevitably include people who actually know both the defendant and the victim. Knowing their families and histories, those jurors bring to the deliberation a greater context in which the crime occurred. Until recently, the judge could also consider that larger context in sentencing. In small places, even the prosecutor could bring into the mix an immediate knowledge of the situation. The positive elements of this familiarity are the ability to think about the matter contextually, as it affects both the individual and the community. This was true for the Saxons on the British Isles and for Americans in the early years in our own lands.

There are those who are building models of conflict resolution that draw on the positive elements of such contextual knowledge. In Baltimore, Maryland, the Community Conferencing Center has developed a model of conflict resolution that has now been used in over 6,000 community-based conferences. The "victim" and the "offender" are brought together, along with their families and all who are affected by the dispute, to discuss and reach agreement about what harm was done, who was responsible, how the harm will be repaired, and what is needed to support the victim and the offender. An agreement is written and signed. While this restorative model resembles the early Saxon justice system, it is actually modeled on native processes in New Zealand (the Maori people) and North America (the First Nations).

The negative aspects of a less directive, law-based approach were revealed during slavery and Reconstruction in our country, when provincial thinking was used to justify and reaffirm social norms that were based on prejudice and influence peddling. The "leveling" of the courts of law and statutes with little room for interpretation was critical for many to survive and seek justice when they were the outsider, or the "other" in color or class. The lessons of leveling are important to maintain when it is an appropriately heinous crime—an actual crime against the state. These formalized processes guaranteeing procedural rights as well as substantive rights are critical to overcome prejudices and to ensure that justice is as colorblind and class-blind as possible.

The Community in Community Development

So why does this justice discussion matter as we think about community development for the twenty-first century? As a field, we have been learning lessons for the past twenty-five years that have moved us forward. But the new challenges that have emerged have moderated these successes. Unless community development is about gentrification and relocation of the current residents so that the *place* is restored, we must create strategies to rebuild the community. "Community in this sense is a form of social capital, a non-market relationship of collective risk-taking. . . . Social capital is constituted by the presence of informal networks of people (family, friends, neighbors) who can collaborate to address shared problems and gain access to city political power" (Bezdek 2006, 88). This collective risk-taking and collaboration on problems is essential to restore order when disordering behavior has taken root. And that requires communities to become active participants in the justice discussion in their boundaries.

Doing so will require new skill sets. Community development corporations (CDCs) have been focused on leadership development and business development skill building. Transactional attorneys have worked alongside residents and nonprofit employees to rebuild houses, develop businesses, and provide services. Skills needed to engage the justice system and strengthen the ability to solve complex interpersonal disputes will require a new set of players: people trained in dispute resolution, lawyers (prosecutors and defenders) committed to solving underlying problems in under resourced communities, and judges willing to think collaboratively about problem-solving remedies and to risk settling in problem-solving courts (drug, mental health, and community courts).

While poor communities are already being asked to solve problems sometimes beyond their training, it is important for community development and justice system professionals to facilitate and encourage community leaders to be part of the problem-solving team. This means reallocating funds to support and develop these collaborations. Until communities can reclaim their public space, as well as their sons and daughters, community development initiatives will be long shots at success. The courts must examine the role they play and return to an equitable and restorative practice so that order—in body, soul, and streets—is restored.

Restorative Justice Initiatives

Whatever may be meant by "justice," it certainly does not mean a court system that stigmatizes and imprisons large segments of poor communities, leaving individuals and communities with a diminished chance of success. In their infancy, courts focused on individuals and communities resolving a problem to the satisfaction of those affected. Over time, however, the judicial treatment changed to a more systematic model, handling the case, not the person, in the name of preserving rights and ensuring equal treatment for similarly situated individuals. This latter approach has brought us to our current situation.

Although communities in need of redevelopment are disproportionately affected by crime, their problems are not eased by the mass imprisonment of their sons and daughters. The effect of our systematic approach to justice on these communities is to destabilize them by constantly removing individuals from the community to put them in prison. Furthermore, communities bear the burden of receiving their neighbors, now ex-convicts, back home and dealing with the fact that their options are even more limited than before. Finally, because imprisonment is so prevalent in these communities, young people begin to see it as a normal experience, and the threat of prison loses its deterrent effect.

Clearly, mass imprisonment has significant and damaging effects on community improvement efforts, not to mention the individuals who are affected personally. This is not to say that criminal behavior should be allowed to continue unchecked, but rather that our standardized, conveyor-belt approach to dispensing justice has fallen short. The pendulum, which started with personalized, community-based problem solving, has swung too far in the direction of sterile, one-size-fits-all management. To correct the entrenched problem of crime in poor neighborhoods in a manner that allows success for the individual and the community, the justice system will have to take into account the individual and the community. Community development lawyers will need new allies and knowledge to navigate this new set of challenges.

References

American Bar Association (ABA). 2006. *Justice Kennedy Commission Recommendations.* www.abanet.org/crimjust/kennedy/JusticeKennedyCommissionReportsFinal.pdf (Accessed 6 February 2008.)
Beale, Joseph H. 1921. "Equity in America." *Cambridge Law Journal* 1: 21.
Bezdek, Barbara. 2006. "To Attain 'The Just Rewards of So Much Struggle': Local-Resident Equity Participation in Urban Revitalization." *Hofstra Law Review* 35 (1): 37–114.
Calabrese, Alex. 2007. Interview with the author.
Cashin, Sheryll. 2004. *The Failures of Integration: How Race and Class Are Undermining the American Dream.* Cambridge, MA: PublicAffairs.

Fifoot, C. H. S. 1993. *English Law and Its Background.* Holmes Beach, FL: Gaunt & Sons (1932, reprinted 1993).

Geohive 2006. Geohive: Global Statistics. www.geohive.com/default1.aspx. (Accessed 15 January 2008.)

Hohfield, Wesley Newcomb. 1913. "The Relations Between Equity and Law." *University of Michigan Law Review* 11: 537.

Ingersoll, Henry H. 1911. "Confusion of Law and Equity." *Yale Law Journal* 21: 58.

Keeton, George W. 1966. *The Norman Conquest and the Common Law.* London: Ernest Benn.

Kennedy, David M. 2002. "A Tale of One City: Reflections on the Boston Gun Project." In *Securing Our Children's Future: New Approaches to Juvenile Justice and Youth Violence,* ed. Gary S. Katzmann. Washington, DC: Brookings Institution Press.

Main, Thomas O. 2003. "Traditional Equity and Contemporary Procedure." *Washington Law Review* 78: 429.

Zehr, Howard. 2002. *The Little Book of Restorative Justice.* Intercourse, PA: Good Books.

Appendix

Redevelopment's Trend Away from Eminent Domain

T. MICHAEL LENGYEL

Redevelopment agencies increasingly play an integral role in rehabilitating older commercial districts that often suffer from blight and disrepair. Under redevelopment law, agencies may invoke eminent domain to assemble land to sell to private developers for privatively financed redevelopment projects. At some point, the improved real estate is then often sold to private concerns at increased property values, which provides the redevelopment agency with tax increment dollars to fund future projects. In 2004, redevelopment consumed $2.9 billion in property tax revenue in California alone; 10 percent of all property taxes statewide.

The *Kelo v. City of New London* U.S. Supreme Court ruling highlighted some of the fundamental concerns of using eminent domain as a redevelopment tool. The Supreme Court's controversial decision allowed the city of New London, Connecticut, to seize private homes and transfer the land to a private developer to build a commercial waterfront project. The ruling struck a deep chord in the American psyche: that the government could seize your house or business in order to build a road for everyone's use was one thing, but the idea that it could hand your property over to private developers was, to many, intolerable.

In response to strong public backlash from the ruling, a number of the states passed laws in one form or another that limit the government's ability to use eminent domain to privately finance development. A measure on the ballot in California in 2006 failed, but only because it was much too broad, affecting such agencies as California's Coastal Commission. An initiative focused on protecting owner-occupied properties is likely to garner voter approval in 2008.

Most redevelopment agencies have always been prudent about when they would invoke eminent domain as a means to eliminate blight. However, it has been a nice tool to have to help prod property owners who may otherwise be disinclined to maintain and/or improve their old and often dilapidated buildings.

With the threat of eminent domain diminished, redevelopment agencies now have to rely more heavily on a carrot approach to stimulate the rehabilitation of these properties. A few of the incentives at their disposal include business improvement districts and maintenance assessment districts, loans, storefront improvement grants, equity funds, new markets tax credits, historic rehabilitation tax credits, and tax incentive zones.

BIDs and MADs—Partnering with the Community

In stark contrast to government agencies using eminent domain to condemn private property, business improvement districts (BIDs) and maintenance assessment districts (MADs) allow business and property owners to advocate for the preservation and enhancement of their commercial districts. Through an external voting process, the owners and tenants choose to assess themselves an annual fee to reinvest money back into the commercial district. Both BIDs and MADs are based on the concept that improvements drive more business to the district, which pays for the assessments through higher profits (for the business owners) or increased rent roles and/or increased property values (for the property owners).

BIDs—Letting the Business Community Take the Lead

BIDs, also known as business improvement associations and special improvement districts, are public–private partnerships between government and small business owners.

Once a BID is established, a constituent-led, neighborhood chamber incorporated as a nonprofit management corporation is formed to administer programs and activities to promote and revitalize the district. In addition to a promotion campaign, BIDs may manage a number of other programs, including public parking, security, public right-of-way maintenance, public improvement and beautification projects, recruiting of new business starts, and sponsoring various neighborhood activities such as farmers' markets and restaurant walks.

Many BIDs also certify with the National Trust for Historic Preservation to become a designated Main Street program. Accredited Main Street programs adhere to the Main Street Four-Point Approach, a comprehensive strategy tailored to meet local needs and opportunities. It encompasses work in four distinct areas—design, economic restructuring, promotion, and organization. The Main Street organization forms committees who plan and implement activities in each of the four points. Depending on the circumstances of the commercial district, the program may also create issue-oriented task forces, such as a parking task force (see www.mainstreet.org).

In 1989, representatives from San Diego's BIDs formed the Business Improvement District Council (BID Council) to disseminate information, resources, and expertise to its member districts and to improve the overall physical, social, and economic environments of San Diego's small business communities. San Diego's BID Council is the only municipal-wide coalition of individual business or property-based special district programs in the nation. A unified council provides strength in numbers to influence citywide initiatives or policies that affect the business community.

MADs—Enhanced Services for Property Owners

A MAD, also known as a landscape maintenance district, is similar in structure to a BID, but specific to property owners. Property owners vote to self-assess a fee to pay for and receive enhanced maintenance services in the public right-of-way. Services may include landscape maintenance, hardscape maintenance, open-space maintenance (safety tree trimming and removal and litter removal), street light maintenance, sidewalk steam cleaning, sign maintenance, banner installation/removal, and seasonal decoration installation/removal.

Redevelopment and BIDs and MADs

Because of the inherent blight conditions in many older commercial districts, BIDs and MADs often overlap with redevelopment projects areas. These special districts can be great development partners for the agency, as they can operate free from most of the city bureaucracy that often impedes agency sponsored projects. The key to BIDs' accomplishments lies in their dissimilarity to big-city government. They operate without civil service rules and red tape; most important, they negotiate labor contracts from a clean slate.

Loan Programs

Often, a lack of access to capital prevents otherwise willing owners and tenants from investing in their properties. The Department of Housing and Community Development (HUD) and the Small Business Administration (SBA) oversee a number of governmental programs to help fill this financing gap. Many cities also directly offer targeted loan funds.

HUD 108 Loans—Seed Capital for Redevelopment Projects

Section 108 is the loan guarantee provision of HUD's Community Development Block Grant (CDBG), providing communities with a source of financing for economic development, housing rehabilitation, public facilities, and large-scale physical development projects. It allows local governments to transform a small portion of their CDBG funds into federally guaranteed loans to pursue physical and economic revitalization projects that can renew entire neighborhoods.

Section 108 loans are not risk-free, however; local governments borrowing funds guaranteed by Section 108 must pledge their current and future CDBG allocations to cover the loan amount as security for the loan. Additional collateral is also required to assure repayment of guaranteed obligations. The additional security requirements are determined on a case-by-case basis and may include assets financed by the guaranteed loan. Projects located in redevelopment areas have an advantage, because tax increment revenue can be pledged for repayment.

SBA 504 Loan Program

The SBA 504 Loan Program allows small business owners to purchase an industrial or commercial building at below-market interest rates with a minimum 10 percent down payment or equity injection. The loan proceeds may be used to purchase or remodel an existing building or construct a new facility (in addition to purchasing equipment).

In the typical structure, a bank makes a loan in the first trust deed lien position for 50 percent of the total project, a nonprofit community development corporation (CDC) issues a loan in the second trust deed lien position for 40 percent of the total project, and the borrower contributes 10 percent of the total project. The CDC loan funds are obtained through the sale of SBA-guaranteed debentures on the private capital market. The rate, term, and fees of the 504 loan are negotiable between the borrower and lender.

The 504 program can be a great tool to help small business owners purchase their property. Once they own it, they have a strong incentive not only to maintain it but also to invest in it to increase sales.

Revolving Loan Funds

SBA has been very successful in expanding opportunities for small businesses. However, for any number of reasons, small business owners often cannot qualify for SBA-guaranteed loan products or can obtain only a portion of the capital they need. Many cities and agencies also manage separate revolving loan funds to supplement the private financing of new or rehabilitated buildings. The loans are typically targeted to small business owners in low-income communities who cannot access standard bank financing but demonstrate credit worthiness and the ability to repay the loan.

The loan funds are often capitalized with federal funds, matched with local dollars. CDBG is a common source of capital, as are grants from the Department of Commerce. As the loans are paid back, the funds are then relent to new borrowers. The interest earned on the loans help offset the costs to run the program.

Storefront Improvement Grants—Cash Incentives to Encourage Action

Redevelopment agencies are often criticized for the amount of property tax revenue they exact from a community. However, most of that revenue is simply passed through the agency and reinvested back into the community. A direct example is grants to small businesses or property owners as an incentive to improve their storefronts within their commercial districts.

The grants are often matched with private capital from the property owner or small business owner and are not disbursed until the project is completed. The cash incentive can often encourage owners to improve their property when they would not do so otherwise. The grants also allow the agency to exact some measure of control over the façade design, insuring deference for the original features of the building and overall design plan on the community. The agency may also require that the grant be returned if the property is not maintained.

Equity Funds—Double Bottom Line Investments

It is also very difficult to attract private equity capital for commercial revitalization projects. Therefore, many cities and local agencies have also been proactive in creating double bottom line equity funds. Consultants such as Belden Daniels with Economic Innovation International have worked with agencies across the country to set up double bottom line equity funds, often capitalized with bank or insurance funds or investments from public pension funds.

The funds provide a financial return to the investors and social return to the communities that are revitalized as a result of an injection in capital. When launching a new fund, it is important to establish investment criteria that insures that the funds are targeted to the communities with the greatest need, while also being flexible enough to ensure strong deal flow. In addition to sourcing deals, the fund managers should be willing to work with developers, the agency, and the community to help overcome barriers to development that may exist in the commercial districts.

New Markets Tax Credits—Quasi-Equity

The New Markets Tax Credit (NMTC) Program was established as part of the federal Community Renewal Tax Relief Act of 2000. The program is administered by the Community Development Financial Institutions Fund within the Department of Treasury (CDFI Fund). Fifteen billion dollars in tax allocation was set aside to award to for-profit community development entities (CDEs). These CDEs in turn offer the credits to taxable investors (usually banks) in exchange for stock or a capital interest in the CDEs. The investors take a credit against their federal taxes for 39 percent of the cost of the investment over a seven-year period. The invested funds are then reinvested into low-income communities, typically in the form of below-market real estate or small business loans or equity investments. The full $15 million in allocation will be awarded to CDEs in 2007. In 2006, Congress approved a one-year extension of the program with an additional $3.5 billion in allocation. Bills have also been introduced in Congress to extend the program through 2013. Funds are available for a wide range of projects in most every city and state. A number of allocation recipients also have national services areas. A full list of recipients is available on the CDFI Fund Web site: www.cdfifund.gov/awardees. They can be searched by region or product type. Another alternative is to call the CRA (Community Reinvestment Act) department of local banks and ask if they invest in NMTC projects. Most of the large banks do, and they may be able to source a CDE that invests in the type of project being considered.

Historic Rehabilitation Tax Credits

The Historic Preservation Tax Incentives program is jointly managed by the National Park Service (NPS) and the Internal Revenue Service in partnership with the State Historic Preservation Officer in each state. The program provides a 20 percent rehabilitation credit for private investment to rehabilitate historic properties, including offices and retail stores. The credit applies to any project that the Secretary of the Interior designates a certified rehabilitation of a *certified historic structure.*

The NPS must approve, or "certify," all rehabilitation projects seeking credit. The NPS assumes that some alteration of the historic building will occur to provide for efficient use. However, the project must not damage, destroy, or cover materials or features, whether interior or exterior, that help define the building's historic character. The owner must hold the building for five full years after completing the rehabilitation, or pay back the credit. For properties held between one and five years, the tax credit recapture amount is reduced by 20 percent per year.

Where available, the historic rehabilitation tax credit is often leveraged with NMTCs. This provides a significant tax incentive that can allow for deep subsidies for a project or provide financing on projects that would not pencil out otherwise.

Incentive Zones—Tax and Financial Incentives

Federal renewal communities (RCs), enterprise zones (EZs), and empowerment communities (and their state counterparts) have the same broad objective as the NMTC program, which is to help spur private investment in communities that have experienced severe economic decline. The primary benefit to businesses located in the zones are wage credits on their employees, but there are also other incentives specific to improving commercial properties.

In RCs, property owners may qualify for a commercial revitalization deduction for investments in commercial properties. If a property owner incurs expenses to build a new commercial building or substantially rehabilitate an existing building located in the RC and used for business purposes, the property owner may be able to take a special tax deduction against federal taxes.

The property owner can deduct either one-half of the capital investment expenditures in the first year the building is placed in service or all capital investment expenditures on a prorated basis over ten years instead of the usual thirty-nine-year depreciation deduction. Each RC in the United States has a yearly maximum of $12 million in commercial revitalization deductions that it may allocate to projects, and there is a $10 million limit on any one project's allocation.

In EZs, state or local governments can issue enterprise zone facility bonds at lower interest rates than standard bond financing to finance construction costs. *Enterprise zone facility* means any qualified zone property the principal user of which is an EZ business and any land that is functionally related and subordinate to such property. Bonds are available for up to $3,000,000 with respect to any one EZ.

A number of states also have implemented similar zones that provided state tax credits and other incentives. The state zones may overlap with federal zones, and both of them often encompass redevelopment project areas. For the redevelopment agency, taking advantage of these programs can be as simple as marketing them within the project area. The agency or local government may also have staff on hand to help the business and property owners take advantage of the incentives.

The Layering Effect of Multiple Incentives

These various incentives work best when offered as a complete package. Grants and tax incentives can encourage a landlord to rehabilitate his or her property and a loan or other investment can help pay for it. A business improvement district can help promote the incentives and also can coordinate a revitalization plan that is consistent throughout the commercial district. The redevelopment agency should take a proactive role to insure that these incentives are available within their project areas, providing resources that help preserve and enhance the community without necessarily having to rebuild it from the ground up.

About the Editors and Contributors

James O. Bates is a career civil servant in Buffalo, New York, who works in the area of community planning and development. He is also adjunct faculty at the State University of New York at Buffalo. His current research focuses on microenterprise development and community leadership practices. Bates has recently published on teaching public leadership and change.

Timothy Bates is Distinguished Professor of Economics at Wayne State University. Prior to his Wayne State appointment, he was professor of policy analysis and chair of the graduate program of urban policy analysis at the New School for Social Research. Bates is the author of five books on urban economic development issues, the most recent of which is *Race, Self-Employment, and Upward Mobility,* published by Johns Hopkins University Press.

Michael Berry joined the Federal Reserve Bank of Chicago's Consumer and Community Affairs division in 1995 as a researcher and special project leader. He now manages the division's Emerging Issues unit and serves as managing editor of the division's economic development publication, *Profitwise.* Prior to joining the Fed, from 1987 to 1995 Berry worked for RESCORP, a real estate development and consulting organization specializing in urban revitalization, heading its market research unit, and from 1985 to 1987 for the Balcor Company, an investment banking subsidiary of American Express, in the investment research group. Berry holds a BA in political science from Susquehanna University, and an MBA from DePaul University.

Brenda Bratton Blom, JD, PhD, is director of clinical law programs at the University of Maryland School of Law. She received her BA in 1989 and JD in 1993 from the University of Baltimore, her MA in policy science in 1993, and her PhD in legal policy in 2002 from the University of Maryland–Baltimore County. Blom worked in public interest law firms after graduating from law school first in the Community Law Center, then as executive director of the Empowerment Legal Services Program. She is chair of the National Law School Consortium Project and serves on the boards of the American Bar Association Forum on Affordable

Housing and Community Development's Legal Educator's Committee, Civil Justice Inc., Maryland Legal Assistance Network, and ABA's Advisory Committee on the Delivery of Legal Services.

Rene Bryce-Laporte is the community-based financial education specialist in the Pennsylvania Office of Financial Education, which seeks to increase the availability and quality of financial education in Pennsylvania schools, communities, and workplaces. Bryce-Laporte is a graduate of Columbia University and the UCLA School of Law.

Terry F. Buss is a project director at the National Academy of Public Administration in Washington, DC. He earned his PhD in political science at Ohio State University. He has held senior policy analyst and adviser positions at the U.S. Department of Housing and Urban Development, World Bank, Congressional Research Service, and Council of Governor's Policy Advisors. He has also served as director of the School of Policy and Management at Florida International University in Miami, chair of public management at Florida International University in Miami, chair of public management at the Sawyer School of Business at Suffolk University, and director of research centers and graduate programs at Ohio State, Youngstown State, and Akron Universities. Buss has published twelve books and nearly three hundred professional articles on many topics within the field of public policy.

Yoel Camayd-Freixas is professor and chairman of the MA and PhD programs in policy and founding director of the Applied Research Center in CED at the School of Community Economic Development, Southern New Hampshire University. Camayd-Freixas is a board member of the Nellie Mae Educational Foundation, Laborers-AGC union national worker training program, and an elected member of the University Senate. His interests include strategic management, economic development, and applied research methods.

Edward J. Dodson retired early in 2005 from the Housing and Community Development division of Fannie Mae, where he was a senior business manager. His professional experience spans over three decades in commercial banking, mortgage lending, and community development. For over twenty-five years, he was on the faculty of the Henry George School of Social Science, and in 1997 he established an Internet-based education and research project, the School of Cooperative Individualism. Dodson is a graduate of Shippensburg and Temple Universities and the author of a three-volume treatise, *The Discovery of First Principles.*

Annie Donovan is chief operating officer of NCB Capital Impact, responsible for innovative community lending, expert technical assistance, strategy formation, product innovation, and policy development. She has been with NCB Capital Impact since 1993 and has been working in the field of community and cooperative development for twenty years, including service in the U.S. Peace Corps. Donovan currently serves on the board of directors for New Markets Tax Credit Coalition, Community Reinvestment Fund, H Street Community Market, CoopMetrics, Inc., and Capitol Hill Day School. She serves on advisory committees for LISC, Coastal Enterprises, Charter School Development Corporation, and Wall Street Without Walls. Donovan has an undergraduate degree in economics and an MBA in finance.

Donna Fabiani has fifteen years of experience in the community development finance field. She is the executive vice president for knowledge sharing at Opportunity Finance Network. Previous positions include research manager at the U.S. Treasury Department's CDFI Fund and director of FINCA USA, a microenterprise finance program in Washington, D.C. Fabiani spent six years doing international development for Catholic Relief Services. She holds an MPP from the Woodrow Wilson School at Princeton University and a BA from Colby College.

Ben Goodwin is the senior grant writer for Southern Financial Partners, the flagship nonprofit affiliate of Southern Bancorp. Southern Bancorp is a $500 million rural development bank holding company and the nation's largest rural development bank. Since joining Southern in January 2006, Goodwin has successfully raised over $20 million in grant funding for projects conducted by each of Southern's three nonprofit affiliates, ranging from affordable housing development to development lending, workforce development, small business support, public policy advocacy, and asset-building services such as matched-savings accounts. He received a BA in mathematics from Hendrix College in 2001 and a BA in politics, philosophy, and economics from Oxford University in 2003.

Lisa A. Hagerman is a doctoral candidate in economic geography at the University of Oxford researching public pension fund investment in urban revitalization. Before starting her research at Oxford, Hagerman worked in regional public–private partnerships as vice president of Economic Innovation International, Boston, a consulting firm that builds privately capitalized community equity funds. Prior to her consulting work, Hagerman was with Wells Fargo Bank, San Francisco, as assistant vice president of government relations. She worked for Citibank, New York, for seven years, marketing transactional banking products to banks in Latin America as assistant vice president in the Latin American Marketing Division. Hagerman received her BA from Bucknell University and her MA in political science, with a concentration in transatlantic studies, from the University of North Carolina at Chapel Hill.

Tessa Hebb is a senior research associate at the Labor and Worklife Program, Harvard University, and the Oxford University Centre for the Environment. Hebb is researching the role of U.S. public-sector pension funds and urban revitalization as the lead investigator on a three-year Rockefeller and Ford Foundation grant. Her doctoral work at Oxford examines the impact pension fund corporate engagement has on the corporate governance, social, and environmental standards of firm behavior. A Clarendon Scholar at Oxford University, Hebb received the prestigious William E. Taylor Fellowship (2003) from the Social Sciences and Humanities Research Council, Government of Canada, and is also a recipient of the York University Schulich School of Business National Research in Financial Services and Public Policy Scholarship (Canada). Hebb is also the director of the Carleton Centre for Community Innovation (3ci), Carleton University, Canada, where her work focuses on the financial and nonfinancial impact of pension fund economically targeted investment in Canada.

Hilary Hunt was appointed director of the Pennsylvania Office of Financial Education in April 2004 by Governor Edward G. Rendell, where she oversees initiatives to increase the availability and quality of financial education in Pennsylvania's school, communities, and workplaces. She currently serves as president of the PA Jump$tart Coalition and is a member of the board of directors of Junior Achievement of Central Pennsylvania. She has served the educational community as an administrator, teacher, and advocate for financial education for ten years. Hunt holds a degree in mathematics from the College of William and Mary.

Dan Immergluck is associate professor in the City and Regional Planning Program at Georgia Institute of Technology. He has authored two books and dozens of studies on community and economic development, real estate and development finance, neighborhood change, and related topics. His research has been published in *Urban Affairs Review, Housing Policy Debate, Economic Geography, Economic Development Quarterly, Urban Studies,* and other journals. His most recent book is *Credit to the Community: Community Reinvestment and Fair Lending Policy in the U.S.* He has received funding from the MacArthur Foundation, the Lincoln Institute of Land Policy, the Aspen Institute, and other organizations. Immergluck has an MPP from the University of Michigan and a PhD in urban planning and policy from the University of Illinois at Chicago.

Gerald Karush is professor of computer information systems at Southern New Hampshire University, and a senior research fellow at the Applied Research Center in CED, where he is involved in several research studies. Karush's principal areas of experience include computer technology, economic development, demography, and market and evaluation research.

Richard Koenig is a research associate at the Applied Research Center and doctoral candidate in the School of Community Development at Southern New Hampshire University. He holds an MCP in urban planning from the University of Illinois at Urbana–Champaign. He recently started his own community development consulting firm in Detroit. Formerly, Koenig served as CEO of the Housing Opportunity Development Corporation, serving Chicago's northern suburbs where he developed two hundred units of affordable housing.

T. Michael Lengyel is a community development specialist with the City of San Diego's City Planning and Community Investment Department, where he co-manages three small business revolving loan funds and serves as a community resource for federal, state, and local financing programs for affordable housing and economic development projects. Lengyel has an MBA in finance and an MS in taxation from San Diego State University and is a certified public accountant. In 2004, the City of San Diego's Business Finance Program was awarded the federal Economic Development Administration's prestigious Excellence in Urban Economic Development Award.

Jane F. Morgan, president of the JFM Consulting Group, is a community planning and program evaluation consultant. As a planner, Morgan works primarily in the metropolitan Detroit area with municipalities, community development organizations, and foundations conducting research while facilitating the development of plans to resolve issues facing urban communities. Morgan has worked with a wide range of organizations and institutions, primarily in the metropolitan Detroit area. Through the JFM Consulting Group, she also provides technical assistance to community-based nonprofit groups through intermediary organizations. Morgan holds an MPA from the LBJ School of Public Affairs at the University of Texas and has completed coursework toward a PhD in urban and regional planning at the University of Michigan.

Kirsten Moy is the director of the Economic Opportunities Program (EOP) at the Aspen Institute. She came to the Institute after serving as project director for the Community Development Innovation and Infrastructure Initiative, a national research project on the future of community development and community development finance. The initiative was incubated at the John D. and Catherine T. MacArthur Foundation in 1998 when Moy was a Distinguished Visitor at the foundation. Previously, Moy served as the first director of the CDFI Fund in the U.S. Department of the Treasury. Before joining the Treasury Department, she was a senior vice president and port-folio manager at Equitable Real Estate Investment Management in New York City, where she was responsible for designing investment products to enable institutional investors to invest in affordable housing and other community and economic develop-ment projects. Her background includes six years as vice president in charge of the Social Initiative Investment Department at the Equitable Life Assurance Society of the United States; serving as a program investment officer with the Ford Foundation; and positions as a management analyst at Equitable and Nabisco, Inc. Moy holds an MS in operations research from the Polytechnic Institute of Brooklyn and a BS in mathematics from the University of Detroit.

Saurabh Narain is chief fund advisor to National Community Investment Fund (NCIF; www.ncif.org) and senior managing director at ShoreBank Corporation ($2 billion bank holding company; www.sbk.com). Narain has had extensive experience in capital markets and risk management, having worked at Bank of America for almost seventeen years in both Asia and the United States. Over the years, he has worked in almost ten countries in Asia and the United States and in dealing with financial institutions, global multinational corporations, and governments. He has experience in raising capital from private and public markets and in client risk–management advisory work across risk classes. He serves on the boards of CDFI Coalition and NMTC Coalition and is a member of the Steering Committee of the Professional Risk Managers' International Association, Chicago Chapter (www.prmia.org). Narain previously served as president of the Board of the Health Clinic of the Asian Human Services, the Council of the United Way of Metropolitan Chicago, the Board of FpML.org, and the Board of the North Asia Steering Committee for International Swaps and Derivatives Association (1999). Narain is a regular speaker at industry conferences. He has a BA (Honours) in economics from University of Delhi and an MBA (1985) from the Indian Institute of Management in Ahmedabad, India.

Melissa Nemon is a doctoral student at the School of Community Economic Development, Southern New Hampshire University, and a research assistant at the Applied Research Center in CED, where she is also involved in studies on small business and community development. Her research interests include sustainable development, employment and labor, and social justice. Nemon is active in the Society for Community Research and Action and the Society for the Psychological Study of Social Issues.

Robin Newberger is a business economist in the Consumer Issues Research Unit of the Federal Reserve Bank of Chicago. Newberger holds a BA from Columbia University and an MA in public policy from the John F. Kennedy School of Government at Harvard University. She is the author of several articles and papers published by the Chicago Fed, including "Financial Access for Immigrants: Lessons from Diverse Perspectives" (2006), "Islamic Finance in the United States: A Small but Growing Industry" (2005), "Savings Account Usage by Low- and Moderate-Income People in the Chicago Metropolitan Area" (2004), and "Financial Institutions as Stakeholders in Individual Development Accounts" (2002). Before working for the Chicago Fed, Newberger lived in Quito, Ecuador, and wrote for the *Economist* Intelligence Unit. Newberger holds a chartered financial analyst designation.

Lynda Petersen earned her MPA from the Evans School of Public Affairs at the University of Washington. She focused her studies on social policy and was the graduate assistant to former Seattle Mayor Norman B. Rice. Petersen currently prepares briefing materials for Seattle Mayor Greg Nickels, works with community groups and constituents on their complaints and concerns, and assists staff in all community outreach efforts to Seattle's neighborhoods and businesses. Petersen believes the two years of direct service she gained with AmeriCorps prior to graduate school helped shape her views on our society and the world.

David Porteous is the director of Boston-based consultancy firm Bankable Frontier Associates LLC. The firm specializes in providing strategic advice to public and private entities on financial sector and financial product development. Particular practice focus areas include the application of technology to increasing financial access, structured housing finance, and the evaluation of public and private entities and programs. Before locating to Boston, Porteous was active in leadership roles within the development finance sector in South Africa, including managing a public housing development finance institution, in charge of strategy for South Africa's largest microfinance banking group, African Bank Investments; and establishing FinMark Trust as a pro-poor market catalyst in the financial sector of southern Africa. Porteous has a bachelor's degree in communication from the University of Cape Town, a master's degree in philosophy from Cambridge University, and a PhD in economics from Yale University.

Gregory A. Ratliff is currently a senior Fellow at the Aspen Institute working with the Economic Opportunities Program. In this capacity, he has been one of the principal investigators for a research project exploring the scalability of community development financial institutions. In addition, he has been an advisor to the Annie E. Casey Foundation as it establishes a social investment program. Ratliff came to Aspen from the MacArthur Foundation, which he joined in April 1991 as a program officer in the area of program-related investments. In 1996, he was promoted to program director of the Access to Economic Opportunity interest area within the Program on Human and Community Development. He was also responsible for program design and grant development focused on questions of economic inequality and access to opportunity. Before joining the Foundation, Ratliff was active in social investing with the ShoreBank Corporation in Chicago. He was responsible for screening the bank's bond portfolio and served as a commercial lender providing small- and medium-sized businesses with SBA loans. Ratliff holds a BA from the University of California, Los Angeles, an MBA from Northeastern University, and has completed graduate work at the Massachusetts Institute of Technology in the Department of Urban Studies.

F. Stevens Redburn is former chief of the Housing Branch at the Office of Management and Budget (OMB). He joined OMB in 1986. He earned his PhD in political science from the University of North Carolina at Chapel Hill. Redburn's scholarly contributions include coauthoring a book, *Responding to America's Homeless,* that helped shape the nation's understanding of a complex problem by delineating subgroups within the homeless population and differences in approaches to service delivery required for each group. He has published twice in *Public Administration Review,* once on models for integrated delivery of human services and again on how to account for the cost of insurance programs in the federal budget. His federal service began in 1979 at HUD, where he led field studies in the Office of Policy Development and Research to evaluate major programs. His most recent book is a collection of essays, co-edited with Terry Buss, *Public Policies for Distressed Communities Revisited.* Redburn is an elected fellow of the National Academy of Public Administration.

Norman Rice is currently serving a three-year term as a Distinguished Practitioner-in-Residence at the University of Washington's Evans School of Public Affairs and is heading up the Civic Engagement in the 21st Century project. The project will involve working closely with professors, students, and civic and community leaders to focus seminars on how to apply the principles of civic engagement in addressing critical issues affecting the Puget Sound region. The project will draw on Rice's own expertise as well as that of other local and national leaders who have been successful at sustaining citizen involvement in resolving tough policy questions. Rice received his MPA from the University of Washington and went on to build an illustrious career that included three terms as a member of the Seattle City Council and two very successful terms as mayor of Seattle. From 1998 to 2004, he served as president and CEO of the Federal Home Loan Bank of Seattle and, until recently, as vice chairman of Capital Access, LLC, an investment banking firm that specializes in strengthening communities and creating a sustainable environment.

Alicia Robb is a research associate at the University of California, Santa Cruz. She is also the founder and president of the Foundation for Sustainable Development, an international grassroots community development organization working in eight countries throughout Latin America, Africa, and Asia. She previously worked as a staff economist for an economic consulting firm and as an economist for the Office of Economic Research in the Small Business Administration and for the Division of Research and Statistics at the Federal Reserve Board of Governors. Her main research interests are minority entrepreneurship, small business lending, community development, and microfinance. She has taught economic development courses at universities in the Washington, D.C., and San Francisco Bay areas, as well as abroad in three countries. Robb graduated summa cum laude in economics and multinational organizational studies from St. Mary's University in San Antonio, Texas. She received her PhD in economics from the University of North Carolina at Chapel Hill, specializing in economic development and econometrics.

Michael Rowett is research and communications manager for Southern Good Faith Fund's Public Policy Program. He previously served as director of communications for the Democratic Party of Arkansas and, before that, spent nine years in journalism as a reporter for Arkansas' two largest daily newspapers. He covered politics and government for the *Arkansas Democrat-Gazette* and government, business, and education for the *Southwest Times Record* in Fort Smith. Rowett is a cum laude graduate of Texas Christian University in Fort Worth, Texas, where he earned a bachelor's degree in journalism.

Julia Sass Rubin joined the faculty of the Edward J. Bloustein School of Planning and Public Policy at Rutgers University in 2003 as an assistant professor of public policy. She spent the prior year as a postdoctoral fellow at the Alfred A. Taubman Center for Public Policy at Brown University. Rubin has advised a number of organizations in the area of developmental finance, including the U.S. Small Business Administration, the John D. and Catherine T. MacArthur Foundation, the Appalachian Regional Commission, the Overseas Private Investment Corporation, and the New Jersey Redevelopment Authority. Previously, she consulted for McKinsey & Company, worked in brand management for the Procter & Gamble and Eastman Kodak companies, and taught strategic management and marketing at Assumption University in Bangkok, Thailand, as a Henry Luce Scholar. Rubin holds a PhD in organizational behavior from Harvard.

William Schweke is vice president of learning and innovation at CFED (formerly, the Corporation for Enterprise Development) and was president of Interchange, a firm specializing in public policy exchange between the United States and Europe. A graduate of the University of Texas at Austin, he is a specialist in development finance, plant closings, small and community business, environmentally compatible development, and local development planning. He has published extensively in the field of community development. In 2004, Schweke delivered the Werner Sichel Lecture at Western Michigan University, entitled, "Getting Beyond Argument and Invective: Can We Bridge the Gap between Free and Fair Trade Advocates?" He was awarded the North Carolina Defender of Justice Award for Advocacy and Policy Research by the N.C. Justice and Community Development Center.

Colin D. Sears is currently economic development manager of the City of Portland's Target Industry Cluster Program at the Portland Development Commission. Before moving to Portland, Oregon, in 1999, Sears worked as a project director at Davidson-Peterson Associates in Maine, where he directed economic research projects for the Bermuda Department of Tourism, the State of Wisconsin, and Duchess County, New York. Sears has skills and experience in applied economic development, strategic planning, and economic impact assessment and research. He is currently leading the development of an economic development strategy for the City of Portland, Oregon.

David W. Sears is currently acting assistant deputy administrator for Cooperative Programs at the U.S. Department of Agriculture. In recent years, he has served as

the acting director of the Empowerment Programs Division at USDA and was director of the National Rural Development Partnership's national office. Earlier in his
career, he was with USDA's Economic Research Service and with the Manufacturing
Extension Partnership at the National Institute of Standards and Technology. Sears
has skills and experience in strategic management, policy assessment, program
evaluation, professional development, and research. He has written numerous
publications on economic development and community development topics, with
an emphasis on rural communities. His edited book, *Rural Development Strategies,* won the Wildavsky Award. He was senior author of *Gearing Up for Success,*
a book aimed at state economic development policymakers.

Joshua Silver, vice president of research and policy at the National Community
Reinvestment Coalition, develops NCRC's policy positions and produces various
research studies with fifteen years of experience in the housing and community
development field. He has written NCRC testimony submitted to the Senate and
House Banking Committees on topics including financial modernization, predatory lending, and the effectiveness of the Community Reinvestment Act (CRA).
In his technical advisory role, Silver helps community organizations and local
public agencies devise neighborhood reinvestment strategies and interpret HMDA
and CRA data on lending activity. He also writes and edits fact sheets and technical manuals. Major NCRC studies produced under Silver's direction include the
Broken Credit System and *Access to Capital and Credit for Small Businesses in
Appalachia.* At the Urban Institute, Silver specialized in housing market analysis
and program evaluation. Silver holds an MPA from the LBJ School of Public Affairs
at the University of Texas in Austin and earned a bachelor's degree in economics
from Columbia University in New York City. He lives in Bethesda, Maryland, with
his wife and daughter.

Anna Steiger is a senior research associate in the Public and Community Affairs
Department at the Federal Reserve Bank of Boston. Her primary areas of research
include community development finance and asset-building programs and policies
for low- and moderate-income individuals and families. She has also worked in
international business and microfinance and served as an emerging markets analyst
at the Federal Reserve Bank of New York. Steiger holds an MPP from the Kennedy
School of Government at Harvard University and a BA in economics from Barnard
College at Columbia University.

Ben Steinberg is president of Southern Financial Partners, a Southern Bancorp
affiliate, which provides both comprehensive community development services in
Arkansas as well as development lending in Arkansas and Mississippi. The comprehensive community development initiative, known as the Delta Bridge Project,
is focused on Phillips County, Arkansas, and is delivering tangible changes to the
community. Before joining Southern, Steinberg accumulated over ten years of

international development experience, including serving as the senior executive for microfinance institutions in Kazakhstan, Armenia, and Tanzania. In Tanzania, the microfinance program became financially sustainable and served over 27,000 customers at the time of his departure. Steinberg has an MPA from the Woodrow Wilson School at Princeton University. He graduated with a BA from the University of California at Davis in economics and international relations.

Hannah Thomas is the Oskowitz Fellow at the Heller School at Brandeis University. She is a doctoral student focusing on questions of assets and inequality, specifically interested in building and protecting wealth for low-income individuals. Thomas was formerly employed at Coastal Enterprises, Inc., a nationally recognized community development organization and CDFI in Maine. At CEI, she helped develop policy platforms around abusive forms of credit and was coauthor of a report on predatory mortgage lending in Maine. She also helped manage data analysis and collation for the organization and performed evaluations for several programs, including a workforce development project in central western Maine for the Department of Labor. Thomas holds an MA from Cambridge University in Geography.

Kate Titford is a second-year student at the University of Maryland School of Law.

Thomas J. Vicino is assistant professor in the School of Urban and Public Affairs at University of Texas at Arlington. He holds a PhD in public policy from the University of Maryland Graduate School, Baltimore. His research focuses on urban development and politics and suburban decline. His recent work has appeared in *Urban Studies, Urban Geography,* and *Encyclopedia of American Urban History.* Vicino's research has also been funded by the U.S. Environmental Protection Agency.

Elisabeth Walden is a third-year student at the University of Maryland School of Law.

Index

A

abusive lending
  multiple abuses, 121–22
  programmatic and policy responses, 118–19
  summarized, 123–25
ACCION New Mexico (ACCION-NM), 17, 18, 21–22
accountability, 5, 229
achievement gap, 48, 50
adjustable rate mortgage (ARM), 121, 122, 129n. 2
adjusted interrupted time series (AITS) analysis, 86–87, 89
affordable housing, 8
  aging-out, 293–300
  foster care, 293–300
    youth emancipation trends, 294
  and land value taxation, 301–7
    current situation, 302–5
    externalities, 302–3
    forecasting, 305
    height restrictions, 302
  median gross rent trend, 295
  multifamily housing permits, 299
African Americans
  achievement gap, 48
  lending disparities, 116–18
aging-out, 293–300
Aid for Families with Dependent Children, 240
American Community Chest. See United Way, strategic philanthropy
American Dream, 144
American Dream Policy Demonstration (ADD), 146, 151
American Housing survey, 242
Annie E. Casey Foundation, 157
anti-busing initiative, Seattle, 209–20
antipredatory lending legislation, 125–26

Appalachian Regional Commission (ARC), 87
Asian Americans
  achievement gap, 48, 50
  lending disparities, 116–18
Asian CDC, 69, 75n. 10
Aspen Institute's Economic Opportunities Program, 15
asset building
  assets framework, 132–42. See also Assets framework for detailed treatment
  community development and, 143–57
    American Dream Policy Demonstration (ADD), 146, 151
    benefits of current policy, 144–45
    community-based development organizations, 150–51
    community economic development, defined, 147
    Community Reinvestment Act (CRA), 151
    competence and, 146–47, 150
    confidence and, 146–47
    connections and, 146–47
    costs of current policy, 144–45
    credit cleaning, 150
    definition, 147
    economic development, defined, 147
    employee ownership, 151–52
    entrepreneurship, 147–48
    entrepreneurship development, 151
    financial literacy, 150
    generally, 5–6
    homeownership, 150
    importance of assets today, 145–46
    new markets, 151
    nexus of asset building, 149–50
    Seed capital, 151
    upward mobility, 144

asset building *(continued)*
  federal policies, 152–53
  lending disparities, 113–31. *See also*
    Lending disparities for detailed
    treatment
  state government, innovation in, 157–66.
    See also Pennsylvania Office of
    Financial Education (POFE)
  state policies, 152–53
  working families, for, 246
Assets and Opportunity Scorecard, 153
Assets for Independence Act, 152
assets framework, 132–42
  CDFI theory, 134–35
  community development finance, 133–34
  market failures, kinds of, 134
  measurement, 141
  program design, 140–41
  program financing, 141
  transformational assets, 135

B
Baltimore, Maryland
  Community Conferencing Center, 332
  land use, 7–8
  suburban decline, 255–73
    age of housing stock, 264
    confrontation of, 267–69
    economic imperatives of Smart Growth,
      269–70
    emergence of, 256–67
    first-tier suburbs, defined, 257
    forecasting, 271–72
    housing, 263–64
    income, 260–63
    labor force, 264–67
    manufacturing employment, 266
    median household income distribution,
      262
    politics and, 269–70
    population, 258–60
    poverty, 260–63
    Smart Growth and Neighborhood
      Initiative, 255
Banks (CDFI), social performance
  measurement, 94–109
  application of SPMs, 103–7
    financial performance, 103–4
    social performance, 104–7
  approaches to performance measurement,
    97–99
  described, 97–98

Banks (CDFI), social performance
  measurement *(continued)*
  development deposit intensity (DDI),
    102–3, 104
    comparisons, 106
    generally, 108
    housing focus, 105
    over time, 106
  development lending intensity (DLI),
    101–3, 104
    comparisons, 106
    generally, 108–9
    housing focus, 105
    over time, 106
  distinguishing features, 102
  housing focus, 105
  mutual fund rating, 98–99
  observations, number in each database in
    each year, 101
  public data bases, summary, 100
  publicly available performance data,
    99–103
    financial performance, 99
    social performance, 99–103
  relative size comparison, 96
  return on assets (ROA), 99, 103, 104, 106–8
  return on equity (ROE), 99
Beaty, Sharon, 70
The Berenstain Bears and the Trouble with
    Money, 161
Bethlehem Steel, 268
bicycling. *See* Positive cycling
borrower-investee types, 76–81
Borrower's Protection Act of 2007, 125–26
Boulding, Kenneth, 155n. 7
British Isles, crime and development, 326–30
"Broken Credit System: Discrimination and
    Unequal Access to Affordable Loans by
    Race and Age" (NCRC), 115, 127
Brown v. The Board of Education, 48
Bush administration
  CDFI fund, 38
  President's Management Agenda (PMA),
    234
business improvement districts (BIDs),
    338–39

C
Calabrese, Alex, 333
California Public Employees' Retirement
    System (CalPERS), 41
California, public pension funds, 61

California State Teachers' Retirement System (CalSTRS), 17
capacity building, citizen engagement and, 6–7
civic engagement, effective, 209–19
Delta Bridge Project, 198–208
Detroit Local Initiatives Support Corporation (LISC), 180–97
multisector collaborations, 180–97
Southern Bancorp's model for community economic development, 198–208
United Way, strategic philanthropy, 169–79
Capital Regional Development Council (CRDC), 70
CARS. See CDFI Assessment Rating System (CARS)
CBO Database, 311, 313, 315–20, 324–25
CDBG. See Community Development Block Grant (CDBG) program
CDCs. See Community development corporations (CDCs)
CDFI Assessment Rating System (CARS), 94
CDFI Coalition and Opportunity Finance Network, 133
CDFI Data Project, 94
CDFI Fund, 38, 94, 96, 133
CDFIs. See Community development financial institutions (CDFIs)
CDLFs. See Community development loan funds (CDLFs)
CECSF. See Credit Enhancement for Charter School Facilities Program (CECSF)
CEI. See Coastal Enterprises, Inc. (CEI)
CEI Capital Management (CCML), 69–70
Center for Community Self-Help (Self-Help), 17, 18
Center for Responsible Lending, 27
charter school facilities financing, 52, 56
loan securitization, expansion, 23
mortgage-backed securities, 32n. 4
nonconforming mortgages, securitizing, 23
Center for Responsible Lending, 27
CFED. See Corporation for Enterprise Development (CFED)
Chafee Act. See Foster Care Independence Act (FCIA)
Chandler Center for Community Leadership, 188
The Charter Coalition, 47
Charter High Schools: Closing the Achievement Gap, 50
Charter School Capital Access Program (CCAP) Fund, 54

charter school facilities financing, 47–59
accomplishments of CDFIs, 51–53
achievement gap, 48
enrollment over time, 50
loans, 52
low-income students, 51
public charter schools defined, 48–50
public sector, role of, 53–56
reason for charters, 51–52
states with charter school laws, 49
Charter School Facility Landscape, 51, 54
Charter School Financing Partnership (CSFP), 56, 58
charter schools, loans to, 24–25
Chase Manhattan Bank, 20
Chicago, Illinois
positive cycling, 287–88
child welfare
aging-out youth, 293–96
as community development, 296–99
citizen engagement, capacity building. See Capacity building, citizen engagement and
civic engagement, effective, 209–19. See also Seattle Education Summit
civic intermediary/aggregator of public funds and resources, 25–27
Clinton administration, charter school facilities financing, 52–53
Clinton, Hillary, 271
Coastal Enterprises, Inc. (CEI), 61, 69
asset framework, 132, 136–39
progressive alliance for careers and training (PACT), 136–37
waterfronts, working, 138–39
Collaborative Lending Initiative, 20
colonial America, crime and development, 330–31
Committee for Economic Development (CED), 326
Community Action Program and Model Cities, 181
community banking models, demonstrating, 27–29
community-based development organizations, 150–51
community-based employment, 245–46
community-based financial education, 162–63
community development. See specific topic
Community development banking institutions (CDBIs), 94

Community Development Block Grant
  (CDBG) program, 7, 181
  CDBG formula, 230–33
    allocating funding based on need and
      fiscal capacity, 231
    immigration, assisting communities
      impacted by, 233
    rewarding communities stressing
      economic development activities,
      232–33
    smaller communities, reducing
      administrative burden, 232
    targeting funding geographically within
      communities, 232
  consolidated plan, reforming, 234
  IDIS, upgrading, 233–34
  immigration, assisting communities
    impacted by, 233
  low-income housing policies and, 249
  overview, 223–24
  performance measurement system reform,
    225–30
    accountability, 229
    alternative performance measurement
      systems, 229
    best- and worst-case scenarios, 229
    community viability analysis, 228
    demonstration projects, 229
    initial negotiated performance measures,
      227
    joint working groups, 225–26
    negotiated performance partnerships,
      225–26
    opportunity costs, 229
    oversight, 229
    program purpose, 226–27
    shift-share, 229
    simulation, 229
    social science attribution, 229
    targeting, 230
    viable communities, 227–29
  reforming, 223–35
  smaller communities, reducing
    administrative burden, 232
  Strengthening America's Communities
    Initiative (SACI), 224–25
Community development corporations (CDCs)
  asset building and, 148
  crime and development, 334
  Detroit Local Initiatives Support
    Corporation (LISC), 182–87
  generally, 60–61

community development entities (CDEs),
  39–40
community development financial institutions
  (CDFIs)
  asset building and, 148
  assets framework. See Assets framework
  banks, performance measurement. See
    Banks (CDFI), social performance
    measurement
  charter school facilities financing, 47–59.
    See also Charter school facilities
    financing for detailed treatment
  defined, 132
  future niche of, 16
  future of, and charter market, 56, 58
  generally, 4
  impact. See Research design, measurement
    of CDFI performance and impact
  interaction between mainstream financial
    institutions, 17–29
  mission-focused and mainstream financial
    organizations. See Mission-
    focused and mainstream financial
    organizations
  performance measurement. See Research
    design, measurement of CDFI
    performance and impact
  research design. See Research design,
    measurement of CDFI performance
    and impact
  subsidy, scarcity of, 34–46
    CDFI fund, 38
    challenges facing field, 38–40
    community development entities
      (CDEs), 39–40
    Community Reinvestment Act (CRA),
      39
    foundations, 39
    individual investors, 42
    market-rate capital, accessing, 42–43
    New Markets Tax Credit Program,
      39–40
    opportunities and industry response,
      40–44
    pension funds, 41–42
    repositioning, 43–44
    Rural Business Investment Company
      (RBIC), 40
    securitization, 42–43
    state and local governments, 41
    structured financing, 42–43
  sustainability, 29–31

Community development institutions
  community development financial
    institutions (CDFIs). *See* Community
    development financial institutions
    (CDFIs)
  generally, 4–5
community development loan funds (CDLFs)
  low-income communities, 36
  multifamily housing, 36
  subsidy, scarcity of, 34–36
    foundations, 39
    individual investors, 42
    opportunities and industry response,
      40–44
    pension funds, 41–42
    repositioning, 43–44
    selling loans, 42–43
  technical assistance (TA), 36
Community Development Venture Capital
  Alliance (CDVCA), 42
community development venture capital
  (CDVC)
  subsidy, scarcity of, 34, 37–38
    foundations, 39
    individual investors, 42
    pension funds, 42
    repositioning, 43–44
community economic development, defined,
  147
Community Impact Program, Heritage
  United Way, 172–73
Community Organized Investment Network
  (COIN), 41
Community partner in economic
  development, 60–75
  case studies, 67–70
    CEI Capital Management (CCML),
      69–70
    Coastal Enterprises, Inc., 69
    Olmstead Green, 68
    Parcel 24, 68–69
    Urban Strategies America (USA) Fund,
      60–61, 67
  CEI Capital Management (CCML), 69–70
  Coastal Enterprises, Inc., 69
  community investments, 60
  credibility pass, 72
  ensuring community benefits, 72–73
  financial engineering, 71
  investment vehicles, 61–67
    financial engineering, 71
    niche industry, developing, 71–72

Community partner in economic development
  investment vehicles *(continued)*
    role of, 70–72
    sourcing deals, 70–71
    structures of, 62, 63
    "toolkit," 64
    types of community partners, 64, 65–66
  Net Market Tax Credit model, 70
  niche industry, developing, 71–72
  Olmstead Green, 68
  Parcel 24, 68–69
  role of community partner, 72–73
  sourcing deals, 70–72
  Urban Strategies America (USA) Fund,
    60–61, 67
Community Preservation Corporation (CPC),
  17, 18
  loan securitization, expansion, 23
Community Reinvestment Act (CRA), 19, 95
  asset building, 151
  civic intermediary/aggregator of public
    funds and resources, 26
  described, 100
  importance of, 30
  lending disparities and
    adjustable rate mortgage (ARM), 122
    failed ratings, 125
    minority neighborhoods, application of
      CRA to, 127–28
    nonbank lending institutions, expansion
      to, 128
    subprime lending, scrutinizing of,
      128–29
  research design, measurement of CDFI
    performance and impact, 81
  retooling, 133
  subsidy, scarcity of, 39
Community Reinvestment Fund (CRF), 17,
  18
  charter school facilities financing, 56
  loan securitization, expansion, 23
  National New Markets Tax Credit Fund,
    Inc., 26
Community Renewal Tax Relief Act of 2000,
  40
Community Tool Box (CTB), 188
competence, asset building and, 146–47, 150
Competitive Inner City (ICIC) study, 312,
  315
Consumer Rescue Fund (CRF), 119–22
  adjustable rate mortgage (ARM), 121
  affordable refinance loan, 120

Consumer Rescue Fund (CRF) *(continued)*
  analysis of terms before and after refinance, 121
  exotic loans, 121–22
  high-cost loans, 121–22
  litigation, 120
  loan modification, 120
  mechanics of, 119–20
  mediation, 120
  multiple abuses, 121–22
  success of, 120–21
Corporation for Enterprise Development (CFED)
  asset building, 146, 152–53
  and Evans, Dwight, 157–58
COSCDA. *See* Council of State Community Development Agencies (COSCDA)
Council of State Community Development Agencies (COSCDA), 225–26
court system, colonial America, 330–31
CPC. *See* Community Preservation Corporation (CPC)
CRA. *See* Community Reinvestment Act (CRA)
CRA Modernization Act, 128
credit cleaning, 150
Credit Enhancement for Charter School Facilities Program (CECSF), 47, 54–55
credit unions (1930s), 133
creditworthiness and lending disparities, 114
CRF. *See* Community Reinvestment Fund (CRF); Consumer Rescue Fund (CRF)
crime and development
  British Isles, 326–30
  colonial America, 330–31
  community redevelopment, crime as deterrent to, 326
  generally, 8
  historical underpinnings, 328–31
  Normans, 327–28, 332
  restorative justice initiatives, 335
  United States, 332–34
  Saxon England, 327–28, 332, 334
  small businesses, impact on, 311–25. *See also* Small businesses, impact of crime for detailed treatment
cycling. *See* Positive cycling

D

Daniels and Economic Innovation International, 61
data availability, research design, 89–91

Davis, California
  positive cycling, 288
DDI. *See* Development deposit intensity (DDI)
Delta Bridge Project
  described, 202–5
  economic impact, 205
  generally, 7
  KIPP program, 205–8
  Phillips County, Arkansas, 200–202
  results from, 205–8
  social impact, 205–8
Departmental Grants Management System (DGMS), 233–34
Department of Commerce (DoC), 224
Department of Housing and Urban Development (HUD), 120
  affordable housing goals, 129
  CDBG program. *See* Community Development Block Grant (CDBG) program
  Departmental Grants Management System (DGMS), 233–34
  generally, 236
  HUD 108 loans, 339
  median rents, 295
  needs, considering, 241
  Notice of Fund Availability (NOFA), 296
  Office of Policy Development and Research (PD&R), 225
  Self-Sufficiency (FSS) program, 246
  Supportive Housing Program, 296
Detroit Local Initiatives Support Corporation (LISC), 180–97
  collaborative planning, 187–90
    challenges and limitations, 189–90
    direction setting, 188
    implementation, 188
    limited empowerment, 190
    multisector collaboration, 188
    problem setting, 188
  Community Action Program and Model Cities, 181
  Community Development Block Grant (CDBG) program, 181
  multisector collaboration, 188, 191–97
    committed catalysts, 191–92
    communication processes, democratic, 194–95
    cooperative culture, 193–94
    democratic decision making, 194
    leadership, effective, 193

Detroit Local Initiatives Support Corporation (LISC)
  multisector collaboration *(continued)*
    political climate, 195–96
    resources and capacity, 196
    social climate, 195–96
    stakeholder engagement, 192–93
    structure and policies, supportive, 195
    sustainability systems, 196–97
  neighborhood level, planning at, 181–83
  neighborhood stewards, CDCs and intermediaries as, 182
  new model, 186–87, 190
  overview, 180–81
  Strategic Investment Areas (SIAs), 180, 183–87, 192–97
Deutsch Bank, 20
development banking industry, expanding, 27–29
development deposit intensity (DDI), 102–3, 104
  comparisons, 106
  generally, 108
  housing focus, 105
  over time, 106
development lending intensity (DLI), 101–3, 104
  comparisons, 106
  generally, 108–9
  housing focus, 105
  over time, 106
disasters, 9–10
discrimination, lending disparities, 113–15. *See also* Lending disparities
DLI. *See* Development lending intensity (DLI)
"Don't Borrow Trouble," 163

E
E.C. Morris Foundation, 206
econometric simulation, 86
economically targeted investments (ETIs), 41
economic development, community partner in. *See* Community partner in economic development
economic development, defined, 147
Elementary and Secondary Education Act Title X, 53
Emergency Shelter Grants (ESGs), 225–26
eminent domain, 9, 337–43
employee ownership, 151–52
Employee Retirement Income Security Act (ERISA), 44

employment, community-based, 245–46
Empowerment Zones, 298
entrepreneurship
  community development and, 148–49, 155n. 10
  development, 151
equity funds, 341
Evans, Dan, 215
Evans, Dwight, 157–58, 163

F
Family and Education Levy, 217–18
Fannie Mae, 129n. 3
  borrowing from, 32n. 4
  and lending disparities, 129
Fannie Mae American Communities Fund, 21
Fannie Mae Foundation, 153
FCIA. *See* Foster Care Independence Act (FCIA)
Federal Deposit Insurance Corporation (FDIC)
  Statistics of Depository Institutions (SDI), 99
  Summary of Deposits (SOD), 95, 100–1, 103
Federal Home Loan Banks, 129
Federal Housing Authority, 141n. 1
federal policy, 7
  Community Development Block Grant (CDBG). *See* Community Development Block Grant (CDBG)
  low-income housing policies. *See* Low-income housing policies, federal
Federal Reserve Board (FRB), 116
  asset framework, 141
  and lending disparities, 127
Federal Reserve Survey of Consumer Finances (FRSCF), 114
Federal Reserve System, 15
FICO, 127
financial literacy, 150
financial output variables, measuring structural impacts via, 87–89
financial performance
  application of SPMs, 103–4
  publicly available, 99
foreclosures, national foreclosure prevention, 125
foster care, 293–300
  youth emancipation trends, 294
Foster Care Independence Act (FCIA), 294, 296–98

foundations, scarcity of subsidy, 39
FRB. *See* Federal Reserve Board (FRB)
Freddie Mac loans, 115, 129
funding innovations impact scale, 29–30
funding subsidies, 4

G
General Motors, 268
George, Henry, 301, 305, 306
GI Bill, 144
Glendening, Parris, 269
Government Accountability Office (GAO), 127
Government Performance and Results Act of 1993, 299
Government Sponsored Enterprises (GSEs), 24, 129
Grameen Bank, 10
Great Northern Paper Company, 73
Greenspan, Alan, 141

H
Harrisburg, Pennsylvania
land value taxation, 306
Harrison, Fred, 305
Harvard University, 48
Heinz Endowments, 162
Heritage United Way, 169, 172–78
Applied Research Center (ARC), 172–76
CIC training, 175
community capacity building, 175–76
Community Impact Program, 172–73
CRT training, 175
intervention, 172–73
lessons learned, 177–78
member agency/applicant training, 175
organizational plan, 176–77
planning program, 174
research, 173–74
Hispanics
achievement gap, 48
lending disparities, 116–18
small businesses, impact of crime, 323
Historic Preservation Tax Incentives program, 342
HMDA. *See* Home Mortgage Disclosure Act (HMDA)
HOME Investment Partnerships Program (HOME), 225–26, 249–50
Home Mortgage Disclosure Act (HMDA)
FICO, 127

Home Mortgage Disclosure Act (HMDA) *(continued)*
lending disparities, 116
data, enhancing quality of, 126–27
social performance measures, 95, 99–101, 103, 108
homeownership, 150
"Homeownership and Wealth Building Impeded: Continuing Lending Disparities for Minorities and Emerging Obstacles for Middle-Income and Female Borrowers of All Races" NCRC, 115
Homeownership Protection and Enforcement (HOPE) Act, 125
Homestead Act, 144
household income, 145
household or firm versus neighborhood or community, 82–84
housing
affordable. *See* Affordable housing
Baltimore, Maryland, 263–64
banks (CDFI), social performance measurement, 105
Housing Act of 1974, 227
Housing Opportunities for Persons with AIDS (HOPWA), 225–26
Housing Partnership Network (HPN), 23, 27, 56
HUD. *See* Department of Housing and Urban Development (HUD)
Hunt, Hilary, 158
Hurricane Katrina, 9

I
ICIC. *See* Competitive Inner City (ICIC) study
IDAs. *See* Individual development accounts (IDAs)
IFF. *See* Illinois Facilities Fund (IFF)
Illinois Charter Capital Program (ICCP), 54–55
Illinois Facilities Fund (IFF), 52, 54
immigration, 9, 233
incentives
multiple, 343
rent, 245–46
incentive zones, 342–43
income
Baltimore, Maryland, 260–63
individual development accounts (IDAs), 136, 141n. 7
and asset building, 146, 147

individual investors and scarcity of subsidy, 42
inner-city small businesses, impact of crime. *See* Small businesses, impact of crime
interpretation of community development, 3–4
investment vehicles
  community partner in economic development. *See* Community partner in economic development

J
Jefferson, Thomas, 144
Jewett, Doug, 210
Jobs-Plus, 246
JP Morgan, 20

K
Kendrick, William, 215
Kennedy Commission Report, 332
KIPP program, 205–8

L
labor force
  Baltimore, Maryland, 264–67
landowners, housing and, 8
land use, 7–8
land value taxation, affordable housing and. *See* Affordable housing
Leadership in Energy and Environmental Design (LEED), 75n. 11
Lena Park CDC, 68
lending consortia, 19–20
lending disparities, 113–31
  abusive lending
    multiple abuses, 121–22
    programmatic and policy responses, 118–19
    summarized, 123–25
  adjustable rate mortgage (ARM), 121, 122, 129n. 2
  African Americans, 116–18
  Asian Americans, 116–18
  Consumer Rescue Fund (CRF). *See* Consumer Rescue Fund (CRF)
  and creditworthiness, 114
  discrimination, generally, 113–15. *See also lines throughout this topic*
  Hispanics, 116–18
  "hypersegmentation" of lending, 116
  literature review, 113–16
  loan pricing, race differences, 5, 113

lending disparities *(continued)*
  low- and moderate-income minorities (LMI), 113
    nonbank lending institutions, expansion of CRA to, 128
    racial disparities, 117–18
    research findings, 116–18
  middle-and-upper income (MUI) minorities, 113
    abusive lending, programmatic and policy responses, 118–19
    racial disparities, 117–18
    research findings, 116–18
    steering, programmatic and policy responses, 118–19
  policy responses, 118–19
  programmatic responses, 118–19
  racial disparities, increases of income level, 117–18
  recommendations by NCRC, 122, 125–29
    antidiscrimination oversight by FRB, 127
    comprehensive antipredatory lending legislation, 125–26
    fair lending enforcement, 126
    fair lending oversight by FRB, 127
    Federal Reserve Board, actions by, 127
    government-sponsored enterprises (GSEs), abiding by anticipatory safeguards, 129
    HMDA data, enhancing quality of, 126–27
    minority neighborhoods, application of CRA to, 127–28
    national foreclosure prevention, 125
    nonbank lending institutions, expansion of CRA to, 128
    programmatic partnerships, 122
    subprime lending, scrutinizing of by CRA, 128–29
  research findings, 116–18
  steering, programmatic and policy responses, 118–19
LIHTCs. *See* Low Income-Housing Tax Credits (LIHTCs)
LIIF. *See* Low-Income Investment Fund (LIIF)
lines of credit, small business term loans, 90–91
LMI. *See* Low- and moderate-income minorities (LMI)
loan pricing, racial disparities, 5

loan programs, 339–40
 HUD 108 loans, 339
 revolving loan funds, 340
 SBA 504 loan program, 340
Local Initiatives Support Corporation (LISC),
 52
low- and moderate-income minorities (LMI)
 lending disparities, 113
  nonbank lending institutions, expansion
   of CRA to, 128
  racial disparities, 117–18
  research findings, 116–18
low-income communities, CDLFs, 36
low-income families
 IDAs, 136, 141n. 7
 mortgages to, 24
low-income housing policies, federal,
 236–51
 effectiveness, doubts about, 237–39
 intellectual foundations
  flaws of current programs, 243–44
  model, possible, 240–41
  needs, considering, 241–43
  rebuilding, 240–45
  stalemates, 239–40
 reforming policy, 245–50
  administrative system, reengineering
   of, 247
  asset building for working families, 246
  community-based employment,
   245–46
  housing subsidies, integrating with
   administration of other social
   services, 247
  institutionalization, avoiding
   unnecessary, 246–47
  rent incentives, 245–46
  separating decisions from decisions
   about households, 247–48
  social objectives, specific, 245
  specific social objectives, 245–47
  streamlined accountability, 248–49
 stalemates, 237–40
Low Income-Housing Tax Credits (LIHTCs),
 64, 236, 248–49, 295
Low-Income Investment Fund (LIIF), 17,
 18, 52
 charter school facilities financing, 56
 loan securitization, expansion, 23
 off-balance sheet capital, 21
low-income students, charter school facilities
 financing, 51

M
MacArthur Foundation, 56
Maine General Rehabilitation and Nursing,
 138
mainstream financial organizations. *See*
 Mission-focused and mainstream
 financial organizations
maintenance assessment districts (MADs),
 338–39
Manpower Demonstration Research
 Corporation (MDRC), 246
manufacturing employment
 Baltimore, Maryland, 266
market failures, kinds of, 134
market-rate capital, accessing, 42–43
Massachusetts, public pension funds, 61
mean equivalent, research design, 84
mega disasters, 9–10
middle-and-upper income (MUI) minorities
 abusive lending, programmatic and policy
  responses, 118–19
 lending disparities
  racial disparities, 117–18
  research findings, 116–18
  steering, programmatic and policy
   responses, 118–19
Mid-State Health Center, 70
minority banks (1880s), 133
minority neighborhoods, application of CRA
 to, 127–28
mission-focused and mainstream financial
 organizations, 15–33
 charter schools, loans to, 24–25
 civic intermediary/aggregator of public
  funds and resources, 25–27
 community banking models, demonstrating,
  27–29
 development banking industry, expanding,
  27–29
 developments and trends, 15–16
 funding innovations impact scale, 29–30
 future niche of CDFIs, 16
 as innovators, 24
 interaction between mainstream financial
  institutions, 17–29
 lending consortia, 19–20
 loan securitization, expansion, 23
 lower-income households, mortgages to, 24
 nonconforming mortgages, securitizing, 23
 off-balance sheet capital, 21
 partnership roles, variations of, 21–22
 pools, 19–20

mission-focused and mainstream financial
organizations *(continued)*
primary market, 19
secondary market, 22
small business loans, non-SBA qualifying,
22–23
sustainability, 29–31
syndications, 19–20
Morningstar, 98
Morrill Act, 144
mortgage-backed securities, 32n. 4
mortgages
to lower-income households, 24
nonconforming, securitizing, 23
single-family mortgages, research design,
89–90
MUI. *See* Middle-and-upper income (MUI)
minorities
multifamily housing, CDLFs, 36
multifamily real estate loans, 90
multiple abuses, Consumer Rescue Fund
(CRF), 121–22
multiple incentives, 343
multisector collaborations, 180–97
mutual fund rating, 98–99

N
National Academy of Public Administration
(Academy), 227, 229
National Assessment of Education Progress, 48
National Association for County Community
Economic Development (NACCED), 225
National Association of Housing and
Redevelopment Officials (NAHRO),
225
National Charter School Research Project, 48
National Community Development
Association (NCDA), 225
National Community Investment Fund
(NCIF), 17, 18, 94
National Community Reinvestment Coalition
(NCRC)
adjustable rate mortgage (ARM), 121, 122
"Broken Credit System: Discrimination and
Unequal Access to Affordable Loans
by Race and Age," 115, 127
Consumer Rescue Fund (CRF), 119–22
adjustable rate mortgage (ARM), 121
affordable refinance loan, 120
analysis of terms before and after
refinance, 121
exotic loans, 121–22

National Community Reinvestment Coalition
(NCRC)
Consumer Rescue Fund (CRF) *(continued)*
high-cost loans, 121–22
litigation, 120
loan modification, 120
mechanics of, 119–20
mediation, 120
multiple abuses, 121–22
success of, 120–21
lending disparities, 113–16
Consumer Rescue Fund (CRF), 119–22
recommendations, 122, 125–29
antidiscrimination oversight by FRB,
127
comprehensive antipredatory lending
legislation, 125–26
fair lending enforcement, 126
fair lending oversight by FRB, 127
Federal Reserve Board, actions by, 127
government-sponsored enterprises
(GSEs), abiding by anticipatory
safeguards, 129
HMDA data, enhancing quality of,
126–27
minority neighborhoods, application of
CRA to, 127–28
national foreclosure prevention, 125
nonbank lending institutions, expansion
of CRA to, 128
programmatic partnerships, 122
subprime lending, scrutinizing of by
CRA, 128–29
National Council of State Housing Agencies
(NCSHA), 225
National Defense Education Act, 144
National New Markets Tax Credit Fund, Inc.,
26
A Nation at Risk, 48
Nature Conservancy, 72–73
NCB Capital Impact, 52, 54, 56
NCRC. *See* National Community
Reinvestment Coalition (NCRC)
neighborhood or community versus
household or firm, 82–84
NeighborWorks, 89
new markets, asset building, 151
New Markets Tax Credit Program
community development, 61
community partner in economic
development, 70
defined, 142n. 8

New Markets Tax Credit Program
  (continued)
  establishment of, 74n. 3, 341–42
  generally, 9
  National New Markets Tax Credit Fund,
    Inc., 26
  subsidy, scarcity of, 39–40
  sustainability of CDFIs, 31
New Markets Venture Capital (NMVC)
  program, 38
New York City
  lending consortia, 19–20
  public pension funds, 61
  single-family mortgages, 89
  suburbs, 256
Niche industry, developing, 71–72
NMCDA. *See* National Community
    Development Association (NCDA)
NMTC. *See* New markets tax credit
Nobel Peace Prize, 10
No Child Left Behind Act, 47
nonbank lending institutions, expansion of
    CRA to, 128
Nonprofit Facilities Fund, 52
Nonprofit Finance Fund (NFF), 17, 18, 26
Norman Conquest, 327–28, 332
nursing profession, 137, 138

O
off-balance sheet capital, 21
Office of Policy Development and Research
    (PD&R), 225
Olmstead Green, 68
OMB. *See* U.S. Office of Management and
    Budget (OMB)
Opportunity Finance Network, 35
outcomes, research design, 79
outputs, research design, 79

P
Parcel 24, 68–69
partnership roles, variations of, 21–22
Payne, Ancil, 210
Penn State Cooperative Extension, 162
Pennsylvania Department of Banking, 158,
    166
Pennsylvania Newspaper Publishers
    Association, 163
Pennsylvania Office of Financial Education
    (POFE), 157–66
  The Berenstain Bears and the Trouble with
    Money, 161

Pennsylvania Office of Financial Education
    (POFE) *(continued)*
  community-based financial education,
    162–63
  "Don't Borrow Trouble," 163
  innovation, 164
  leadership vs. stewardship, 164
  lessons learned, 163–66
  operations, 159–63
  origin, 157–59
  partners and, 165
  prioritization, 165–66
  school-based financial education, 160–61
  workplace-based financial education, 161–62
  Your Money's Best Friend, 160
pension funds
  public pension funds, 61
  subsidy, scarcity of, 41–42
performance attainment, 4
performance management, 5
performance measurement
  banks (CDFI). *See* Banks (CDFI), social
    performance measurement
  CDBG program, system reform, 225–30
    accountability, 229
    alternative performance measurement
      systems, 229
    best- and worst-case scenarios, 229
    community viability analysis, 228
    demonstration projects, 229
    initial negotiated performance measures,
      227
    joint working groups, 225–26
    negotiated performance partnerships,
      225–26
    opportunity costs, 229
    oversight, 229
    program purpose, 226–27
    shift-share, 229
    simulation, 229
    social science attribution, 229
    targeting, 230
    viable communities, 227–29
  community development financial
    institutions (CDFIs). *See* Research
    design, measurement of CDFI
    performance and output
Phillips County Strategic Community Plan
    (PCSC), 202–4, 206, 208
PNC Bank, 55
POFE. *See* Pennsylvania Office of Financial
    Education (POFE)

pools, mission-focused and mainstream financial organizations, 19–20
population
Baltimore, Maryland, 258–60
Portland, Oregon
positive cycling, 286–87
positive cycling, 274–89
case studies, 286–88
Chicago, Illinois, 287–88
Davis, California, 288
forecasting, 288–89
institutions, 286
Portland, Oregon, 286–87
promotion of community development success, 275
theory of, 274–77
ultimate bicycle-friendly community, 278–86
bicycle encouragement events, 282
bicycle route network, 279–80
certified bicycle shops, 283–84
characteristics of, 278
courtesy and, 285
creating, 278–86
maintenance of bicycles, 283
modeling, actors, 282
parking, 280–81
pilot programs, 285
public schools, pro-bicycle message, 283
rental bicycles, availability, 281
safety and courtesy classes, 283
subsidies for, 282–83
tax credits, 282–83
poverty
Baltimore, Maryland, 260–63
President's Management Agenda (PMA), 234
product groups, research design, 76–81
product lines, research design, 76–81
experimental methods for impact evaluation, 84–85
home-improvement loan product line, 79
typology, 78
Program Assessment Rating Tool (PART), 224
programmatic partnerships, 122
Progressive Alliance for Careers and Training (PACT), 132, 136–37
propensity-scoring techniques, research design, 86
property values, research design, 84

public housing agencies (PHAs), 238
public pension funds, 61
public sector, charter school facilities financing, 53–56

Q
Quality Housing and work Responsibility Act of 1998, 240

R
randomization, research design, 84
Raza Development Fund, 56
Red Hook Justice Center, 333
Reed, Jack (Senator), 125
Reed, Stephen R., 306
reforms, low-income housing policies. See Low-income housing policies, federal
Reigle Community Development/Regulatory Improvement Act, 141n. 3
The Reinvestment Fund (TRF), 17, 18
charter schools, loans to, 25, 52, 54–55
civic intermediary/aggregator of public funds and resources, 27
loan securitization, expansion, 23
motto, 32n. 2
Rendell, Edward G., 157–58, 163
rent
incentives, 245–46
median gross rent trend, 295
research availability, 89–91
research design, measurement of CDFI performance and impact, 76–93
adjusted interrupted time series (AITS) analysis, 86–87, 89
borrower-investee types, 76–81
Community Reinvestment Act (CRA), 81
data availability, 89–91
econometric simulation, 86
end outcome, 79
financial output variables, measuring structural impacts via, 87–89
geographic areas, experiments using, 84–85
household or firm versus neighborhood or community, 82–84
mean equivalent, 84
multifamily real estate loans, 90
neighborhood or community versus household or firm, 82–84
outcomes, 79
outputs, 79
product groups, 76–81

research design, measurement of CDFI
performance and impact *(continued)*
product lines, 76–81
experimental methods for impact
evaluation, 84–85
home-improvement loan product line, 79
typology, 78
propensity-scoring techniques, 86
property values, 84
purported effect, 79
quasi-experimental methods for measuring
impact, 85–87
randomization, 84
research availability, 89–91
single-family mortgages, 89–90
small business term loans, lines of credit,
90–91
strategic space, 83
structural impacts, measuring via financial
output variables, 87–89
summative impact evaluation (SIE),
performance measurement versus,
79–81
targeting places, people, or both, 83
unit of analysis, 82–84
return on assets (ROA), 99, 103, 104, 106–8
return on equity (ROE), 99
revolving loan funds, 340
Rice, Constance, 210–11
Rice, Norman B., 209–10, 212, 216, 218–19
ROA. *See* Return on assets
Rockefeller, David, 20
Royal Bank of Canada, 21
Ruppersberger, "Dutch," 267–284
Rural Business Investment Company (RBIC),
40
Rural Opportunities Enterprise Center
(ROECI), 72

S
Savings for Working Families (SWFA), 152
Saxon England, crime and development,
327–28, 332, 334
SBA. *See* Small Business Administration
(SBA)
Schenck, A. William III, 158, 163
school-based financial education, 160–61
School Lunch Program, 55
School of Community Economic
Development in Southern New
Hampshire University (SNHU)
Applied Research Center (ARC), 172–76

Schumer, Charles (Senator), 125–26
SCORE Act. *See* Suburban Core Opportunity
Restoration and Enhancement (SCORE)
Act
Seattle Education Summit
anti-busing initiative, 209–20
celebration of end of, 216–17
citizen involvement mission, 210
citywide summit, 214–16
community summit meetings, 212–14
Family and Education Levy, 217–18
generally, 209
Save Our Schools (SOS), 209–10
theory, underlying, 211–12
secondary market, 22
securitization, scarcity of subsidy, 42–43
Seed capital, 151, 339
Self-Help. *See* Center for Community Self-
Help (Self-Help)
Self-Sufficiency (FSS) program, 246
Sen, Amartya, 143
September 11, 2007 terrorist attacks, 9
ShoreBank Corporation, 17, 18
community banking model, 27–29
financial output variables, measuring
structural impacts via, 88
SIAs. *See* Strategic Investment Areas (SIAs)
single-family mortgages, 89–90
small banks, return on assets (ROA), 104
Small Business Administration (SBA), 22
elimination of leverage, 44
SBA 504 loan program, 340
small businesses, impact of crime, 311–25
analysis matrix, 316
CBO Database, 311, 313, 315–20, 324–25
Census Bureau data, 313
Competitive Inner City (ICIC) study, 312, 315
evidence, 312–15
firm and owner traits, 314
logistic regression analysis, 319
market segments impacted by serious
crime, 320–22
traits of urban firms and owners, 321, 322
small business investment companies
(SBICs), 37
small business loans
non-SBA qualifying, 22–23
term loans, lines of credit, 90–91
smart growth
community investment and, 255–73
political impact, 269–70
and positive cycling, 283–84

Smart Growth Areas Act of 1997, 269
Smith, Adam, 145
Smith, James, 267–68
social performance measurement. *See*
     Banks (CDFI), social performance
     measurement
Southern Bancorp's model for community
     economic development, 198–208.
     See Delta Bridge Project for detailed
     treatment
  Delta Bridge Project, 198
  overview of Southern Bancorp, 198–99
  theory of change, 199–200
Southern Community Development
     Corporation, 199
Southern Financial Partners, 199, 205
Southern Good Faith Fund, 199
Southwestern Pennsylvania Community Loan
     Fund (CLF), 52
spending, federal, 3
Spies, Charlie, 70
start-up small businesses, impact of crime.
     See Small businesses, impact of crime
state and local governments, scarcity of
     subsidy, 41
state government, innovation in, 157–66. *See
     also* Pennsylvania Office of Financial
     Education (POFE)
Statistics of Depository Institutions (SDI), 99
storefront improvement grants, 340–41
Strategic Investment Areas (SIAs), 180,
     183–87, 192–97
strategic space, research design, 83
Strengthening America's Communities
     Initiative (SACI), 224–25
structural impacts, measuring via financial
     output variables, 87–89
structured financing, 42–43
subprime lending, scrutinizing of by CRA,
     128–29
subsidy, scarcity of
  CDFI fund, 38
  challenges facing field, 38–40
  community development entities (CDEs),
     39–40
  community development loan funds
     (CDLFs), 35–36
     foundations, 39
     individual investors, 42
     opportunities and industry response,
         40–44
     pension funds, 41–42

subsidy, scarcity of
  community development loan funds
     (CDLFs) *(continued)*
     repositioning, 43–44
     selling loans, 42–43
  community development venture capital
     (CDVC), 34, 37–38
     foundations, 39
     individual investors, 42
     pension funds, 42
     repositioning, 43–44
  Community Reinvestment Act (CRA), 39
  foundations, 39
  individual investors, 42
  market-rate capital, accessing, 42–43
  New Markets Tax Credit Program, 39–40
  opportunities and industry response, 40–44
  pension funds, 41–42
  repositioning, 43–44
  Rural Business Investment Company
     (RBIC), 40
  securitization, 42–43
  small business investment companies
     (SBICs), 37
  state and local governments, 41
  structured financing, 42–43
Suburban Core Opportunity Restoration and
     Enhancement (SCORE) Act, 271
Summary of Deposits (SOD), 95, 100–1, 103
summative impact evaluation (SIE),
     performance measurement versus, 79–81
Supported Independent Living Programs
     (SILPs), 296–97
Sustainable Jobs Fund, 135
syndications, 19–20

T
Task Force for Working Families (TFWF),
     157–59
taxation
  land value, affordable housing and. *See*
     Affordable housing
tax credits
  Historic Preservation Tax Incentives
     program, 342
  Low Income-Housing Tax Credits
     (LIHTCs), 64, 236, 248–49, 295
  new markets tax credit. *See* New Markets
     Tax Credit Program
  positive cycling, 282–83
Temporary Assistance for Needy Families
     (TANF), 240

transformational assets, 135
TRF. *See* The Reinvestment Fund (TRF)

U

United Way, strategic philanthropy, 169–79
  Heritage United Way, 169, 172–78
    Applied Research Center (ARC),
      172–76
    CIC training, 175
    community capacity building, 175–76
    Community Impact Program, 172–73
    CRT training, 175
    intervention, 172–73
    lessons learned, 177–78
    member agency/applicant training, 175
    organizational plan, 176–77
    planning program, 174
    research, 173–74
  overview of strategic philanthropy, 170–71
  overview of UWA, 169–70
unit of analysis, research design, 82–84
upward mobility and asset building, 144
UrbanAmerica, 44
urban renewal, 7'0
urban small businesses, impact of crime. *See*
  Small businesses, impact of crime
Urban Strategies America (USA) Fund,
  60–61, 67
U.S. Department of Agriculture (USDA)
  low-income housing policies, 236
  School Lunch Program, 55
U.S. Department of Education (DoE)
  Charter High Schools: Closing the
    Achievement Gap, 50
  charter school facilities financing, 47

U.S. Department of Treasury
  CDFI Fund, 94
    qualifying Investment Area, defined, 96
U.S. Office of Management and Budget
  (OMB), 225
  low-income housing policies, 238
  Program Assessment Rating Tool (PART),
    224, 227
UWA (United Way of America). *See* United
  Way, strategic philanthropy

V

venture capital. *See* Community development
  venture capital (CDVC)
Virginia Constitution of 1776, 144

W

war on poverty, 7
Watt, Bob, 212, 218
Western Mass Enterprise Fund (WMEF), 73
West Oak Lane, 157
Working Waterfronts Program, 132
workplace-based financial education,
  161–62

Y

York and Trust, 139
young urban small businesses, impact of
  crime. *See* Small businesses, impact of
  crime
Your Money's Best Friend, 160
Yunis, Muhammad, 10

Z

Zehr, Howard, 332

For Product Safety Concerns and Information please contact our EU
representative GPSR@taylorandfrancis.com
Taylor & Francis Verlag GmbH, Kaufingerstraße 24, 80331 München, Germany